The Uncommonly Common

The Story of James Wilson of Maine

and

His Topsham Descendants

by

Delia Wilson Lunsford

Table of Contents

CvilleGenie, a division of WizTech, Inc.
Charlottesville, Virginia

ISBN: 978-0-692-58424-8
First edition, hardback, IngramSpark, printers

Book Jacket
Photos front and inside front cover, canstockphoto.com
Delia's portrait, Gitchell's Studio, Charlottesville, VA
James Wilson's gravestone, author photo

Jefferson C Wilson grave photo used with permission from Barb Butcher, Iowa, email, 26 Oct 2015
Photos of Hugh Wilson houses on Winter Street, Virginia cabin, excerpts from the Pejebscot Papers, author
Tontine Hotel and maps from Wheeler's History of Topsham
Emery and Addie Wilson provided by Donna Carano-Cooper

Preface

This is the culmination of family tree research gone horribly wrong. Sigh. Not really, but close, as I never intended to start a study of 20,000 family members. I am writing this as a gift to the descendants of James Wilson of Topsham, Maine, who arrived on America's shores in the very early 1700s. I might as well since I have all this information (and can write) - I do not know what else to do with it!

So here are some facts and information you need to know before you start plowing through this (or when you get confused later in your reading):

First, this not intended to be a study of the history but a story that uses history. I have used a variety of sources but part of the historical information outside the actual genealogical facts is based on website sources such as WikiPedia and not on academic historical texts. Where appropriate I have included sources in the chapters, but I also have included a source list in the appendix for reading that I think readers might be interested in.

Secondly, I am a writer and a genealogist. The writer came first and I mind my grammar and such like but I prefer to produce readable material. My relaxed style of writing is intentional - I hope you enjoy it. I do actually break some writing rules in this book - I made some decisions on how I wanted things done and feel a little guilty at not minding my grammar p's and q's. It probably won't bother most readers but I do have to apologize for that because it does bother this English teacher and grammarian.

The one thing I have used occasionally to keep the stories more manageable is to put in parentheses the ancestor names such as (4th generation surname or full name[4], 3rd generation[3], 2nd generation[2], James[1]). Hopefully, this convention will help. Each person has an added number as they are discussed to assist, like this - name[6]. I do suggest using the table of contents pdf on the website as a guide when reading chapters. If you have the table of contents genealogy to look at, it will help you keep your place in the story.

- **There is no one who was born after 1900** included in this book unless that person is dead and is memorable in some way or is my generationally immediate family. After finding my family in a similar book with some mistakes, I realized that living people do not take kindly to their information being incorrect. I hope to avoid offense, and it was also necessary to put an arbitrary cut off date on families due to the size of the task. Full genealogies, which will be updated as information becomes available, are available on my website. Please see the appendix for more information.
- **Women are only referred to by their maiden name** (or former married name if maiden is not known).
- **Abbreviations**: a. for about, b. for born, m. for married, d. for died, unc. for unconfirmed.
- Unlike many genealogies, I am **not giving precedence to the surname line** - I generally am treating the daughters as equal to the sons as this is a study of all descendants and not just Wilson surnamed descendants.
- I have pulled vital records directly from the sources used to create the digital records where possible such as Mary Pelham Hill's Topsham records. She uses some abbreviations throughout and those are noted in the appendix. Specifically, P.R. stands for private record and T.R. stands for town record.
- **I have taken other liberties with the footnotes and annotations.** After I realized where the original records came from, I started just copying over the information and putting the town name and page number in parenthesis. Totally against any writer rules but a convention that cuts down on the number of footnotes and adds a bit of interest and often even information. If ever in doubt about the source, just refer to the appendix as all books and record sources are there.
- Once I added those original records I realized there need to be some more explanation about those records so that is provided on the page after next.
- **Since many sources come with on line URLs, I have added them in lieu of explicit genealogical proof footnotes.** In doing so, I also used Google to shorten the links. This was all about conserving space and making the book more readable.
- I also want to state one other thing. **If I have the source, I foot-**

note it. If there is no footnotes on a date, that may mean there is no confirmation but it also may mean that there are several dates and the footnote may be later in the sentence or paragraph. If you use this book as source material, please make sure you are using data that is confirmed. Check those footnotes!

- One unfortunate bit of news: I have determined that the deeds in Lincoln County from about 1826 to 1854 are not available. As of this writing, the Registry of Deeds is not admitting this problem so I don't know whether the actual deeds are missing or if the index is incomplete. This did put a wrench into this project and adds a bit of uncertainty into the data for those years. They are in the process of digitizing the records prior to putting them on line so I am hoping this will be either corrected or explained sometime within the next year.
- One point about naming that you should know before you get started, though this is usually explained when you find it. Junior is used to designate which person, not son of. Numbers are also used this way. So James Junior is the second James in the area. The other may not even be related. James 2, 3 and 4 are also possible. That's birth order of the like-named people, not related people.

Last but not least, I'm as human as the next person; I make mistakes. I'm sure I don't have everything correct and would love to know when I'm wrong. Tell me: contact me via my website at http://cvillegenie.com. The only thing about a book in print is that corrections are hard. I will be posting a list of incorrect facts from the print edition once I receive confirmed data.

If you want to add to the story of your family, I welcome everything but don't promise to use it. I did try contacting folks for more information and offered up some of it for proofing by family members but found little interest from most of those I tried to contact.

One of the strongest possibilities is that I didn't find a marriage and children for someone. I list folks as never married - anytime I do that, the truth is that the person may have and I just didn't find the information. So I simply may have missed a lot of folks! There are plans for updates....

Vital Records Abbreviations

Most of these hold true throughout the various record sources. The last (after widr) are only Topsham.

Marriages were declared as intentions first and then the marriage happened later much like today's engagements. So the second date mentioned in a marriage entry is the wedding.

Also, birth dates can sometimes be found by pure mathematics. Many stones had death dates with age at years, months and days, so some of the records only have death dates but with the information to figure out the birth dates.

I did occasionally truncate these records for space so the original record could have a bit more in them.

b. born
m. married
h. husband
w. wife
int. publishment of intention of marriage
inf. infant
s. son
d. daughter, died, day
U.S.C. - United State Census for 1850
wid. - widow
widr. - widower
L.V. - list of vaccinations given by Dr. Isaac Lincoln in 1810, incorporated in the Topsham Town Books viewable on microfilm.
G.R.I - grave stone record, First Parish Burying-ground, adjoining First Parish Church
G.R.2 - grave stone record, Haley Burying-ground
G.R.3 - grave stone record, Riverview Cemetery
G.R.4 - grave stone record, Eaton Cemetery
N.P. - newspaper record
P.R. 22 - family Bibles of James and Ezekial Purinton
P.R. 80 - Early History of Topsham by Cyrus Woodman in the Maine Historical Society, Portland, citation above.

“What’s in a name?”

“That which we call a rose by any other name would smell as sweet”

The Backstory

I really hated my Shakespeare class in college. I had hoped I would gain some appreciation for the "Bard" but it was so boring! Yet, when I reached for a quote to use, lo and behold, up pops the above phrase from Romeo and Juliet.

Shakespeare was asking a question that has come to haunt me in my adult years. He wanted to know if the name makes the man (or woman as in my case).

Names do come with connotations for most of us. The more recent phenomenon of giving boys or non-sex names to girls recognizes that Jane Doe is obviously female but Madison Doe could be a guy. Parents frequently do this to give their "girls" an edge in today's still male-dominated world.

Growing up as a Delia in Gainesville, Georgia, in the 1950s and 1960s was fraught with name problems for me. First, because there were no connotations to my name. There was not anyone I ever met there who had my name. In fact, I met my first other Delia at age twenty in college. I have met very few since then.

I did occasionally see my name in print: the Irish maid in so many stories from years ago was so frequently named Delia. A maid! Not the heroine, not the story's main character, a maid, for heaven's sake. Oh, dear. What is in a name?

Additionally, I (okay, my name) was the subject of 2 hit songs back in the early '60s. (Waylen Jennings sang about "my" adultery and murder in "Delia's Gone".) Then in the 1970s or 1980s a soap opera character was christened Delia. I did not even check to see what they had done to me that time.

My teachers could not pronounce my name correctly (and I was too embarrassed to teach them how to say it). The other kids used my name as a taunt: I was obviously a good victim.

My name is always being misspelled. I get called Debra or Delilah or Julia or Belia in writing or out loud. (My handwriting probably does not help this process.)

Once I started my own business back in the '80s, I decided to use that uniqueness to my advantage and to teach the world how to pronounce and spell my name. "I will take this opportunity teach the world! I will become pronounceable, spellable!" I ended up constantly spelling my name anew to customers, vendors, sales people, etc. Constantly, they were apologizing for mangling the pronunciation. I have received uncountable apologies, more than enough to make up for the teachers' and children's misuse of my name in those early years.

But, then, the unthinkable happened. It started some years ago. Somebody named a company Delia's. This company sells clothing and such to pre-teens and others of tender age. Type "my" name in a internet search and this company hogs the scene!

Then a specific author rose to some prominence, Delia Ephron, sister of Nora Ephron, movie director. Nora brought us the movie, You've Got Mail, and has helped to bring her sister to wider acclaim.

Now you say that's not much. How could this be problematic for me? Well, it seems like all of a sudden every author in the world has decided to include a Delia in their opus. I do read voraciously but now I can check 10 books out of the library and find my name in two or three!

For those of you who are accustomed to seeing "your" names in print, you cannot fathom how truly disconcerting and upsetting this is for me. For most of my life, my name virtually did not appear in print. If Delia was mentioned, it was me someone was talking about me, like in a newspaper article. I was important, unique and fortunate to have something different. My own name.

As always, I read along, enjoy my fiction, my escapism. But now,

I am getting jolted out of my fantasy, my stories. Hey, my name again! Hey, what does this mean about me? I'm not the Irish maid any longer. I'm not so unique. My lifelong self-assumed identity does not work anymore.

I'm just Delia, one of many fictional characters who exist only in other authors' imaginations; for you see, I still rarely meet other Delias. People are only beginning to name their children with my name. It remains a more common name for my great-grandparents' and my grandparents' generations.

Well, I guess it is a step up, from total obscurity to a type of infamy. Today I am still only a figment of someone else's imagination!

And there is the family tree...

I was named after my great-grandmother, Delia McCarron Wilson, from Ireland. I think somewhere someone said it was a family name, but since I cannot find evidence of her existence before she married my great-grandfather, I have not been able to prove that.

I always assumed that Delia was a very common name in Ireland but I was informed by a techie Irish friend of mine that it is not so. Delia does appear to be more common in the British Isles than here in the states but not by much.

It turns out that Delia in Ireland may well be a nickname for someone named Bidelia, Biddie, or Bridget. So much for an identity grounded in my "name".

And then there is the rest of the family tree.

I am a Wilson - one of those Maine Wilsons. Well, I declare! I had no idea until December of 2013. For some unknown reason I had decided my family up New Jersey / Massachusetts way were all immigrants from Ireland and Poland.

Nope, the original James Wilson came here about 1719 landing in

Maine with his wife and children. Such a common name, Wilson. Can that really mean anything?

In my digging through my Maine family tree I do see the introduction of Delia - as a shortened form of Cordelia, Perdelia and many more interesting and forgotten names. I was able to pinpoint where in my family women were named Delia instead of using a nickname of Delia. Oh, well, I am now firmly grounded in my roots.

So Delia Wilson. An uncommonly common name.

And you'll come to see that the commonly-named Wilsons of Topsham, Maine, are not so common after all.

Thus begins the tale of the Wilsons of Maine, a story of Maine, Massachusetts, and New England from the Mayflower until today.

The Wilsons - a Scotch Irish Family

I'm starting this off just like most genealogies - about the name Wilson - but I am warning you, this is a story of more, for it is a tale of a number of entwined families of early Maine.

According to Ancestry.com, Wilson is the tenth most common name in the United States:[1] it is even more common in Great Britain - the seventh most common name there.[2] As normal with a name with 'son' on the end, Wilson at one time probably meant the son of Will, a popular medieval name.

First recorded in England in 1324, the name Willeson[3] gave rise to the present day Wilsons and Willsons, the more common American spellings. It is found among the Scottish and Irish as well as the British. There are multiple coats of arms (over 70!) so I am not even going to talk about the possibilities of that. I'm pretty sure my forebears were not worried about that kind of thing: they worried about survival instead.

The origin of the name William (where Will probably came from) is actually quite important in genealogy because of DNA. William the Conqueror, the first Norman king of England, was a descendant of the Vikings. His 1066 entry into England brought the blood of those Vikings into Anglo-Saxon England.

If your ancestors are from the British Isles, your DNA test is quite likely to show Scandinavian origins.[4] Mine does, my husband's does (he is mostly English) and, as the footnoted ancestry.com page tells you, "even individuals with deep British pedigrees often have some Scandinavian" ancestry. So there is almost no such thing as pure English, Irish or Scottish.

In fact, origins can to get really murky for us of Scotch Irish de-

1. Hello, Mr. and Mrs. Smith: America's Most Common Surnames, http://goo.gl/lE-5Hdf accessed 9 Feb 2015.
2. Wilson (name), https://goo.gl/xEppnD, accessed 9 Feb 2015.
3. Reaney, Percy Hilde (1995), Wilson, Richard Middlewood, ed., A Dictionary of English Surnames (3rd ed.), Oxford University Press, p. 495.
4. Got Scandinavian? Why your DNA results may have unexpected ethnicities, http://goo.gl/iHrNb3, acccessed 4 April 2014.

scent as my line of Wilsons (and one of my southern lineages) is. My DNA test is right on the mark with Irish, Scandinavian, British, Scottish, French and Polish origins. (Nice to have that confirmation!)

Wilsons can be solely English or Scottish but the Scotch Irish Wilsons of Maine make no claims to either. This Scotch Irish background is extremely important for these Wilsons as it explains a lot of things I found in this family tree.

I had been told I had Scotch Irish origins and years later I was totally confused about whether my Scotch Irish Presbyterian southern ancestors on my Mom's side originated in Scotland or Ireland and what difference did it make?

I found the answers while rooting around in my Yankee tree. The Scotch Irish background is a tale of survival starting back in Scotland originally for some but this American term is more likely used to describe the Protestant inhabitants of Northeastern Ireland or Ulster with Scottish roots who came to America in the 1700s and the 1800s. The term Scotch Irish is said to have been adopted by the Protestant Irish to distinguish themselves from the influx of Catholic Irish after the Great Irish Famine of the 1840s[5] and is not a term most Englishmen are even familiar with.

This Scotch Irish pride is manifested in one 1910 book written by a little known but important New England author named Charles Knowles Bolton. He writes, "They came to America, not as discoverers, but as the pioneers of their race; they defended the frontiers against Indians, and their numbers in the South so much augmented the forces in the Revolutionary army that they may fairly be said to have saved Washington from defeat."[6]

His book is an interesting look into the early Scotch Irish pioneers starting in New England as many American stories do. One par-

5. Scotch-Irish American , https://goo.gl/uzIsvC, accessed 4 Jan 2014.
6. Bolton, Charles Knowles, Scotch Irish Pioneers in Ulster and America (Boston: Bacon and Brown, 1910), 6.

ticular relevant fact is found in his appendix - a list of ships that arrived from Ireland between 1714 and 1720. Interestingly, among those ships is the first one to Maine in 1718 with a master named John Wilson.[7] No, he's not my original ancestor and he most likely did not settle in the New World but my James Wilson did arrive on one of those ships.

The history of these "Scotch Irish" immigrants is a tale of a people looking for religious freedom and opportunity denied to them, first in Scotland and later in Ireland. First sent to Ireland by James VI, the king of Scotland who inherited the English and Irish thrones in the 1500's, the original Scotch Protestants left an overpopulated low country Scotland with its high rents and harsh conditions.

By the end of the seventeenth century, a third of the Ulster, Ireland, population was Scottish. Conditions, however, worsened as time went on because there was no government support there for Protestantism and the long term Irish leases started expiring. A well-written description of this piece of history is available at http://www.scottishtartans.org/ulster.html if you desire a more detailed account of this time period.

Bolton tells us: "Under Queen Anne (1702-1714) the Presbyterians in Ireland again lost almost every advantage that had been gained, and became by the Test Act of 1704 virtually outlaws. Their marriages were declared invalid, and their chapels were closed. They could not maintain schools nor hold office above that of a petty constable."[8]

This lead to a rush to immigrate between 1717 and 1727 that was encouraged by American colonists such as those in the Massachusetts colony. Massachusetts did not desire the Scotch Irish as their neighbors though; they only wanted them for protection.

As early as 1706 the well-known Rev. Cotton Mather wrote, "I write letters unto diverse persons of Honour both in Scotland and

7. Bolton, 319.
8. Bolton, 15.

in England; to procure Settlements of Good Scotch Colonies, to the Northward of us. This may be a thing of great consequence." It was Mather's plan to settle hardy families on the frontiers in Maine and New Hampshire to protect the towns and churches of Massachusetts from the French and Indians.[9] This was actually common all over the Eastern seaboard - delving into my South Carolina roots found the same story down there.

So the Scotch Irish arrived after generations of migration, upheaval and, in Ireland, the isolation of being surrounded by and increasingly suspicious of the Irish Catholics. They tended to be as clannish as the Scottish and this shaped many things in Maine - not marrying out of their extended family, for example.[10] This marks the Maine Wilsons in many ways and actually has assisted me and other family researchers because the only other Wilsons in the Topsham area in the 1700's and early 1800's were not Scotch Irish but English or Irish. The family patterns are obviously different between these Wilson families and there was very little intermarrying.

In addition, they used different first names; whether by design or because of naming traditions in the different Wilson families, I just don't know. For example, you'll find very few Thomas Wilsons among James' descendants; there's only two. The Irish Wilson original ancestor was Thomas and there were plenty of Anns in his family as well. James' family used Ann as a middle name and not as a first name. Between the clannishness of James' family and the naming traditions, separating out who was who was much easier than one would think. (except for those Marys - I swear the most common first name back then for a woman was Mary!)

9. Bolton, 17.

10. W.J. Montgomery, A Montgomery Family Genealogy, http://goo.gl/TYALBh, accessed April 4, 2014.

Maine, the Only Foreign Country in the United States

As this book is not written just for New Englanders, I feel that a description of Maine, a bit of its history and the Maine persona is necessary.

I found a description online that summarizes some of the unique things about Maine:

"It has been observed that Maine is the only foreign country in the United States.

These Yankees are highly independent, resourceful, frugal, rugged and hardworking individualists who have learned to wrest a living from the land or the sea, no matter the weather, oftentimes working at two or three jobs or trades to make ends meet. And all with a "wicked" sense of humor.

Maine has the traditional form of New England government - home rule - said to be the only existing type of "pure" democracy. This means that state government has relatively little power, and that the town and cities make all their major decisions by citizen vote through the vehicle of annual town meetings, usually held in March. In many of Maine's 450 smaller towns and plantations, this is one of the major social events of the year, usually with refreshments and, more often than not, a potluck dinner or supper."[1]

This is so not the South and the states I have lived in!

But...I never felt that I fit in down in Georgia. I just was not a typical Georgia girl. I know that part of the reason was because my brother and I were close and did many things together growing up - things that were not the norm for girls in the '50s and '60s in Georgia. I was a tomboy. Strike one.

Also, family dysfunction lead to a feeling of aloneness, of not belonging. And...I had a Yankee dad who, though he never stuck out as that, just was not a typical southern father. He mostly dropped

---

1. Maine's Guide to Coastal and Lakefront Real Estate, http://goo.gl/pwLyCD, accessed online 4/9/2014.

his New Jersey accent so it was not obvious, but his pronunciation of four and fourth was truly Boston. My mother was typical in some ways but was not the normal passive sweet southern mother or wife. Strike two and three.

Maybe I would feel more comfortable in New England.

I was able to contact via email and phone a number of New England born cousins, some close and some quite distant. I knew I was not fighting southern communication when speaking with those plain talking folks. I saw pictures of some of my cousins - they looked familiar (and cute!) I met one cousin on his way south when he dropped into Virginia. A taciturn native of Massachusetts, he was also trying to find family he did not know and had not known about until his late teens.

His gal said we looked alike. There is some definite physical similarities and ... hey, he is pretty cool! I don't know that the things we have common have anything to do shared blood but it was wonderful to explore the similarities and get accustomed to that Massachusetts accent.

I befriended a number of New England cousins on Facebook and started to get to know them and their home states. I began feeling more and more comfortable in the company of those "damn Yankees".

I kept reading and researching for this book. I knew I needed to make a trip to New England and missed the seasonal opportunity in 2014. In 2015, I was able to score a house sitting job in Boston for two weeks. This scheduled me and committed me to a trip north. I was finally going to experience it all! So I went.

Weeks after I got back from that New England trip, I was still trying to collate the information I had gathered while I was there and to figure out what I experienced. First, I found that if I were to start talking family trees while in the Topsham/Brunsick area, I would usually discover another cousin. I think that is typical for any area where one might have deep family roots (as a Charlottesville, VA, friend told me, "I am my own cousin!").

But not typical for me. I had no known relatives in Gainesville, GA, where I grew up besides my immediate family and a cousin of my grandfather's generation. This is probably not abnormal for a post-war child as the movement of troops exposed many to other states in the US as well as overseas. That is exactly how my dad ended up in Georgia, via the army.

Though most of my mom's family had arrived in North America in the early 1600's or 1700's, most of them arrived in Georgia generations later - even as late as 1870 as in the case of the Vances though the rest came earlier in the 19th century. My mother's Vance grandfather was born in Tennessee. He and some of his grown children moved to Georgia around 1870. Her other grandparents straddled that Georgia - South Carolina line, Edgefield, SC, to Lincoln County, GA, earlier than that but still middle 1800's - nothing to compare with the 1700s and the family staying in one place as they did up in Maine.

The realization that the kind of movement my family experienced actually weakened those family ties was truly eye opening. Perhaps that was another part of the reason for that movement. Less family meant more movement? Of course, there were other reasons in the south, over-farming and large families simply required new lands and new states. But that was more true of the English ancestors than my Vance Scotch-Irish / Presbyterian ministers from Tennessee. I haven't even been able to determine the original ancestors of one of my southern lines. It's as if they popped into existence in 1830. Again, a difference between my southern and northern ancestors.

So I gained more awareness of family in Maine which continued to increase a feeling of coming home. While in New England I got more validation as a Wilson when cousins remarked on how much I looked like a cousin who had died. I caught a glimpse of a shy smile from another that struck to the heart of me: it obviously was a

Wilson smile.

Interestingly, I actually look more like my mom than my dad compared to my siblings. They have his jaw (I suspect that's a Polish jaw from his mother) but mom's ears. Though my Wilson ears have gained more attention than I would have liked ('Thanks, Henry, I never knew I looked like Minnie Mouse.' I so do wish I had a clever retort back in 1968 for that one.) I guess I don't mind not having that strong jaw either. That lack of jaw, however, is more a Wilson thing anyway.

I certainly appreciated the weather. I've not enjoyed the heat in Georgia as an adult and have struggled with allergies and a mild asthma that increased the discomfort of southern summers. Moving north to Virginia (that was 500 miles north) netted milder summers which I really appreciate. I did experience mild in western Washington state - I actually never used allergy medicine the whole time I was there back in the 1970s. I do think humidity increases that misery.

My New England trip allowed me to experience spring three times this year. Virginia was all abloom when I left in late April though I missed the full affect of the new azaleas in my front yard. Boston burst out by the time I left there in mid May with gorgeous stands of forsythias and muted rusts and reds of the new tree leaves. And then to watch the unfolding of early spring in Maine added to the continued seasonal display. It was cool there still - not so much when I abruptly hit Virginia again. I found myself longing for the cooler climes once I got back south.

Now of course I timed my trip accordingly, missing the cold and incredibly heavy snow this past year up there and missing the black fly season which sounds unappealing. But still, it was really nice. I now truly understand the snow bird syndrome and am looking to make plenty money off this book so I can do the same. Ha. Nice thought at least.

The most incredible part of the trip, however, was my name. It is a

New England, a Maine name. When I was working the Wilson family tree, I watched names being shortened to Delia. Later there were also frequent occurences throughout this tree of Delia as a given name.

So what does that mean? Does it matter? Well, as it turns out, it does.

When in Maine, not one person asked me to spell or repeat my name. Not one person mispronounced it. Not one person said, "Oh, what a pretty name." They just understood. They knew the name.

It's really funny in some ways since I was named after my Irish great-grandmother, the original Delia Wilson. I wasn't named after any of those Wilsons. Daddy was born and raised in New Jersey. I don't know that he ever went any further north than that.

But they gave me a familiar Maine name.

So in short, I felt comfortable there. Hmmm.

But I digress.

The Mainers

I went to Maine to find out about Maine. My conclusions from my first visit:

1. It's gorgeous.
2. It's clean - they were sweeping the interstate as I came into the state. It's cleaner than you can imagine.
3. No billboards.
4. A bit cool but not cold. My host kept the windows open - and perhaps ran the heat, too. But at those temps further south, I would not be comfortable with the windows open.
5. Everyone obeys the traffic laws. It's quite bizarre. Conformity inside that "foreign country".
6. They are quite polite.

7. They have more boundaries than many southerners.

That last one was an eye opener. No one mentioned my southern accent, no one. Finally, one person did ask me where I was from. I asked her why no one had asked. She said because they are private people.

I asked at the historical society how would a homeowner react if I knocked on his front door and asked about his house (the oldest house in Topsham) - in the city. The answer was I could get shot.

They are polite. They don't meddle with strangers nor do they profess to welcome them. (I did feel welcomed by the way.)

As opposed to the southerners who profess to being friendly and are polite but love to meddle. They get into your business. One example is when I came back to Georgia in 1980. I had been friends with a New Jerseyite while on Okinawa, Japan, so my southern accent was mostly non-existent. I went into the local "mercantile" store trying to find out where to pay my water bill in a tiny rural town.

The reply was a gruff question, "whar yew from?" Once I said "Gainesville" in a very twangy Georgia hill accent, he said "Oh, okay."

Nosy neighbors, neighbors and family who think my religion is their business, etc. That's part of my southern experience.

Since I haven't lived in Maine, these comparisons may not be completely valid. Just my first look. Perhaps I'll get the chance to dig deeper into Maine and Mainers. Snow birding does appeal....

The Project, 2014 - 2015

I just do not tend to do things in a small way and my genealogy project is a good example of this. Do not ask me why; I do not want to think what causes such excesses.

My curiosity started me tracking all the descendants of that original ancestor, James Wilson. I had finished the main part of finding out who my ancestors were but was left with more questions than answers. I did not know my family hailed from Maine. I had never been further north than Utica, New York - had never been to New England and had never been that interested. Sure, I hoped for one of those leaf peeping trips one autumn and my curiosity was mildly piqued that fall with my sister's account of her Acadia National Park trip to a wedding.

But obsessively intrigued? No way. But oh, dear, oh, yes, that happened.

I was raised in Georgia and though I never felt I fit into the role of a Southern woman of my times, my identity is firmly rooted in the south. I knew about southern farming families who birthed many babies each generation. I knew of the hardships and continuing repercussions of the Civil War. I know towns intimately that were destroyed or spared by General Sherman and his march to the sea.

I have never dwelled on it like some southerners do. My husband, for example, in some ways is still fighting the Civil War; I heard that kind of sentiment all my life but I never internalized it. But about halfway through the over 18,000 descendants, I suddenly whipped around in my chair and proclaimed to said husband, "Oh, my God, now I really understand why the Civil War was fought."

He looked at me as to say, "Duh..." I explained to him that I could not get into the heads of my northern ancestors, that I just did not understand them. I told him that if I cannot understand, after living on both coasts and two foreign countries with all my education and knowledge of history, then "How in the world were southerners and northerners in the late 1800s supposed to begin to understand each other?"

Wow, just wow.

What started as a family tree morphed into the history of the early colonists of New England, the Civil War, WWI, WWII, the influenza and smallpox outbreaks, migration patterns across the United States and more as well as a dip into genetics (an ongoing education).

So first the parameters of my study:

I initially used Ancestry.com to trace all the descendants of James Wilson: every man, woman and child I could find. For the first 100 or more years, I also traced the lineages of those who married into the Wilson clan and made connections between their ancestors and the Wilson ancestors. I ended up tracking a number of families, including the Alexanders, the Toothakers, the Purintons, the Hinkleys, the Linscotts, the Farrins and many more.

At first I was extremely careful and watched sources obsessively. Later, after many thousands of folks, I eased up on the sources and stopped tracking the parents of every one who married into the tree especially if they were born after 1850 and if they were in part of the tree that had wandered far enough away from Topsham.

I started with William Alexander and his wife Jennett and it turned out this was a well-documented family tree. Descendants of Robert, king of Scotland, this particular branch of their family descends from another Scotch Irish settler, David Alexander, who may well have arrived on the same ship as James and his family.

I watched the occupations found in these sea going families and saw how that affected home life and families and watched the birth rate at times drop far sooner than other parts of the country.

I watched the Topsham families stay in Topsham for generations, hunkered down as it were. I compared that to the same generations in my southern families who kept moving almost generation to generation, state to state. I watched and wondered at the young deaths; marveled at the ships lost in far flung places and noted the drownings in this coastal family.

The family patterns in both the Alexanders and the Wilsons helped me keep on track and led me to some possible conclusions about the accuracy of my tree. I dug deeper into my part of the tree due to meeting "new" cousins, one of which had been trying to get accepted into the Mayflower society. I picked up his quest to ferret out the needed documentation and arguments. I found helpful information for this in the outlying families, the Thompsons and the Purintons, who also were some of the early settlers of Topsham.

I started tracking down more sources, more verifiable details; I developed a thirst for solving the myriad puzzles I uncovered.

I became a genealogist. Uh, wait, what? Life altering? Well, yes, in fact it was.

So, in the end, this book is about all the Wilson descendants, though I will focus on my specific line in detail - a family gift.

The Arrival, 1719 - 1722

Ships laden with the Scotch Irish started arriving in Maine in 1718 and continued up to 1722. One particular one is of interest. Bolton teased out what details were available about the ships[1] and lists three arriving in 1718 and 1719 from Ireland and Londonderry and bound for the Kennebec (river) and Casco Bay. Most likely it was one of those ships that carried James and his family to the New World. Perhaps this one:

> *[Name Not Given. Joseph ?] Philip Bass, master, from Londonderry; arr. Aug. 21, at Kennebec River (N. L. Aug. 17-24, 1719). 200 passengers.*[2]

These were among the ships arranged by Robert Temple. Bolton states, "Temple could not persuade [Captain] Law and his company to continue their voyage to Connecticut, and on the eighth of September the "Maccallum" sailed out of Boston harbor, for the territory owned by the Gentlemen Proprietors of Eastern Lands, at the mouth of the Kennebec River."[3]

Settlers from the Maccallum and the succeeding ships spread towards Nutfield, New Hampshire, and into the Merrymeeting Bay cities of Brunswick (established as Township May 1717) and Topsham (subsequently laid out in 1717).[4] Much of this land was purchased from the Indians in the later 1600s after King James granted a charter in 1620. Many of the Indians had vacated the area by 1713 after the Treaty of Portsmouth ended most of the regional strife. (Anyone with an interest in the particulars of the early history and founding of Topsham and Brunswick will find details in the Wheelers' History of *Topsham, Brunswick and Harpswell*. There is a digital copy on line provided by the Curtis Library in Topsham of this book as well as various PDFs available of the original book.[5])

But by 1721, war with the Indians once again reigned. In 1722 war was declared that lasted 3 years. Named Father Rales, Lovewell's or Dummer's war, the root cause was disputed territory east of the

---

1. Bolton, 133-153.
2. Bolton, 321.
3. Bolton, 142.
4. George Augustus Wheeler, M.D. and Henry Warren Wheeler, History of Topsham, Brunswick and Harpswell including the ancient territory known as Pejebscot (Boston: Alfred Mudge and Sons, Printers, 1878), 29.
5. Digitized version: http://community.curtislibrary.com/CML/wheeler/index.html

Kennebec, the agreed upon boundary in the treaty. Settlers started moving into the area and Indians of the Wabanaki Confederacy eventually started pushing back.[6]

In June of 1722, Indians seized (and released) nine entire families in Merrymeeting Bay, not very far north of the Brunswick area where early settlers were living - bringing home the war to my ancestors.[7] The next month on the twelfth Brunswick was "reduced to ashes".[8]

Bolton describes life then in Maine: "During these days of Indian warfare, pillage and reprisal, men were impressed for sentinel duty, and distributed in small groups at garrison houses throughout the frontier towns in Maine, which was then under the jurisdiction of Massachusetts. One of the unpleasant experiences of young Scotch Irishmen was to be met in the street by an officer and his attendants, and forced into military service. Many fell sick under the strain of such a life in the Maine woods, and through rough usage at the hands of officers. This ill-treatment fell heaviest upon the 'Irish', and particularly at the outset of the Indian troubles."[9]

At this point some of the more affluent (I assume) settlers fled permanently south towards Boston and to Pennsylvania. The ones left behind would be those who owned land and those who had no where to go. Some of hardy Scotch Irish would be included in that population who had no where to go.

A number tried to sail to Boston but were "warned off". Included in those lists on "July 28, 1722 from the Eastward viz.1 [the following who from their names, notably that of McFarland, evidently came from about Merrymeeting Bay.]" is a Jean Wilson with 4 Children.[10] Bolton also lists Jean and a James Wilson as settlers of Merrymeeting Bay Scotch Irish Settlers, 1718-1722.[11] So it's possible that James'

6. Father Rale's War, https://goo.gl/rhq4zh, accessed online 4/12/2014.
7. William Durkee Williamson, The History of the State of Maine: from its First Discovery, AD 1602, to the Separation, AD 1820, Inclusive, Vol. II (Hallowell: Glazier, Masters & Co., 1832), 114.
8. Williamson, 191.
9. Bolton, 227.
10. Bolton, 231.
11. Bolton, 238.

wife, who might have been Jean, was fleeing Brunswick within weeks of the incursion on July 12.

When did James and his family actually arrive? Most likely the year was 1719.

In a 1914 volume about the Alexanders of Topsham, we find William Alexander "married Jennet, daughter of James Wilson, who came from Ulster, Ireland, to Topsham, Maine, in 1719".[12] The Wheelers describe the Wilsons in Topsham, "Among the early settlers of Topsham were Hugh, Samuel, Robert, William, and Thomas Wilson ; and an Alexander Wilson settled at Harpswell. Hugh, Samuel, Robert, William, and Alexander were probably brothers. Thomas, according to family tradition, was of no relation to the others of the name. A James Wilson is called the father of Hugh, and so was probably father of Robert, Samuel, William, Alexander, and Jane, who m. William Alexander of Topsham, afterwards of Harpswell."[13]

The Wheelers go on to describe the sons in more detail, thus laying the foundation for the known information of James Wilson (my sixth great grandfather), his sons, Hugh, Robert, William, Samuel and daughter, Jane or Jennett.

So starts my genealogy - which quickly ballooned into more.

---

12. William M. Clemens, Alexander Family Records. An Account of the First American Settlers and Colonial Families of the Name of Alexander, and Other Genealogical and Historical Data, Mostly New and Original Material Including Early Wills and Marriages Heretofore Unpublished (New York: the author, 1914), 15.

13 Wheeler, 860.

Life and Times of the Scotch Irish in Early Maine

In trying to imagine what life must have been in the early 1700s, I found the Wheelers' book helpful with insights into our ancestors' lives. We do know that when James Wilson, his wife Jean and children arrived there was almost nothing.

"In Brunswick...there were in 1718 no dwelling places for the families, except within the walls of the fort...A little before that time, three families settled in Topsham; all of whom were afterwards destroyed in Lovewell's war."[1] The Wilsons may have arrived in 1719, only a year later. The Indian wars heated up in 1722 and we see Jean leaving the area with the children immediately afterwards.

Families lived far apart initially and mainly traveled by water as there were no inland avenues.

These Scotch Irish "were usually called 'wild Irish' by the native New-Englanders. It is said of these early settlers that "they used to peek out through a crack or partly opened door, to see whether their callers were friends or foes, and that the same habit of peeking out through a half-open door to see whom their callers may be, is noticed to this day in their descendants." These settlers were nearly all poor, and often suffered for the necessaries of life. They had to work hard for their living, and dress in the plainest manner."[2]

They were understandably not happy:

> *During the period embraced by the Indian wars, the character of the people differed materially from what it afterwards was. Instead of gayety and dissipation, a melancholy spirit prevailed. Almost the only topic of conversation with the people was in regard to their troubles with the Indians and the individual difficulties of their situation. Their chief relaxation consisted in singing psalms and doggerel rhymes. The only news that reached them was of cruel murders, by the savages, of their friends and acquaintance, or else of the wonderful escapes and marvellous exploits of the latter.*[3]

Though official churches were not established until much later in the 1700s, a meeting house was first on the agenda of many. A mis-

1. Williamson, 88.
2. Wheeler, 205.
3. Wheeler, 206.

sionary from Massachusetts started preaching at the Brunswick fort first in 1717 and continued on into 1718. The Brunswick First Parish building was probably started in 1718 but it was many years before they had a settled and permanent minister. According to Wheeler, it was of Presbyterian thought.[4]

I assume they were pragmatists but also like the Pilgrims whose religion figured so prominently in their desire to settle (and conquer) the New World. Their life in Ireland would have been a preview for this lifestyle without formal religion since their communal and church life was dismantled before they left.

A few tales survive that frequently described one aspect of life in Maine - Indian encounters. One involved David Alexander, father of William who married James Wilson's daughter, Jennet. William and a friend of him were set upon by Indians:

> *The boys' outcries at length attracted the attention of the settlers up and down the river, and his father being first to comprehend the true state of things outstripped all others in going to the relief of his son, guided partially by the voice of the lad and partly by the zigzag trail of the furrowed earth which was a conspicuous mark and was made by the boy's stubborn obstinacy and resistance. The father at length came in full sight of his son and was hastening to his rescue when the Indian, letting go the lad, fired, killing Mr. Alexander, who fell instantly dead. The son, the moment he saw his father fall, ran. and the Indian, fearing pursuit, desisted from attempting his recapture.*[5]

Bolton's description of these Scotch Irish settlers is truthful even though a bit lyrical:

> *The Scotch Irish have never claimed that they brought literature or art to these shores. They knew little of the former and nothing of aesthetics. Diaries and letters of the migration period do not exist and perhaps never did exist. Let us speak frankly. Every race brings to our western civilization a gift of its own. These people from Ulster cared very little for the beautiful, with the single exception of the wonderful and beautiful Bible story.*[6]

He goes on to say:

> *The Scotch Irish could not see that the severe lines of a cabin are softened by a sumac against the south wall or a creeper at the corner. They did not trim the edge of the roadway that led to the front door. In short, utility required nothing of these things and utility was their law. For the same reason, if the soles of their feet were tough*

4. Wheeler, 365.
5. Wheeler, 208.
6. Bolton, 301-302.

they saw small need of shoes in summer. Their bare feet, however, gave something of a shock to century-old New England. This rude development of taste was based possibly upon a primitive state of education.[7]

So utilitarian, no-frills, not educated (I prefer that to uneducated) - just survivors as our ancestors needed to be or else we would not be alive today. Bolton phrases it this way: "It is evident that whether we view the Scotch Irish pioneers from the standpoint of education, or culture, or material success of the larger kind, they were in 1718 in their proper place when Cotton Mather consigned them to the frontier."[8]

But they were literate. This is proven by the fact that all of that second generation were able to sign their names to documents. In fact very few signatures appear with mark in any of the paperwork I found.

These Scotch-Irish," says Professor Perry, of Williams College, "were all in general one sort of people. They belonged to one grade and sphere of life. They were for the most part very poor in this world's goods. The vast majority of all the adults, however, could read and write. If they had but one book to a family, that book was surely the Bible, and if there were two volumes to a family, the second place in most cases was disputed between Fox's 'Book of Martyrs' and Bunyan's 'Pilgrim's Progress.' Their personal habits, their mental characteristics, their religious beliefs and experiences, and their very superstitions, were held largely in common.[9]

And in addition, they were poor. These were not moneyed classes but "were subjected to many hardships and privations".[10]

If by any possibility we could be transported back to the early days of old Pejebscot we should find a vastly different condition of affairs and widely different customs than those we have today. If the old Puritans were gloomy the people of Topsham were much more so. In the age when the falling of every rustling leaf was mistaken for the stealthy footfall of a savage foe gladness and hilarity found no lodgement in the human heart. The only topics discussed were those relating to the last cruel murder and the probabilities as to who the next victim would be.[11]

I only started looking at the role of the Scotch Irish after I had worked my way through numerous generations and thousands

7. Bolton, 303.
8. Bolton, 306.
9. De Alva Stanwood Alexander, The Alexanders of Maine (Buffalo, NY: The Peter Paul Book Company, 1898), 7.
10. Old Slavery Days in Topsham, Lewiston Journal, April 25-29, 1908. From Cyrus Woodman's Scrapbook.
11. Newspaper excerpts from Cyrus Woodman's Scrapbook.

of descendants. I think this is why so much of early Maine was so hard for me to comprehend; it is a story very different from much of what we know about the early colonies. We are fed a diet of heroic ancestors and doings and never introduced to real life.

Even the tragedy of Jamestown is more interesting. Talk of the "seasoning" that the English had to undergo, getting used to the heat of the south, the oft-told romanticized tale of Pocahontas - it all adds up to marvelous stories.

The story of James Oglethorpe, a social reformer, who founded the colony of Georgia is another tale that I, as a Georgia native, was raised with. Not only did he rescue debtors from prison but he also laid out a well-thought out city in Savannah. As anyone who been there knows, it is a gorgeous city with incredible history.

Comparing those stories to Indian horrors? Not much of contest there! Once again, however, someone had to do it and the Scotch Irish settlers of early Maine performed their duty well.

James and His Family

It has not been proven who James married or exactly where he came from originally. We believe he came from Scotland to Ireland just to go to across the ocean. They may have lived in northern Ireland for a while; I doubt if we will ever know for sure.

According to various sources, none definitive, James and his wife, who was probably Jean, arrived in Maine with four children. Two more children were born in Maine. I have found no other mention of a Jean Wilson in Maine and for the moment feel safe in assuming she was James' wife. It may be a bit of stretch to say her last name was Shaw but it is a possibility. There are Scottish traces of a Jean Shaw married to a James Wilson though I do not feel comfortable with any of that data. It appears to be common to have an ancestor come through or from Ireland in the 1700s and the only information here in the new world is that they came from Ulster.

Tracing ancestors who were born or lived in Ireland has proved to be a daunting task. Record keeping in Ireland for Protestants may well be found in the Presbyterian churches but those records are not as well digitized as those in England and Scotland.

Also, the missing data can also be explained by what was happening in Ireland under Queen Anne as noted in chapter two of Bolton's Scotch Irish Pioneers.[1] If marriages were declared invalid and chapels closed, the protestants / Presbyterians may well have lost those church records (or they were destroyed by others) that would assist us now.

James did live in Brunswick first; his son Samuel[2] claimed in depositions that he was born there. The family did live in Topsham, however, before James' death on 9 September 1743. The Pejebscot Papers list Widow Wilson living with Hugh[2] and Samuel[2] on lot 57 in 1746 with William[2] living on lot 56.[2] There is also a list from that same time period (undated) that is a sign up list of those who want to live in Topsham. Those appear to be signatures with marks next to the ones who can't write. It is entitled "A list of Settlers to be at

1. Bolton, 15.
2. Pejebscot Papers, 3-35.

Topsham (some of whome came) no date."[3] James Wilson's name is on that list with a mark instead of a signature.

Wheeler says there were only 36 settlers there in 1746.[4] A note in the Pejebscot list says 25 residents were there in 1747 and a number of people are listed as dead and or killed, such as William and John Mustard and James Potter with the last ones being James McFarland and James Crain.

Note the lot numbers on the left. This is dated 9 April 1746.[5]

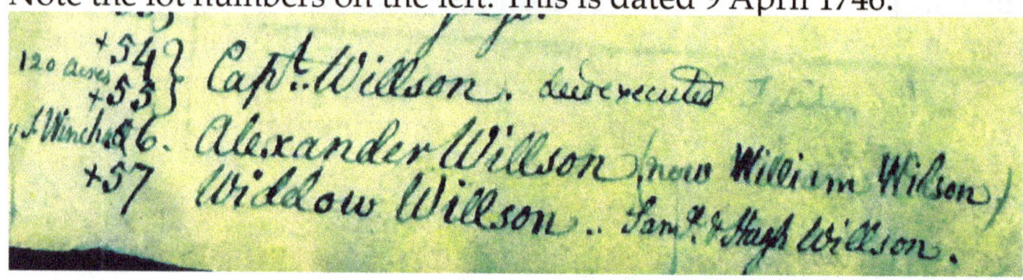
120 acres +54 } Capt. Willson.
+55 }
56. Alexander Willson (now William Wilson)
+57 Widdow Willson .. Saml. & Hugh Willson.

Two deeds, one for Hugh[2] and one for Samuel[2], mention that the land had been previously "taken up by his Father James Wilson". [6] So James did live and work the land in Topsham before his death.

James is buried in First Parish Cemetery (Marquoit) in Brunswick. The gravestone inscription makes his birth year around 1670.

Here lies Buried
The Body of M^{r}.
JAMES WILSON
Who Departed this Life
September ye 9th 1743
in the 73^{d} year
of his Age.[7]

His granddaughter, Hannah[3] (Samuel[2] and Mary's daughter) who died in 1762 is also buried in First Parish[8] and, as her parents' graves cannot be found today, they may be buried there as well. The First Parish Church was established just prior to James' arrival

3. Pejebscot Papers, 4-73.
4. Wheeler, 43.
5. Pejebscot Papers, 3:35.
6. Lincoln County Deeds, 3:206, 3:235.
7. Findagrave.com, gravestone and personal photograph, http://goo.gl/CvMTWt.
8. Findagrave.com, gravestone and personal photograph, http://goo.gl/vle5Fb.

in 1717 and there wasn't an church in Topsham during James' life. Son William[2] may also have been a member as a William is listed in one parish record in December of 1762.[9] The church seems to have been a mixture of Church of Christ and Presbyterian.

The Children

The eldest known child was the daughter, Jane[2] or Jennet as she is frequently referred to. She was born 1706; her headstone lists her age as 92 when she died 7 March 1798.[10] Her husband, William Alexander, was born that same year in Ulster, Ireland. They married prior to the birth of their first son, David b.1737, probably in 1736.[11]

Either William[2] or Robert[2] was James Wilson's oldest son; the dates are very close.

Robert[2] may have been born about 1714 and though he is mentioned in the Wheelers history, little information has been found about him. All indications are that he never married but did have a share in the saw mill. There is a deed dated 1763 selling that portion of the sawmill to his brother Alexander[2] that he didn't register until after Robert's death in about 1783. (Lincoln County Deeds, 17:149) A probate record of the administration after his death by Samuel[2] Wilson is dated 12 Aug 1783. He was declared insolvent then so I don't see how that came to pass as the numbers of assets to liabilities do not add up. Besides the saw mill portion, he also had one old boat, an old bedstead, some plates and bottles (3:113)

> *Probated 12 Ap., 1783. [II. 187.] Robert Wilson, late of Topsham. Samuel Wilson, residing at little River. so called, Adm'r, 4 June, 1783. [II, 188.] David Reed, of Topsham, and Enoch Danford, of Brunswick, sureties. Inventory by Andrew Dunning, of Brunswick, Actor Patten and James Wilson, both of Topsham, 12 Aug., 1783, .£36: o: o. [III, 113.] John Merrill and Actor Patten, both of Topsham, commissioners to examine claims. [III, 113.] Account filed 4 Jan., 1787. [Ill, 129.]* [12]

There are some references to Robert in a list for Captain Adam

9. Wheeler, 375.
10. Findagrave.com, gravestone photograph, name is Jennet http://goo.gl/6d1Oiy
11. Clemmons, 15.
12. William Davis Patterson, The Probate Records of Lincoln County, Maine: 1760 to 1800 (Portland, Me, 1895), 121.

Hunter's militia company from 1757. The four Wilsons listed together are the brothers: Hugh[2], Robert,[2] Samuel[2] and William[2].[13]

He did live in Harpswell, proven by deeds that read "Robert Willson of Harpswell" (3:172) and it was his brother in Harpswell to whom he sold that sawmill portion.

Born about 1715, William[2] married Isabella Larrabee, the daughter of Benjamin Larrabee, a well-known figure at the time. William[2] and Isabelle are my fifth great grandparents.

Alexander[2] was the third son born around 1716; he married Catharine Swansea (Swanzey) around 1746 but moved about 16 miles away to Harpswell closer to the ocean and raised his family away from Topsham. It is his family that also intermarried with a family of English Wilsons a few generations later.

The two youngest brothers, Hugh[2] b.1729 and Samuel[2] b.1722 or 1732, would have been late in life children for James. As we know that Jean tried to flee the Indian wars in 1722, no telling where she actually went and how long they might have been separated.

Wheeler says "In 1722 the fourth Indian, or Lovewell's, war commenced, and the situation of the settlers here became so disagreeable that they nearly all abandoned their homes, and it was not until about 1730 that the settlement was renewed."[14]

It is quite understandable if they had put off having additional children until the area was safer - after the Dummer's War treaty in 1727. Permanent Topsham settlers did not appear until after 1730 and many families that did remain did not even have homes in years prior to that but resided inside fortifications.

The oldest daughter, Jennett[2], did wait until about age 30 to marry and bear her first child in 1737. William[2] may have been 35 when he married in 1749; Samuel[2] was nearly 30; Robert[2] most likely did not

13. Wheeler, 879.
14. Wheeler, 37.

marry at all. All details that lend more indicators of the hard times in the area; interestingly, all marriages except one happened after James' death. Both William^2 and Hugh^2 married in 1749, Alexander^2 in 1746, Samuel^2 in 1761 and possibly James' wife remarried in 1750.

There is a record of a Mrs. Elisabeth Wilson announcing intentions to marry Walter McDonall of Georgetown on 31 Dec 1750.[15] I cannot find any Elizabeth Wilsons married or not from any Wilson family in the area before 1750, so that Elizabeth may have been James wife (maybe even a second wife). There is no actual marriage record however for a McDonall marriage. Vital records of Georgetown show a large concentration of "Mc" names - but only one listing for Walter and that is the marriage intention.

Land

All brothers owned property in early Topsham and were major players in the area's early history as entrepreneurs. The large map included in Wheeler's book is a visual layout of the land ownership and though I can include parts of it in this book, if you are really interested, try to find a library copy to view that map. The full map is available on line at the Curtis library site.

Jennet's husband was also a land owner and person of influence in Topsham and Harpswell. Samuel^2, Hugh^2 and William^2 settled permanently in Topsham; Alexander^2, Robert^2 and Jennett^2 moved downstream to Harpswell.

Hugh Wilson's house was built in Topsham in 1750 and is still the oldest house standing in Topsham. I did get the opportunity to tour the house (and no, I didn't just knock on the door. It's for sale and the owner was eager to show me around and talk about the house and the remodeling that's happened in the past 16 years.)

The original lots in Topsham were 100 acres each but Hugh^2, Samuel^2 and William^2 added more land as they could.

15. Hill, II, 284.

These maps are available on line at mainememory.net:

Hugh Wilson's 200 acres, 1761: https://goo.gl/OwVCfU
Samuel's 60 acres, 1762 : https://goo.gl/KPdCwp
https://goo.gl/uklc4l William Alexander dated 1764
Samuel and Hugh lot, 1758 https://goo.gl/Uhu1ay

Religion

According to Wheeler, the majority of the western side of Brunswick were Scotch Irish and Presbyterian. The first Baptists started meeting around 1783 in Brunswick.[16] In 1790 the first protests appear in the records about paying taxes for the First Parish ministers.

In Topsham, the First Parish Church there was officially started after the incorporation of Topsham in 1764.[17] According to Wheeler, it was decidedly Presbyterian in nature. A few of the Wilsons are buried in that cemetery, located on Middlesex Road, including Hugh^2, the eldest and his son, Hugh^3, and William^2 the Eldest's son, William^3. All of them died before 1800.

The first Baptist meetings in Topsham began around 1779 with the first incorporation in 1794. Here we find the names of the children who remained in Topsham and their spouses and in-laws: Hugh Wilson^3, John Wilson^3, Ebenezer Farren, Samuel Wilson^3, James Purington, and Humphrey Thompson.[18] Most of these original members were born around 1750 to 1760 and there were a few of their parents as well. A number were revolutionary war veterans. The first minister was John Wilson's son-in-law, Elihu Purington.

The Haley Cemetery, where some of the descendants of William^2 and Hugh^2 Wilson are buried, is the site of the "old yellow meeting house" principally built by the Haleys, among others, and whose name now graces that cemetery. It is the site of that Baptist meeting

16. Wheeler, 377.
17. Wheeler, 406.
18. Wheeler, 419-420.

house.

That does strike me as funny - my father was Catholic and I had always assumed that the Wilsons were too. One of the first questions from my newly found New England cousins was where did the Catholicism come from in my family. I was startled to realize that Catholicism was an aberration in my Dad's family and not the norm.

My southern family was strongly Presbyterian on the Scotch Irish side of the Vances, some of whom were well-known ministers in Tennessee. So my roots are firmly just Christian but with a bigger mix than some others. Baptist. Well, I'll be.

Military

Wheeler's appendix includes rosters from the several Indian wars. Robert² and William² are listed in Captain Benjamin Larrabee's company for 1748. Hugh², Robert², Samuel² and William² all show up in a list of Captain Adam Hunter's company in 1757.[19]

The Willsons, Wilssons

Wilson was spelled with two 'll's throughout this generation. The gravestones have Willson but the deeds spell it all three ways. The 1790 census has Wilson. In writing I found it frequently spelled with one 'l' and two 's' as represented by what looks to be a kind of 'f' during that time.

19. Wheeler, 874-877.

First Generation

During their lives...

Between years of 1742 to 1750 Maine experienced what is termed a great depopulation due to Indian Wars and smallpox.[1]

By the American Revolution, Massachusetts and, therefore Maine, still did not have defined borders.[2]

Maine did not become a separate state until after the turn of the century.

Primary exports of Maine in the eighteenth century were lumber and fish so nearly all occupations were in logging, sawmills, fishing and transportation of those items. Initially those went to Boston but larger ships made longer voyages to England, the West Indies, the Mediterranean and the wine islands.[3] It was trade and the tightening of trade laws in the 1700s that led to the American Revolution. That started in Massachusetts and in coastal Maine. Riots broke out in seaport cities after the passing of the Stamp Act in 1765[4]. There was unrest!

Hugh (James[1]), Hugh the Eldest

Hugh[2] was the first cabinet maker in Topsham. He was also the first of the family born in Maine in about 1729. He amassed quite a bit of property quickly and seemed to have been a bit of a controversial fellow. He was part owner of the first dam and saw mill with his brother William[2] in 1753[5] and served as Topsham's first constable after its incorporation in 1764.[6]

He built a house in Topsham in 1750 which is on present day Win-

---

1. W. S. Rossiter, A Century of Population Growth (Washington, Government Printing Office, 1908), 5.
2. Rossiter, 17.
3. Duncan, Roger E., Coastal Maine: a Maritime History (New York: Norton & Company, 1992), 195.
4. Duncan, 200.
5. Pebscot Papers.
6. Wheeler, 183.

ter Street and is listed on the walking tour of Topsham[7] as an example of the Center Chimney Cape style. The present owner told me that there used to be a tunnel under the house from the basement to the edge of the land where it drops down. That was an escape tunnel to use if threatened by the Indians. One of the advantages of placing your house on little land surrounded by cliffs!

This is the photo I took this year which is the driveway side, not the road side which would normally be the front.

Here is almost the same view from the 1995 brochure which is closer to the original house. The picket fence on the right delineates the road.

Hugh holds a permanent place in Topsham history for an accident that led to his leg being amputated when he caught his legs between mill logs on the eastern branch of the Cathance River. He died early about age 40 after the operation on 9 June 1769.[8] Wheeler says this was the first work-related accident in the area.[9]

His marriage to Elizabeth Hewey produced at least three sons, including Hugh[3] and William[3]. There was also a James[3] who died early and two daughters, Martha[3] and Elizabeth[3], as well.

> *"Elizabeth and Hugh Wilson (the eldest), [ ], P.R.80. [Elizabeth Henry and Hugh Wilson of T., int. Sept. 5, 1759, p.R.106.] [Mrs. Elizabeth Hewey of Brunswick,*

---

7. Topsham, Maine, Historical Walking Tour, A Publication of the Topsham Historic District Commission, 1995, 1997.
8. Topsham II, 398.
9. Wheeler, 318.

T.R.4.]" (Topsham II, 130)

Hugh did not prepare for his death; he died intestate while his children were all under the age of 11.

"Hugh Wilson, late of Topsham. Elizabeth Wilson of Topsham, widow, Adm'x, 30 Aug., 1769. [I, 173.] Thomas Willson and Samuel Wilson, sureties. Inventory by Thomas Wilson, Robert Gower and Actor Patten, all of Topsham, 3 Oct., 1769, £649: 11: o. [I, 191.] Account of Elizabeth Weymouth, Adm'x, 9 Mar. 1787. [111, 137 and 245.J Samuel Thompson, of Brunswick, guardian unto William minor son, 17 Sep., 1787. [111, 160.]"[10]

Elizabeth did remarry 9 years after Hugh's death so the children were raised by their mother, a step-father (for a while) and William's guardian, Samuel Thompson. Samuel Thompson is the father-in-law of my fourth great grandfather, John[3] Wilson.

Weymouth, Timothy of T., formerly of Berwick, and Mrs. Elizabeth (Hewey) Wilson, wid. of Hugh the eldest, [ ]; they parted, he d. in Brunswick, she in T., P.R.80." (Topsham II, 273)

As I said, Hugh[2] bought land.

His first recorded purchase in 1759 was the 100 acres allowed him on the Cathance River, the unnumbered lot on the map from 1761. (1:441). He then bought half a lot "taken up by his Father James Wilson" which becomes lot 58. (3:206) He, William[2], Samuel[2] and others bought 3/4 of an acre with the privilege of building mills in what came to be named Granny's Hole. (LC 1:443) He kept adding bits and pieces over the next few years: 15 acres (LC 3:207), 53 acres (LC 2:213), 50 acres (PP 4:205-207) and 5 acres (LC 4:145). I either missed some deeds at Lincoln County or not all of the older deeds were there: some of this I pulled out of the Pejebscot Papers.

But also in the Pejebscot Papers was a surveying mistake that Hugh[2] obviously didn't want to deal with. Stephen Getchell, the surveyor, made some error that had to be corrected later. Belcher Noyes wrote a letter afterwards that called Getchell a "poor, miserable, shufling Fellow" and said he had received numerous complaints about him.[11] That mistake was settled by giving someone else more land but then in 1768 Hugh[2] was accused of altering a deed, changing 40 rods to 50 rods so that he had laid claim to 25

10. Patterson 45.
11. Pejebscot, 164-165.

acres more than the deed was supposed to contain.[12] The deed to this day, however, still reads 50 rods so though the Pejebscot Proprietors had decided to pursue this in the courts, they must not have prevailed.

He also was embroiled in other controversies sometimes alone and sometimes with his brothers - it might have been all about water rights and trespass to get the rights they needed. I suspect this was about the saw mills but more study is needed in the Pejebscot Papers to untangle all of it.

In 1789 three men were appointed to split his estate. This would have been as the youngest, William[3], was close to 21.

Elizabeth was given 1/3 of the home lot that ran from the Androscoggin to the Cathance which should be where the 1750 house is today. (That is the widow's dowry which by law, the widow was to receive 1/3 of the estate.) That was carried to an extreme as she also got 1/3 of the house, 1/3 of the barn and two days in the saw mill every week.

Son Hugh[3] received 30 acres of the homestead, 1/3 of the barn, 2/3's of the house and 1/5 of the 5 acre meadow lot. William[3] Junior (called that because there was an elder William[2], his uncle) received 66 acres and 2/3 of an acre in the meadow lot. Martha[3] (and husband Ebenezer Farrin) got 30 acres of the home lot, 1/3 of the barn, 1/6 of a pasture and 1/2 of the small meadow lot. Daughter Elizabeth's children received 61 and 1/3 acres of the home lot and 1/3 of the pasture lot. Each also was allowed five and 1/2 days of the saw every four weeks.

At the end of this probate record (19:378), Hugh[2] is refusing to agree because he says he has paid some bills that should be shared by the others. This controversy was never resolved before he died in 1799.

The rest of the Hugh Wilson story is told in the chapter entitled

12. Pejebscot, 2:18.

"Hugh's Descendants".

Hugh's signature & requested meadow acreage, Pejebscot Papers

William (James^{1}), William the Eldest

William^{2} b.abt 1715 is my fifth great-grandfather. He married the daughter of Captain Benjamin Larrabee, Isabella.

> *"[----] and William Wilson the eldest, the Innholder, [—], P.R.80. [Isabella, int. July 29, 1749, p.R.106.] [she of Brunswick, he of T., T.R.4.]" (Topsham II, 158, under Larrabee)*
>
> *William the eldest, the Innholder, and [ ], Larrabee, [----], p.R.80. [Isabella, July 29, 1749, int. p.R.106.] [he of T., she of Brunswick, T.R.4.] (Topsham II, 288)*
>
> *Mr William Willson of a place Called Topsom and m^{rs} Isabella Larrabee of Brunswick intends marrige to each other Brunswick Jully 29 1749 (Brunswick, 117)*
>
> *Isabella Larrabee Daughter of the above named Benjamin and Mary Larrabee was Born November 27th 1731.*
>
> *"Isabella, Widow, Oct. —, 1798, a. more than 70 y., C.R.I. [w. William, Oct. 17, in 66th y. of a., G.R.2.]" (Topsham II, 398)*

Capt. Benjamin Larrabee was the agent of the Pejepscot company who had been given in 1737 "full power of attorney to execute deeds to the settlers in Brunswick and Topsham".[13] So though William married into an influential and rich family, he did so a year after Benjamin's death in 1748.

William^{2} and Isabella had at least seven children, sons William^{3}, John^{3}, and Samuel^{3} were listed in his will dated 1762 as were daughters Mary^{3} and Isabella^{3}. Other daughters not mentioned in the will were Hannah^{3} and Elizabeth^{3} who must have been born after the will. He probably wouldn't have worried about changing the will since it states there should be money given to his daughters in a equal share.

According to Wheeler, "In 1762, Samuel Wilson was licensed as an innholder, and for each successive year, down to September, 1766, when his last license was granted....This last year, William Wilson

13. Wheeler, 31.

is mentioned in the Pejepscot Papers as an innholder in Topsham. He was licensed in 1761, and an Isabella Wilson in 1767. The precise locality of the two inns kept by the Wilsons is not known, but they were doubtless within the limits of what now constitutes the village of Topsham. The reason for this supposition is, that Samuel and William Wilson owned lots in 1768 opposite the fort, and in 1773 there was a tavern kept at Topsham Ferry by a Mr. Wilson."[14]

In the vital records and in deeds and other papers, William[2] is frequently referred to as William the Innkeeper. I didn't run into any information about a tavern at the Topsham Ferry so it must have been in the town records. I did go through a fair amount of them but it would have been easy for me to miss it due to the quality of the microfilm and handwriting.

William was one of the prime people involved in the Granny's Hole saw mill. He purchased the land for it from John Patten in 1762 (3:2) and then divvied it out to the others (3:23). In the end his boys inherited his portion.

The Church of the First Parish in Brunswick lists "William Wilson, received December, 1762"[15] two months after his will in October. A new minister was ordained in November which may have prompted his joining. The estate inventory does include a pew in the Brunswick meeting house but also there is mention of "half of the ground for a pew in Topsham meeting house".

William's will was written on 1 Oct 1762 when he obviously got very ill and was thinking he would die; two daughters, Elizabeth and Hannah are not mentioned but the will was probated on 13 Aug 1766 so they must have been born between 1762 and 1766. Elizabeth's husband was born in 1766, however, so I doubt she was born much before his death.

> *"In the Name of God Amen the Twenty first Day of October 1762 I William Wilson of Topsham in the County of Lincoln Husbandman being Very Sick and Weak in Body but of Perfect Mind and Memory. Thanks be Given to God : Therefore Calling unto mind the mortality of my Body and knowing that it is appointed unto all men*

14. Wheeler, 298.
15. Wheeler, 374.

once to die do make and ordain this my Last Will and Testament That is to say, Principally and first of all I Give and Recommend my soul into the Hands of God that gave it and my Body I recommend to the Earth To be Buried in decent christian burial at the discretion of my Executors, nothing doubting but at the General Resurrection I shall receive the same again by the mighty Power of God and as touching such worldly Estate wherewith it hath pleased God to bless me in this Life I give demise and dispose of the same in the following manner and form

Imprimis. I give and bequeath to my well beloved sons viz, William Wilson, John Wilson & Samuel Wilson all and Singular my Lands Messuages and Tenements with all the Right I have in any Saw Mill or Mills Together with all my Household Goods, Chattles, Debts and moveable Effects by them and each of them freely to be possessed & enjoyed I likewise give and bequeath to my well beloved Daughters Mary and Isabella Willson so much money to be raised & levyed out of my Estate by the aforesaid William John and Samuel Wilson to pay to the aforesaid Daughters as shall make all my Children to have an Equal Share--

Item. Constitute make and ordain Isabella my dearly and well beloved Wife my Sole executrix of this my last Will and Testament and she the said Isabella to have the Income of said Estate till all the heirs come of age unless she Should marry before that Time And I do hereby utterly I disallow revoke and disannul all and every other former Testament, Wills, Legacies and Bequests and Executors by me in Any ways before named, willed and Bequeathed, ratifying and Confirming this and no other to be my Last will and Testament In Witness whereof, I have hereunto Set my Hand and Seal the Day and year above Written William Wilson and a Seal

Signed Sealed published pronounced and declared by the Said William Willson as his Last Will and Testament in the Presence of us the Subscribers Thos Willson James Potter Sam[el] *Moody Wm Alexander Executors*

Probated 13 Aug., 1766. (1:94)
Inventory by Thomas Willson, William Alexander and John Merrill, 1 Sep., 1766, £297: 12: 6. (3:195)

I thought at first that he was buried in Haley cemetery next to his wife. There are bits of stone left at the head and the foot of that grave but no cemetery records exist that list him or the next graves which I believe to be his son Humphrey and his wife Nancy. Then I realized that Haley Cemetery didn't exist at that time. Isabella was one of the first buried there. He could have been buried in Topsham First Parish or even in Brunswick First Parish since he seems to have joined before his death. That was where his father and niece were buried - they were the only deaths previous to his in the family. That may have been the reason he joined First Parish after he wrote the will. He may wanted to have been buried there.

There is one mention about Isabella in Wheeler's history.

> *As an illustration of the indefinite manner in which many of the roads are recorded, the following is copied : "The Road begining at Issabella's Barn Running to William Alexander's house was laid out by the Selectmen in October 1774." It is, perhaps, needless to say that we have found no allusions to Isabella's barn elsewhere.*[16]

That may have put the road he is talking about up in the meadow lands near the Cathance since the only the only piece of land that William Alexander's name is on to was next to William's (on the 1768 map), possibly near and/or parallel the path of route 201 today.

Last but not least, William's legacy lived on after his death when the children donated a hundred acres to be designated for a school.[17] I'm not sure how that land was originally obtained or which parcel was donated. On the map dated 1768 there is a school lot above lot 56 which William owned. The donation is dated 1769. It could possibly be that the boys donated lot 56 to be added to the other existing lot or else the boys had already told them about the donation but it had not been officially recorded when the map was made. I think the knowledge was there before the map was drawn.

I can find no evidence of any of William's children living in the area of lot 56. All the later deeds I found were on the Cathance River, not the Androscoggin. The inventory taken at the time of his death does not actually describe where the land and buildings were, but they were assessed at 160 pounds. That may have been only on the plots where the mills were but it only says "land and buildings thereon". Five acres of meadow land were also listed.

Also included were two Bibles, five books, various farm tools, animals, a dozen plates, a looking glass, two guns, two pistols and more for a total estate worth about 297 pounds.

William's children and descendants are continued in the chapter entitled "William's Children".

16. Wheeler, 542.
17. Pejebscot Papers, 2:19.

Samuel (James[1])

Samuel's signature & requested meadow acreage, Pejebscot papers

Samuel's birth year may be 1722 or 1732. Both Alexander and Hugh's graves still exist and the dates combined with the ages makes Alexander born in 1718 and Hugh in 1729 but in depositions still in existence in the Pejebscot Papers Samuel states his age, 55, 61 and 63. These are dated in a different hand, obviously after the fact and the ink is darker as if years later. Those dates and ages make Samuel's birth year 1732 but he also states in one that a brother is seven years older than him. 1732 makes Hugh 5 years older and 1722 makes Alexander possibly 7 years older. I also found another deposition summary that said a deposition where he states he is 67 is supposedly from 1796 - making him born in 1722.[18] So the numbers don't add up completely.

The Pejebscot papers hold several copies of depositions, letters and deeds - they are not always marked as copies though it is obvious that some are since duplicates exist. That lowers my trust level in them as factual documents. One deposition where Samuel states he was 55 in June in 1787 is viewable on line at the MaineMemory.net site.[19] The full collection is held by the Maine Historical Society in Portland.

Samuel married Mary Reed and then later Elizabeth Snow[20] after Mary's death.

> *Samuel and Mary Reed, a sister of Col. John Reed, [---]. He rem. to Lisbon prior to 1790, P.R.80. [int. Dec. 11, 1761, P.R.106.] [both of T., T.R.4.] (Topsham II, 288)*
>
> *Mr Sam[l] Willson & M[rs] Mary Ried Ju[r] both of Topsham Intend Marriage Brunswick Dec[r] 11th 1761 (Brunswick, 122)*

---

18. Pejebscot papers, 9:38
19. Maine Memory network,https://goo.gl/S24snK, accessed 21 May 2015.
20. Woodman, Cyrus, A History of Topsham, Maine, Scrapbook, 1835 (Archival material, Maine Historical Society, Coll. 1498), 65.

Holbrook, Elizabeth (Snow), Mrs. (wid. of Abijah H. of Harpswell) and Samuel Wilson (his second w., no issue), p.R.80. (Topsham II, 135)

No birth or death days or even months are known for either Samuel or his wives but it appears that Mary was still alive in 1781 and received 6 shillings at the death of her father, John Reed. Mary is listed as the wife of Samuel Wilson in that will.[21]

Item I give to My Daughter Mary the wife of Samuel Wilson Six Shillings to be paid by my Executor.[22]

But then in 1 Jan 1799 we find in a probate record for David Reed, Samuel's brother-in-law:

Division of personal estate among widow, mother, Jane, wife of Joseph Foster, Martha, wife of Joseph Randall, Hannah, wife of Robert Potter, Margaret, wife of Robert Jack, Elizabeth, wife of John Soule, Charlotte, wife of John Herrin, ***the representatives of Samuel Wilson and wife, deceased,*** *and the representatives of John Reed, deceased, 4 Jan., 1799.*[23]

So Mary died between 1781 and 1798. Since she was not removed from her father's will by the time he died in 1795, her death date then might have been between 1795 and 1798.

The only Elizabeth Snow I could find traces of was born 3 Nov 1743 in Brunswick[24] and married Abizir Holbrook in 1762 in Brunswick.[25] I could not find a death date for Abizir to help pinpoint when she and Samuel may have married.

Samuel² was the only Samuel in the area except for his nephew, son of William².

According to Wheeler, Samuel² was "licensed as an innholder at Topsham, by the Court of Sessions for Lincoln County, in Oct. 1762, and for each successive year down to Sept. 1766, when his last license was granted."[26] He is listed in one deed as Samuel the Innkeeper.

Samuel² did get the ferry license:

21. Patterson, 258.
22. Patterson, 258.
23. Patterson, 261.
24. Brunswick, 19.
25. "Maine, Marriages, 1771-1907," https://goo.gl/e41xvP.
26. Wheeler, 860-861.

> *On September 8, 1761, Samuel Wilson was licensed to keep a ferry over the Androscoggin River, about one hundred rods below the falls, and gave bonds in the sum of £20 for the faithful discharge of his trust. He was permitted to demand and receive of every passenger three " coppers," and three "coppers" for each horse ferried across. The Topsham landing-place was at first, probably, a short distance east of the present village burying-ground. Later, about 1783 to 1796, it was near the point at the end of the iron railroad bridge, which then went by the name of Ferry Point. During this later period, the ferry was kept by Brigadier Samuel Thompson.*[27]

From that description I assume the ferry then was somewhere near where the railroad bridge is today.

He was a surveyor of highways in 1764[28] and was involved in the saw mills along with Hugh^2 and William^2.

Wheeler claims "He removed to Lisbon prior to 1790, and lived and died on the farm owned in 1835 by Charles Thompson."[29] He did move to Lisbon (Little River Plantation) but he did not die in 1835. The first mention of Little River was in a deed from 1787 where it is said that he was of "a place called Little River".[30] The Little River Plantation was part of the Pejepscot Purchase and is now in the area of Lisbon Falls.[31]

Other deeds also mention Little River (Lincoln County 27:195, 40:60, 40:65) and in the probate records he is said to be late of Lisbon. (14:320)

Another deed (3:25) he buys land "taken up by his Father James".

The original mention of the move and death was in the Cyrus Woodman papers with no mention of death date. It also said the farm in Lisbon was 'now' owned by Charles Thompson, not owned at the time of Samuel's death. Wheeler was incorrect.

That probate record was to name his second wife Elizabeth administrator of his estate because he died without a will. That first notice

27. Wheeler, 547.
28. Wheeler, 183.
29. Wheeler, 861.
30. Lincoln County, 27:195.
31. Lisbon, Maine, http://goo.gl/ezKrNQ, accessed 21 May 2015.

is dated 30 July 1810. The inventory of his estate recorded on 20 Aug 1810 does not include any land and is valued at only $81.44 but there are debts totalling $475.17 - all signed notes. In the inventory are listed 3 bed quilts, bedstead, chest, trunks, table, desk, chairs, rocking chair, linens, cow, pig, flat irons, crane and dishes/crockery. (14:401).

He had sold by deed his part of the sawmill in 1772, recorded in 1802 (65:98), and his part of the long dam to son James in 1797 (40: 65). He had amassed a fair amount of land, 190 acres in 1787 (27:195), 65 acres in 1761 (4:195), 30+ in 1764 (3:235), and 100 in 1757 (3:8). I don't know where the sales of those lots are but I certainly could have missed something in the records though missing all of that is odd. I keep getting the feeling that there are missing records between Lincoln and Sagadahoc Counties. Topsham became part of Sagadahoc in 1854 and this all had to be put together between two court houses.

Samuel^2 and Mary had five known children: Hannah^3, James^3, Susanna^3, John^3 and William^3 but I was only to trace the children of one, James^3.

The rest of Samuel's story is told in the chapter named "Samuel's Descendants".

Alexander (James^1)

Alexander Wilson was born before the family's arrival in New England; his tombstone lists his age at about 56 which means he would have been born around 1718 probably in Ulster. Settling in Harpswell before his marriage around 1746, he, like others at that time, waited until he was about 30 to marry.

> *Alexander dug his cellar next to G----- lot and cleared about 3 acres of land, got ye timber for his house ready for raising, but was drove off by ye Indians after he had been at ye fight wth Col. Harmon at Summerset all which cost him considerable.*[32]

In 1758 at the first recorded meeting of the district it is noted that

32. Watson, S M, Maine Historical and Genealogical Recorder, vol. IX (Portland, Maine: 1898) 198..

"Alexander Wilson and Andrew Dunning should be a committee to settle with North Yarmouth, and to receive whatever money was due the town."[33] (Andrew Dunning would provide one daughter-in-law to him later.) As the town's representative, his name appears regularly in Wheeler's history.

He also was a tradesman: by about 1762 "Andrew Dunning and Alexander Wilson were also in trade; that is, they were licensed retailers, and had a stock of goods which they disposed of to the settlers when called upon, but they probably did not confine themselves exclusively to that business."[34]

> *Alaxander Willson and Katherin Swainey Both of Brunswick intends marriage to each other Agust the 19 1746 (Brunswick, 116)*

Catharine Swanzey b.1727 d.5 Jan 1764[35] of Harpswell is said to be the daughter of an Irishman, Robert, and his wife, Lillie May Isaacs. There is nothing on record for any Swanzeys in the 1700s and there are very few Swanzeys in the United States. Swanzey, New Hampshire, is said to be a spelling of Swansea and seems to be the main origin in the US of the name spelled that way. Most genealogical records spell her name as Swanzey but the children and grandchildren named Swanzey seemed to spell it in various ways. Alexander died 26 March 1774 according to his tombstone.[36]

Alexander's name is on lot 56 in Topsham but William must have taken it when he got of age after Alexander moved to Harpswell. Alexander and Catharine left a legacy in their property now called Wilson's Point. Their descendants occupied that land until 1949.

"We have been told that the first dwelling on the property was a simple 'log cabin' near the high cliff on the shore. It was likely to have been built by Alexander Wilson, who also established a small shipyard on his land in Wilson Cove near the point. Alexander and his nephew John Alexander built the first craft there. Its size and name are not known, but, in May 1763, the town voted to pay

33. Wheeler, 163.
34. Wheeler, 621.
35. Findagrave.com, gravestone, http://goo.gl/D1hjdp.
36. Findagrave.com, gravestone: http://goo.gl/Adg3CT

Benjamin Jaques, Alexander Wilson, and John Alexander the sums assessed against them for the sloop built the previous year."[37]

They had nine children, James³, Mary³, Elizabeth³, David³, Esther³, Jennet³, Alexander³, Swanzey³, and Catharine³. Eight of those children survived but only three had children, James³, David³, and Alexander³.

Alexander married a second time after Catharine's death to a Sarah Cloof; however, I was not able to find any other information about her.

Alexander Willson of Harpswell and Sarah Cloof resident at Harpswell were married Aug 12 1766 (Harpswell, 22)

The tale of Alexander's family is continued in the chapter entitled "Alexander's Family in Harpswell".

Jane "Jennet" (James¹) A Dynasty All Her Own - The Alexanders

Last but not least is Jennet, Jean or Jane, the only known daughter. Wheeler refers to her as Jane, as do the notations in Hill's vital records and commonly the plain jane name of Jane is variably treated - I have run across Jennett, Jennet, and Jenet more often than Jane for the 1700s in Maine. Her gravestone has Jennet.

Her husband, William Alexander, was one of two children of David Alexander and his mother is unknown. His father came to Maine in 1719[38] with the Robert Temple ships just as James and Jean Wilson did, possibly on the same ship.

Alexander, William of T. and Harpswell, and Jane Wilson, sister of Elder Hugh, [ ], P.R.80. (Topsham I, 38)

There is a lot near the Cathance River marked with his name near a lot marked for whom we assume was his brother, Robert. He did sell his or give up his lot on the Pejebscot, number 48 to Samuel

37. Harpswell Heritage Land Trust, http://goo.gl/2Goy6K, accessed 29 March 2015.

38. Passenger and Immigration Lists Index, 1500s-1900s Ancestry.com. Original data: Filby, P. William, ed. Passenger & Immigration Lists Index, 1500s-1900s. (Farmington Hills, MI, USA: Gale Research, 2012), 29. Bolton, lists them as well.

Thompson. There are references to William Alexander in Topsham continuing into the 1800s but whether that was the original William or not I simply don't know. Dipping into the Topsham Alexanders, I did find Alexanders that weren't even related to David and William.

Jane and William had seven children, David[3], James[3], William[3], Elizabeth[3], John[3], Samuel[3], and Hugh and they together produced almost 50 grandchildren for William and Jane[2].

A summary of those children and grandchildren is found in a later chapter named "William & Jennet Alexander in Harpswell".

The Life and Times in Maine for the Children of Jane, Alexander, William, Samuel and Hugh.

The first dam between Topsham and Brunswick was built as they were being born in 1753. Topsham was incorporated in 1763.

They all married after the Revolution but not many went to war. Agriculture was the chief occupation - mostly, survival required tending to crops, leaving little time for going off to war.

The father-in-law of William is famous for the so-called Thompson's War,[39] an early Revolutionary confrontation. In 1790, following the Revolution, the Scotch Irish in Maine still clung in greatest numbers about the Kennebec.[40]

There was only one carpet in Topsham in 1799. Wagons were not introduced until 1816 or 1817 though a few carts did exist before then.[41]

Maine didn't became a state until 1820.

Change defined their lives.

39. Thompson's War, https://goo.gl/PysDq3 accessed 13 Oct 2015.
40. Bolton, 307.
41. Wheeler, 217.

Maps

Maps, Topsham 1768 & Brunswick 1741

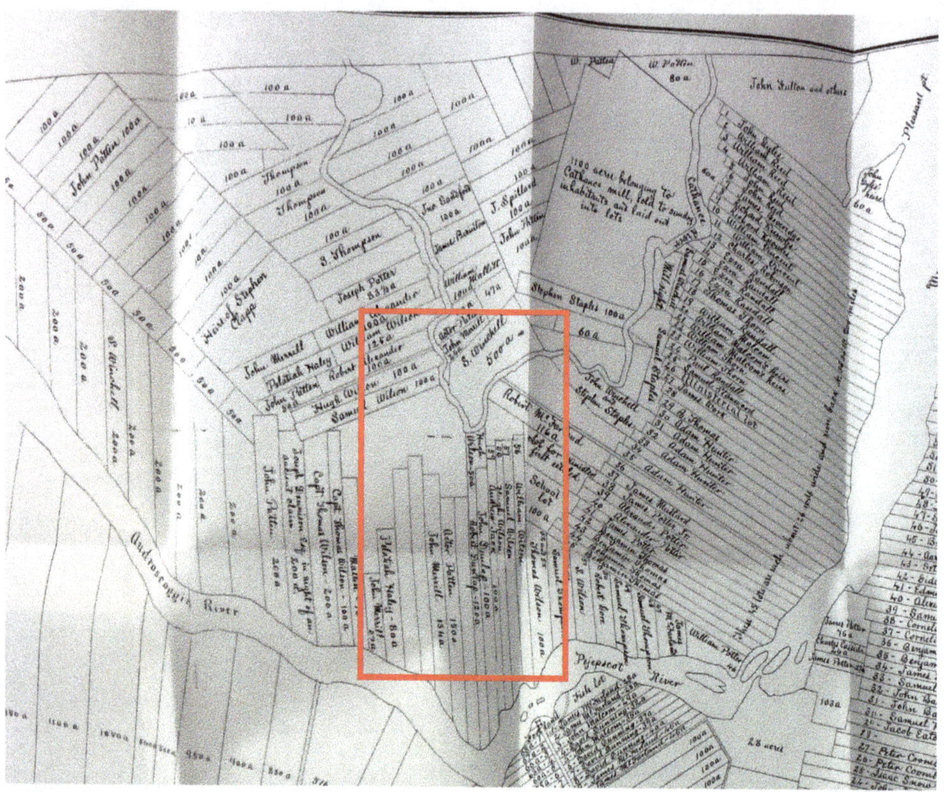

This is a photo of the folded map included in Wheeler's history. Measuring 18 inches by 18 inches, it is not attached to the second edition and not available for viewing in the PDF. Some books will be missing it. The red box is shown on the next page enlarged.

The lots that are running vertically in the bottom half of the box stretch from the edge of the Androscoggin River to the Cathance River. Those original lots ran two miles back from the river and averaged twenty-six rods wide. That is about .08 of mile or 429 feet wide.

The farms are to the north bordered on the right hand side by the Cathance River.

Web version of the larger map available here: http://goo.gl/jZIDD8

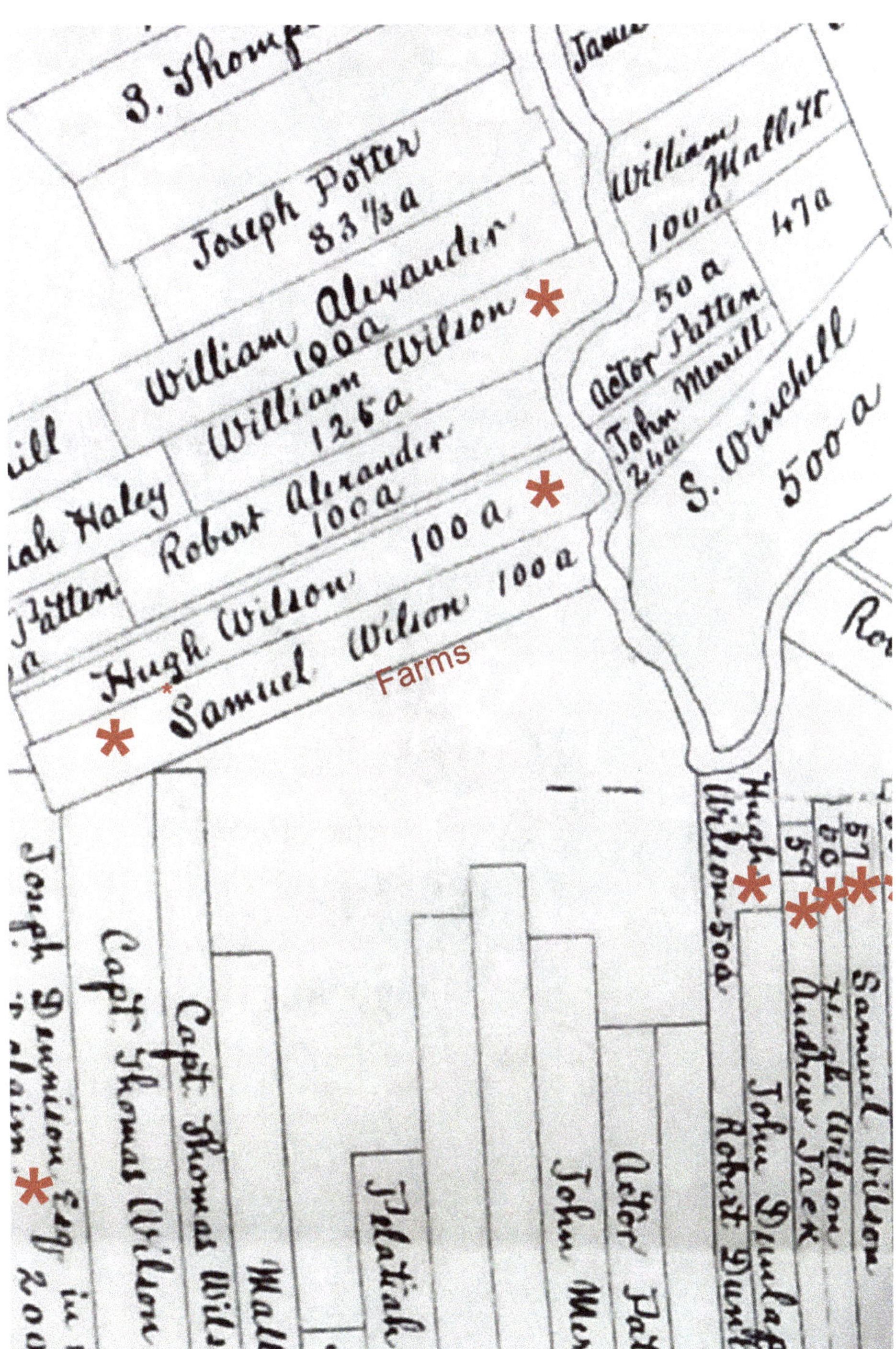

Each lot that Wilson family owned is shown here with a large asterisk. This is not all but most of the lots.

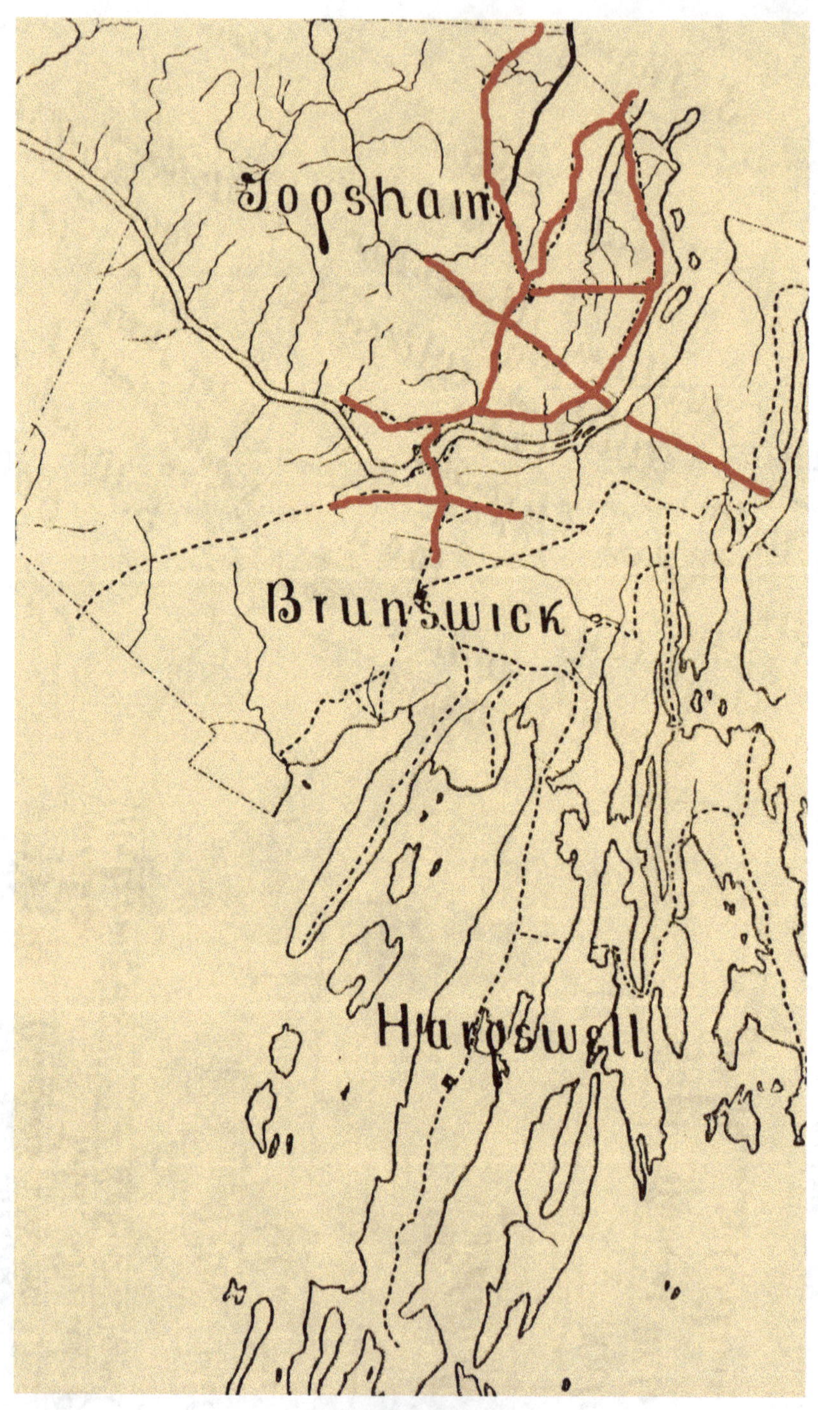

Roads in 1764
(red and dotted lines)

The roads in 1764 weren't much - obviously just tracks, not really roads. They followed the same paths today's roads do and they cut through the lots. Winter Street, Elm Street/24, 201, 196 and Cathance Road were the main ones back then.

Zoomable maps are also are available here:
http://cvillegenie.com/topsham-maps/

Samuel's Descendants

Samuel[2] only had one child, James[3], who married and that we have any children for but others exist in the records including Hannah[3], who died at 13 months on 26 Nov 1763[1] and is buried in the Brunswick First Parish cemetery with her grandfather, James.

Hannah, ch. Samuel and Mary, Oct. 27, 1762. (Topsham I, 209)
Susanna, ch. Samuel and Mary, May 18, 1766. (211)
John, s. Samuel and Mary Reed (sister of Col. John Reed), [----], P.R.80. (32)
William, s. Samuel and Mary Reed (sister of Col. John Reed), [----], p.R.80. (33)

There is a deed for the heirs to sell the John Reed property. The names are all spelled out including Hannah, a minor child of Mary and Samuel. That deed is dated 1799 so all of the children were alive that year. Hannah would have been born after 1778 in order to be a minor in 1799. Both John and William would have been born before 1778 since they were of age. Both James and William were said to be of Durham. Hannah is first referred to as Hannah Ross Wilson and then as Hannah Ross. The buyer is a Thomas Reed whose last name is dropped in the deed as well so her name is a bit uncertain.[2]

Susanna[3] (Samuel[2], James[1])

Susanna married Amasa Smith. According to that deed they lived in Thompsonborough in 1799 - that is the old name of Bowdoin. I found an 1800 census in Thompsonborough that lists Amasa, his wife and three boys under ten.[3] Subsequent censuses has an Amasa in Gardiner and in Orrington but I could find nothing else.

William[3] (Samuel[2], James[1])

The 1800 census in Durham lists a William whose age was 16 to 26 with a wife in the same age bracket and two boys.[4] That would make his birth year 1774 to 1778. Looking back on sources towards the end of the project, I realized that Stackpole had listed this Wil-

1. "Maine, Nathan Hale Cemetery Collection, ca. 1780-1980," (https://goo.gl/1xGQWv).
2. Lincoln County Registry of Deeds, 44:119.
3. Year: 1800; Census Place: Thompsonborough, Lincoln, Maine; Series: M32; Roll: 6; Page: 330; Image: 319; FHL Film: 218676.
4. Year: 1800; Census Place: Durham, Cumberland, Maine; Series: M32; Roll: 6; Page: 84; Image: 20; FHL Film: 218676.

liam in addition to James.[5]

He married Dorcas Parker on 8 Dec 1796 in Durham.[6] One of their children was named Mary Reed, named after her grandmother - that was the clincher for me.

I couldn't find them in the 1810 census but Mary Reed married at 16 in Campbell, Kentucky, so most likely the Wilsons headed west.

There were at least two other children listed in Stackpole, James b.10 May 1797[7] and William Jr b.30 Mar 1802[8] but Mary is the only one I could find information for.

Mary Reed[4] (William[3], Samuel[2], James[1])

Mary b.12 Feb 1800[9] d.26 Dec 1859 married Benjamin Jewett Ricker b.7 Jul 1796[10] of Poland, Maine, on 24 Nov 1816 in Kentucky.[11]

She and Benjamin are seen together in the 1850 census with their youngest still at home. She died on 26 Dec 1859 (unc) in Pleasant Hill, Ohio. The cemetery there does not list any Rickers, however. Most of the dates for the next generation is provided by family and possibly from the Ricker Family Genealogy.[12]

They had Benjamin[5] who died in infancy about 1829 and Adeline Wilson[5] b.16 Nov 1824 d.19 Dec 1912[13] who married but didn't have children. There is no information on either Susan[5] b. 22 Dec 1821 d.26 May 1891 or Mary Ann[5] b.20 Nov 1827 d.12 Sep 1891. Elbridge Gerry[5] and William Wilson[5] both had children.

---

5. Stackpole, Everett S, The History of Durham, Maine, with Genealogical Notes (Lewiston, Maine: Press of Lewiston Journal Company, 1899), 217.
6. "Maine Vital Records, 1670-1907 ", (https://goo.gl/C51M91).
7. "Maine Vital Records, 1670-1907 ", (https://goo.gl/tNG5Wb).

"Maine Vital Records, 1670-1907, (https://goo.gl/JmgWx0).

9. "Maine Vital Records, 1670-1907 ", (https://goo.gl/zMz9yQ).
10. "Maine Births and Christenings, 1739-1900," (https://goo.gl/k8iSrx).
11. Stackpole, 288
12. Ricker, Percy Leon, Holland, Edwin R, A Genealogy of the Ricker Family, (Heritage Books, 1996).
13. "Ohio Deaths, 1908-1953," (https://goo.gl/c3kIcd)

Elbridge Gerry[5] Ricker (Mary[4], William[3], Samuel[2], James[1])

Elbridge Gerry Ricker[5] b. 31 Jul 1818 d.10 Mar 1876 married Margaret Foster b.29 Jul 1818 d.31 Mar 1897 on 13 Dec 1838.[14] Their children who never married or had children were Edward[6] b.8 Oct 1846 d.8 Jul 1872, Maria[6] b.24 Jan 1845 d.8 Jul 1872, Thomas Foster[6] b.23 Sep 1843 d.11 May 1874,[15] and Benjamin Jewett[6] b.14 Sep 1840 d.12 Sep 1907.[16]

Those who had children were Sarah "Sally" Foster[6], Dr. Joseph Trimble[6], and Rosella Ann[6].

Sarah "Sally" Foster[6] b.22 Nov 1855 d.11 May 1935[17] married William Thomas Simpson b.12 Sep 1855 d.30 Mar 1915[18] and had one child, Robert Ricker[7] b.1881 d.1885.

Dr. Joseph Trimble[6] b.18 May 1848 d.4 May 1926[19] married Catherine Elmira Winspear b.5 Jun 1850 d.26 Nov 1936. They had three children, Dr. Joseph Winspear[7] b.12 Mar 1880[20] d.9 Oct 1962,[21] Catherine Elmira[7] b.2 Dec 1881[22] d.21 Mar 1934[23] and Elbridge Gerry[7] b.28 Aug 1883[24] d.5 Dec 1967.[25]

Rosella Ann[6] b. d.5 Apr 1899[26] married Edwin Zoeth Freeman. They had four children, Zolette Foster[7] b.7 Feb 1867 d.bef 1880, Dr. Edwin Ricker[7] b.7 Feb 1865 d.26 Jul 1912,[27] Dr. Leonard Ricker[7] b.16

14. "Ohio Marriages, 1800-1958," (https://goo.gl/JodFjO).
15. "Ohio Deaths and Burials, 1854-1997," year only (https://goo.gl/UgsANZ).
16. "Ohio Deaths and Burials, 1854-1997," year only, (https://goo.gl/kWfTi0).
17. Spring Grove Cemetery, http://goo.gl/jCiYnD
18. Ohio, Deaths, 1908-1932, 1938-2007, https://goo.gl/8AZcXa
19. "Ohio Deaths, 1908-1953," (https://goo.gl/ufpIVV).
20. "Ohio Births and Christenings, 1821-1962," (https://goo.gl/fI3M5R).
21. Ohio Dept of Health. Ohio, Deaths, 1908-1932, 1938-2007, cert # 72760; vol: 17050.
22. "Ohio Births and Christenings, 1821-1962," (https://goo.gl/pViBFN).
23. New York, New York City Municipal Deaths, 1795-1949, (https://goo.gl/NP3bWE)
24. "Ohio, County Births, 1841-2003," (https://goo.gl/cDDl1P).
25. Social Security Adminstration, Number: 305-42-5812; Indiana; Date: 1956-1957.
26. "Ohio, County Death Records, 1840-2001," (https://goo.gl/Q9dRQX).
27. Ohio, Deaths, 1908-1932, 1938-2007, Ancestry.com.

Dec 1860[28] d.27 Dec 1935[29] and Rosella[7] b.5 Sep 1873 but only Leonard[7] had children that I could find.

William Wilson[5] Ricker (Mary[4], William[3], Samuel[2], James[1])

In 1850 William is listed next to a Cynthia Wilson who is also 17. That looks like a wife to me but there's no other information.[30]

William Wilson Ricker b.1 Aug 1832 d.28 Oct 1904 married Mary French Doane b. d. on 25 Oct 1854.[31] They had two daughters Elmira French "Mina"[6] b. 21 Aug 1855 d.22 Sep 1940[32] who married William George Caldwell and had three children (only one had children): Nellie Ricker b.12 Feb 1876 d.28 Jun 1878,[33] Ralph Ricker b.1 May 1877 d.29 Aug 1960[34] and Mary Louise b.26 Jan 1879 d.7 Jun 1964[35] (Merrell, 2 children). The second daughter was Fanta Doane Belle[6] b.17 Dec 1868 d.15 Nov 1949[36] who married Warren P Bell and had one child, Frances Louise b.19 June 1889 d.Sep 1980[37] (Wohlgemuth, three children).

James[3] (Samuel[2], James[1])

James, ch. Samuel and Mary, July 2, 1764. (Topsham I, 210)

James[3] d.26 Mar 1829[38] married Elizabeth McGray b.10 Mar 1769,[39] daughter of Captain William McGray and Susanna Turner.

James and Elizabeth McGraw, Mar. 20, 1788. (Topsham II, 285)
Mr James Willson J^r^ without the Bounds of any town & Mrs Elisebath McGraw of Royalstown Intend marriage Octr 10. 1787. (Brunswick, 134)

James Wilson married 20 March 1788 Elizabeth McGray. Their children were : Mary b. 10 Dec. 1788; Lemuel b. 15 Oct. 1790; Sarah b. 20 Jan. 1793, m. Simeon

---

28. Passport Applications, January 2, 1906 - March 31, 1925; Roll #: 2278; Volume #: Roll 2278 - Certificates: 296350-296348, 25 May 1923-26 May 1923.
29. Findagrave.com, year only, http://goo.gl/uv5sSJ
30. Year: 1850; Census: Ohio, Clermont, Ohio; Roll: M432_667; Page: 418A; Image: 275.
31. "Ohio, County Marriages, 1789-2013," (https://goo.gl/w3bxFm).
32. "Ohio Death Index, 1908-1932, 1938-1944, and 1958-2007," https://goo.gl/8TWJzq
33. Spring Grove Cemetery, http://goo.gl/Cxx5lv
34. Findagrave.com, http://goo.gl/a0Rf14, accessed 25 Oct 2015.
35. "Ohio Death Index, 1908-1932, 1938-1944, and 1958-2007," https://goo.gl/BkDLMA
36. Findagrave.com, http://goo.gl/lrxf8O, accessed 25 Oct 2015.
37. Findagrave.com, http://goo.gl/VW6fEH, accessed 25 Oct 2015.
38. "Maine, Nathan Hale Cemetery Collection, ca. 1780-1980," (https://goo.gl/tIkcz1).
39. Stackpole, 217.

Snow; Mercy b. 17 Mch. 1795; and Timothy Horn b.4 Aug. 1797.[40]

Continuing the confusion surrounding this family, James' location in the years before Durham is in question. The above Brunswick record does appear to be his marriage intentions complete with misspellings and incorrect information but it does say "without the Bounds of any town".

They moved to Durham by the 1790 census there and then moved to Unity by 1810. The boys include Lemuel[4] and Timothy Horn[4] but there was probably one other.

Since so much information is not available for his children, I looked to the censuses to help reconcile them. In 1790[41] there were two boys and one girl besides Elizabeth. In 1800[42] there were a boy 10 to 15 (Lemuel, 10) and three girls under 10: Sarah, 7, Mercy, 5, and Mary, 12. In 1810[43] there was one boy under 10 (possibly James), one 10 to 15 (Timothy), one 16 to 25 (Lemuel), one girl under 10 (Betsey), one 10 to 15 (Mercy, 15), one 16 to 25 (Sarah, 17). In 1820 there are only two girls under 10 (Betsey and Olive).[44]

The entry of James[4], Olive[4] and Betsey[4] comes from the Nathan Hall Cemetery collection where the three children are listed on the sheet along with Mary[4] McDonald but the only date at all is James' death date. The cemetery is cited as being named Durham - which I cannot find. Even those that know the area do not know where that cemetery might be. This leads me to believe that James[4], Betsey[4] and Olive[4] may have died young. Elizabeth herself is listed as dying in New Albany, Indiana, but with no date.[45] That is truly a mystery.

---

40. Stackpole, 288.
41. Year: 1790; Census Place: Durham, Cumberland, Maine; Series: M637; Roll: 2; Page: 270; Image: 156; FHL Film: 0568142.
42. Year: 1800; Census Place: Durham, Cumberland, Maine; Series: M32; Roll: 6; Page: 84; Image: 20; FHL Film: 218676.
43. Year: 1810; Census Place: Unity, Kennebec, Maine; Roll: 11; Page: 733; Image: 00722; Family History Library Film: 0218682.
44. I apologize but I have lost the source for this one. If I can't find it again, well, it may not be true.
45. "Nathan Hale Cemetery Collection, ca. 1780-1980," (https://goo.gl/ahCeMp).

I found a Waldo marriage record for a Lemuel to Elsa Melvin on 23 Dec 1810[46] and a military record for Sgt. Lemuel M of Durham with an enlistment date of 27 Apr 1813 for the 33rd U.S. Infantry.[47] I found a pension record that was rejected that also listed Lemuel but it lists no dates only the state with no city. He did serve one year.

Timothy Horn[4] is also a mystery as the only records I find for any Timothy in Maine during this period is a birth record with James as a father and a marriage to Mary B Kimball in Shapleigh on 22 May 1841.[48]

I could find nothing else for either man.

Mary[4] (James[3], Samuel[2], James[1]) - The McDonalds

Mary, w. Joseph, Dec. 17, 1841, a. 53, g.r.i. (Belfast deaths, 585)
Joseph, h. Mary, Apr. 17, 1835, a. 59, g.r.i. (585)

James[3] and Elizabeth's oldest child was Mary[4] b.10 Dec 1788 who married Joseph McDonald b.23 Nov 1779[49] of Gorham. After their marriage on 1 Aug 1805,[50] they had at least ten children in Waldo County. There are children that there are no information for and may have died in infancy, including James[5] and one infant. Sophronia[5] (no birth or death dates) married Thomas Cunningham b.24 Mar 1814[51].

Saphronia of Belmont and Thomas Cuningham, int. Nov. 15, 1834, "Certificate Issued Dec 6th." (Belfast II, 267)

Jonathan Frye McDonald[5] was born around 1820 and never married. He is listed in the 1880 census with Harry as single with an occupation of shoemaker.[52]

Ann[5] McDonald (Mary[4], James[3], Samuel[2], James[1]) - The Cooksons

Ann[5] was born in late October 1807 and died on 4 Nov 1873.[53]

46. "Maine, Marriages, 1771-1907," (https://goo.gl/uFTIv9).
47. "US Registers of Enlistments in the U.S. Army, 1798-1914," https://goo.gl/tNF3WQ
48. "Maine, Vital Records, 1670-1907 ," (https://goo.gl/2FumM2).
49. "Maine, Births and Christenings, 1739-1900," (https://goo.gl/e9j3f8).
50. "Maine, Marriages, 1771-1907," (https://goo.gl/suO0Fr).
51. Maine, Births and Christenings, 1739-1900," (https://goo.gl/H3WBVK).
52. "United States Census, 1880," (https://goo.gl/iOw2Da),.
53. Findagrave.com, gravestone: http://goo.gl/xuVIMY.

She married Josiah Cookson b.9 Feb 1813[54] d.Feb 1888[55] on 18 July 1835.[56] The strongest proof that she is part of this McDonald family is both the census of 1850 and 1860. Her brothers, John and Frye, are living with them.[57] They had three boys, William Harrison, Adelbert and Daniel b.abt 1848[58] d.bef 1860.

William Harrison[6] Cookson b.abt 1839[59] married Annie E Verrill b. June 1845[60] on 2 April 1866. They had three children Wesley Oland b.15 Apr 1873 d.25 Aug 1943 (unc), Edith J b.1 May 1881 d.30 Apr 1980[61] and William J b.16 Mar 1878 d.11 Jan 1880.[62]

Adelbert Austeen[6] Cookson b.abt 1842 d.4 May 1909[63] married Aurilla Brown Murch b.1852 d.1934[64] on 18 Nov 1869.[65] They had five children, Hatti Melvina (Page) b.19 May 1870 d.27 Apr 1942, Luthia A (Rose) b.abt 1873, Lorintha M b.8 May 1875[66] d.21 Nov 1875, Grace M (Marden) b.Oct 1883 d.5 Aug 1953, and Winnet I (Parker) b.29 Jul 1887 d.1 Dec 1978.[67] Most dates are provided by family members as I can find no digital records for the children's births.

Harrison G.O.[5] McDonald (Mary[4], James[3], Samuel[2], James[1])

Harrison b.4 Feb 1814 d.1884[68] is the next known child of Mary's. He married Albinia Ann Brown b.1827 d.21 Apr 1911[69] and they had four boys, James[6] b.1855, Nathaniel[6] b.1857, Joseph Franklin

54. "Maine, Births and Christenings, 1739-1900," (https://goo.gl/CzzUJ4).
55. Maine State Archives; Pre 1892 Delayed Returns; Roll #: 23
56. "Maine, Marriages, 1771-1907," (https://goo.gl/9ajV2C).
57. Year: 1860; Census Place: Bangor Ward 5, Penobscot, Maine; Roll: M653_447; Page: 3; Image: 4; FHL Film: 803447
58. Year: 1850; Census Place: Montville, Maine; Roll: M432_271; Page: 271A; Image: 529
59. Year: 1850; Census Place: Montville, Maine; Roll: M432_271; Page: 271A; Image: 529
60. Year: 1880; Census Place: Kenduskeag, Penobscot, Maine; Roll: 485; FHL: 1254485; Page: 34D; District: 019; Image: 0525
61. Social Security Administration, Number: 004-64-4989; State: Maine; Date: 1973.
62. "Maine Vital Records, 1670-1907 " (https://goo.gl/9Cdnuq)
63. Massachusetts, Death Records, 1841-1915 [database on-line]. Ancestry.com.
64. Massachusetts, Death Index, 1901-1980 Ancestry.com Operations, Inc., 2013.
65. "Maine, Marriages, 1771-1907," (https://goo.gl/MTP2Tr)
66. "Maine, Vital Records, 1670-1907 ", (https://goo.gl/Fb0JsW)
67. Massachusetts Death Index, 1970-2003 [database on-line]. Ancestry.com.
68. Findagrave.com, year only photograph, http://goo.gl/JE0PZp
69. Maine State Archives; 1908-1922 Vital Records; Roll #: 36

b.1872 d.1874,[70] Charles[6] b.1858 and Harry Reed[6] b. 25 Aug 1869[71] d.27 Sep 1909.[72] Harry Reed[6] and his wife, Adwina C Flagg b.abt 1871 d.1 Apr 1961,[73] had one son, Walter Ray[7] b. 1893 d.21 Feb 1895.[74] Charles B[6] and his wife, Eva, had four children, J Merrill[7], Agnes B[7], Lennie A[7], and Ruth A[7].

William[5] McDonald (Mary[4], James[3], Samuel[2], James[1])

The third son, William b.1 Mar 1820, was a Methodist minister whose obituary tells the story. He joined the Methodist Episcopal church at age 18 and "1840 was granted a license to preach and took a circuit". He was a world traveler, editor, and writer.[75] He died on 11 Sep 1901, leaving his wife, Frances Jordan b.31 Aug 1827 d.1919,[76] one daughter, Mary Wheatie[6] b.6 Jun 1860 and one son, William[6] b.31 Jul 1863 d.1938. William[6] married Harriet Bliss b.17 Feb 1864 d.1944[77] and they had one child, John Haskell b.1 Sept 1896.[78]

Mary Wheatie[6] married Frederick Webster Farley b.29 Jun 1859[79] on 27 Dec 1882[80] and had four children, Arthur James[7] b.2 Sep 1885[81] d.Aug 1967,[82] Alice Francis[7] b.8 Jan 1890[83] and Mary Louise[7] b.28 May 1893.[84] The oldest, William[7] b.18 Dec 1883[85] d.5 Mar 1966,[86] was the only one who married and had children that I could find.

---

70. Findagrave.com, gravestone photograph, http://goo.gl/MW9kRi
71. "Maine, Births and Christenings, 1739-1900," (https://goo.gl/WlC68u).
72. Maine State Archives; 1908-1922 Vital Records; Roll #: 36.
73. Findagrave.com, http://goo.gl/eclngB, accessed 26 Oct 2015.
74. Maine State Archives; 1892-1907 Vital Records; Roll #: 37.
75. Somerville Journal, Sept. 13, 1901, page 6, column 1 as posted on ancestry.com, http://goo.gl/SqTLiq, accessed 23 April 2014.
76. Findagrave.com, http://goo.gl/TLLiiV, 26 Oct 2015.
77. Findagrave.com, both on gravestone, http://goo.gl/PsI1Eu
78. Maine State Archives; 1892-1907 Vital Records; Roll #: 37
79. "Massachusetts, Births and Christenings, 1639-1915," (https://goo.gl/C2yhXq).
80. "Massachusetts, Marriages, 1695-1910," (https://goo.gl/NfhIQS)
81. "Massachusetts, Births, 1841-1915," (https://goo.gl/4lW4Pi)
82. Social Security Administration Number: 142-30-8299; New Jersey; 1955-1956.
83. "Massachusetts, Births, 1841-1915," (https://goo.gl/AsRVa7)
84. "Massachusetts, Births, 1841-1915," (https://goo.gl/43S21Q)
85. "Massachusetts, Births, 1841-1915," (https://goo.gl/X6AEHX)
86. Findagrave.com, http://goo.gl/QhYBGV, accessed 26 Oct 2015.

Susan McDonald[5] (Mary[4], James[3], Samuel[2], James[1]) - The Scovills

Susan b.2 Jan 1826 married Ezekial Scovill b.abt 1820 who must have been a seaman because he died at sea in 1864. They had five children according to the 1860[87] census: Sarah Frances[6], Harriet[6] A b.abt 1848, Mary E[6] b.1851 d.1866, Addie Susan[6] and Ella[6] b.1857 d.27 Oct 1875.[88] Another was born before Ezekial's death, John b.abt 1861.[89] The children were not living with Susan in 1870; John was with the Cooksons and Ella was living with another family.[90] Susan[6] married Major H. Paine b.20 Nov 1825 d.10 Dec 1900 on 23 Dec 1870, three years after Ezekial's death and after the Civil War in which he fought.[91]

Sarah Frances Scovill[6] b.1846 d. 1929[92] married George Washington Vickery b.1 Nov 1845[93] d.1922 on 8 Aug 1868.[94] They had three children Gilbert Scovil[7] b.13 Jun 1869 d.2 Jul 1928,[95] Myra Frances[7] b.18 Mar 1875[96] d.1964,[97] and Ethel[7] b.19 Mar 1889 d.30 Dec 1907.[98]

Addie Susan Scovill[6] b.1854 married George F Smith.[99] I have no information for them beyond the fact that he was from Brooklyn, New York, and they lived in Massachusetts where she died in an auto accident on 3 Jul 1916.[100]

Mary[5] McDonald (Mary[4], James[3], Samuel[2], James[1]) - The Ames

Mary E. and Nathan[ie]l G. [int. 0.] Ames, Sept. 9, 1849. (Belfast II, 267)

Mary[5] McDonald b.abt 1830 d.28 Sep 1903[101] married Nathaniel O.

87. "United States Census, 1860," (https://goo.gl/QsgdMb)
88. "Maine Vital Records, 1670-1907 ", (https://goo.gl/970iEh) & http://goo.gl/I06Qj2
89. "United States Census, 1870," (https://goo.gl/W1Q4KQ)
90. "United States Census, 1870," (https://goo.gl/VPnQK0)
91. "United States 1890 Census of Union Veterans", (https://goo.gl/YxwxEH)
92. Findagrave.com, tombstone photo, http://goo.gl/zSUyU7
93. "Maine, Births and Christenings, 1739-1900," (https://goo.gl/d4S7do)
94. "Maine, Marriages, 1771-1907," (https://goo.gl/i2pp8O)
95. Pennsylvania, Death Certificates, 1906-1963 [database on-line]. Ancestry.com.
96. "Maine, Births and Christenings, 1739-1900," (https://goo.gl/sEhEja)
97. Findagrave.com, http://goo.gl/mIygiY, accessed 22 Oct 2015.
98. Findagrave.com, gravestone photograph, http://goo.gl/7GdgB0
99. Year: 1900; Census Place: Cambridge Ward 4, Middlesex, Massachusetts; Roll: 657; Page: 8A; Enumeration District: 0717; FHL microfilm: 1240657
100. "Massachusetts State Vital Records, 1841-1920," (https://goo.gl/BAlttj)
101. California State Library Mortuary Records, 1849-1900; Sacramento; Reel #: 1.

Ames b.abt 1825 d. 11 Dec 1895[102] and moved to California before their first child was born. There were at least six: John[6], Caroline[6], Hattie Lou[6] or Lulu b.Feb 1863 d. 12 Aug 1926,[103] Mary[6] b.abt 1864, and Edward[6] b.abt 1866.[104]

Caroline[6] b.May 1857 d.2 May 1926[105] married Shelley Ornon Inch b.abt 1854 d.14 Jan 1939[106] from England on 11 Feb 1877.[107] They had two sons, Leonard Perkins[7] b.3 Mar 1879 d.29 May 1959[108] and Shelley Ornon[7] b.10 Feb 1879 d.29 Oct 1918.[109] John Ames b.1855 d.29 Jan 1886 married Rose B Winger b.1951 d.4 May 1910[110] and had four daughters, Mariel Joyce b.23 Nov 1876 d.4 Apr 1942,[111] Rose E b.abt 1858 d.bef 1940, Maude M b.21 Feb 1958 d.20 Feb 1881,[112] and Caroline Cecelia b.19 Dec 1883 d.17 May 1956.[113]

Sarah[4] (James[3], Samuel[2], James[1]) - The Dickeys

Daughter Sarah "Sally"[4] b.20 Jan 1793[114] d.26 Apr 1876 or 1864 married Robert Dickey b.12 Sep 1782[115] d.4 May 1862 who was from New Hampshire. A farmer and a shoemaker, he was a descendant of an Irishman who had come to New Hampshire in the early 1700s. Few records exist for this family and we have to rely on an 1898 genealogy by Everett Stackpole for much of the information.

They lived in Northport and had ten children, but only two had families - most never married: Mary A[5] b.16 Feb 1812 d.8 Jan 1870, Elizabeth W[5], James W[5], master mariner, b.31 May 1820 d.12 Mar 1895[116] in Waltham, MA, Benjamn Franklin[5] b.8 Jun 1823 d.18 Mar

102. California State Library Mortuary Records, 1849-1900; Sacramento; Reel #: 1.
103. California, Death Index, 1905-1939, Ancestry, Findagrave http://goo.gl/mEhyfV
104. "United States Census, 1870," (https://goo.gl/WjALUm)
105. California, Death Index, 1905-1939 [database on-line]. Ancestry.com.
106. California, Death Index, 1905-1939 [database on-line]. Ancestry.com.
107. "California, County Marriages, 1850-1952," (https://goo.gl/v3kNJp)
108. "California, Death Index, 1940-1997," (https://goo.gl/QH15o2)
109. California, Death Index, 1905-1939 [database on-line]. Ancestry.com.
110. Findagrave.com, both of them, http://goo.gl/5Xo4id
111. California, Death Index, 1940-1997 [database on-line]. Ancestry.com.
112. "California Death Index, 1940-1997," (https://goo.gl/wtZyOw)
113. Findagrave.com, http://goo.gl/kRD7CA, accessed 26 July 2015.
114. Maine Birth Records, 1621-1922. Augusta, Maine: Maine State Archives.
115. "New Hampshire Birth Records, early to 1900." Concord, New Hampshire.
116. Massachusetts, Death Records, 1841-1915 Ancestry.com,

1850 in New Orleans,[117] William^{5} E. b.11 Mar 1826 d.2 Feb 1855, sailor, David^{5} A b.20 Mar 1832 d.6 Jul 1848 drowned, and Emma J B^{5} b.30 Apr 1839 d.1 May 1860.[118]

I can't find either Robert or Sally's grave and the death dates are not confirmed. What I do know is that I know that Sally is not in the 1870 census in Northport. A search did not turn her up anywhere else so the 1876 death date may not be correct. Both Robert's and her 1864 date is given in the Dickey genealogy.

Elizabeth W^{5} b.10 May 1816 was said to have married a Dolbin from New Brunswick, Canada, but she is listed as late as 1860 with her family and without a married name.[119] Also, the genealogy lists Harriet as never married but that is definitely not so.

Since Stackpole lists Simeon Snow as Sarah's husband instead of Robert Dickey, take the Stackpole genealogy dates with a caveat that more could be incorrect.

(Simeon Snow did marry a Sarah Wilson but she was born in 1803 as evidenced by her gravestone that lists her age death at 73 as well as her death record.)[120]

The Dickey children who did marry were John Wilson^{5}, Harriet^{5} and Frederick Augustus^{5}.

John Wilson^{5} Dickey (Sarah^{4}, James^{3}, Samuel^{2}, James^{1})

John^{5} b.14 Feb 1814 d.19 Feb 1874[121] married Lydia Richards b.Nov 1815 d.27 Jan 1868 on 17 Jun 1835.[122] He was a sea captain, master mariner. The children started the year after their marriage: Charles F.^{6}, Caskidelia "Cassie"^{6}, William^{6}, Ellen^{6}, Hartwell^{6} D, and Sarah^{6} all died early between the ages of five and twenty-four, 1858 to

117. Findagrave.com, David, Benjamin, William gravestone http://goo.gl/2if6xe
118. David Dickey, Genealogy of the Dickey Family (Worchester, MA: F.S. Blanchard & Co.), 182.
119. "United States Census, 1860," (https://goo.gl/0NECT4)
120. Maine State Archives; Pre 1892 Delayed Returns; Roll #: 93
121. Findagrave.com, http://goo.gl/oct8Z4, accessed 27 June 2015.
122. "Maine, Marriages, 1771-1907," (https://goo.gl/baSR03)

1864. His wife died in 1868 and he followed only 6 years later. The pattern of deaths and spacing suggests consumption but I cannot find one death record. All dates are from findagrave.com.[123]

John^{6} b.abt 1843 was the only surviving child marrying Julia A Wadlin. They had Lydia J^{7} b.1869 d.1956 (unc), Ellen b.abt 1870, Annie^{7} b.abt 1874, Olivia Rebecca^{7} b.1877 d.1944[124] and Emma^{7}. It may be their youngest child that suggests the full story of the family deaths. Emma^{7} b.abt 1881 d.23 Oct 1898[125] died of consumption.

Lydia and Olivia both married and had eight children between them.

Harriet^{5} Dickey (Sarah^{4}, James^{3}, Samuel^{2}, James^{1}) - The Stones

In the 1850 census Harriet^{5} b.25 Aug 1818 d.June 1860 is living with her parents and her children. Her last name is Stone and there is a death record on 26 Aug 1871 for her child, Anna^{6}, which lists the father as Porter Stone.[126] They had three children, twins, Emma^{6} and Anna Dickey^{6} b.April 1843, and son, William^{6} b.abt 1845, all in Massachusetts. The children were in care of their grandparents in 1860. Robert Dickey died two years later and no more traces exist of either William^{6} or Emma^{6}.

In addition, the 1860 census has a three year old, Hattie Waterman, also born in Massachusetts. From that I was able to find a birth record of 26 Apr 1857. Her parents were Ansel Waterman b.1822 d.1883 and Harriet A^{5}. They were married 17 Dec 1856 in Boston[127] but she is not living with him in 1860.[128] The 1865 census has Ansel with his children and no Harriett and he listed as a widower. The Dickey genealogy says she died June of 1860 and that does look likely though I could find no records.

123. Findagrave.com, http://goo.gl/R1HFIw, accessed 5 July 2015.
124. Findagrave.com, http://goo.gl/wpndjn, accessed 23 July 2015.
125. Ancestry.com. Maine, Death Records, 1617-1922 [database on-line]. Ancestry.com.
126. "Massachusetts, Deaths, 1841-1915," (https://goo.gl/Bco2zc)
127. Massachusetts, Town and Vital Records, 1620-1988. Ancestry.com
128. Year: 1860; Census Place: Brookline, Norfolk, Massachusetts; Roll: M653_514; Page: 786; Image: 702; FHL Film: 803514

Hattie Waterman was living with her half-sister, Anna, in 1870[129] but she died in 27 Dec 1873 at age sixteen.[130]

Harriett's daughter, Anna[6], married Silas May Penniman of Connecticut b.23 April 1842[131] and had three girls born in Massachusetts. Silas was a Civil War veteran having served in the infantry, company D, regiment 18 of Connecticut and did receive a pension after he moved to Pennsylvania.[132] Their three daughers were Mable Adelia[7] b.8 Dec 1867 d.12 Dec 1958,[133] Emma Louise[7] b.19 Jun 1869 d.4 Dec 1916,[134] and baby Elizabeth Dickey[7] b.19 Jul 1870 (unc) d.19 Sep 1870.[135] Anna died 26 Aug 1871 of consumption in Massachusetts.[136] That increases the chance that her mother, Harriet, also died of consumption.

Frederick Augustus[5] Dickey (Sarah[4], James[3], Samuel[2], James[1])

Frederick[5] b.29 Aug 1829 d.11 Feb 1911[137] married Harriet L Knowlton b.7 Dec 1832 d.5 Dec 1916[138] on 2 Jan 1853.[139] His death certificate lists him as a retired carpenter but he also owned the family farm in Northport.

> *He is a man of tact and ability in business affairs. Nearly all the public town offices have been filled by him. He was one of the Selectmen ten years in succession, and often chosen unanimously. He was marshal for taking the census in i860, and has been, at different times, candidate for clerk of the court and for judge of probate, but being in the political minority he was defeated.*[140]

Four of their six children married. Those that did not were Frederick A[6] b.1 Aug 1853 d.18 Aug 1879 and George K[6] b.28 Dec 1858

129. "United States Census, 1870," (https://goo.gl/nyiiBV)
130. Massachusetts, Death Records, 1841-1915 [database on-line]. Ancestry.com.
131. "Connecticut, Births and Christenings, 1649-1906," (https://goo.gl/YQ1MXV)
132. "United States Civil War Pension Index, 1861-1917," (https://goo.gl/Y90MF5)
133. Vermont State Archives and Records Administration; Montpelier, Vermont; Vermont Death Records, 1909-2008; User Box Number: PR-02116; Roll Number: S-31393; Archive Number: PR-1398-1399
134. Pennsylvania, Death Certificates, 1906-1963 [database on-line]. Ancestry.com.
135. "Massachusetts, Deaths, 1841-1915," (https://goo.gl/gmt2Nm)
136. Massachusetts, Death Records, 1841-1915 Ancestry.com Operations, Inc., 2013.
137. Maine State Archives; 1908-1922 Vital Records; Roll #: 15
138. Findagrave.com, gravestone, http://goo.gl/B9LIc3, accessed 23 July 2015.
139. "Maine, Marriages, 1771-1907," (https://goo.gl/2HS1XW)
140. Stackpole, 193.

d.10 Apr 1863. The younger Frederick[5] was lost when the schooner, Helen B. Condon, foundered on a trip between Pennsylvania and Boston.

Fannie M[6] Dickey b.19 Nov 1854 d.1932 married Bartlett Wadlin, master mariner, b.1851 d.1930.[141] Bartlet was the brother of Julia, John's wife. John[6] was the son of John Wilson[5] Dickey.

Dickey, Fannie M. of Northport & Bartlet Wadlin of Northport, Dec. 5, 1873. (Belfast II, 118)*

Their five children were Frederick Bartlett[7] b.5 Sept. 1874[142] d.1933, Hattie L[7] b.27 Aug. 1878, Olive Clara[7] b.15 Oct 1889 d.aft 1940 (never married), Mabel[7] b.28 Jun 1893[143] d.aft 1930 (never married) and George Knowlton[7] b.5 June 1895 d.19 Aug 1981 who served in WWI.[144] Many of them and their children are buried in the East Northport Cemetery.

Frederick Morse[6] Dickey b.9 Apr 1855 d.27 Nov 1947[145] married Grace A Lindsley of New York b.11 Oct 1871 and had seven children born between 1892 and 1908. I was not able to find out what he did for work but there is no question they moved around. Birth locations for the children include South Dakota, Vermont, Pennsylvania and Maryland. Fred died in California where two of his children also died. He is not listed in the Dickey genealogy at all so I am sure there is an interesting story there. His death certificate does state that he was the son of Robert and Sally.

Charles O[6] Dickey, farmer, b.28 Feb 1861 d.27 Nov 1937[146] married Josephine Knowlton b.30 July 1864 d.3 Apr 1931. She was possibly a distant relation to her mother-in-law, Harriet. They had three boys, Charles A[7] b.13 Apr 1889 d.8 Mar 1907,[147] Fred Roy[7] b.14 Nov 1891

---

141. Findagrave.com, gravestone, http://goo.gl/HY2RDB, accessed 19 July 2015.
142. WWI, Registration State: Maine; Registration County: Waldo; Roll: 1654019.
143. "Maine, Vital Records, 1670-1907 ," (https://goo.gl/gidTPW)
144. Findagrave.com, http://goo.gl/rtBDS9, accessed 19 July 2015.
145. California, Death Index, 1940-1997 Ancestry, Findagrave http://goo.gl/OSC3Tn
146. Findagrave.com, gravestone, http://goo.gl/kJ111z, accessess 26 July 2015.
147. Findagrave.com, gravestone, http://goo.gl/bkjYCz, accessed 19 July 2015.

d.21 Aug 1951,[148] and Walter[7] b.13 Apr 1893[149] d.31 Jul 1983.[150]

The youngest, Franklin I[6] Dickey b.1863 d.1945, married Henrietta Pierce b.1872 d.1930 and had three children, Albert W[7] b.1890 d.1961, Harold F[7] b.15 Nov 1892 d.1945, and Annie[7] b.18 Feb 1894[151] d.Dec 1977.[152] All of them are together on one gravestone[153] though the social security record I found for Annie is not the same as the gravestone year (1971) which makes me wonder.

Mercy[4] (James[3], Samuel[2], James[1]) - The Fryes

Mercy [ ], w. Jonathan, Mar. 17, 1795, in Durham, g.r.i. (Belfast I, 79)
Mercy, Mrs., consumption, Apr. 13, 1864, a. 60. [w. Jonathan, G.R.I.] (II, 545)
Jonathan, h. Mercy, July 21, 1788, in Pembroke, N. H., g.r.i. (I, 79)
Jonathan, old age, May 19, 1864, a. 72. [h. Mercy, g.r.i.] (II, 545)

Mercy Wilson[4] and Jonathan Frye's oldest child was Jonathan Lowell b.23 Feb 1815 d.8 Mar 1900[154] in Boston who married twice but had no children. Benjamin b.18 Dec 1821 may not have married and Esther b.9 Apr 1829 d.18 Sep 1908[155] did not marry. Jonathan is listed as a brick mason on numerous death certificates.[156] Mercy died early of tuberculosis but unfortunately her youngest daughter's family was hard hit and one other of Mercy's granddaughters was also lost to consumption. The family that went to Massachusetts escaped the TB; those that stayed behind were not so fortunate.

Their children who did marry were Joseph B[5], Sarah Mariah[5] and Celia J[5].

Joseph B[5] Frye (Mercy Wilson[4], James[3], Samuel[2], James[1])

Joseph B. and Betsy C. Emery, int. June 21, 1840. [Betsey C, m. July 14, CO.R.] (Belfast II, 162)

148. Findagrave.com, http://goo.gl/ytyJnP, accesssed 26 July 2015.
149. Social Security Administration: Number: 005-18-7985; Maine; Before 1951.
150. Findagrave.com, year only, http://goo.gl/NOVeZ0, accessed 19 July 2015.
151. "Maine, Vital Records, 1670-1907 ," (https://goo.gl/oxyBES)
152. Social Security Administration. Social Security Death Index, Master File.
153. Findagrave.com, gravestone, http://goo.gl/gLsrDj, accessed 19 July 2015.
154. Findagrave.com, gravestone, http://goo.gl/U6bf3R, 19 July 2015.
155. Findagrave.com, gravestone, http://goo.gl/bVXDFp, accessed 19 July 2015.
156. Maine State Archives; 1892-1907 Vital Records; Roll #: 6.

Joseph B Frye b.1 Apr 1817 d.15 Apr 1895[157] married Betsey C Emery b.abt 1817 and had four children, Frances S^{6} b.21 Nov 1843,[158] Joseph Franklin^{6}, Charles ^{6}, and George^{6}.

Joseph Franklin^{6} Frye b.4 May 1845[159] married Amanda P Berry b.8 Feb 1849 d.1937 of Massachusetts on 4 Sep 1869.[160] Their children were Blanche E^{7} b.27 Oct 1869,[161] Maud Shute^{7} b.abt 1872, Amy Allen^{7} b.abt 1873 d.10 Jul 1912,[162] Franklin Willard^{7} b.4 Nov 1879[163] d.aft 1940, Franklin Mossman^{7} b.1875 d.14 Sep 1876, Celia Ella^{7} b.1878 d.1879, Lois Amanda^{7} b.9 May 1883[164] d.18 Apr 1890,[165] and Dorothea^{7} b.6 Dec 1890[166] d. 1926.

Charles William^{6} Frye b.9 Apr 1847[167] d.1926 married Amy Frances Allen b.12 Sep 1851 d.1941 on 13 Jan 1876. Settled in Scituate, their children were Ralph Bridges^{7} b.10 July 1877[168] d.1955, Allen^{7} b.5 Sept 1879[169] d.6 Nov 1886,[170] George Minot^{7} b.2 Mar 1882[171] d.30 May 1909[172] of typhoid, Howard Otis^{7} b.19 Sep 1886[173] d.June 1963,[174] and Dean Boynton^{7} b.29 April 1884[175] d.28 May 1918 in France.[176] Only Ralph and Howard married and had children. Nearly all are on a marker together in the Union Cemetery, Scituate, MA.[177]

---

157. Maine State Archives; 1892-1907 Vital Records; Roll #: 20
158. "Maine, Births and Christenings, 1739-1900," (https://goo.gl/4U5Rpa)
159. "Maine, Births and Christenings, 1739-1900," (https://goo.gl/p2V0Rg)
160. "Massachusetts, Marriages, 1695-1910," (https://goo.gl/1pSZFj)
161. "Massachusetts, Births, 1841-1915," (https://goo.gl/BmqZL6)
162. "Massachusetts, Deaths, 1841-1915," (https://goo.gl/nyvTq0)
163. Massachusetts Vital Records, 1840–1911. NEGHS, Boston, Massachusetts.
164. "Massachusetts, Births, 1841-1915," (https://goo.gl/lBCRdv)
165. Massachusetts, Death Records, 1841-1915 [database on-line]. Ancestry.com.
166. "Massachusetts, Births and Christenings, 1639-1915," (https://goo.gl/tkwQax)
167. "Maine, Births and Christenings, 1739-1900," (https://goo.gl/VwJsBZ)
168. "Massachusetts, Births, 1841-1915," (https://goo.gl/4Krudt)
169. "Massachusetts, Births, 1841-1915," (https://goo.gl/BUcgqr)
170. Massachusetts Vital Records, 1840–1911. NEGHS, Boston, Massachusetts.
171. "Massachusetts, Births, 1841-1915," (https://goo.gl/eaOTss)
172. Massachusetts Vital Records, 1840–1911. NEGHS, Boston, Massachusetts.
173. "Massachusetts, Births and Christenings, 1639-1915," (https://goo.gl/5TVV26)
174. "United States Social Security Death Index," (https://goo.gl/0rzHVm)
175. "Massachusetts, Births, 1841-1915," (https://goo.gl/giiVHK)
176. Findagrave.com, http://goo.gl/2lFdlf, accessed 27 Oct 2015. WWI, WWII, and Korean War Casualty Listings, Ancestry.com.
177. Findagrave.com, gravestone photograph, http://goo.gl/ElJqAD

George Russell[6] Frye b.17 Oct 1849[178] married Laura Spinney b.abt 1853 d.12 Feb 1908 on 25 Jul 1876.[179] His Massachusetts death certificate lists his occupation as farmer.[180] Their children were Lottie M[7] b.Jan 1887[181] who never married, Chester E[7] b.abt 1879 and Laura E[7] b.abt 1887, both of whom last appear in the 1900 census.[182]

Sarah Mariah[5] Frye (Mercy[4], James[3], Samuel[2], James[1]) - The Boyntons

Sarah Mariah W. & Amos R. Boyinton, int. Nov. i, 1840, "Certificate Issued Decmber 16th." (Belfast II, 162)

Boynton, Amos R., Sept. 20, 1816, in Bangor, g.r.i. (I, 33)

Annie C, only ch. Amos R. and Sarah M., Nov. 9, 1847, g.r.i. (I, 33)

Sarah[5] Frye b.23 Sep 1819 d.17 Dec 1906[183] married Amos Russell Boynton d.19 Apr 1892.[184] They had one child, Annie Celia[6] who died at age 39 unmarried on 1 Dec 1886 of consumption[185] in Waldo.

Celia J[5] Frye (Mercy[4], James[3], Samuel[2], James[1]) - The Woods

Celia J. and William M. Woods, May 1 1850. [Celia P., P.R.151] (Belfast II, 162)

William M., h. Celia J. (Frye), Nov. 9, 1821, g.r.i. P.R.151. (I, 212)

Celia[5] b.31 Aug 1826[186] d.7 May 1902[187] married William McGray Woods and had one child, Emily Pierce[6] d.25 Nov 1896.[188] Emily[6] married Lendall T Shales d.11 Jun 1913[189] and also had one child, Alice G[7] who, though twice married, never had children and William Arthur[7] who never married. Celia[5], Lendall, William Arthur [7]and Emily[6] all died of tuberculosis in Belfast.

Emily P., w. L. T. Shales, July 20, 1852, g.r.i. [d. William M. & Celia J, p.R.151. w. Lendal T. Shales, P.R.152.J (I, 212)

Emily [int. Emma] P. & Lendall T. Shales, Nov. 13, 1876. [Emily P., c.R.3. Emily P. and Lendal T. Shales, P.R.151.] (I, 171)

Lendall T., h. Emily P. (Woods), May 27, 1847, g.r.i. [Lendal T., p.R.152.] (I, 212)

178. "Maine, Births and Christenings, 1739-1900," (https://goo.gl/4QZOcm)
179. "New Hampshire, Marriages, 1720-1920," (https://goo.gl/DOsiae)
180. "Massachusetts, Deaths, 1841-1915," (https://goo.gl/QHIQSN)
181. Year: 1880; Eliot, York, Maine; Roll: 491; FHL: 1254491:254D; District: 191: 0250.
182. Year: 1900; Census: Eliot, York, Maine; Roll: 602:5A; District: 0234; FHL: 1240602.
183. Maine State Archives; 1892-1907 Vital Records; Roll #: 6.
184. Findagrave.com gravestone photo, http://goo.gl/RoZ2Np
185. Waldo County, Maine Deaths, 1743-1892: Belfast Ancestry.com.
186. "Maine, Births and Christenings, 1739-1900," (https://goo.gl/mNZ3FS)
187. Maine State Archives; 1892-1907 Vital Records; Roll #: 62.
188. "Maine, Vital Records, 1670-1907 ," (https://goo.gl/YREWUn)
189. Maine State Archives; 1908-1922 Vital Records; Roll #: 50.

Shales, Alice G., d. Lendal T. and Emily P. (Woods), Sept. 27, 1877, p.R.152. (I, 212) (d.after 1940)
William A., s. Lendal T. and Emily P. (Woods), Oct. 23, 1889, p.R.152. (I, 212) (d.30 Jan 1916[190]*)*

190. Maine State Archives; 1908-1922 Vital Records; Roll #: 50

Hugh's Descendants

Though James' son, Hugh the Eldest, died at only age 40 in the accident where he lost his leg, he had amassed a solid estate which eventually passed to his son, Hugh[3], once he became of age. His four children that lived and married were Hugh[3], Martha[3], Elizabeth[3] and William, Jr.[3] One other son born around 1767 was the first recorded consumption death in the Wilson family.

James, s. Hugh and Elizabeth Hewey, , —, 1786, unmarried, P.R.80. Died of consumption, 1786, unmarried. (Topsham II, 398)[1]

Hugh[3] (Hugh[2], James[1])

Hugh, Jan. 7, 1799, a. abt. 40 y., C.R.I. [a. 36 y., G.R.I.] (Topsham II, 398) (b.1759)
Duggon, Mary [int. Miss Mary Dugin] & Hugh Wilson, Feb. 27, 1785. [int. adds, both of T.] P.R.80.] (Topsham II, 85)

He was one of the original members of that Baptist Religious Society in Topsham.[2] He probably lived in the original 1750 house until his death.

It was he that objected to the original settlement of his father's estate in 1789, saying that he had paid bills that the others should share. Only 10 years later, however, he was dead. He was the same age as his father at his death.

I was able to find his death record in the town records on microfilm, and I believe it says 'of consumption'. The word is not fully spelled out, 'consumpt' and the first c is faint. His is the second mention of TB in the records followed by his cousin's wife, Priscilla, in 1818.

Mary Durgin Wilson survived him and was the administrator of the estate. (19:8) The inventory totals the real estate at $1446.20 and included the homestead farm of 30 acres, two and half acres of meadow at Cathance, the pasture lot, one shop, sawmill part and the "Dwellinghouse with 30 acres. The personal estate was extensive and totaled $1712.14. There were farm implements, two oxen, two steers, a heifer, half a pew in the meeting house, a loom, apparel, three candlesticks and more. (8:19-20)

The final dispensation Hugh the Eldest's estate happened after

1. Woodman Scrapbook, 65.
2. Wheeler, 420.

Elizabeth's death in 1816. It was valued at over $2200. Martha[3] Farrin got the part of the homestead and another lot and had to pay William $168 and Elizabeth[3] Davis's heirs $51. William Jr[3] got the one third of the Cathance 100 acres where he was already living. Elizabeth's children got part of the homestead, 3 1/2 acres and one twelfth part of the saw. Hugh II's heirs received part of the homestead and part of the pasture lot. (20:305)

In a deed dated May 1818 Hugh III bought out Elizabeth's dower portion of Hugh the Eldest's estate for a total of $560. It is not delineated but is called the estate and dower of Elizabeth Weymouth so essentially a third of the estate. (102:74)

Then Hugh II's estate was settled in September, 1818. As his children ranged in age from ten to three at his death, this could not have been done until they came of age, just like his father's family. The valuation was way higher than in 1789, a total of $2973. A third went to Mary and that was used to compensate the others for what she got. She also was detailed what exactly, and I mean exactly, what she physically ended up with.

> *In the "dwelling-house the South west room in the second Story also the two north chambers on the same story the North stairs leading to the same with a privilege of washing & baking in the kitchen also making soap - also a passage way at all times in the west door. Also in the cellar one third part of the arch the North side of the same. Also in the North west corner of said cellar six feet wide & eleven feet long Southerly - with a passage way to & from the same. Also a privilege of laying fire-wood at or the near the west door of said dwelling house."*

She also got part of Hugh's acreage and one half the pew. All of the children signed the agreement. What I do find interesting is that Mary left her mark as did her daughter Mary so they didn't read and write but everyone else did. (20:319-321)

Another probate record shows how the children divvied up their portions but it's highly complicated. Son James was still alive and he was bought out completely by Hugh. Hugh also paid each of his siblings in order to get what he wanted which included the saw mill portion and half of the pew as well as the bulk of the land in Topsham. (20:324)

So in the Hugh III ended up with the largest portion.

> *James, s. Hugh and Mary Durgin, [ ], unmarried, went south, P.R.80. (Topsham II, 31)*
> *[ ], ch. Hugh, May 7, 1793, C.R.I. (I, 211) Perhaps this is James birth record.*
> *James 3d, under "head of family of Wid. W.," a. 18 y. in 1810, L.V. (I, 210) This probably him as well.*

Hugh II had as many as eight children with one girl with no confirmed birth date, Mary[4]. In the 1800 census there is one girl age 16 to 25. Since there were three females besides Mary[4] in the 1790 census,[3] I expect Mary[4] was born before 1790. Esther[4] and Hannah[4] were twins born 26 Dec 1797. Mary[4] and Esther[4] never married:

> *Esther, twin d. Hugh and Mary Durgin, [ ], unmarried, P.R.80. (Topsham II, 31)*
> *Mary, d. Hugh and Mary Durgin, [ ], (unmarried), p.R.80. (II, 32)*
> *[ ], [twin] d. Hugh, Dec. -------, 1797, C.R.I. (I, 212) (microfilm of the original town records says "daughters at one birth")*
> *[ ], [twin] d. Hugh, Dec. -------, 1797, C.R.I. (212)*

Also, no records of either death or burial can be found for Mary[4] and Esther[4] but the censuses are an indication of when they might have died.

The twins were under age when Hugh died and David Foster was appointed guardian. I was surprised to see a guardianship of someone I had never heard of. There are some Fosters in the deeds but no one that seems to be related to the family.

It does appear that Esther[4] lived with her mother until 1840 as there is a woman born in the 1790s in each census. In 1820[4], there is also a girl under 10 but that is the only year she appears. There is an addition of a boy 5 to 10 in 1830[5] and he's there again in 1840[6]. There is no census record in Topsham for Esther[4] (the other unmarried daughter) or Mary[4] in 1850 nor is there an appearance of a new Wilson in Topsham for the boy of 1830 or 1840 if an unmarried

3. Year: 1790; Census Place: Topsham, Lincoln, Maine; Series: M637; Roll: 2; Page: 260; Image: 151; Family History Library Film: 0568142.
4. 1820 U S Census; Census Place: Topsham, Lincoln, Maine; Page: 163; NARA Roll: M33_36; Image: 95.
5. 1830; Census Place: Topsham, Lincoln, Maine; Series: M19; Roll: 49; Page: 302; Family History Library Film: 0497945.
6. Year: 1840; Census Place: Topsham, Lincoln, Maine; Roll: 144; Page: 23; Image: 51; Family History Library Film: 0009705.

daughter had given birth.

Daughter Esther[4] is probably the female age 16 to 26 in the 1820 census but she is gone by 1830. So Mary most likely died between 1840 and 1850 and Esther between 1820 and 1830.

It looks like James was in the 1830 census so though it was said he went south, he didn't leave before then. There is a James 2 in the 1840 census that could be him. James 1 would have been his cousin James, son of Samuel born 1790. There are children in that census but I found no birth records or a marriage record for another James. A lot of unknowns and with a plain name like James and other families with James as a name, it is a mystery I couldn't solve.

Mother Mary's birth and death dates are also unknown but she did not remarry and so shows in all censuses between 1800[7] and 1840. They married in 1785 and most of the family waited into their twenties to marry. Hugh[4] was about 26 at the time of their marriage. Based on the censuses she probably died between 1840 and 1850. She went over 45 between 1800 and 1810[8]. If she was 44 in 1800, her birth year would have been 1756. If she was 45 in 1810, her birth year would have been 1765. No mention of her grave can be found. If she was buried with Hugh, she should be in First Parish Cemetery. There is empty space between Hugh[2] the Eldest and Lt. William[3], son of William[2] the Eldest. There is not an empty space next to her husband.

One interesting side note is that on 3 May 1801, the town records reflected that the selectmen "voted to discharge the widow Mary Wilson from any taxes assessed against her by the town in the year of 1800."[9]

Hannah[4] (Hugh[3], Hugh[2], James[1]) - The Crams

Hannah, twin d. Hugh and Mary Durgin, [----], w. Stephen Crain, p.R.80. (Top-

7. Year: 1800; Census Place: Topsham, Lincoln, Maine; Series: M32; Roll: 6; Page: 487; Image: 457; Family History Library Film: 218676.
8. Year: 1810; Census Place: Topsham, Lincoln, Maine; Roll: 12; Page: 15; Image: 00023; Family History Library Film: 0218683.
9. Topsham, Town Records, Microfilm, Maine State Archives, Augusta, Maine.

sham II, 31)
CRAMM, Stephen and Hannah Wilson, both of T., int. Aug. 16, 1818. [cert. Sept. 7, Cram.] (73)
Hannah [----], w. Stephen, Dec. 26, 1797, in T (I, 45)

There is a Cram family is buried in the Riverview Cemetery and was fairly easy to trace but I first had to make sure that Hannah Cram was Hugh's daughter. I found three Hannahs only in Topsham thru ancestry.com and various family trees in the area born between 1780 and 1800, twenty years before the marriage date for this couple.

"Hannah, ch. James and Ann, Jan. 6, 1783" (Topsham II, 209) - she's the guess of whoever wrote the Riverside Cemetery history on the Topsham Library website.[10] Hannah Cram's gravestone, however, says she died 9 Aug 1844 and was 46 years old[11] making her birth date about 1798 and confirming the birth date we have for our Hannah.

One Hannah born in 1798 was the daughter of Samuel and Priscilla b.Jun 1798:

Hannah of T. and John Whitmore of Lisbon, int. Mar. 10, 1825. [cert, issued Mar. 25, "Wilson." (Topsham II, 285)

She and the Whittemores are buried in Lisbon.

I found no other Hannah Wilsons in Topsham. It does look like to me that the only reference to Crain was a transcription or misspelling of Cram in a source; that entry was from another manuscript by Cyrus Woodman who had pulled information from newspaper accounts and other sources. There were Crains/Cranes in Topsham later as evidenced by deaths listed in Topsham's volume 2 on page 308 but there are no Stephen Crane/Crain in Maine between 1790 to 1850 except one in a Mount Vernon census in 1840.[12] There were other Stephen Crams in Maine during much of his life, just not in Topsham.

I was able to find Stephen with his last name spelled variously as

10. Riverview Cemetery Life Stories, http://goo.gl/oFbnRs accessed 14 April 2015.
11. Findagrave.com, gravestone photograph, http://goo.gl/3J5RWg.
12. "US Census, 1840," (https://goo.gl/33RKJZ)

Crom and Crane in nearly every census in Topsham however.

Hannah[4] and Stephen had four children born between 1819 and 1842, two years before Hannah died on 9 Aug 1844 at 1:30 of consumption, the same day as one of her adult children, Catherine P[5] and months after another, Mary Jane[5] (no proof of consumption but very likely). Those consumption deaths tie Hannah Cram even closer to Hugh's family. A macabre family tradition as it were.

Catherine, ch. Stephen and Hannah, Nov. 7, 1821, in Brunswick. (Topsham I, births, 45)
Hannah [ ], w. Stephen, Dec. 26, 1797, in T.
Mary Jane, ch. Stephen and Hannah, Apr. 5, 1819, in Brunswick.
Stephen, h. Hannah, Sept. 10, 1796, in Lynsboro, N. H. [a. 51 y., in u.s.c]

Catherine, ch. Stephen and Hannah, Aug. 9, 1844, at 7.30 A.M., a. 22 y. 9 m., in T., consumption. [Catherine P., G.R.3.] (II, deaths, 308)
Hannah, w. Stephen, half past 1 o'clock P.M., consumption, Aug. 9, 1844, a. 46 y. 8 mo., in T.
Mary Jane, Jan. 6, 1844, in T. [a. 24 y., G.R.3.]
Stephen, Oct. 24, 1885, a. 39 y., in T., N.P.6.

The two other children were Olive[5] and William[5].

Olive[5] Cram (Hannah[4], Hugh[3], Hugh[2], James[1]) - The Gilmans

Olive Ann, ch. Stephen and Hannah, July 8, 1826, in T. (Topsham I, 45)
Gilman, Christopher M., Sept. 29, 1873, a. 42 y. 4 m., G.R.3. (II deaths, 322)

The only surviving daughter was Olive[5] who married Christopher M Gilman b.abt 1831 on 22 Mar 1855[13] in Randolph, Vermont, and they had one child Eva Ann[6] b.Jan 1856[14] who never married. She was born in Vermont according to the 1900 Brunswick census; they were living in Sutton, Vermont, in 1870.[15] They also lived in Massachusetts in 1865.[16]

Christopher died after 1870, supposedly in 1873 but I cannot find a death record for him. Olive is last seen in the 1910 census but I have not been able to find the 1920 census with her daughter who is last seen in the 1930 census.[17] None of the three of them has a grave that

13. "Vermont, Vital Records, 1760-1954," (https://goo.gl/khsqbW)
14. "United States Census, 1900," (https://goo.gl/0OWtH0)
15. Year: 1870; Census Place: Sutton, Caledonia, Vermont; Roll: M593_1616; Page: 244B; Image: 494; Family History Library Film: 553115.
16. Massachusetts, State Census, 1865 Ancestry.com Operations, Inc., 2014.
17. Year: 1930; Census Place: Brunswick, Cumberland, Maine; Roll: 830; Page: 2A;

I can find in Topsham or Brunswick. I can find no death records in Maine, Vermont or Massachusetts for any of them.

William[5] Cram (Hannah[4], Hugh[3], Hugh[2], James[1])

William C, ch. Stephen and Hannah, Aug. 8, 1833, in T. (Topsham I, 45)

William[5] moved to Massachusetts before 1860[18] where he married Laura Ann Dinsmore b.1839 d.9 Jun 1892[19] on 6 Jul 1871.[20] She had been married before to a Joshua Evans and had several children by him but he died in 1919; his death certificate lists her as his wife and says he was widowed.[21] Did they divorce? No records clear that up.

The 1880 census has all children with the name of Cram but Cora A[6] and Lillian Olive[6] were both Evans based on their birth dates. Lillian's death certificate lists William as her father but she was born in 1870 and William's and Laura's marriage was the year after her birth.

They had six more children, two who died young, Ethel[6] b.12 Dec 1880[22] d.4 Jul 1884[23] and Emma Josephine[6] b.5 Feb 1879[24] d.12 Dec 1888[25] who were born in Rhode Island. William[6] C b.20 Oct 1872[26] d.25 May 1940[27] may not have married and Cora A Evans b.abt 1865[28] was alive in 1880.[29] The others did marry but I can find no children for Pearl[6] F b.25 Dec 1881 d.Feb 1965.[30]

Edith Laurie[6] Cram married Alfred Chapleau[31], a French Canadian,

---

Enumeration District: 0007; Image: 211.0; FHL microfilm: 2340565.

18. Year: 1860; Census Place: Boston Ward 10, Suffolk, Massachusetts; Roll: M653_523; Page: 261; Image: 261; Family History Library Film: 803523.
19. Massachusetts, Death Records, 1841-1915 Ancestry.com Operations, Inc., 2013.
20. Massachusetts, Town and Vital Records, 1620-1988 Ancestry.com.
21. "Massachusetts State Vital Records, 1841-1920," (https://goo.gl/6NHylD)
22. "Rhode Island, Births and Christenings, 1600-1914," (https://goo.gl/Rp3ujU)
23. Massachusetts, Town and Vital Records, 1620-1988 Ancestry.com.
24. "Rhode Island, Births and Christenings, 1600-1914," (https://goo.gl/m64LC6)
25. Massachusetts, Death Records, 1841-1915 Ancestry.com Operations, Inc., 2013.
26. "Massachusetts, Births, 1841-1915," (https://goo.gl/G4WxQQ)
27. "New Hampshire, Deaths and Burials, 1784-1949," (https://goo.gl/on9Vb9)
28. "Massachusetts, State Census, 1865," (https://goo.gl/Vo8mQt)
29. Year: 1880; Census Place: Providence, Providence, Rhode Island; Roll: 1212; Family History Film: 1255212; Page: 163A; Enumeration District: 042
30. Social Security Administration Number: 025-14-7302; Massachusetts; I Before 1951
31. "Massachusetts, Marriages, 1841-1915," (https://goo.gl/lI44El)

which resulted in a son, Walter, b.June 1895.[32] She seems to have married again later but I find no records for her after 1915.

Lillian[6] Cram b.26 May 1870 d.9 Nov 1911 (in Massachusetts from tuberculosis)[33] married Frank A Drummond[34] and had one daughter, Emma[7] b.23 Sep 1889.[35]

Harry Wallace[6] Cram b.13 Jul 1878[36] married Anna Lucinda Edmundson[37] b.25 Oct 1882[38] which resulted in five children born after 1901.

Margaret[4] (Hugh[3], Hugh[2], James[1]) - The Wentworths

Margaret[4] married Captain John Wentworth (not a descendant of one of the original Topsham landowners also named John Wentworth) and there are census records for the family that help in establishing who the children were. Margaret was his second wife. He had three children (one died young) by his first wife, Eleanor, and six by Margaret.

John, Capt., h.Eleanor, Dec. 26, 1788, in Lisbon. (Topsham I, 296) (Lisbon 25, Dec 27th 1789)
Margaret [ ], [second w. Capt. John], May 4, 1793, in T. (I, 296)
Margaret, d. Hugh and Mary Durgin, [ ], w. of John Wentworth, P.R.80 (I , 32)
John and Margaret Wilson, both of T., int. Jan. 29, 1815. [cert. Feb. 18.] (II, 273)

I found records for a number of children: Mary Eleanor[5] born only months after the wedding, Charles[5], Alfred I Stone[5], and Benning[5] in Topsham. The Topsham records don't include either Otis[5] or Frances Jane[5] because the original birth records were recorded in 1824 before their births;[39] their death records confirm their place of birth as Topsham.

Mary E., ch. Capt. John and [second w. Margaret], May 16, 1815, in T. (I, 196)

---

32. "United States Census, 1900," (https://goo.gl/VsAb76)
33. "Massachusetts, Deaths, 1841-1915," (https://goo.gl/IrVDUS)
34. "Massachusetts, Marriages, 1841-1915," (https://goo.gl/DtkPMe)
35. "Massachusetts, Births, 1841-1915," (https://goo.gl/bVZ3ee)
36. "World War II Draft Registration Cards, 1942," (https://goo.gl/ZkKQns)
37. "Massachusetts, Marriages, 1695-1910," (https://goo.gl/3msaM6)
38. "Massachusetts Births, 1841-1915," (https://goo.gl/vRPtZW)
39. Hill, Mary Pelham: Family records, Topsham, Me. (Mss C 3518). R Stanton Avery Special Collections Department, New England Historic Genealogical Society. (loose leaf family records)

Alfred I. Stone, ch. Capt. John and [second w. Margaret], May 3, 1821, in T(196)
Benning, ch. Capt. John and [second w. Margaret], Feb. 1, 1817, in T (196)
Charles, ch. Capt. John and [second w. Margaret], May 1, 1819, in T. (196)

The 1820 census has 2 boys and 1 girl under 10 (Mary, Charles and Benning).[40] 1830 has 2 boys under 5 (unknown), one 5-9 (Otis), 2 10-14 (Charles, Benning) and 2 girls 10-14 (Frances Jane and unknown) and one 15-19 (Mary).[41] There is no 1840 census and it is said that both Margaret and John died in 1832/33 in Lisbon but I can find no records or burials in Topsham or Lisbon. John's first wife and infant daughter are not buried locally either. John's brother, Foster, has one additional family member in 1840[42] that is Frances Jane's age which then would be more evidence that John and Margaret died prior to that census.

If you had any doubt about the benefits of being connected with this illustrious branch:

This same year Hugh Wilson and Major William Frost owned the Granny-Hole Mill, and James Rogers owned the Rogers Mill, on the upper dam. In the fall of this same year, David Scribner engaged in the business and continued in it, in Topsham until 1838. James Haley and John Wentworth were also engaged in the business in 1817. (Wheeler, 607)

Alfred[5] was living with his brother, Otis[5], in 1850 in Auburn[43] but was not living with them in 1860 in Massachusetts.[44] I could find no other records for him.

Charles[5] was an engineer and living with a French family in Algiers, Louisana, in 1860.[45]

Benning[5] Wentworth (Margaret[4], Hugh[3], Hugh[2], James[1])

Benning[5] married Elizabeth B b.1821 d.1900 and his gravestone states that he died in 1862 and was buried at Malvern Hill in Vir-

40. 1820 Census; Census Place: Topsham, Maine; Page: 163; NARA Roll: M33_36:95.
41. 1830; Census: Topsham, Maine; Series: M19; Roll: 49;:300; FHL Film: 0497945.
42. 1840; Census: Webster, Maine; Roll: 145; Page: 353; Image: 719; FHL Film: 0009705.
43. Year: 1850; Census Place: Auburn, Maine; Roll: M432_250; Page: 26B; Image: 248.
44. "United States Census, 1850," (https://goo.gl/mU4FGB)
45. Year: 1860; Census Place: Algiers, Orleans, Louisiana; Roll: M653_415; Page: 1078; Image: 110; Family History Library Film: 803415.

ginia.[46] He was a private in Company B, 22nd Regiment of the Massachusetts Volunteers[47] and Elizabeth did receive a pension after his death.[48] They had moved to Massachusetts prior to 1860[49] but both gravestones are together in Auburn, Maine.

The Massachusetts 1865 census lists her with children, Lizzie B[6], Charles A[6] and George[6]. Two doors down is a rooming house with another Charles Wentworth age 36, a telephone operator from New Hampshire.[50] There was a third child, Emma F[6], who died in Auburn 9 Oct 1850.[51]

Charles A[6] Wentworth b.26 May 1853 d.27 Feb 1885 (consumption)[52] was working in a tailor shop in 1870 and George H[6] (engineer in 1870)[53] married Carrie S Witherbee[6] on 8 Dec 1870[54] but supposedly died in 1880. Lizzie[6] married Arthur Joshua Scott and they are buried together in Auburn but there is no death date for her on the gravestone.[55]

Otis[5] Wentworth (Margaret[4], Hugh[3], Hugh[2], James[1])

Otis[5] b.14 May 1826 (unc) d.18 Jul 1905[56] married Nancy Haskins of Grafton, New Hampshire, and first settled in Auburn but moved his family to Massachusetts by 1854. They had five children, Flora[6] b.abt 1852, Charles Otis[6], Herbert[6] b. 9 Oct 1855,[57] and Clara E[6] b.1858 d.14 Aug 1884[58] who never married. It is Clara's death record that says Otis was born in Topsham.

---

46. Findagrave, http://goo.gl/ldfx9b
47. "Maine, Veterans Cemetery Records, 1676-1918," (https://goo.gl/L1Tprw)
48. "United States General Index to Pension Files, 1861-1934," (https://goo.gl/N9DVwJ)
49. Year: 1860; Census Place: Boston Ward 9, Suffolk, Massachusetts; Roll: M653_522; Page: 758; Image: 766; Family History Library Film: 803522
50. "Massachusetts, State Census, 1865," (https://goo.gl/0ix1eJ)
51. Findagrave.com, gravestone, http://goo.gl/GuUd3Q, accessed 6 June 2015.
52. "Massachusetts, Deaths, 1841-1915," (https://goo.gl/AJ8Mj8)
53. 1870; Census Place: Newton, Middlesex, Massachusetts; Roll: M593_630; Page: 132B; Image: 271; Family History Library Film: 552129.
54. "Massachusetts, Marriages, 1841-1915," (https://goo.gl/FKlr7r)
55. Findagrave.com, gravestone, http://goo.gl/JZqdes, accessed 6 June 2015.
56. "Massachusetts, Deaths, 1841-1915," (https://goo.gl/42KSGI)
57. "Massachusetts, Births, 1841-1915," (https://goo.gl/Th4tAJ)
58. "Massachusetts, Deaths and Burials, 1795-1910," (https://goo.gl/x4JL1V)

Charles Otis[6] b.29 Jan 1854,[59] married Susan Augusta Capelle on 29 Dec 1876[60] and had two daughters, Avaughnie Capelle[6] b.26 Dec 1877[61] and Elizabeth C[6] b.abt 1883 d.aft 1940 who never married.

Francis Jane[5] Wentworth (Margaret[4], Hugh[3], Hugh[2], James[1]) - The Drews

Francis Jane[5] b.Nov 1830[62] d.28 Feb 1910[63] was born only a little over a year before her father's death and her mother died shortly after that. It appears that she might have been raised by her uncle Foster Wentworth in Webster. She married Nicholas Brown Drew b.1823 d.1 Mar 1897[64] in Massachusetts before 1850 where they resided in Natick. They had five children before they divorced prior to 1878 when he married a 22 year old who died of alcoholism in 1903.[65]

Untangling this family was complicated by the presence in Natick, Massachusetts, of another Drew family that had a son named John F and whose mother was a Frances J W. His father was John B Nicholas and Frances' son, John, has a death record that states his mother was born in Topsham as well.

John F[6] Drew[6] b.23 May 1848[66] d.27 Mar 1870 died from consumption.[67] Though his middle initial is listed as F nearly every single time, his birth record records his middle name as Wentworth and in the first census he is enumerated as John W. His father was a shoemaker - a dangerous occupation in Massachusetts during this period. John had probably worked in that industry as well. Just five years after John's death, his brother-in-law, Joshua P Clough b.abt 1845 d.11 Sep 1875,[68] died of typhoid two years into his marriage to Ella Frances[6] Drew b.abt 1849 d.bef 1910. She married again to Ed-

59. "Massachusetts, Births, 1841-1915," (https://goo.gl/VEEwCw)
60. "Massachusetts, Marriages, 1695-1910," (https://goo.gl/hlt5XB)
61. Massachusetts, Town and Vital Records, 1620-1988 Ancestry.com.
62. Year: 1900; Census Place: Natick, Middlesex, Massachusetts; Roll: 663; Page: 10B; Enumeration District: 0886; FHL microfilm: 1240663.
63. "Massachusetts, Deaths, 1841-1915," (https://goo.gl/3jpmLM)
64. Massachusetts, Death Records, 1841-1915, Ancestry.com.
65. Massachusetts, Death Records, 1841-1915: Ancestry.com Operations, Inc., 2013.
66. "Massachusetts Births and Christenings, 1639-1915," (https://goo.gl/knSxdk)
67. Archive Collection: T1204; Archive Roll Number: 22; Census Year: 1870; Census Place: Natick, Middlesex, Massachusetts; Page: 329.
68. Massachusetts, Death Records, 1841-1915,Ancestry.com.

ward Howe Wilson b.26 Sep 1848 d.5 Aug 1927, another shoemaker, after her mother's death in 1910.

Charles O[6] Drew b.27 Jun 1856[69] married Fanny E Banks in 1881[70] but she died 27 Mar 1894 from consumption.[71] Abby E[6] b.28 May 1858[72] married Frank Clough Jameson b.abt 1859 and they had a son, Alfred Arthur[7] b.2 Jun 1881. The last daughter, Luetta A[6] b.abt 1858 d.9 Dec 1917[73] married Alfred Coolidge Atwater also in the shoe industry and had one daughter, Hortense Frances b.16 Oct 1889 d.May 1981.[74]

In 1900, the census lists Frances[5], Charles[6], Abbie[6], Luetta[6] and the children, Alfred[7] and Hortense[7]. Alfred[7] has the last name as Clough and both Abbie[6] and Luetta[6] are listed as married. Ella[6] and Frances[5] are widows. Luetta's husband, however, married again in 1905. In 1915 she is listed in a city directory as the widow of the very alive Alfred Atwater.[75] Her death certificate tells us that she is divorced and had been in the state mental hospital in Westborough for months before her death.

Luetta[6] and John F[6] are the only ones with known death dates. I could not anything for Ella[6], Abbie[6] or Charles[6]. All in all, one very confusing family.

John[4] (Hugh[3], Hugh[2], James[1])

John, s. Hugh and Mary Durgin, [ ], h. [ ] Hodgkins, P.R.8O. (Topsham I, 32)
Mary Hodgkins of Bath and John Wilson, 4th, of T., int. May 18, 1822. [cert, issued June 2.] (II, 135)
John, h. Mary, Nov. 11, 1797, in T. (II, 210)
Mary [— — —], w. John, Aug. 16, 1801, in Bath. (II, 211)
John, Aug. 6, 1850, a. 53 y. in T. [a. 53 y. 9 m., G.R.3.] (II, 398)

He is listed as John Wilson 3 on the gravestone[76] which is correct, not 4. His wife, Mary, was still alive in 1870 when she is living with

69. Massachusetts, Town and Vital Records, 1620-1988 Ancestry.com.
70. "Massachusetts Marriages, 1695-1910," (https://goo.gl/92g9ev)
71. Massachusetts, Death Records, 1841-1915, Ancestry.com.
72. "Massachusetts Births, 1841-1915," (https://goo.gl/cL9hMM)
73. "Massachusetts State Vital Records, 1841-1920," (https://goo.gl/GD2dPC)
74. Social Security Death Index, Number: 085-32-3610; New York; 1957-1958.
75. U.S. City Directories, 1821-1989, Natick, Mass, ancestry.com.
76. Findagrave.com, gravestone, http://goo.gl/vzmtOh, photographed, 3 May 2015.

Benjamin but she is gone by 1880. This is probably the correct death record then:

Mary, Mrs., Mar. 3, 1874, in T. [a. 72 y. 8 m., N.P.6.] (Topsham II, 399)

Between census records and vital records I have found three children for John and Mary: Benjamin B[5], James[5] (buried with his father), and Josephine Jane[5]. Jane[5] was only 16 when her father died and I can find no trace of her after the 1850 census.

Josephine, ch. John and Mary, June 16, 1834, in T. (Topsham II, births, 210)
James, ch. John and Mary, Oct. 20, 1826, in T. (II, 210)
James, May 11, 1846, drowned at T. [s. John and Mary, a. 19 y. 8 m., G. R.3.] (Topsham II, 398)

Benjamin[5] (John[4], Hugh[3], Hugh[2], James[1])

Benjamin B., ch. John and Mary, Mar. 9, 1824, in T. [dup. h. Priscilla.] [, —, 1822, h. Priscilla J. Buzzell, G.R.3.] [a. 27 y., in u.s.c] (Topsham II, 208)
Benjamin B. of T. and Priscilla Buzzell of Winthrop, int. Nov. 9, 1845. [cert. Nov. 24.] (II, 283)
Priscilla [—— —], w. Benjamin, Aug. 3, 1824, in Winthrop. (II, 211)
Priscilla, [Priscilla J. Buzzell, G.R.3.] w. Benjamin B., Sept. 28, 1877. (II, 399)

Benjamin[5] d.20 Jan 1907 (Boston)[77] was with the pioneers who sailed around Cape Horn to California in 1849 and remained in the gold fields for about two years. He was a carpenter by trade and built the paper mills in Topsham and also the old red mill which burned. He was the first in this vicinity to manufacture match blocks, as an industry.[78]

Three children never married and the two girls are buried with Benjamin and Priscilla:

Harriet Eliza, ch. Benjamin and Priscilla, Oct. 1, 1846, in T. (Topsham II, 209) d.1899[79]
Mary Emma, ch. Benjamin and Priscilla, July 25, 1853, in T. [1863, G.R.3.] (II, 211) d.6 Nov 1896[80]
Edwin J., ch. Benjamin and Priscilla, Jan. 6, 1849, in T. (II, 209)

I can find no records for what happened to Edwin[6]. The last record was the 1870 census[81] where he was still at home.

77. "Massachusetts Deaths, 1841-1915," (https://goo.gl/6au3aX)
78. Topsham Library Website, http://goo.gl/oFbnRs, accessed 4 May 2014.
79. Findagrave.com gravestone, http://goo.gl/vf64ct
80. Maine State Archives; 1892-1907 Vital Records; Roll #: 61.
81. Year: 1870; Census Place: Topsham, Sagadahoc, Maine; Roll: M593_557; Page: 442A; Image: 433; Family History Library Film: 552056.

Lizzie, ch. Benjamin and Priscilla, Jan. 17, 1862, in T. (II, 210)

The youngest daughter, Elizabeth 'Lizzie' Maria[6] d.1955 married Emerson Hershey Nye b.1862 d.1935 in Boston on 10 Jun 1890.[82] He was Boston police officer and they spent vacations in Topsham and then retired to Topsham. They had daughters who never married, Priscilla Matilda[7] b.12 Feb 1894[83] d.1965 and Elsie Augusta[7] b.31 July 1900[84] d.1975. The four of them are buried in the Riverview Cemetery in Topsham.[85] The oldest daughter, Marion Bertha[7] b.11 Jan 1891[86] d.11 Nov 1972[87] did marry but had no children.

Hugh[4] (Hugh[3], Hugh[2], James[1])

Hugh[4] and Mary's oldest child was Hugh[4] .

Hugh, s. Hugh and Mary Durgin, [ ], h. [ ] Staples, p.R.80. (Topsham II, 31)
Hugh, h. Susan S., Mar. 23, 1789, in T. [under "head of family of Wid. Wilson," a. 21 y. in 1810, L.V.] (Topsham I, 209)
Hugh, Nov. 9, 1860, a. 71 y. 8 m., G.R.3. (II, 398)

He married Susan Staples of Brunswick.

Hugh and Susan Stapel, both of T., Feb. 3, 1818. (Topsham II, 285) '
Susanna Staples was born to them feb[y] 10. 1796 (Brunswick, 55)
Susan, Oct. 30, 1846, in Vassalboro. [w. Hugh, a. 49 y. 4 m. 20 d., G.R.3.]

It must have been him who built the beautiful home across the street from the homestead at 11 Winter Street. It is said that it was built in 1802,[88] three years after his father's death. The house is presently empty but has been extensively remodeled after being left to decay for years.

82. Massachusetts, Marriage Records, 1840-1915 Ancestry.com Operations, Inc., 2013.
83. "Massachusetts, Births and Christenings, 1639-1915," (https://goo.gl/yt8o67)
84. "Massachusetts, Births and Christenings, 1639-1915," (https://goo.gl/JYympa)
85. Gravestone and personal photograph, http://goo.gl/0Ov5GC, May 2015.
86. "Massachusetts, Births, 1841-1915," (https://goo.gl/IkNecm)
87. "Massachusetts, Death Index, 1970-2003," (https://goo.gl/E2L299)
88. Topsham Walking Tour Brochure.

Left, side view; right, front view

It is impressive. It was remodeled in the Victorian era around 1880 so we really don't know what it looked like his son, Hugh, lived there. I didn't get to get inside this one unfortunately.

Hugh was quite active in the community according to the town records. A perusal of the microfilmed records show Hugh at various times was a fire warden or a fence viewer, field driver and hog viewer. Those last three are essentially an official that arbitrates and possibly even prosecutes livestock trespassing, a serious offense in early New England.

There were four children that died young:

Francis, ch. Hugh and Susan S., Mar. 23, 1824, in T. (Topsham I, 209)
Francis, Oct. 3,1831, in T. [s. Hugh and Susan, a. 7 y. 6 m.] (397)
Angelia, ch. Hugh and Susan S., July 7, 1834, in T. (208)
Angelia, Dec. 7, 1841, in T [Angella D, d.Hugh & Susan, Dec. 7, a. 4 y. 6 m.] (397)
William H., ch. Hugh and Susan S., July 31, 1837, in T. (211)
William H., Oct. 3, 1837, in T. [s. Hugh and Susan] (400)
Ellen Maria, ch. Hugh and Susan S., Nov. 5, 1838, in T. (209)
Ellen Maria, Jan. 5, 1842, in T. [d. Hugh and Susan, a. 38 m.] (397)

I never found any indication of why they died but one can think consumption or something else that might have affected them all.

Hugh^4 is listed as a lumberman in the 1850 census with a $2000 value of real estate.[89] He did remarry in 1849 after Susan's death. Her married name was Nancy Andrews and she and her daughter, Ellen, are listed in the 1850 census with Hugh, Frances and Hugh's mother, Mary. Her husband of 21 years, Shirley Andrews, died in 1844; her maiden name was Felch and she was from Wayne originally.[90]

Andrews, Nancy, Mrs., of Lisbon and Hugh Wilson of T., int. Sept. 15, 1849. [cert. issued Sept. 30.] (Topsham II, 40)

There is a census entry in 1860 for a Hugh (teamster) and Nancy Wilson in Lisbon with three adult children with the last name of Andrews. The children are a blacksmith, shoemaker and tailoress.

---

89. Year: 1850; Census Place: Topsham, Lincoln, Maine; Roll: M432_261; Page: 346B; Image: 480.
90. Lisbon, 46, 82.

This does appear to be Hugh with the ages of both Hugh and Nancy within 3 years of their birth dates.[91] He is buried with Susan and several of his children in Topsham after dying on 9 Nov 1860.[92]

The other children were Elizabeth Ann[5], Mary Jane[5], Althea[5], Francis D[5] and Charles L[5].

Elizabeth Ann[5] (Hugh[4], Hugh[3], Hugh[2], James[1])

Elizabeth Ann, ch. Hugh and Susan S., Jan. 29, 1820, in T. (Topsham I, 209)
Elizabeth Ann of T. and William H. Whittier of North Vassalborough, int. Sept. 5, 1838. [cert, issued Sept. 25-] (284)

Elizabeth Ann[5] married William Henry Whittier b.31 Mar 1814 d.27 Aug 1895[93] and later Melthiah H Marsh (or March) on 8 Nov 1863[94] in Somerville, Massachusetts, where she died 12 Apr 1895.[95] She seems to have had no children.

Mary Jane[5] (Hugh[4], Hugh[3], Hugh[2], James[1]) - The Nowells

Mary Jane, ch. Hugh and Susan S., May 1, 1826, in T. (Topsham I, 211)
Mary J. of T. and John Nowell of Vassalboro, Aug. 17, 1846. (Topsham II, 287)

Mary Jane[5] married John Nowell b.1822 d.26 Nov 1897. She died on 25 Oct 1862[96] in Vassalboro. He was listed as a dyer in the 1870 census but with real estate value of $4300.[97] That 1870 census also give us his children and their birth years: Lizzie[6] b.1847, Charles W[6] b.1848, and Ellen M[6] b.24 Jan 1851 d.28 May 1885.[98]

Lizzie[6] married George Homans on 7 Dec 1880[99] but there's a possibility that his name is spelled incorrectly. I could find no other records.

---

91. Year: 1860; Census Place: Lisbon, Androscoggin, Maine; Roll: M653_432; Page: 157; Image: 157; Family History Library Film: 803432.
92. Findagrave.com, http://goo.gl/hjlWBT, accessed 7 Mar 2015.
93. Findagrave.com, gravestone, http://goo.gl/HDNYU2.
94. "Massachusetts, Marriages, 1841-1915," (https://goo.gl/V0p4si)
95. Massachusetts, Death Records, 1841-1915 Ancestry.com Operations, Inc., 2013.
96. "Faylene Hutton Cemetery Collection, ca. 1780-1990," (https://goo.gl/eS4tSM)
97. Year: 1870; Census Place: Vassalboro, Kennebec, Maine; Roll: M593_547; Page: 507A; Image: 298; Family History Library Film: 552046.
98. Findgrave.com, description, http://goo.gl/xUSuu7, accessed 29 April 2015.
99. "Maine, Marriages, 1771-1907," (https://goo.gl/E7DKvJ)

Charles[6] married Emma D Williams on 27 Jan 1877[100] and is found with a daughter, Alice[7] b.abt 1878, in the 1880 census[101] but he died four years later on 11 Dec 1884.[102] Alice[7] did marry and had four children. That 1880 census lists his occupation as druggist.

Ellen[6] married George Southwick Hawes b.17 Jul 1845[103] d.30 Mar 1925[104] and had one known child, Grace Kimbal[7] b.21 Oct 1874[105] d.30 Oct 1943.[106]

Althera[5] (Hugh[4], Hugh[3], Hugh[2], James[1])

Althera, ch. Hugh and Susan S., Nov. 1, 1828, in T. (Topsham I , 208)

Althera married Andrew Couch b.Aug 1823 d. 16 Jan 1901[107] of Massachusetts on 3 Jun 1882[108] but they had no children.

Her birth record is spelled Althera but most census records spell her name as Althea. She was living with her sister, Elizabeth, and husband in 1850 according to the Bangor, Maine, census[109] but also appeared in the Topsham 1850 census with her family. She most likely died in Massachusetts but I cannot find burial records for her. Andrew is buried in the same cemetery as his first wife in Boxboro. Althea[5] was alive at the time of the 1900 census.[110]

Francis D[5] (Hugh[4], Hugh[3], Hugh[2], James[1])

Francis, ch. Hugh and Susan S., Aug. 27, 1831, in T. (Topsham I, 209)

Francis D[5] d.7 Jun 1901[111] in Lynn, Massachusetts, married Sarah Jane Clough b.24 May 1837[112] on 15 Sep 1858.[113] I found records

---

100. "Maine, Marriages, 1771-1907," (https://goo.gl/qdAWPT)
101. Year: 1880; Census Place: Vassalboro, Kennebec, Maine; Roll: 482; Family History Film: 1254482; Page: 429C; Enumeration District: 105; Image: 0178.
102. "Faylene Hutton Cemetery Collection, ca. 1780-1990," (https://goo.gl/xM7byX)
103. "Maine, Births and Christenings, 1739-1900," (https://goo.gl/oioZnu)
104. "Faylene Hutton Cemetery Collection, ca. 1780-1990," (https://goo.gl/17TDRe)
105. "Maine, Births and Christenings, 1739-1900," (https://goo.gl/mxxpA9)
106. Findagrave.com, gravestone year, http://goo.gl/PCBTGF accessed 29 April 2015.
107. Findgrave.com, gravestone, http://goo.gl/k6qINj, accessed, 14, Feb 2015.
108. Massachusetts, Marriage Records, 1840-1915 Ancestry.com Operations, Inc., 2013.
109. Detail: Year: 1850; Census Place: Bangor, Maine; Roll: M432_264; Page: 103B:213
110. "United States Census, 1900," (https://goo.gl/dQ4cK1)
111. Massachusetts, Death Records, 1841-1915 Ancestry.com Operations, Inc., 2013.
112. Massachusetts, Marriage Records, 1840-1915 Ancestry.com Operations, Inc., 2013.
113. Massachusetts, Marriage Records, 1840-1915 Ancestry.com Operations, Inc., 2013.

for two children who may not have survived childhood: Willie, b.21 Oct 1862[114] and Marcia E b.22 Nov 1860.[115] They had one son, Charles Hugh[6] b.17 May 1861[116] who married twice. His marriage on 16 Sept 1885 to Florence J Hutchinson[117] b.1860 d.2 Dec 1895[118] produced one daughter, Melita[6] b.3 Apr 1886[119] d.28 Dec 1931.[120] Melita[6] married Clarence Pomeroy Davis b.7 May 1887[121] d.1932[122] of Maine on 27 July 1909.[123]

Charles L[5] (Hugh[4], Hugh[3], Hugh[2], James[1])

Charles L., ch. Hugh and Susan S., Mar. 3, 1818, in T. (Topsham I, 209)

Hugh[4] and Susan's eldest was Charles L[5]. He moved to Florida just before Florida became a state. His convoluted tale is told in the chapter entitled "Charles L. Wilson, Sheriff, Alachua County, Florida" on page 143.

Martha[3] (Hugh[2], James[1]) - The Farrins

Martha[3] b.1763 d.11 Jun 1838[124] married Ebenezer Farrin on 17 Mar 1787.

Ebenezer and Martha Wilson, Mar. 17, 1787. [int. adds both of T.] [d. of Hugh the eldest and Elizabeth Hewey, p.R.80.] (Topsham II, 94)
Ebeneezer Farren was born to them Nov[r] 23 1764 (Brunswick, 25)

Ebenezer was the son of John and Hannah Farrin of Brunswick. They were original settlers: John Farrin was hired as a teacher in 1759 (Brunswick);[125] Ebenezer was their third son. Some documentation of the Farrins exists in a Rev. Charles Sinnett typewritten manuscript of a few pages now held in the New England Historic Genealogical Society in Boston. Stamp dated Nov. 21, 1922, the lineage of only two of the sons are outlined but only Ebenezer's birth

114. "Maine, Births and Christenings, 1739-1900,"(https://goo.gl/64bjqK)
115. "Maine, Births and Christenings, 1739-1900," (https://goo.gl/gW2krW)
116. "Massachusetts, Births, 1841-1915," (https://goo.gl/168naq)
117. "Massachusetts, Marriages, 1841-1915," (https://goo.gl/626IaV)
118. "Massachusetts, Deaths and Burials, 1795-1910," (https://goo.gl/9SkQb4)
119. "Massachusetts, Births, 1841-1915," (https://goo.gl/v3BfMr)
120. Findagrave.com, http://goo.gl/oXAHsP, accessed 27 Oct 2015.
121. "Maine, Births and Christenings, 1739-1900," (https://goo.gl/5QlX7W)
122. Massachusetts, Death Index, 1901-1980 [database on-line]. Ancestry.com.
123. "Massachusetts, Marriages, 1841-1915," (https://goo.gl/LcwkFk)
124. Findagrave.com, gravestone photograph, http://goo.gl/KKsGlI.
125. Wheeler, 458.

date is listed for him. As Wheeler says, all Farrins in the area are descendants of those children though.

Using the census data and the only two graves I found in Topsham, I have pieced together what looks to be correct for the Farrins. There are plenty of Farrins and I had to dig into Ebeneezer's siblings' families in order to make sure the ones I was looking at are not part of their families. In short, their son William lived at home after marriage until after 1820.

By 1790 Martha and Ebeneezer had one boy and one girl.[126] By 1800 they had three boys under 10, two 10 to 05, and two girls under 10 - total of seven children.[127] In 1810, the census shows three boys under ten (Washington, George and an unknown) two 10 to 15 (William and an unknown), one girl 10 to 15 and one girl 16 to 25.[128] In 1820[129], the census shows multiple families. There is one boy under ten (John, son of William), one boy 10 to 15 (George W), one male 16 to 18 (Washington), one male 18 to 25 (William), one male 26 to 45, three girls 10 to 15 (Martha, Eliza, Mary Ann) and only one adult female 25 to 45 which would be Mehitable, William's wife, at age 28. Martha, age 53, is absent. If the census taker got it wrong by only a few years, that could be reversed. At any rate, one of the adult women is not there. There are also listed two foreigners not naturalized which might explain the unknown adult male. All in all, this matches with most of the family data but not all.

In 1830, listed together in order are the households of William Farrin, John Wentworth, John Wilson, Hugh Wilson and Ebenezer; all members of the same extended family. living out near the Cathance River on the meadow lands. It appears that Washington may be the only child left at home in 1830 with Ebeneezer and Martha.[130]

Martha died in 1838. So in 1840 Ebenezer has no wife in his house-

---

126. Year: 1790; Census Place: Topsham, Lincoln, Maine; Series: M637; Roll: 2; Page: 260; Image: 151; Family History Library Film: 0568142.
127. Year: 1800; Census: Topsham, Maine; Roll: 6; Page: 486:456; FHL Film: 218676.
128. Year: 1810; Census: Topsham, Maine; Roll: 12; Page: 6:0218683; FHLFilm: 00014.
129. 1820 U S Census; Census: Topsham, Maine; Page: 154; NARA Roll: M33_36:91.
130. 1830; Census: Topsham, Lincoln, Maine; Series: M19; Roll: 49:300; FHL: 0497945.

hold but one male 30 to 39 and one female 30 to 39[131] who could be Washington and Rebecca. They are listed together in the 1850 census but no occupation entered for either of them.[132] I could find no traces of either of them after that.

I was convinced, once I saw "Nettie's" grave in the Riverview Cemetery, that her father, George W[4], was Martha and Ebenezer's son. Nettie is buried almost next to Martha. There is a grave size space between them so Ebeneezer was probably buried there as well.

George W[4] Farrin (Martha[3], Hugh[2], James[1])

George W[4] is found in the 1870 census with his wife, Mary Jane, and his daughter 'Genette' who was working in a cotton mill.[133] Also, in that census is a Sarah Farrin, age 71, perhaps a sister or sister-in-law. There definitely are other children of Ebenezer and Martha that I could not name. There are no other Sarahs as wives or daughters in the John Farrin family that I can find so she most likely is their child but also could be the wife of one of the unnamed sons.

Mary Jane [— — —], w. George W., Oct. 14, 1830, in Brunswick. (Topsham I, 65)
Susan Jeanett, ch. George W. and Mary Jane, Aug. 18, 1848, in Brunswick. (65)
Almond Augustus, ch. George W. and Mary Jane, Dec. 25,1854, in T. (65)

Nettie, Aug. 7, 1873, a. 25 y., G.R.3. (Topsham II, 318)
George W., Mar. 4, 1874, in T. [a. 70 y., N.P.6.] (318)

Almond[5] was last seen in the 1900 census in Topsham at age 45, with a housemate named Berry Dunham in Topsham - both are day laborers.[134] Mary Jane cannot be found again.

William[4] Farrin (Martha[3], Hugh[2], James[1])

William, Capt., h. Mehitable, , —, , in T.
Mehitable [ ], w. Capt. William, Dec. 22, 1792, in Harpswell.
William of T. and Mehetible Leavitt of Harpswell, int. Jan. 2, 1813. [cert. Jan. 20.]
George, ch. Capt. William and Mehitable, July 29, 1828, in T

131. Year: 1840; Census: Topsham, Maine; Roll: 144; Page: 14:33; FHL Film: 0009705.
132. Year: 1850; Census Place: Topsham, Maine; Roll: M432_261; Page: 346B: 480.
133. Year: 1870; Census Place: Topsham, Sagadahoc, Maine; Roll: M593_557; Page: 441A; Image: 431; Family History Library Film: 552056
134. Year: 1900; Census Place: Topsham, Sagadahoc, Maine; Roll: 599; Page: 21B; Enumeration District: 0217; FHL microfilm: 1240599

John E., ch. Capt. William and Mehitable, May 27, 1819, in T .
William Jr., ch. Capt. William and Mehitable, May 17, 1826, in T.

William's birth date is unknown but according to the censuses, he was born between 1780 and 1790. Since his parents married in 1787, his birth year is probably between 1788 and 1790.

In 1830 William[4] has almost exact match in the census with daughter Martha's age group missing.[135] 1840 is an exact match. Not all of the children married. Topsham lists four marriages and I found two more. George[5] is probably the namesake for one of Jesse's children and I expect that he died as a young adult possibly away from Topsham as he and Jesse[5] would have been the two in ocean occupations in 1840. I couldn't find what happened to John E[5] either.

Margaret Jane[5] is found in the 1850 census with her married sister Almira in Bath at age 18.[136] That is the year that William disappears from the census and Mehitable is living with her daughter, Mary Ann[5], in Bath.[137]

Mehitable died 2 Feb 1863 and is buried with her son, William J[5], in Cranberry Horn Cemetery (he died 17 Mar 1866, having never married).[138] His father's grave location is unknown.

The children who married were Eliza[5], Martha[5], Margaret Jane[5] and Almira[5].

Eliza[5] Farrin (William,[4] Martha[3], Hugh[2], James[1]) - The Leavitts

Eliza, ch. Capt. William and Mehitable, Aug. 13, 1813, in T. (Topsham I, 65)
Eliza and John W. Leavitt, both of T., , —, 1833. [cert, issued Feb. 2.] (II, 93)

Eliza[5] and John W Leavitt had one boy, Charles, who drowned.

Charles J., s. John W. and Eliza, July 16, 1839, a. 4 y. 2 m., drowned, G.R.2. (Topsham II, 346)

Charles is buried in the Haley cemetery but his parents are not. I wasn't able to find records for other children but Eliza appears in

135. 1830; Census: Topsham, Lincoln, Maine; Series: M19; Roll: 49; Page: 300; Family History Library Film: 0497945.
136. Census, 1850, (https://goo.gl/6jBd59)
137. Year: 1850; Census: Bath, Lincoln, Maine; Roll: M432_261; Page: 189A; Image: 167
138. Findagrave.com, gravestones, http://goo.gl/AvCYGC, accessed 11 May 2015.

the census in 1840 with one girl under 5 and one girl 15 to 19.[139] John is not there but that may mean that he died between 1835 and 1840. I found no other records for the family.

Martha[5] Farrin (William,[4] Martha[3], Hugh[2], James[1]) & Abraham Snow

Martha, ch. Capt. William and Mehitable, July 24, 1817,in T . (Topsham I, 66)
Martha of T. and Abraham Snow of Brunswick, int. May 7, 1836. [cert, issued May 23.] (II, 93)

Martha[5] married Abraham Snow b.3 Mar 1815.[140] The 1840 census in Topsham shows two boys under 5.[141] The 1860 census shows a boy named William born about 1833 and a woman named Fanny born about 1837.[142] Fanny may be William's wife but I have found no other records for either Fanny or William that I can be sure are them. Abraham was a sailor, noted as just a mariner in 1850. Martha died 25 April 1859[143] and is buried without her husband. He appeared in the 1860 census but he was not next door to his brother in 1870. I can find no death record for him.

Almira[5] Farrin (William,[4] Martha[3], Hugh[2], James[1]) & Daniel Snow

Almira D., ch. Capt. William and Mehitable, Oct. 2, 1823, in T. (Topsham I, 65)
Almira D. of T. and Daniel Snow of Bath, int. Nov. 3,1844. [cert, issued Nov. 18.] (II, 93)

Almira[5] married her brother-in-law's brother, Daniel b.12 Oct 1813.[144] He was a Master Mariner just like his brother and in 1850 and 1860 the brothers were living next door to each other. Almira[5] and Daniel had two children, Mary E[6] b.1846 and Edwin Herbert[6] b.1848 d.21 Dec 1895.[145] Mary[6] was still living in 1860 but I found no trace of her after that.

Edwin Herbert[6] Snow married Adelaide Elizabeth Allen b.1849

---

139. Year: 1840; Census Place: Topsham, Lincoln, Maine; Roll: 144; Page: 17; Image: 39; Family History Library Film: 0009705.

140. "Maine, Births and Christenings, 1739-1900," (https://goo.gl/rWW58C)

141. Year: 1840; Census Place: Topsham, Lincoln, Maine; Roll: 144; Page: 21; Image: 47; Family History Library Film: 0009705.

142. Year: 1860; Census Place: Bath, Sagadahoc, Maine; Roll: M653_448; Page: 195; Image: 195; Family History Library Film: 803448.

143. Findagrave.com, http://goo.gl/IlzUjO, accessed 29 July 2015.

144. "Maine, Births and Christenings, 1739-1900," (https://goo.gl/LMgrvz)

145. Maine State Archives; 1892-1907 Vital Records; Roll #: 53.

d.1928[146] on 7 Jan 1869.[147] They had five children: Myra D[7], Charles Edwin[7], Ethel A[7], May Baston[7] and Daniel H[7] b.1872 d.1877.

Myra D[7] Snow b.1868 d.1958 married Alvah D Kelley b.1869 d.1932 on 23 Dec 1891[148] and they had Ethel May[8] b.4 Mar 1893 d.1915.[149] Charles Edwin[7] Snow b.14 Aug 1870[150] d.1940[151] married Evelyn Miller b.1876 d.1956 on 23 Aug1894[152] and had one daughter, Myra Miller Snow[8] b.26 Apr 1895 d.28 Apr 1919.[153] Ethel A[7] Snow b.23 May 1878[154] d.7 Jul 1939 also married (Walter Murtaugh b.1879 d.7 Jul 1939[155]) but had no children. May Baston[7] Snow b.17 Aug 1880[156] married Karl Liberty from Switzerland on 15 July 1909[157] but also had no children.

Mary Ann[5] Farrin (William,[4] Martha[3], Hugh[2], James[1]) - The Blaisdells

Mary Ann, ch. Capt. William and Mehitable, July 22, 1815, in T. (Topsham I, 66)
Mary Ann of T. and Joseph Blasdell of Brunswick, int. Nov. I I , 1832 [cert, issued Nov. 25], T.R.4. (II, 94)

Mary Ann[5] d.22 Aug 1899[158] and Joseph Blaisdell b.abt 1813 d.1898 (unc) had three children, Octavia Ann[6], George Henry[6] and Joseph William[6]. They lived in Harpswell and Bath. According to Octavia's death record, Joseph was a blacksmith. I could find no proof of his birth or death dates beyond the census.

I found two marriage records for the oldest, Octavia Ann[6] b.1832 d.30 Dec 1902.[159] She married a Matthew Potter when she was very young. They are seen together living with her parents in 1850[160] but

146. "Nathan Hale Cemetery Collection, ca. 1780-1980," (https://goo.gl/Rx6mc4)
147. "Maine, Marriages, 1771-1907," (https://goo.gl/3ifzCv)
148. "Maine, Marriages, 1771-1907," (https://goo.gl/83FJCe)
149. Findagrave.com, gravestone, http://goo.gl/EJzDER, accessed 24 May 2015.
150. "Maine, Vital Records, 1670-1907 ," (https://goo.gl/S0X9JA)
151. "Nathan Hale Cemetery Collection, ca. 1780-1980," (https://goo.gl/BYvPjZ)
152. Maine, Vital Records, 1670-1907 ," (https://goo.gl/iOR9J8)
153. Maine State Archives; 1908-1922 Vital Records; Roll #: 44.
154. "Maine, Vital Records, 1670-1907 ," (https://goo.gl/iirtth), Augusta; FHL microfilm 1,205,246.
155. New York, New York, Death Index, 1862-1948 Ancestry.com.
156. "Maine, Vital Records, 1670-1907 ," (https://goo.gl/1MLYpf)
157. "Maine, Marriage Index, 1892-1966, 1977-1996," (https://goo.gl/iaDYLr)
158. Maine State Archives; 1892-1907 Vital Records; Roll #: 5.
159. Maine State Archives; 1892-1907 Vital Records; Roll #: 37.
160. Year: 1850; Place: Bath, Lincoln, Maine; Roll: M432_261; Page: 189A; Image: 167.

she married Isaac J Maxwell b.abt 1842[161] on 16 Aug 1854.[162] She and Isaac had one daughter, Ida[7] b.abt 1858, according to the 1870 census.[163]

George Henry[6] Blaisdell b.5 Dec 1853 (unc) d.12 Jun 1908[164] married Mary Estelle Stover b.20 June 1865 (unc) whose family tree is an interesting mix of Wilson - Alexander names such as Merryman, Curtis and Webber. It looks like they had no children.

Joseph William[6] Blaisdell b.1853 d.31 Jan 1898[165] married Albertina/Albertena C Conant b.27 Feb 1854.[166] They had four children, Georgie[7] b.1883 d.29 May 1895,[167] Helen L[7] b.1890 d.2 Nov 1895,[168] William W[7] b.9 Feb 1885[169] d.5 Dec 1970[170] and Fanelia Frances[7] b.1888 d.13 Jul 1922[171] who married Harold Leroy[7] Powlesland.[172]

Jesse W[5] Farrin (William,[4] Martha[3], Hugh[2], James[1])

Jesse W., ch. Capt. William and Mehitable, Nov. 24, 1821, in T. (Topsham I, 65)

Jesse W[5] married Emeline Newall on 13 Apr 1847[173] and had seven children, every one of whom lived to be an adult and have children. He was a rigger. He must have died after the 1880 census because that is the last time he or Emeline appear in the records.

The youngest, Jesse H[6] Farrin b.abt 1869 d.28 Apr 1895,[174] however, died early of consumption and so did his son, Herbert[7] b.4 Feb

161. Year: 1880; Census Place: Harpswell, Cumberland, Maine; Roll: 478; Family History Film: 1254478; Page: 357D; Enumeration District: 037; Image: 0102.
162. "Maine, Marriages, 1771-1907," (https://goo.gl/8NeeOK)
163. Year: 1870; Census Place: Harpswell, Cumberland, Maine; Roll: M593_540; Page: 342B; Image: 159; Family History Library Film: 552039.
164. Massachusetts, Death Records, 1841-1915 [database on-line] Ancestry.com
165. "Maine, Deaths and Burials, 1841-1910," (https://goo.gl/cbDF24)
166. Brunswick, 436.
167. "Maine, Vital Records, 1670-1907 ," (https://goo.gl/t23I2y)
168. "Maine, Deaths and Burials, 1841-1910," (https://goo.gl/dyxC6M)
169. Social Security Adminstration, Number: 004-14-8835; Maine; Before 1951.
170. Maine Death Index, 1960-1997 [database on-line]. Provo, UT, USA: Ancestry.com.
171. Maine State Archives; 1908-1922 Vital Records; Roll #: 45
172. Maine State Archives; Augusta, Maine, USA; 1908-1922 Vital Records; Roll #: 45.
173. "Maine, Marriages, 1771-1907," (https://goo.gl/ucJDPV)
174. "Maine, Vital Records, 1670-1907 ," (https://goo.gl/QkeOXJ)

1893[175] d.3 Dec 1894.[176] The mother was Jesse C Norris b.Feb 1870[177] d.aft 1920.

Franklin R[6] Farrin b.1848 d.9 Mar 1916[178] married late in life. According to the 1880 census, he, a blacksmith, had "chronic rheumatism".[179] He married Hannah A Holmes of New Brunswick, Canada, in Bristol and they had Lottie A[7] b.abt 1884, Edison[7] b.13 Aug 1892[180] d.5 Jul 1985[181] and Alton Holmes[7] b.14 Jun 1885.[182]

John William[6] Farrin b.13 Jun 1851 d.16 Dec 1904[183] married Mary Frances Muir b.May 1852 d.aft 1930 of Scotland on 5 Jan 1871[184] and had one child, William Henry[7] b.7 Sep 1876.[185]

Ella[6] Farrin b.4 Jan 1853 (unc) d.1 Jun 1915[186] married Charles M McDonald b.abt 1848 d.4 Sep 1897. They had two children, Jesse Garfield[7] b.13 Aug 1881[187] d.17 Oct 1955[188] and Charles Fred[7] b.Feb 1876[189] d.8 Jun 1952.[190]

Henry R[6] Farrin b.1855 d.1889 married Ann S Hardie b.1851 d.1939[191] on 3 Sep 1879.[192] They had twin daughters, Lucy Agnes[7] b.24 Aug 1885[193] d.Jul 1986[194] and Ann S[7] b.24 Aug 1885 d.Mar

175. "Maine, Vital Records, 1670-1907 ," (https://goo.gl/gMd9iU)
176. "Maine, Vital Records, 1670-1907 ," (https://goo.gl/8aiipw)
177. "United States Census, 1870," (https://goo.gl/vCSyOS)
178. Tennessee State Library and Archives; Nashville, Tennessee; Tennessee Death Records, 1908-1959; Roll #: 58.
179. Year: 1880; Census Place: Bath, Sagadahoc, Maine; Roll: 488; Family History Film: 1254488; Page: 10D; Enumeration District: 142; Image: 0024.
180. "Maine, Vital Records, 1670-1907 ," (https://goo.gl/hyRvsx)
181. Ancestry.com. Maine Death Index, 1960-1997 Ancestry.com.
182. WWI. Maine; Registration County: Lincoln; Roll: 1653911. Ancestry.com.
183. Findagrave.com, gravestone, http://goo.gl/xB0GjO, accessed 26 May 2015.
184. "Maine, Marriages, 1771-1907," (https://goo.gl/aBGkZ3)
185. WWI, Registration State: Mass.; County: Middlesex; Roll: 1674432; Draft Board: 2.
186. New Hampshire, Death and Disinterment Records, 1754-1947. Ancestry.com.
187. "Massachusetts, Births and Christenings, 1639-1915," (https://goo.gl/BNSxUy)
188. "New Hampshire, Death Certificates, 1938-1959," (https://goo.gl/FdZCca)
189. Findagrave.com, gravestone, http://goo.gl/4rfVMR, accessed 27 May 2015.
190. Connecticut Death Index, 1949-2012 Ancestry.com
191. "Maine, Nathan Hale Cemetery Collection, ca. 1780-1980," (https://goo.gl/FngnLc)
192. "Maine, Vital Records, 1670-1907 ," (https://goo.gl/dHPidg)
193. "Maine, Births and Christenings, 1739-1900," (https://goo.gl/awm6ho)
194. Number: 004-36-1681; Issue State: Maine; Issue Date: 1953-1954.

1977.[195]

Almira S[6] Farrin b.1857 d.1887 married Samuel D S Thompson b.1849 d.1928 and had three children; he was a ships joiner in 1880.[196] The three children were Lucy Thompson[7] b.1884 d.1886,[197] Luther[7] b.7 Jan 1879 d.Jan 1963[198] and Gertrude[7] b.25 Dec 1882 d.Jan 1965.[199]

George Leavitt[6] Farrin b.1862 d.1926 married Clara Ellen Ragon b.1866 d.1932[200] on 26 Apr 1884.[201] They had Nellie E[7] b.1884 d.27 Jul 1912,[202] George Henry[7] b.9 Oct 1886[203] d.1955,[204] Elmira Snow[7] b.8 Aug 1888 d.Sep 1973,[205] John David[7] b. 14 Aug 1890[206] d.13 Apr 1935,[207] Annie J[7] b. 1892 d.10 Sep 1894, Arthur L[7] b. 1897 d. 18 Feb 1900,[208] and Ruby Mae[7] b.25 Aug 1898.[209]

Margaret Jane[5] Farrin (William,[4] Martha[3], Hugh[2], James[1]) - The Websters

Margaret Jane, ch. Capt. William & Mehitable, July 13, 1832, in T. (Topsham I, 66)

The youngest daughter, Margaret Jane[5], married Ruel Webster b.abt 1837 and had four children, Ida[6] b.1858, James[6] b.1858, Eugene[6] b.1867 and Fred[6] b.12 July 1870.[210] I can't find death dates for any of them except Margaret[5] who died on 25 Mar 1902[211] of dementia. Considering that her death certificate is devoid of the normal information, I believe that none of the children survived to even help fill out the certificate. Only Ida[6] is with her mother in 1860. In 1870,

195. Number: 004-64-2365; Issue State: Maine; Issue Date: 1973.
196. Year: 1880; Census Place: Bath, Sagadahoc, Maine; Roll: 488; Family History Film: 1254488; Page: 8D; Enumeration District: 142; Image: 0020.
197. "Nathan Hale Cemetery Collection, ca. 1780-1980," (https://goo.gl/oO9gv3)
198. "United States Social Security Death Index," (https://goo.gl/D0Zf08)
199. "United States Social Security Death Index," (https://goo.gl/dBPWcg)
200. Findagrave.com, gravestone, http://goo.gl/XVpxTf, accessed 27 May 2015.
201. "Maine, Marriages, 1771-1907," (https://goo.gl/qEKrFz)
202. Maine State Archives; 1908-1922 Vital Records; Roll #: 16.
203. "Maine, Vital Records, 1670-1907 ," (https://goo.gl/3GPgof)
204. Findagrave.com, gravestone, http://goo.gl/6zbxh6, accessed 27 May 2015.
205. Number: 004-64-2945; Issue State: Maine; Issue Date: 1973.
206. WWII, Registration State: Mass; County: Suffolk; Roll: 1684776; Draft Board: 05.
207. Pennsylvania, Death Certificates, 1906-1963 Ancestry.com Operations, Inc., 2014.
208. "Maine, Vital Records, 1670-1907 ," (https://goo.gl/giWO2R)
209. "Maine, Vital Records, 1670-1907 ," (https://goo.gl/JG8nn4)
210. "Maine, Vital Records, 1670-1907 ," (https://goo.gl/DuId4p)
211. "Maine, Vital Records, 1670-1907 ," (https://goo.gl/MpsPlo)

Ida[6] was gone.[212] In 1880[213] Margaret is by herself as widowed and no children at home. Only Ruel[6], James[6] and Eugene[6] were present in 1870. I thought at first husband Ruel was a sailor but one census identified his occupation as blacksmith. Definitely some sort of traumatic life for Margaret.

Elizabeth[3] (Hugh[2], James[1]) & Jesse Davis

Elizabeth [int. Miss] and Jesse Davis [int. of Burnt Meadow], June 8, 1784. [(d. of Hugh the eldest and Elizabeth Hewey).
Jesse, h. Elizabeth (Wilson), July 16, 1757, in Action, Mass., P.R. 101. [Head of family, P.R.87.] (Bowdoin I, 78)

Elizabeth "Betsey"[3] b.1765 (unc) d.bef 1789 married Jesse Davis d.15 Mar 1792[214] of Acton, Massachusetts. They had two children before she died: Jonathan[4] and Rebecca[4]. Jesse was a Revolutionary War soldier according to the Son's of the American Revolution application of one of his descendants.[215] Both Jesse and Betsey died while their two children were quite young.

The family lived in Bowdoin/Bowdoinaham but Jesse died in Lisbon, Maine, after surgery to amputate his leg wounded during the war. He had remarried after Betsey's death in early 1789 to a Hannah Curtis b.1760 d.22 Dec 1843[216] who was left with Betsey's two and her own two children. He was buried with Hannah but Betsey's burial location is unknown and her birth date is suggested, not confirmed. Before his death, he built the Davis Bryent house which, if still standing, would be the oldest house in Sabattus, Maine.

That leg amputation information probably came from the Cyrus Woodman scrapbook[217] where there was a handwritten note:

Jesse Davis died suddenly in 1792 of loss of blood caused by the amputation of a leg made necessary by the breaking out of a mind received at the battle of Lexington. He came from Roxbury in 1786 to build mills and develope a settlement on the land

212. "United States Census, 1870,"(https://goo.gl/ebqAvK)
213. Year: 1880; Census Place: Bath, Sagadahoc, Maine; Roll: 488; Family History Film: 1254488; Page: 33A; Enumeration District: 143; Image: 0069.
214. "Maine, Veterans Cemetery Records, 1676-1918", (https://goo.gl/yxoSws,)
215. Volume: 163; SAR Membership Number: 32436.
216. Findagrave.com, gravestone, http://goo.gl/6PWHMJ
217. Woodman, History of Topsham.

owned by his uncle.

Jesse Davis was a descendant of early settlers of Massachusetts. There actually were quite a few of that name that came in the early 1600s from England. There's an interesting source on line by a Sabattus researcher that delineates this family.[218] Some of these descendants are well known but if there is a footnote for a date, there's a possibility only the year is confirmed. Some of the dates seem to come from family sources but I simply have not been able to confirm all of the dates.

His descendants stayed in the Lisbon area and seemed to be mainly engaged in farming according to the censuses in the Lisbon and Wales area.

Jesse Davis, late of Bowdoin. Hannah Davis, of Bowdoin, widow, and Joshua Davis, of Sidney, Adm'rs, 2 Oct., 1795. [V, 106.] Ezekiel Thompson, of Topsham and James Curtis, of Brunswick, sureties. Inventory by Isaac Hinkley and Samuel Tibbets, both of Bowdoin, and James Wilson, of Topsham 30 Oct., 1792, £359: 4 : 3. [VI. 1 16.] John Merrill, of Topsham and Samuel Tibbets, of Bowdoin, commissioners to examine claims. [VI, 117.] Widow's dower set off by Isaac Hinkley, John Merrill and Samuel Tibbets, 15 July, 1795. [VI, 120.] Advertisement of sale of real estate 16 Sep., 1795. (VI, 139·] Account filed 2 7 May, 1 796. [VI, 140.] Distribution ordered 30 May, 1796. [VI, 149-151.] Seth Hinkley, of Bowdoin, guardian unto Jonathan and Rebecca, minor children, 10 Jan., 1799. [IX, 178.] Rachel, minor daughter, chose Seth Hinckley, of Lisbon, to be her guardian, 25 Aug., 1804. [IX, 252.][219]

Jonathan[4] Davis (Elizabeth[3], Hugh[2], James[1])

Jonathan, s. Jesse & Elizabeth (Wilson), May 7, 1785/84, P.R.101. (Bowdoin I, 78)
Rebecca Larrabee was born to them Oct[r] 31, 1785 (Brunswick, 33)
1808 Dec[r] 1 Jonathan David & Rebecca Larrabee (Brunswick, 102)
Rebeckah Davis wife of Jon[a] Departed this life Feb 16th 1839 (Lisbon, 27)
Mary Davis was born March the 22[d] AD 1809 (27)
Rebekah Davis was born March the 24th AD 1817 (27)

Jonathan[4] d.6 Apr 1865[220] married Rebecca Larrabee. She was the niece of William[2] Wilson (James[1]) and Isabelle Larrabee. They had three boys, John L[5], Jesse[5] and Benjamin[5] and three daughters, Mary[5], Rebekah[5], and Azelia[5]. Their father, Jonathan, "became quite wealthy in real estate".[221] Mary may have married a William Max-

218. David C. Young , Early Families of Sabattus, Maine, http://goo.gl/d89Zui, accessed 14 Feb 2015.
219. Patterson, 226-227.
220. Findagrave.com, gravestone, http://goo.gl/V5mKqc.
221. Young, David C.

well but I can't find any more information. (Lisbon, 343)

John L[5] Davis (Jonathan[4], Elizabeth[3], Hugh[2], James[1])

John L Davis was born February the 9th AD 1812 (Lisbon, 27)
Marriage is intended between John L Davis of Lisbon & Eunice Cary of Turner Lisbon Feb 1837 (352)
Eunice C Davis the wife of John L Davis Departed this life Feby the 18th AD 1846 (157)
Abigail Davis 2nd wife of John L Davis Died April 13th AD 1859 (157)
Mary Elen Davis was born April the 3d AD 1838 (156)
Clara C Davis was born May the 6th AD 1840 (156)
Jonathan Davis was born October the 27th AD 1845 (156)

John[5] L d.30 Mar 1892[222] married three times, outliving two wives. His first and mother of his children was Eunice S Cary b.28 Dec 1816.[223] They married 2 Mar 1837.[224] Daughter Mary Elen[6] disappears from view after the 1850 census[225] and Clara[6] also disappeared after the 1870 census.[226]

Son Jonathan[6] d.23 Dec 1917[227] married Izanna Moulton on 2 Aug 1871.[228] They had 6 sons, Albert[7] b.28 Feb 1873 d.22 Jul 1890,[229] Arthur[7] b.1875 d.1949,[230] Edwin[7] b.19 Oct 1877 d.26 Apr 1902,[231] Jesse[7] b.4 Oct 1879[232] d.6 Jun 1967,[233] John L[7] b.13 Aug 1883 d.1947,[234] and Clarence Benjamin[7] b.6 May 1886 d.15 Jul 1976.[235]

Jesse[5] Davis (Jonathan[4], Elizabeth[3], Hugh[2], James[1])

Jesse Davis was born July the 21st AD 1814 (Lisbon, 27)

Jesse[5] d.16 Feb 1897[236] was a public figure in Lisbon and was said

222. "Maine, Vital Records, 1670-1907 ," (https://goo.gl/9d45Iw)
223. "Maine, Vital Records, 1670-1907 ," (https://goo.gl/nJ9OS7)
224. Maine State Archives; Augusta, Maine, USA; Pre 1892 Delayed Returns; Roll #: 27.
225. Year: 1850; Census: Lisbon, Maine; Roll: M432_261; Page: 417A; Image: 621.
226. Year: 1870; Census Place: Lisbon, Androscoggin, Maine; Roll: M593_537; Page: 342A; Image: 56; Family History Library Film: 552036.
227. Maine, Births and Christenings, 1739-1900," (https://goo.gl/mROVBW)
228. "Maine, Marriages, 1771-1907," (https://goo.gl/X12jkX)
229. "Maine, Births and Christenings, 1739-1900," (https://goo.gl/uSV2uK)
230. Findagrave.com, gravestone, http://goo.gl/hKr6WQ
231. "Maine, Births and Christenings, 1739-1900," (https://goo.gl/dPtlKP)
232. Social Security Administration, Number: 005-36-6275; Maine; Issue Date: 1954
233. "Maine, Death Index, 1960-1996," (https://goo.gl/FRjZYB)
234. Findagrave.com, gravestone, http://goo.gl/hKr6WQ
235. "United States Social Security Death Index," (https://goo.gl/VdWijU)
236. Findagrave.com, (http://goo.gl/DsxJIM)

to have inherited a considerable fortune from his father, Jonathan. His picture is included in a history book from the American Historical Society and there is lengthy collection of stories.[237] He was a justice of the peace and married many couples starting about 1870. His own marriage was to Mary Ann Woodbury b.10 Oct 1824 d.26 Oct 1899[238] on 15 Feb 1845.[239] They had Albert[6] b.5 Oct 1846[240] d.abt 1870, Ada Elizabeth[6] b.22 Jun 1851[241] d.3 Jul 1867, Emily Jane[6] b.17 Nov 1852,[242] and Sarah Louise[6] b.Aug 1861.[243] Sarah Louise[6] is listed as just Louise or Louisa in census records but her marriage record from 20 Dec 1892 in Boston[244] reads Sarah L. Her husband was Morrill Newman Drew b.17 May 1862 d.27 Sep 1917,[245] a lawyer. They had one child, Jesse Albert Drew[7] b.6 Aug 1896 d.13 Jul 1981.[246]

Benjamin[5] Davis (Jonathan[4], Elizabeth[3], Hugh[2], James[1])

> *Benjamin Davis was born April the 13th AD 1822 (Lisbon, 27)*
> *Elizabeth Jane of T & Benjamin Davis of Webster, Jan. 29, 1863 in T (Topsham II, 284)*
> *Elizabeth J., ch. Arthur L. and Elizabeth B., Dec. 27, 1835, in T. [Elizabeth Jane, 1836, P.R.43. (Topsham I, 209)*

Benjamin[5] b.13 April 1822 d.18 May 1901[247] married Elizabeth Jane Wilson of Topsham d.1918[248] and had two children, Lee Wilson[6] b.4 Mar 1867 d.31 Jan 1930[249] and baby Mary Alice[6], born and died 1878.[250] Lee did marry and had at least six children born after 1900.

Elizabeth was a cousin, the great-great-granddaughter of Hugh Wilson, the daughter of Arthur Lee Wilson. I had all the pieces to

---

237. Louis Clinton Hatch, Maine, a History, Biographical (New York: American Historical Society, 1919), 5-6. https://goo.gl/aYPu1C (part of the book).
238. Findagrave.com, gravestone, http://goo.gl/cfQ0X0.
239. "Maine, Marriages, 1771-1907," (https://goo.gl/XV9SAN)
240. "Maine, Births and Christenings, 1739-1900," (https://goo.gl/LBVSXU)
241. "Maine, Births and Christenings, 1739-1900," (https://goo.gl/9sQSZM)
242. "Maine, Births and Christenings, 1739-1900," (https://goo.gl/rbt8rA)
243. Year: 1900; Census Place: Portland, Cumberland, Maine; Roll: 591; Page: 12B; Enumeration District: 0072; FHL microfilm: 1240591.
244. Massachusetts, Marriage Records, 1840-1915 Ancestry.com.
245. Maine State Archives; 1908-1922 Vital Records; Roll #: 16.
246. "Massachusetts, Death Index, 1970-2003," (https://goo.gl/uRbdwB)
247. "Maine, Vital Records, 1670-1907 ", (https://goo.gl/43q2Br)
248. Findagrave.com, gravestone, http://goo.gl/bvwPWK, accessed 11 Feb 2015.
249. Findagrave, com, http://goo.gl/gn6Uqz, accessed 11 Feb 2015.
250. Gravestone, http://goo.gl/d27llL, accessed 11 Jan 2015.

this puzzle but did not make the connection until late in the project. My original info simply had an incorrect assumption - that Elizabeth had died and not married. Once I started looking closer, I realized the marriage record wasn't so odd. It's just rare that a Topsham resident would marry someone from outside the area. Once I realized they were actually distant cousins, it came into focus. The relationship is proven by Arthur Lee's will where he states that she, his daughter, is married to Benjamin.[251]

Azelia[5] Davis (Jonathan[4], Elizabeth[3], Hugh[2], James[1]) - The Sanborns

Arzelia Davis was born November the 27th AD 1824 (Lisbon, 27)

Azelia[5] d.22 Oct 1897[252] married David Scribner Sanborn b.18 Aug 1821 d.26 Feb 1891.[253] He was a farmer like her father (censuses of 1850,[254] 1870,[255] 1880[256]) and they had six boys with one who died young, Herman M[6] b.31 Mar 1864 d.29 Aug 1869.[257] The other five boys all married and lived into the 20th century. They were George Irving[6], Frank Leslie[6], Davis[6], Milan B[6] and Albert Jesse[6].

George Irving[6] Sanborn b.19 Jan 1851[258] d.14 Sep 1906 married Laurette E "Laura" Colby b.19 Jul 1856 d.19 Oct 1917[259] on 1 Mar 1876.[260] They had three children, Lizzie[7] b.abt 1878[261] d.30 Apr 1888,[262] Frank Sleeper[7] b.13 Nov 1881 d.22 May 1966,[263] and Addie D[7] b.23 July 1884[264] d.15 Nov 1971[265] who married a Wilson but for once it wasn't a Wilson from this family!

---

251. Sagadahoc County Probate Court, 1892, Arthur Lee Wilson Will.
252. Maine State Archives; 1892-1907 Vital Records; Roll #: 50.
253. Findagrave.com, gravestone, http://goo.gl/ZgZtwP, accessed 11 Feb 2015.
254. Year: 1850; Census: Webster, Maine; Roll: M432_261; Page: 438B; Image: 663
255. Year: 1870; Census: Wales, Maine; Roll: M593_537; Page: 445A; Image: 262.
256. Year: 1880; Census Place: Wales, Androscoggin, Maine; Roll: 475; Family History Film: 1254475; Page: 480A; Enumeration District: 021; Image: 0957
257. "Maine, Births and Christenings, 1739-1900," (https://goo.gl/puHnJZ)
258. "Maine, Births and Christenings, 1739-1900," (https://goo.gl/q4BkTS)
259. Maine State Archives; 1908-1922 Vital Records; Roll #: 49.
260. "Maine, Marriages, 1771-1907," (https://goo.gl/XYyXgE)
261. Year: 1880; Census Place: Webster, Androscoggin, Maine; Roll: 475; Family History Film: 1254475; Page: 468A; Enumeration District: 021; Image: 093.
262. Findagrave.com, gravestone http://goo.gl/liAqbN, accessed 11 Feb 2015.
263. Findagrave.com, gravestone, http://goo.gl/7CDsYM, accessed 11 Feb 2015.
264. "United States Social Security Death Index," (https://goo.gl/yrPdwa)
265. "Maine, Death Index, 1960-1996," (https://goo.gl/YCsWGp)

Frank Leslie[6] Sanborn b.22 Aug 1852 d.27 Feb 1908 and his wife Anvella Getchell b.20 Jan 1854 d.1 Mar 1912[266] had one son, David Amzi[7] b.11 Sep 1875 d.7 Feb 1923.[267] David[7] did marry and had four children.

Davis[6] Sanborn b.29 Apr 1856 d.4 May 1889 married Arabella M Thompson b.1859 d.1933[268] and had two children, Mima b.19 Sep 1887 d.16 Mar 1970[269] and Davis b.16 Sep 1889 d.9 Jan 1974.[270]

Milan B[6] Sanborn b.13 Apr 1862 d.15 Aug 1947 married Mellie J Thompson b.22 Sep 1866 d.19 Jul 1950, Arabella's sister. They had one son, Jesse Lee b.25 Aug 1892 d.2 Dec 1980.[271]

Albert Jesse[6] Sanborn b.19 Jan 1866 d.3 Apr 1952 married Olive May Beal b.5 Feb 1875 d.4 Jul 1920.[272] They had three children.

Rebecca[4] (Elizabeth[3], Hugh[2], James[1]) - The Donnells

Rebecca, d. Jesse and Elizabeth (Wilson), May 4, 1786/87, P.R.101. (Bowdoin I, 79)

Elizabeth Donnell born Nov[r] 7th 1811 (Lisbon, 13) d.30 Sep 1848 (unc)
Benjamin Donnell Jr born Octr 17th 1815 (Lisbon, 13) d.30 Sep 1834[273]
Rebecca Donnell ... born March the 9th AD 1828 (Lisbon, 13) d.29 Oct 1837 (unc)
William Donnell was born March the 1st AD 1820 (Lisbon, 13) d.31 Aug1864[274]

Rebecca[4] b.4 May 1786[275] d.15 Jan 1859[276] married Benjamin Donnell b.8 Mar 1787[277] d.28 Sep 1869.[278] Benjamin was the son of Nathaniel Donnell from York, Maine. Though the Donnells were one of the Maine families Rev. Charles Sinnett documented, he did not mention Benjamin unfortunately.[279]

---

266. Findagrave.com, gravestone photograph, http://goo.gl/0mmsBJ
267. Findagrave.com, gravestone photograph, http://goo.gl/9YF8BN
268. Findagrave, com, gravestone photograph, http://goo.gl/QKSHmQ
269. Social Security Administration, Number: 013-14-4809; Mass; Before 1951.
270. Social Security Administration, Number: 021-07-5034; Mass; Before 1951.
271. Findagrave.com, http://goo.gl/c4bOlr, accessed 29 July 2015.
272. Findagrave.com, gravestone photograph, http://goo.gl/OVwCgO
273. "Maine, Nathan Hale Cemetery Collection, ca. 1780-1980," (https://goo.gl/fd1Jix)
274. "Maine, Veterans Cemetery Records, 1676-1918", (https://goo.gl/BU0PIL)
275. "Maine, Births and Christenings, 1739-1900," (https://goo.gl/nTnX6i)
276. Findagrave.com, gravestone, http://goo.gl/etdRBq.
277. "Maine, Births and Christenings, 1739-1900," (https://goo.gl/O8AZwG)
278. Findagrave.com, gravestone, http://goo.gl/dcvMnf
279. Sinnett, Rev. Charles N., The Donnell Family in Maine (Brainerd, Minn: ca. 1922) The Donnell family in Maine (Mss A 8650). R Stanton Avery Special Collections, New En-

Their children who married were Nathaniel[5], Charles Kingsbury[5], Isaiah[5], Jessie Davis[5], and Samuel[5].

Nathaniel[5] Donnell (Rebecca[4], Elizabeth[3], Hugh[2], James[1])

Nathaniel Donnell born Sept[r] 8th 1809 (Lisbon, 13)
The intentions of marriage between Mr. Nathiel Donnell of Lewiston and Mrs. Olive D Williams of West Bath have been entered in the town clerks office and published in the town of Lewiston according to law, This 27th day of Augst. A.D. 1848 Certificate granted Sept. 11th 1848 (Lewiston, 538)

Nathaniel[5] Donnell d.26 Feb 1879 married Olive D Williams b.1808 d.13 Feb 1891.[280] According to the 1850 census[281] they had at least three children though I'm pretty sure there were more. The 1860 census adds another possible daughter and I also found a death record from 1838 that might well be another. They were Benjamin[6] b.abt 1833, Mary[6] b.abt 1836, Nathaniel[6] b.abt 1840 and Elizabeth[6] who would have been a late baby born about 1853. None of them show up buried in the Bath area on findagrave.com. So this information is all provided with caution.

Isaiah[5] Donnell (Rebecca[4], Elizabeth[3], Hugh[2], James[1])

Isaiah Donnell born Sep[r] 20th 1813 (Lisbon, 13)

Isaiah[5] Donnell d.12 Apr 1895 married Sophia A Thompson b.24 Mar 1812 d.10 Mar 1896.[282] They had 8 children all born in Monmouth: Albert B[6] b.2 May 1842 d.11 July 1843, Wesley C[6] b.13 Mar 1845 d.25 Aug 1865, Marietta[6] b.24 Aug 1847 d.8 Oct 1865, Loring[6] b.12 Apr 1849 d.5 Oct 1862 in Washington, DC, Alonzo M[6] b.13 Nov 1849 d.8 Jul 1935,[283] Florella[6] b.3 Sept 1851 d.17 May 1873, Elwood L[6] b.1 Jan 1854 d.23 Oct 1865,[284] and Stillman W[6] b.23 Dec 1855 d.5 Nov 1934.[285]

Only two lived long enough to marry: Stillman[6] and Alonzo[6] who married Annie Hamilton on 25 Mar 1871. They had 5 children, Ina

---

gland Historic Genealogical Society.

280. Findagrave.com, gravestone, http://goo.gl/JRHRHY, accessed 11 Feb 2015.
281. Year: 1850; Census Place: Bath, Maine; Roll: M432_261; Page: 178A; Image: 145.
282. "Nathan Hale Cemetery Collection, ca. 1780-1980," (https://goo.gl/WWMSJj)
283. North Carolina, Death Certificates, 1909-1975 Ancestry.com Operations Inc, 2007.
284. "Nathan Hale Cemetery Collection, ca. 1780-1980," (https://goo.gl/EERmTy)
285. Findagrave.com, gravestone, http://goo.gl/YsCcrc, accessed 11 Feb 2015.

W[7] b.17 Jul 1872 d.12 Mar 1940,[286] Ralph Loring[7] b.23 Feb 1874 d.28 Nov 1941, Merton Elwood[7] b.28 Dec 1876 d.3 Oct 1964,[287] Wallace Alonzo[7] b.31 Dec 1879 d.24 Nov 1954 and Henry[7] b.12 Jan 1884 d.1937. Stillman[6] married Nellie Blake b.16 Sept 1854 d.12 Apr 1939 on 7 Sept 1878[288] and they had one child, Wilbur[7] b.abt 1883 d.10 Aug 1898.[289]

Jesse Davis[5] Donnell (Rebecca[4], Elizabeth[3], Hugh[2], James[1])

Jesse Davis Donnell was born March the 17th AD 1818 (Lisbon, 13)

Jesse Davis[5] Donnell d.16 Feb 1902 married his brother's wife's sister, Sarah Thompson b.9 Jun 1820 d.9 Jun 1848 on 3 July 1843. They had three children, Edwin L[6] b.14 Jul 1844 d.31 Mar 1921, Winfield S b.26 Nov 1847 d.1 Feb 1848[290] and Almon B[6] b.1846 d.3 October 1924.[291] Almon[6] was a Civil War veteran and is buried in Arlington National Cemetery. Edwin was also a Civil War Veteran. Shortly after Sarah's death, Jesse married Roxanna Warren b.1811 d.21 Oct 1882 and had two more children, Ella F[6] b.25 Jun 1850 d.7 May 1902[292] and Henry Miles b.23 Apr 1854 d.1897.[293]

Charles Kingsbury[5] Donnell (Rebecca[4], Elizabeth[3], Hugh[2], James[1])

Kingsbury Donnell was born February the 9th AD 1822 (Lisbon, 13)

Dr. Charles Kingsbury[5] Donnell d.25 Mar 1897[294] married Mary Harris b.7 Mar 1827 d.22 Jun 1909[295] on 15 Oct 1851.[296] Their marriage resulted in five children: Benjamin Franklin[6] b.30 Jul 1852[297] d.15 Oct 1910,[298] Rebecca J[6] b.11 Mar 1854 d.23 Mar 1863, John[6] b.1856 d.22 Feb 1871,[123] and Lucinda Etta[6] b.1861 d.1883,[299] but only one, Charles K[6], married.

286. "Faylene Hutton Cemetery Collection, ca. 1780-1990," (https://goo.gl/xU8k5H)
287. Photo of death certificate, Ancestry.com. http://goo.gl/jXZjiE
288. "Maine, Marriages, 1771-1907," (https://goo.gl/4bNCCm)
289. Maine State Archives; 1892-1907 Vital Records; Roll #: 15.
290. Findagrave.com, gravestone photograph, http://goo.gl/urw3tj.
291. Findagrave.com profile, http://goo.gl/nTYR9S, accessed 13 Oct 2015/
292. Maine State Archives; 1892-1907 Vital Records; Roll #: 31.
293. Findagrave, gravestone photograph, http://goo.gl/QQOfH0.
294. Maine State Archives; C 1892-1907 Vital Records; Roll #: 15.
295. Maine State Archives; 1908-1922 Vital Records; Roll #: 16.
296. "Maine, Marriages, 1771-1907," (https://goo.gl/DCJvYd)
297. The New England Historical & Genealogical Register, 1847-2011 Ancestry.com.
298. Maine State Archives; 1908-1922 Vital Records; Roll #: 16.
299. Findagrave.com, gravestone, http://goo.gl/nuS0Ek, accessed 11 Feb 2015.

Dr. Charles K[6] Donnell b.1866 d.abt 1934 married Isabelle M Coolidge on 4 Dec 1892.[300] They had Charles Everett[7] b.8 Oct 1893[301] d.3 Aug 1898,[302] Levi Kingsbury[7] b.12 Oct 1894[303] d.22 Oct 1918,[304] Ruby Gertrude[7] b.19 Jun 1896[305] d.13 Oct 1985,[306] Dr. Floyd Everett[7] b.29 Mar 1899[307] d.1946,[308] and Clarence Leslie[7] b.6 Sep 1901[309] d.12 Aug 1970.[310] Charles[6] outlived three wives and was probably survived by a fourth.

Samuel[5] Donnell (Rebecca[4], Elizabeth[3], Hugh[2], James[1])

Samuel Donnell was born July the 15th AD 1825 (Lisbon, 13) d.10 May 1911[311]
Mr Samuel Donnell of Webster and Miss Sarah Whittemore of Lisbon Intend marriage Dated at Lisbon the 1st day of June 1850 Recorded by me Robert Jack Town Clerk of Lisbon (Lisbon, 237)
Sarah Whittemore was born April the 12th AD 1860 (Lisbon, 111) d.10 Feb 1908[312]

Samuel[5] Donnell and Sarah Whittemore had six children born in Webster: Clara Eunice[6] b.31 May 1852 d.24 Mar 1892, Minerva P[6] b.8 Sep 1855 d.30 May 1887,[313] Watson H[6] b.1 Feb 1860 d.21 Nov 1922,[314] Augusta Louise[6], May L[6], and Willis Burton[6]. He and Sarah moved to Bowdoinham by 1870.[315]

Augusta Louise[6] Donnell b.28 Jul 1861 d. 6 Sep 1947 married James Edwin Cornish b.abt 1855 and had two children, Donald Edwin or Owen[7], b.9 Dec 1886 d.6 Feb 1938[316] and Gladys M[7] b.22 Jun 1889[317]

---

300. Maine State Archives; Augusta, Maine, USA; 1892-1907 Vital Records; Roll #: 15.
301. "Maine, Vital Records, 1670-1907 ," (https://goo.gl/BKk4Bl)
302. Maine State Archives; 1892-1907 Vital Records; Roll #: 15.
303. "Maine, Vital Records, 1670-1907 ," (https://goo.gl/WzwClg)
304. Maine State Archives; 1908-1922 Vital Records; Roll #: 16.
305. Social Security Administration, Number: 007-50-5954; Maine; 1965-1966
306. Maine Death Index, 1960-1997 [database on-line]. Ancestry.com.
307. Maine State Archives; 1892-1907 Vital Records; Roll #: 15
308. Findagrave.com, gravestone, http://goo.gl/3XkPlb, accessed 28 May 2015.
309. Maine State Archives; 1892-1907 Vital Records; Roll #: 15
310. Massachusetts Death Index, 1970-2003 [database on-line]. Ancestry.com.
311. Maine State Archives; 1908-1922 Vital Records; Roll #: 16.
312. Maine State Archives; 1908-1922 Vital Records; Roll #: 16.
313. Maine State Archives; Pre 1892 Delayed Returns; Roll #: 30
314. "Texas, Death Index, 1903-2000," (https://goo.gl/yEefQZ)
315. Year: 1870; Census: Bowdoinham, Sagadahoc, Maine; Roll: M593_557; Page: 366B; Image: 280; Family History Library Film: 552056.
316. Massachusetts, Mason Membership Cards, 1733-1990 Ancestry.co.
317. "Maine, Births and Christenings, 1739-1900," (https://goo.gl/KHHY3q)

d.Sep 1981.[318]

May L[6] Donnell b.24 Apr 1864 d.3 Feb 1943[319] married Herbert Horace Nealey b.1860 d.24 May 1900.[320] They had Herbert D[7] b.8 Sep 1884 d.6 Aug 1970,[321] Phillip Carlton[7] b.17 Jun 1886[322] d.aft 1940, Lester Horace[7] b.5 Sep 1889 d.8 Dec 1971,[323] Samuel Purington[7] b.3 Aug 1893 d.17 Nov 1978,[324] and Courtney May[7] b.8 Nov 1895 d.18 Oct 1948.[325]

Willis Burton[6] b.21 Sep 1867 d.1944[326] married Mary Patten b.1872 d.1945[327] in Brunswick and had two children, Orrin Smith[7] b.25 Dec 1894 d. 8 Mar 1959[328] and Dorothy[7] b.4 Nov 1896 d.23 Oct 1973.[329]

William[3] (Hugh[2], James[1])

William, Jr., and Sally Chace (Chase) , both of T., int. Nov. 15, 1793. [William, s. of Hugh Wilson] (Topsham II, 288)
1793 Dec[r] 25 William Wilson to Sally Chase (Brunswick, 97)
William, Mar. 7, 1837, a. 68 y., G.R.2. (Topsham II, 399)

William[3] b.1769 married Sally Chase b.1771 d.2 Dec 1823.[330] Three of their children died as young adults:

James A., Oct. 26, 1830, a. 21 y., G.R.2. (Topsham II, 398)
Harriet, d. William and Sally, Mar. 9, 1825, a. 25 y., G.R.2. (398)
Mary, Feb. 18, 1830, a. 26 y., G.R.2. (398)

They are all buried with their parents and stepmother, Deborah Page b.1783, in Haley Cemetery.[331]

Page, Deborah, Mrs., and William Wilson, both of T., int. Jan. 26, 1829. [cert, issued Feb. 9.] (Topsham II, 188)
Deborah, w. William, Oct. 25, 1862, a. 79 y., G.R.2. (397)

---

318. Social Security Administration, Number: 004-46-0284; Maine; Issue Date: 1962
319. Ancestry.com. California, Death Index, 1940-1997 Ancestry.com.
320. Gravestone & description, http://goo.gl/1rByk3, accessed 28 May 2015.
321. Ancestry.com. California, Death Index, 1940-1997 Ancestry.com.
322. WWI, Registration State: Maine; Registration County: Sagadahoc; Roll: 1654016.
323. California, Death Index, 1940-1997 [database on-line]. Ancestry.com.
324. Gravestone, http://goo.gl/VMRGi8, accessed 28 May 2015.
325. California, Death Index, 1940-1997 [database on-line]. Ancestry.com
326. Findagrave.com, gravestone, http://goo.gl/89I9Xh, accessed 28 may 2015.
327. Findagrave.com, gravestone, http://goo.gl/GvS99u, accessed 28 May 2015.
328. Findagrave.com, gravestone, http://goo.gl/iTL6bT, accessed 28 May 2015.
329. Florida Death Index, 1877-1998 USA: Ancestry.com Operations Inc, 2004.
330. Findagrave.com, gravestone & personal photograph, http://goo.gl/svQ0T7.
331. "Maine, Nathan Hale Cemetery Collection, ca. 1780-1980," (https://goo.gl/4Bbltv)

William did leave a will (Lincoln County Probate 48:505-506). He gave one third of everything to Deborah as long as she did not remarry. He gave $50 each to William F[4], Hugh[4], Jesse D[4], John H[4], Horace[4], Rebeckah[4] and Elbridge G[4] and the remainder of his estate to the youngest, Arthur Lee[4], who was also the executor of his will.

According to the division of his father's estate, he was also called William Wilson, Jr, rather than the William Wilson 2 I would have expected. This made the records quite confusing as there were other Williams, both in his family and in Thomas Wilson's family.

What is odd about this family is that not one of the childrens' births was recorded until Jesse D married. The only reason why I have the following information any where near complete was William's will.

I was able to track all of his children except Hugh. He could not have been born before 1795 as the eldest was John, born less than 6 months after the marriage in 1826. The other children are spaced between 1 to 2 years apart except a gap of 4 years between Rebecca and Harriet who could have been born in 1799 so I suspect he was born about 1798. I can find no information on him though. He was alive in 1837 when his father died but I guess did not stay in Topsham like most of his siblings who moved away.

Rebecca[4] (William[3], Hugh[2], James[1]) - The Huntingtons

> *Rebecca of T. and Daniel T. Huntington of Litchfield, int. Mar. 5, 1830. [cert, issued Mar. 22.] (Topsham II, 287)*

Rebecca "Rebeckah" D b.1796 d.6 Sep 1885[332] and Daniel True Huntington b.16 Jun 1806 d.22 Aug 1882[333] had three children, Alvin[5], Rebecca[5], Ann[5], and Daniel[5] in Litchfield. Only Alvin[5] lived to marry and have children.

Alvin T[5] (John H[4], William[3], Hugh[2], James[1])

Alvin[5] married Cordelia Jordan b.13 Mar 1837[334] d.24 Jan 1899[335] of

332. "Nathan Hale Cemetery Collection, ca. 1780-1980," (https://goo.gl/yXXYC6)
333. Findagrave.com, http://goo.gl/HLlrhD, accessed 27 Sept 2015.
334. "Maine Births and Christenings, 1739-1900," (https://goo.gl/nRACj9)
335. Maine State Archives; 1892-1907 Vital Records; Roll #: 28.

Freeport. This Orrs Island family was large as the island families tend to be. Only one did not marry Alwin A[6] b.1869 d.21 Oct 1892 (typhoid).[336] The others were John Jacob Astor[6] b.19 Mar 1858 d.17 Dec 1938[337] who married three times and had thirteen children, Frances Delia[6] b.19 Sep 1859[338] d.28 Oct 1910[339] who married James W Field and had three children; James Alvin Huntington b.26 Jan 1863[340] d.1943[341] who married Lizzie Ardell Moody and had three children; Harriet "Hattie" A[7] Huntington b.5 May 1866 (unc) d.15 Oct 1901[342] who married Frank O Stevens and had six children, Mary Emma[7] Huntington b.9 Oct 1871 (unc) who married Joseph E[7] Doughty and had one daughter, Cora Belle[7] Huntington b.5 Feb 1877 (unc) d.1942 (unc) who married Elmer Lucien[7] Wilson and had eight children, and Lettie Fay[7] Huntington b.8 Apr 1880 (unc) d.1952[343] who married John Irving Field and had three children. Out of those 37 grandchildren, I could find only 13 marriages.

Elmer Lucien Wilson was the son of Robert Getchell Wilson who had married Mary Wilson, daughter of Alexander II. Lucien, however, was a son of Robert's second marriage and therefore not related to the Huntingtons.

Horace[4] (William[3], Hugh[2], James[1])

Horris and Almira Twitchell, both of T., int. Sept. 24, 1831. [cert. Oct. 9.] (Topsham II, 285)

Sept 10. 1838 Horace Willson of Bath & Sally Snow of Brunswick (Brunswick, 209)
Sally Snow was born Febury 21st 1804 in Brunswick (190)

William's son Horace[4] b.1807 d.31 Mar 1882[344] married Jesse D's sister-in-law, Almira b.8 Jan 1811.[345] Almira must have died before 1838 but Sally b.1804 d.9 Apr 1857[346] is buried in Maple Grove cemetery in Bath. There are no pictures on findagrave.com or relation-

336. Maine State Archives; 1892-1907 Vital Records; Roll #: 28.
337. Findagrave.com, http://goo.gl/aJhPXI, accessed 28 Sep 2015.
338. "Maine Births and Christenings, 1739-1900," (https://goo.gl/TxOSTq)
339. Maine State Archives; 1908-1922 Vital Records; Roll #: 19.
340. "Maine Births and Christenings, 1739-1900," (https://goo.gl/FX03w0)
341. Findgrave.com, http://goo.gl/sIqHIg, accessed 28 Sept 2015.
342. Maine State Archives; 1892-1907 Vital Records; Roll #: 54.
343. Findagrave.com, http://goo.gl/22N1Sk, accessed 28 Sep 2015.
344. Findagrave.com, http://goo.gl/wCQSna, accessed 27 Sept 2015.
345. "Maine Births and Christenings, 1739-1900," (https://goo.gl/wf5CEf)
346. Findagrave.com, http://goo.gl/d5oIsQ, accessed 27 Sept 2015.

ships listed. I actually tried to find the graves but was not able to spot them where they were supposed to be.

So his and Almira's daughter was Ellen M^5 b.1832 d.28 Mar 1872,[347] and Horace and Sally had Francis^5 b.1841 d.27 Sep 1867[348] and Horace^5 b.1856 d.26 Sep 1865.[349] Horace outlived both wives and all of his children.

John H^4 (William^3, Hugh^2, James^1)

John H. and Experiance Lufkin, both of T., Apr. 29, 1821. (Topsham II, 286)

(Brunswick, 398-399)

Parents:	*John H Wilson*	*March 24 1794*	*Augt 8 1852*
	Experience Lufkin Wife	*Feby 9 1798*	*Feby 28 1876*
Children:	*Charles H. Wilson*	*April 10 1822*	*Feby 18 1859*
	John H	*Feby 16 1825*	*Decr 3 1848*
	Harriet E	*Augt 22 1831*	*Decr 2 1851*
	Rachael L	*Feby 8 1834*	*Decr 2 1856*
	William E	*July 1 1836*	*Oct 12 1857*
	Esther M	*Jany 14 1851*	*July 21 1859*

'Tis a sad list of children; with so many dying as young adults, I can think tuberculosis. Father John was one of those deaths as well. Only Sarah J^5, Charles H^5 and Jesse D^5 married and had children.

Charles H^5 (John H^4, William^3, Hugh^2, James^1)

Charles H. Wilson	*April 10 1822 Feby 18 1859 (399)*
April 12th 1854	*Charles H Willson & Rhoda L. Hunt both of Brunswick (by Rev. Andrew Rollins) (298)*
Rhoda Hunt	*Oct 12 1822 (199) d.7 Jul 1908*[350]

Charles^5 did live to see his daughter born. She was Harriett Ellen^6 b.1859[351] d.24 Dec 1950. She married Holman Douglas Waldron b.16 Jun 1857 d.9 Apr 1917[352] and had four children in Portland: Caroline Howard^7 b.2 Nov 1881 d.18 May 1882, Howard H^7 b.4 Dec 1888

347. Findagrave.com, http://goo.gl/j6HN6s, accessed 27 Sept 2015.
348. Findagrave.com, http://goo.gl/8VWnZI accessed 27 Sep 2015.
349. Findagrave.com, http://goo.gl/RaAmsU, accessed 27 Sept 2015.
350. Maine State Archives; 1908-1922 Vital Records; Roll #: 26.
351. Year: 1860; Census Place: Brunswick, Cumberland, Maine; Roll: M653_437; Page: 24; Image: 861; Family History Film: 803437.
352. Findagrave.com, http://goo.gl/E90LIX, accessed 27 Sept 2015.

d.21 Aug 1946,[353] Arthur Wilson[7] b.6 May 1883 d.17 Sep 1943[354] and Annie Louise[7] b.26 Nov 1893 d.Dec 1984.[355] There were two grandchildren.

Sarah J[5] (John H[4], William[3], Hugh[2], James[1])

Sarah J	*Sept 2 1828 (399) d.12 Mar 1880*	
1849 Nov. 24th	*Algernon W. Hinkson & Sarah J. Willson both of Brunswick intend marriage Decr 8th (248)*	
Algernon W. Hinkson	*May 19 1826*	*July 13 1866 (391)*
Emma M. Hinkson	*March 15 1852*	*d.1927[356]*
Alice G.	*May 30 1855*	*d.1941[357]*

Unfortunately Sarah's[5] husband, Algernon Wellington, also died young leaving two children behind. Emma May[6] married William K Thomas b.1848 d.1924[358] and had three children, Arthur Lee[7] b.19 Mar 1874 d.6 Feb 1939,[359] Winfred Samuel[7] b.21 Mar 1880 d.13 Nov 1940[360] and Alice H[7] b.28 Jan 1890 d.Apr 1983.[361] Emma's sister, Alice G[6], also married but may not have had children.

Jesse D[5] (John H[4], William[3], Hugh[2], James[1])

Jesse D	*Decr 26 1823 (Brunswick, 399) d.17 Sep 1910[362]*
Mary Hunt	*Novr 3 1820 (499) d.28 Feb 1902[363]*

Jesse[5] married Mary Hunt, brother Charles' sister-in-law. They had one child, Anna Maria[6] b.3 Mar 1858 in Portland who married but may not have had children.

Elbridge G[4] (William[3], Hugh[2], James[1])

Elbridge[4] b.1807 d.7 Dec 1885 moved to Bath after he married and first appears in 1850 with his first wife, Lucy Ann Dunn b.26 Apr

353. Findagrave.com, http://goo.gl/A7mkDv, accessed 27 Sept 2015.
354. U.S., Social Security Applications and Claims Index, 1936-2007 Ancestry.com.
355. US Social Security Administration, Number: 004-64-9782; Maine; 1973.
356. Findagrave.com, http://goo.gl/akuHyF
357. Findagrave.com, gravestone, http://goo.gl/zLvW5P
358. Findagrave.com, gravestone photograph, http://goo.gl/o7co1F
359. U.S., Social Security Applications and Claims Index, 1936-2007.
360. U.S., Social Security Applications and Claims Index, 1936-2007.
361. U.S., Social Security Applications and Claims Index, 1936-2007.
362. Findagrave.com, http://goo.gl/We7Ot2, accessed 27 Sept 2015.
363. Maine State Archives; 1892-1907 Vital Records; Roll #: 61.

1812[364] d.3 Mar 1856[365] from Hallowell, and their seven children.[366]

He married Elizabeth Buswell also of Hallowell after Lucy's death on 13 Feb 1859.[367] In his will he left his personal possessions, home and store to her and to her sister but divided the money between his heirs.[368] His occupation was listed as trader in 1860 but of what I could not discern.[369]

The children were Harriet Cornelia[5] b.18 Aug 1836[370] d.31 Mar 1885[371] who married Charles Deering but had no children and died in New York, John Dunn[5] b.17 Sep 1841,[372] last seen in San Francisco in 1866,[373] and Frederick Eugene[5] b.14 May 1849 (unc) d.20 Sep 1889 in Boston.[374] The others who did have children were Lucy Ann[5], Henry Augustus[5] and Mary Elizabeth[5].

Mary Elizabeth[5] (Elbridge[4], William[3], Hugh[2], James[1]) - The Taylors

Two of his children died before him; Mary Elizabeth[6] b.1847 d.19 Oct 1883 married a Lt. F. Beers Taylor and had one child who was named in Elbridge's will, Mary Rosamund Taylor[7]. That is also where her father's name comes from but we know nothing else. Mary[7] was born in Georgia about 1871 according to the census reports. She married Henry B Kerr and had three children born around 1900. They lived in Colorado, Texas and California. He was some sort of investigator or detective.

Lucy Ann[5] (Elbridge[4], William[3], Hugh[2], James[1]) - The Knights of New York

---

364. Maine State Archives; Pre 1892 Delayed Returns; Roll #: 32.
365. Findagrave.com, photograph, http://goo.gl/Fqzzs5
366. Year: 1850; Census: Bath, Lincoln, Maine; Roll: M432_261; Page: 170A; Image: 129.
367. Maine State Archives; Pre 1892 Delayed Returns; Roll #: 104.
368. Sagadahoc County Probate Records, 1854-1901; Docket, 1854-1876.
369. Year: 1860; Census Place: Bath, Sagadahoc, Maine; Roll: M653_448; Page: 170; Image: 170; Family History Library Film: 803448.
370. "Maine Births and Christenings, 1739-1900," (https://goo.gl/58OD6T)
371. New York, New York, Death Index, 1862-1948.
372. "Maine Births and Christenings, 1739-1900," (https://goo.gl/MSERuc)
373. California State Library, California History Section; Great Registers, 1866-1898; Collection Number: 4 - 2A; CSL Roll Number: 41; FHL Roll Number: 977096.
374. Massachusetts, Death Records, 1841-1915 Ancestry.com Operations, Inc., 2013.

Lucy Ann[5] b.25 Sep 1843[375] d.14 May 1885[376] married George Wakefield Knight b.Apr 1843[377] d.Apr 1893[378] of London, England. They married and lived in New York, having one child, Charles R Knight[6] b.21 Oct 1874 d.1952 or 1953.[379] Charles[6] married Annie Humphrey Hardcastle b.abt 1874 and they had one daughter Julia Hardcastle Knight[7].

Henry Augustus[5] (Elbridge[4], William[3], Hugh[2], James[1])

A sailor, Henry[5] b.16 Nov 1837[380] married a Sarah or Sally b.abt 1849 from Pennsylvania and had at least one child, Eva[6], but there is no information on the family beyond that.

Jesse Davis[4] (William[3], Hugh[2], James[1])

Jesse D., h. Clarissa, Aug. 30, 1800, in T. [a. 49 y., in u.s.c] (Topsham I, 210)
Jessee D., Feb. 11, 1885, c.R.5. [Jesse, a. 84 y., G.R.3.] [a. 84 y. 5 m., in T., N.P.6.] (II, 398)

Jesse D[4] married Clarissa Twitchell and had eight children.

Clarissa [ ], w. Jesse D., Mar. 27, 1808, in Bethel. (Topsham I, 209)
Clarisa, May 21, 1886, C.R.5. [Clarissa, w. Jesse D., a. 78 y., G.R.3.] (II, 397)
Jesse D. of T. and Clarary Twitchell of Bethel, int. Sept. 2, 1827. [cert. Sept. 17.] (II, 286)

He is listed as a retired lumberman in the 1880 census.[381] Three who either never married or died as young adults were:

Eliza Ann, ch. Jesse D. and Clarissa, July 13, 1834, in T. [a. 14 y., in u.s.c] (I, 209)
Eliza Ann, ch. J. D. and C , Aug. 1, 1856, a. 19 y., G.R.3. [Aug. 1, 1853, in T., d. Jessie D., N.P.6.] (II, 397)
Almira, ch. Jesse D. and Clarissa, Mar. 3, 1833, in T. [a. 16 y., in u.s.c] (I, 208) d.19 Apr 1917[382]
Henry Clay, ch. Jesse D. and Clarissa, Jan. 16, 1846, in T. (I, 210)
Henry C , Aug. 28, 1847, in T. [ch. J. D. and C , a. 19 m., G.R.3.] (II, 398)

---

375. "Maine Births and Christenings, 1739-1900," (https://goo.gl/cNdFsi)
376. Green-Wood Cemetery Search, http://goo.gl/x7Cepj
377. FreeBMD. England & Wales, FreeBMD Birth Index, 1837-1915 Ancestry.com.
378. Web: Brooklyn, New York, Green-Wood Cemetery Burial Index Ancestry.com.
379. U.S., Social Security Applications and Claims Index, 1936-2007 Ancestry.com
380. "Maine Births and Christenings, 1739-1900," (https://goo.gl/59iwB0)
381. Year: 1880; Census Place: Topsham, Sagadahoc, Maine; Roll: 488; Film: 1254488; Page: 183B; District: 151; Image: 0377.
382. Maine State Archives; 1908-1922 Vital Records; Roll #: 60.

The others who did marry were Frances Jane[5], Eveline[5], Albion Davis[5], Frederick Henry[5] and George E[5].

Frances Jane[5] (Jessie Davis[4], William[3], Hugh[2], James[1]) - The Humphreys

Frances Jane, ch. Jesse D. and Clarissa, Aug. 23, 1831, in T. [a. 18 y., in u.s.c] (Topsham I, 209)
Humphreys, John H of Brunswick & Frances Jane Wilson of T, July 22, 1851 (II, 139)
John H Humphreys Feby 11 1825 (Brunswick, 419)

The oldest child, Frances Jane[5], d.18 May 1915 married John H Humphreys d.6 Jun 1891 and had one child, Frederick[6] W b.31 May 1852 d.11 May 1877. The 1870 and 1880 census says John was a bank cashier. They are all buried together in the Maple Grove Cemetery in Bath.[383]

Eveline[5] (Jessie Davis[4], William[3], Hugh[2], James[1]) - The Thompsons

Everlina, ch. Jesse D. and Clarissa, Aug. 28, 1836, in T. (Topsham I, 209)
Thompson, Andrew J., Dr., of Guilford [int. Laconia], N. H., and Everline Wilson of T., May 22, 1861, in T. (II, 258)

Eveline d.8 Apr 1932[384] married Dr. Andrew Jackson Thompson b.23 Jul 1833 d.26 Apr 1879 and moved to his home state of New Hampshire. He was a physician who served in the Civil War.[385] They had two boys, Fred[6] b.1864 and Willis[6] b.1868 and moved to Salem, Massachusetts, before his death on 26 Apr 1879.[386] Their son, Fred[6], was also a doctor in Massachusetts.[387] He married late and had no children. Willis[6] also married but had no children. I can find no traces of either son after 1920.

Albion D[5] (Jessie Davis[4], William[3], Hugh[2], James[1])

Albion D., ch. Jesse D. and Clarissa, Dec. 6, 1842, in T. (Topsham I, 208)

Albion Davis[5] d.19 December 1923[388] was a druggist. He married Lunette Evelyn Potter b.4 Mar 1853 (unc) d.aft 1940 on 22 Oct

---

383. Findagrave.com, gravestone photographs, http://goo.gl/YkYTyl
384. Massachusetts, Death Index, 1901-1980 [database on-line]. Ancestry.com
385. U.S., Civil War Soldier Records & Profiles, 1861-1865 Ancestry.com.
386. "Massachusetts, Deaths, 1841-1915," (https://goo.gl/OKbM24)
387. Year: 1920; Census Place: Orleans, Barnstable, Massachusetts; Roll: T625_679; Page: 10A; Enumeration District: 16; Image: 399.
388. Portland, Maine, City Directory, 1924. Ancestry.com.

1877.[389] They had three sons, Frank Albion[6] b.18 Feb 1879[390] d.aft 1930, Robert Potter[6] b.28 Feb 1883[391] d.25 Jan 1970[392] and Richard Luther[6] b.28 Dec 1884 d.bef 1900.

Frederick H[5] (Jessie Davis[4], William[3], Hugh[2], James[1])

> *Frederick H. of T. and Mary E. Stinson of North Vassalboro, [ ], in North Vassalboro. [rec. between Nov. 1 and 2, 1870.] [int. Nov. 5.] (Topsham II, 162)*
> *LUKE, Ensena E. of Falmouth and Frederick H. Wilson of T., int. Nov. 18, 1879. [cert, issued Nov. 23.] [d. Capt. W. W. Luke, N.P.6.] (162)*

Frederick Henry[5] b.1848 d.1915[393] married Mary Ellen Stinson and then Ensena E Luke b.1854 d.1949. Another druggist, he was in the 1910 census in Brunswick.[394] Frederick and Ensena had several children that I found and there may be more, Margaret Luke[6] b.abt 1884, Jesse Davis[6] b.21 Jan 1881 d.Nov 1967[395] and Frederick Henry[6] "Fritz" b.9 Feb 1891 d.11 Oct 1969.[396]

George E[5] (Jessie Davis[4], William[3], Hugh[2], James[1])

George E[5] b.16 Jan 1851 d.19 Feb 1931 was a druggist as well. He married Ella Frances Curtis b.1853 d.1935 on 28 Nov 1876[397] and had one child, Eva[6] b.1877 d.25 July 1895.[398]

William F[4] (William[3], Hugh[2], James[1])

> *William F. and Judah Huntington, both of T., int. July 23, 1825. [cert. Aug. 6.] (Topsham II, 288)*

Unfortunately, many of the birth and death dates in this family branch were supplied by ancestry.com. I tried confirming as many as I could but it appears that the families lived in some of the areas that never supplied the vital records to the state. Any date without a footnote may be from ancestry.com or findagrave.com. In some

389. "Maine, Marriages, 1771-1907," (https://goo.gl/sTHlW1)
390. WWI, Maine; Registration County: Cumberland; Roll: 1653906; Draft Board: 2.
391. "United States Social Security Death Index," (https://goo.gl/sIY2ZA,
392. Maine Death Index, 1960-1997 [database on-line]. Ancestry.com
393. Findagrave.com, gravestone photograph, http://goo.gl/TAjAtC
394. Year: 1910; Census Place: Brunswick, Cumberland, Maine; Roll: T624_538; Page: 13B; District: 0044; FHL microfilm: 1374551.
395. Social Security Administration, Number: 004-34-9621; Maine; 1952.
396. Findagrave.com, http://goo.gl/x7FD4Z, accessed 30 July 2015.
397. "Maine, Marriages, 1771-1907," (https://goo.gl/D0Qi2K)
398. "Nathan Hale Cemetery Collection, ca. 1780-1980," (https://goo.gl/Mp9yWN)

cases, findagrave.com provided a photograph with a year only when I had both day and month as well. Also due the number of family members born so close to 1900, I've eliminated detailing the some of the sixth generation children completely.

William F[4] b. 30 Mar 1802[399] d.9 Mar 1884[400] married Judith Huntington b.11 April 1808 d.23 Jun 1884[401] and left Topsham after 1830. They lived in Bangor and finally settled in Atkinson where they both died within months of each other. They had five children who did not have children of their own: Benjamin G[5] b.8 Aug 1833 d.22 Aug 1862,[402] George H[5] b.10 Feb 1839 d.2 Nov 1864[403] who was a civil war navy veteran,[404] Mary E[5] b.abt 1843,[405] Emery Lee[5] b.April 1849[406] d.aft 1930, and Harriet b.1852[407] d.4 Apr 1904.

The children who married and had children were Charles Henry[5], Jesse David[5], Randall N[5] and Ann Judith[5].

Charles Henry[5] (William F[4], William[3], Hugh[2], James[1])

Charles Henry[5] b.15 Aug 1827 d.30 Dec 1907[408] married Elizabeth W Gross b.19 Jul 1832 d.22 Jul 1905[409] from Deer Isle on 6 Dec 1857. Their children were Bertha A[6] b.14 Mar 1856 d.31 Dec 1865 and Charles Henry[6] Jr b.3 Nov 1858 d.24 Nov 1863 who died young. The others who lived to be adults were Judith A b.8 Nov 1863 d.4 Aug 1903, Addie E[6], Sarah M[6], Amy M[6] and Horace C[6]. Four of the children's dates are on their parents' monument.

---

399. "Maine, Births and Christenings, 1739-1900," (https://goo.gl/hCV0UX)
400. Maine State Archives; Pre 1892 Delayed Returns; Roll #: 105.
401. Findagrave.com, gravestone photograph, http://goo.gl/BAwdhA
402. Findagrave.com, gravestone photograph, http://goo.gl/5zKSqX
403. "Maine, Vital Records, 1670-1907 ," (https://goo.gl/qR4F9X)
404. Weekly Returns of Enlistments at Naval Rendezvous ("Enlistment Rendezvous") Jan. 6, 1855-Aug. 8, 1891, roll 24, v 33, p 343.
405. Year: 1850; Census: Atkinson, Maine; Roll: M432_267; Page: 307A; Image: 259.
406. Year: 1900; Census Place: Bangor, Penobscot, Maine; Roll: 597; Page: 1A; Enumeration District: 0084; FHL microfilm: 1240597.
407. Year: 1860; Census Place: Atkinson, Piscataquis, Maine; Roll: M653_433; Page: 763; Image: 7; Family History Library Film: 803433.
408. Findagrave.com, gravestone photograph, http://goo.gl/od3JX2
409. Findagrave.com, gravestone photograph, http://goo.gl/ThdtIG.

Addie E[6] b.16 Dec 1859 d.21 Jan 1943 married Franklin Levi Philpot b.6 Nov 1843 d.19 Jan 1946[410] and had four children and 13 grand-children. Sarah M[6] b.1 Oct 1861 d.20 Jun 1931[411] married George M Farnham b.26 Jul 1853 d.28 Jul 1917 and one had one child. Amy M[6] b.7 Sep 1867 d.1926[412] married Luther Martin Averill and had four children. Horace C[6] b.16 Aug 1871 d.28 Sep 1944[413] married Martha Ann Sudbury and had three children.

Ann Judith[5] (William F[4], William[3], Hugh[2], James[1]) - The Gowens

Ann Judith[5] b.1 Nov 1831 d.13 Feb 1877[414] married Ruel Gowen b.29 Jan 1830 d.17 Nov 1899[415] on 20 May 1853.[416] They had one son, Frank E[6] b.7 Sept 1864[417] d.8 Sept 1938[418] who married Sarah Emma McCartney b.7 Jun 1862 d.21 Jul 1944[419] of Canada. Frank and Emma had Edgar A[7] b.29 Jul 1898 d.7 Feb 1974.[420]

John H[5] (William F[4], William[3], Hugh[2], James[1])

John H[5] b.31 Jan 1835 d.24 Jun 1899[421] married Sarah E Henderson on 12 Nov 1863.[422] John[5] and Sarah's children were George Orrington[6], William F[6], Allen Carl Tibbets[6] and Chandler Moses[6].

Their oldest son, George Orrington[6] b.1864 d. 22 Dec 1912[423] went west to California, marrying Ada Maye Abbot b.15 Jun 1871 d.10 Sep 1945 [424] on 6 Dec 1893.[425] They had two children, Alfred George

410. "Nathan Hale Cemetery Collection, ca. 1780-1980," (https://goo.gl/kOWVQ1)
411. "Faylene Hutton Cemetery Collection, ca. 1780-1990," (https://goo.gl/KPlhrO)
412. Findagrave, http://goo.gl/DcevK5, accessed 31 July 2015.
413. Findagrave.com, gravestone photograph, http://goo.gl/1nXqeQ
414. Findagrave.com, gravestone, http://goo.gl/tnGTbd, accessed 28 May 2015.
415. Findagrave.com, gravestone, http://goo.gl/g1Zg7C.
416. "Maine, Marriages, 1771-1907," (https://goo.gl/f21JgV)
417. "Maine, Births and Christenings, 1739-1900," (https://goo.gl/feIPYH)
418. Findagrave.com, http://goo.gl/oOC37f, accessed 28 May 2015.
419. Findagrave.com, http://goo.gl/sgqAld, accessed 28 May 2015.
420. Findagrave.com, http://goo.gl/VbYtPC, accessed 28 May 2015.
421. "Maine, Vital Records, 1670-1907 ," (https://goo.gl/0b7Vfb)
422. "Maine, Marriages, 1771-1907," (https://goo.gl/aNUmTt)
423. Findagrave.com, http://goo.gl/xw06KC, accessed 29 May 2015.
424. California, Death Index, 1940-1997 Ancestry.com.
425. "California, County Marriages, 1850-1952," (https://goo.gl/jIqzRF)

b.17 Oct 1894 d.16 Sep 1983[426] and Sadye Mae b.6 Feb 1898 d.7 Dec 1990.[427] Neither of them had children.

I can find no other data for William F[6] b.29 Jan 1870[428] after the 1880 census but Alan Carl Tibbetts[6] b.22 Mar 1867[429] d.1952 married Mary V McIntosh b.1873 d.1940[430] on 25 Dec 1900.[431] They had five children born 1900 - 1911.

Chandler Moses[6] b.26 Dec 1873 d.20 July 1955 married and had two children but his wife, Lizzie Head b.9 Nov 1873, died within a year of the birth of her second son on 17 May 1903.[432]

Randall N[5] (William F[4], William[3], Hugh[2], James[1])

Randall N.[5] b.1841 d.1927[433] married Mary Yeaton b.1851 d.20 Feb 1914.[434] They had three children, Eugene M[6] b.abt 1872,[435] Lester[6], b.abt 1875[436] and Adelbert[6] b.29 Sep 1873[437] d.1953.[438]

Jessie David[5] (William F[4], William[3], Hugh[2], James[1])

Jessie David[5] b.19 Aug 1847 d.3 Sep 1926[439] married Hannah French b.1 June 1849 d.30 July 1926 and had Bernard Aubrey[6] b.14 May 1878[440] d.21 Jul 1940 (mth,day unc) who never married but all the others did marry.

---

426. California, Death Index, 1940-1997 [database on-line]. Ancestry.com
427. Oregon State Library; 1966-1970 Death Index; Year Range: 1981-1990.
428. "Maine, Births and Christenings, 1739-1900," (https://goo.gl/4Kv9q0)
429. "Maine, Vital Records, 1670-1907 ," (https://goo.gl/cNvw2b)
430. Findagrave.com, http://goo.gl/kzmT66, accessed 29 May 2015.
431. "Maine, Marriage Index, 1892-1966, 1977-1996," (https://goo.gl/edRdCn)
432. Maine State Archives; 1892-1907 Vital Records; Roll #: 61.
433. Findagrave.com, gravestone, http://goo.gl/nj28Gy
434. Maine State Archives; 1908-1922 Vital Records; Roll #: 60.
435. Year: 1920; Census Place: Kenduskeag, Penobscot, Maine; Roll: T625_646; Page: 6B; Enumeration District: 101; Image: 385.
436. Year: 1900; Census Place: Kenduskeag, Penobscot, Maine; Roll: 598; Page: 7B; Enumeration District: 0104; FHL microfilm: 1240598.
437. WW I, Maine; Registration County: Penobscot; Roll: 1654011; Draft Board: 1.
438. "Maine, Nathan Hale Cemetery Collection, ca. 1780-1980," (https://goo.gl/Ur7Fls)
439. Findagrave.com, gravestone year, http://goo.gl/MnErVa, accessed 28 May 2015.
440. WWI, Registration State: Maine; Registration County: Piscataquis; Roll: 1654013.

Arthur Lee[6] b.Apr 1868 d.14 Nov 1903 married Nellie Marie Chase b.Oct 1864[441] on 12 Aug 1893.[442] They had four children born 1895 to 1905.

Lenora A[6] b.24 Jan 1870 d.23 Nov. 1917[443] married Nellie's brother, Charles A Chase b.21 Jan 1863 d.13 Aug 1944[444] and had four children and at least 6 grandchildren.

Edwin Richmond[6] b.30 Nov 1873[445] d.1932[446] married twice and had two children with each wife.

Arthur Lee[4] (William[3], Hugh[2], James[1])

Arthur Lee[4] was the biggest mystery. I could find no information about his parents until I looked at his death record dated 2 July 1892.[447] It lists a William born in Topsham as his father. William Jr is the only possibility of a father during those years in Topsham. Arthur is found living next door to another Wilson of his generation, Humphrey Wilson in 1850.[448] He had a nephew named after him, a son of Jesse David's as well. I was confident of his parentage but it was a circumstantial fact until I found William's will which states Arthur Lee[4] is his son. Arthur[4] inherited 240 acres and an eighth part of the saw mill from his father.

Arthur L., h. Elizabeth B. [first w., P.R.43], Sept. 25, 1811, in T. (Topsham I, 208)
Page, Elizabeth [Elizabeth Chase, P.R.43] & Arthur L. [Lee, p.R.43] Wilson, both of T., int. Nov. 26, 1831. [cert. issued Dec. 11.] (II, 188)
Elizabeth B, w. Arthur L., Aug. 15, 1805. [first w. Arthur, 1808, P.R.43.] (I, 209)

Potter, Henerette [Henrietta, second w., P.R.43] & Arthur L. [Lee, P.R.43] Wilson, both of T., int. Sept. 11, 1840. [cert, issued Sept. 25.] [m. Sept. 27, p.R.43.] (II, 203)
Henrietta Potter, second w. Arthur Lee, June 2,1806, P.R.43. (I, 209)
Henrietta, w. Arthur L., [2d. w., P.R.43.], Jan. 19, 1884, a. 77 y., G.R.3. (II, 398)

James, s. Arthur Lee and Elizabeth, [ ], P.R.43. (1834) (I, 210)

---

441. Year: 1900; Census Place: Atkinson, Piscataquis, Maine; Roll: 598; Page: 4A; Enumeration District: 0127; FHL microfilm: 1240598.
442. "Maine, Marriage Index, 1892-1966, 1977-1996," (https://goo.gl/SYYrFY)
443. Maine State Archives; 1908-1922 Vital Records; Roll #: 10.
444. Findagrave.com, gravestone, http://goo.gl/44I4le, accessed 29 May 2015.
445. "World War I Draft Registration Cards, 1917-1918," (https://goo.gl/ZBoQz7)
446. Findagrave.com, gravestone, http://goo.gl/drXxWQ, 29 May 2015.
447. "Maine, Vital Records, 1670-1907 ," (https://goo.gl/74RN3m)
448. Year: 1850; Census: Topsham, LMaine; Roll: M432_261; Page: 358A; Image: 503

James S., s. Arthur L. and Elizabeth, Jan. 10, 1835, a. 1 y.,G.R.3. (II, 398)

Mary A., ch. Arthur L. and Elizabeth B. [first w., P.R.43], Mar. 7, 1832, in T.(211)
Bailey, James H. of Brunswick & Mary A. Wilson of T., Feb. 5, 1856. [Mary Ann, T.R.4.] (II, 42)
Mary A. Bailey, d. A. L. and E., June 4, 1892, a. 58 y., G.R.3. (II, 399)

Arthur Lee[4] had two wives; Elizabeth Page d.15 Aug 1838[449] was the first. They had four children that survived childhood, Mary Ann[5], James S[5], Elizabeth[5] and George Lamb[5]. He and his second wife, Henrietta Potter, adopted Clara Etta[5] but, though she appears in the 1860 census,[450] there is no trace of her after that.

Clara Etta, [adopted] ch. Arthur L. and Elizabeth B., Dec. 5, 1850, in Brunswick. (Topsham I, 210)

Though Mary Ann[5] did marry, only George Lamb[5] and Elizabeth[5] had children. Elizabeth Jane[5] married Benjamin Davis (earlier in this chapter).

George Lamb[5] (Arthur Lee[4], William[3] F, Hugh[2], James[1])

George Lamb, ch. Arthur L., and Elizabeth B., Jan. 11, 1838, in T. (Topsham 209)
George Lamb, Mar. 19, 1877, a. 39 y. 2 m. 8 d., G.R.3. (398)
George L. of T. and Mary E. Parks of Richmond, int. Dec. 23, 1863. [cert, issued Dec. 29.] (II, 284)
Mary E., w. George L., Sept. 20, 1864, a. 23 y., G.R.3. (II, 399)

George L. & Lovina C. Thompson, both of T., int. Nov. 28, 1865. [George Lamb & Lavina Carr, d. Benj. & Hannah (Pennell) Thompson, Dec. 5, at Auburn.] (II, 285)
Lovina C. (Lavina Carr, d. of Benj. & Hannah (Pennell) Thompson) & George L. (Lamb) Wilson, both of T., int. Nov. 28, 1865. (m. Dec. 5 at Auburn.) (II, 260)
Lavina Carr, ch. Benjamin and Hannah, Aug. 15, 1838, in T. (I, 186)
Lavina C , w. George L., May 2, 1885, a. 46 y., G.R.3. (II, 398)

Hattie Emma, d. George Lamb & Lavina Carr, Jan. 1, 1874, P.R.44. (I, 209)
Jennie May, d. Goerge Lamb and Lavina Carr Thompson, June 7, 1871, p.R.44. (210) d.1958

Hattie Emma[6] d.6 May 1893 did marry but died six months later of consumption at age 19 on 6 May 1893.[451] Jennie May[6] married Nathan H Pierce b.1868 d.1943[452] on 14 Sep 1892.[453] They had one child, Dwight Wilson[7] b.5 Sep 1894 d.8 Jun 1972.[454]

449. Findagrave.com, gravestone, http://goo.gl/A2dyst
450. Year: 1860; Census Place: Topsham, Sagadahoc, Maine; Roll: M653_448; Page: 441; Image: 439; FHL Film: 803448.
451. Maine State Archives; 1892-1907 Vital Records; Roll #: 60..
452. Findagrave.com, gravestone photographs, http://goo.gl/O7LA1n
453. Maine State Archives; Augusta, Maine, USA; 1892-1907 Vital Records; Roll #: 45
454. Social Security Administration, Number: 004-09-9363; Maine; Before 1951.

Charles L. Wilson, Sheriff, Alachua County, Florida

And One Went South

One of the most interesting things I found in working through this family tree was how the Mainers "hunkered" down and did not leave the state for generations. My southern families all kept moving almost with each generation to new areas in both the eighteenth and nineteenth centuries. They moved south first - along the eastern seaboard to North Carolina, South Carolina and Georgia, then headed west at some of those points, spreading through eastern and southern states and finally crossing the Mississippi. Some went north but the point is, they really moved.

The reason for this migration in the South is easily explained by several factors prevalent in farming in the early and mid nineteenth century. First is the idea of rotating crops was not even conceived until 1850 or so. They wore out the land quickly. Secondly, the southerners had more children on average than the Mainers in my family. This means that inheritance sometimes broke up the plantations as with my third great grandfather, George Elam who died in about 1845. He parceled out his land to his four sons and split up his 49 of his 84 slaves among his six children in his will.[1] Two sons stayed in or moved to Edgefield, SC, one went to Mississippi and my great-great-granddad, William Francis, had settled earlier on the Lincoln County, GA, plantation purchased in late 1840. His three brothers eventually sold their share of the plantation to William before they moved or took up new ventures.

The southerners had an advantage with milder winters and more seaboard with available land. The Mainers, however, moved mostly to Massachusetts and by the end of the 1800s were poised for more movement. Sometimes, families went west to other cold climes such as Minnesota and Wisconsin but a few went south, either deliberately or, in Edward Paul Dyer's case, with the military during the Civil War. In each case outlined, Edward Paul Dyer (in a later chapter) and Charles L, there is a story to tell.

1. Earl H. Elam, From Virginia to Texas: A History of the Elam Family (Baltimore, MD: Gateway Press, Inc, 2001), 165 -175.

Charles L[4] Wilson (Hugh[3], Hugh[2], James[1])

We'll probably never know why Charles L Wilson went south but I found a great quote when I was rummaging around the Edgefield Discovery Museum in South Carolina. In 1826 Robert Mills, a South Carolina architect, wrote "the disposition to emigrate originated from three causes: first from the wearing out of lands, second from the increase in families, requiring more land; third, from inclination to wander, arising from exaggerated descriptions of new and better countries, which operate like a talisman upon the minds of many, particularly the idle part of mankind".[2]

Not a glorious insight in to the minds and psyches of our "pioneers"! But still, an insight as to what might have happened to Charles L Wilson to spur him on to leaving Maine at an early age.

Florida became a territory in 1822 and the result of the Second Seminole War of 1835 to 1842 was the exile of most of the Seminole Indians to lands west of the Mississippi. At the time at its statehood in 1845, Florida was a slave state, with almost half the state's population being "enslaved African Americans working on large cotton and sugar plantations, between the Apalachicola and Suwannee rivers in the north central part of the state" - in other words, the Alachua area where our Wilson cousin settled.[3] Still not a settled and safe area even into the late 1850s, this was more like the Maine frontier of the 1700s as the last Indian war in Florida occurred 1855 to 1858.

This must have appealed to Hugh[4] and Susan's eldest, Charles L[5].

Charles L., ch. Hugh and Susan S., Mar. 3, 1818, in T.

By the time he came of age, Topsham, Maine, was becoming a tame place to live. The War of 1812 was only a memory, temperance reform was in full swing[4], a fire engine company was in use[5], and the impressive Tontine Hotel had been built to the cost of nearly

2. Robert Mills, Statistics of South Carolina: Including a View of Its Natural, Civil, and Military History, General and Particular, (Charleston, SC, Hurlburt and Lloyd), 527.
3. History of Florida, https://goo.gl/3qDIQo, accessed 22 June 2014.
4. Wheeler, 250-251.
5. Wheeler, 272.

THE TONTINE HOTEL.

$7000 in 1829. Topsham was no longer a frontier town.

Charles lost his first brother in 1831 while his mother was pregnant with the next son and then he may have witnessed the loss of the next four children who died in 1826-30, 1837, 1841 and 1842. I can only imagine the emotional strain on the family from this high rate of child death. His mother Susan died in 1846, only a few years later but after Charles moved to Florida. Did he watch his mother decline in health or depression? I can understand wanting to get away from such sorrow.

One recurring theme in this family is consumption. His great uncle and grandfather had died of tuberculosis and even though Charles' father lived a long life, those children and even his mother may well have had that family curse. I keep seeing this same pattern - frequently a number of small children with some young adults dying in a space of 10 to 15 years. That could be even worse - to know that perhaps to stick around could be your death.

But maybe because his family was rich, he was able to afford travel. Maybe he saw it was best to take some of that inheritance and leave. Perhaps a good thing since his father did not die until 1860? One other scenario is that he didn't get along with father and was gifted with an early inheritance to assist his leaving.

Keep in mind this is a wealthy family but this is the fourth generation. Wealth and ambition frequently dissipates by then. His great-grandfather and grandfather were men known for an ability to stir controversy. Surely he grew up with those tales ringing in his ears. Perhaps those stories helped him leave Topsham to find his own fortune.

He may have gone south before 1840; I do know that he was not living with his parents that year as there was no male that age at home.[6] I did find an 1840 census record from the Nassau, Florida,

6. 1840 Census; Topsham, Lincoln, Maine; Roll: 144:23; Image: 51; FHL Film: 0009705.

area for a Charles L Wilson.[7] There were 48 slaves and this Charles was the only free person and head of household; he is listed as 30 to 39 which is, of course, older than our Charles.

He certainly could have lied about his age, however, in order to get the job. That type of census record indicates that this was a group of slaves sent south to clear a land for a new plantation with an overseer. This transient group that may have been sent down from South Carolina was a common practice as plantation owners reached out for untouched lands after they depleted the existing land in South Carolina. If that is the case and this is the correct Charles, it's also possible that he took his payment in slaves. That would have given him a stake once he moved on to Alachua county.

The best way to travel south during this period from Maine was via the sea and I expect that Charles did just that. One of the biggest ports was Charleston so there's a very strong possibility that Charles traveled to South Carolina and perhaps met up with some like minded explorers who either continued by sea to Florida, landing in the Nassau territory on the present day Georgia / Florida border or by the land routes that could have taken him more directly to Alachua county. Since he later became the guardian of a child born in South Carolina, perhaps that child might have been part of family group that Charles got to know before he got to Florida. We may never know any of the details of his trip south but the possibilities are interesting!

If not the Nassau territory Charles L in the 1840 census, then he was not the head of any household that year as no other record can be found which is a plausible scenario for twenty-two year old. He did consistently use that middle initial which should make it easier to find a census record with his name on it.

He was registered to vote in 1845 in the Mineral Springs district of Columbia County.[8] Voters in that first statewide election had to

7. 1840 Census," p. 129, NARA microfilm publication M704, roll 36, FHL 0006712.
8. Florida Memory Project, image of voter list, https://goo.gl/1sMijF

own land in that county and "had to demonstrate that it had been his 'place of permanent abode' for at least the six months preceeding the election in which he offered to vote, and that he also had resided within the Territory and State of Florida for the two years immediately prior to the election of Monday, 26 May 1845. Also, only free white citizens of 21 years of age and older could vote, and able-bodied men under age 45 were obliged to become members of the State Militia before voting." So he was in Florida by May of 1843.

When I started researching Charles, I stumbled across "Ancient" probate records from Alachua County and when a database search turned up numerous references to Charles L, I was really taken aback. Criminal? Deadbeat? Oh, dear, what in the world? Ta da, a Sheriff!

As I dug further, I found a website and, in the end, a new cousin who had worked on the Wilson genealogy in Florida. She knew that Charles was from Maine but no more than that. It was a thrill to email her and let her know that I had just filled in all the gaps in her family tree!

Charles was appointed roads commissioner 16 Sep 1846[9] and then ran for county commissioner in 1847 but got only one vote.[10]

Next he ran for Sheriff in 1849 and served in that position until 1855.[11] He also was appointed Elisor of Levy County (tax collector, coroner, process server, etc.) in Dec 1850.[12] That same year the census lists his occupation as farmer.[13]

He was a plantation and slave owner having purchased 635 acres in May 1849[14] before he won his election in October at age 31. His

---

9. Commission Minutes Book 1, http://goo.gl/r09Ene
10. Alachua County Commission Minutes Book 1, http://goo.gl/8VB04n
11. Alachua Sheriff, http://goo.gl/VqmvWN, accessed 30 April 2014.
12. Alahua County Clerk of Court Records, Judgment Record A:17, http://goo.gl/qbona9 accessed 27 April 2014.
13. 1850 Census; Division 14, Alachua, Florida; Roll: M432_58; Page: 18A; Image: 42.
14. Alachua County, Deed Record A:172, http://goo.gl/38V68Q.

first payment on his mortgage was the transfer of a slave named William; the total cost was $997.49. For him to carry and be trusted with that high a mortgage, I think that he may have arrived in area with money - making the 1840 census more likely that he was in Nassua Territory that year. He could have taken pay in the form of slaves but he does seemed to have easily convinced folks of his worthiness. Perhaps he did arrive in Florida with his inheritance.

Charles' first wife was Lydia Gillet b.abt 1830.[15] Lydia had a bit of history of her own. On March 16, 1838, her parents and siblings were all killed in an Indian attack. Lydia was spending the night at a neighbors so she didn't witness this. She did spend the next day on foot with others fleeing. According to George Gillett Keen, they "tried to make a woods route and got lost; walked all night and the next day, till about one hour by sun in the afternoon, trying to make fifteen miles. They were torn up with briers and bushes and they had just clothes enough to say they had on a few rags. Their persons were scratched, I would say in not less than five hundred places."[16] Nothing is known about the rest of her childhood but the terror engendered by that experience must have been an indelible memory for Lydia.

Charles would have been close to thirty at the time of their marriage and Lydia was only about seventeen. The marriage date is not known but most likely would have been by 1847, the birth year of their oldest child. They had four girls, Susan Elizabeth[5], Martha[5], Frances E[5] and Matilda Jane[5] but they divorced on 15 December 1854.

Lydia sued him for divorce claiming that he had

> *deserted the Said Lydia Wilson the complainant for more than the Term of one year and that the Said Defendant Since his marriage with the complainant illicit intercourse with another woman, thereupon it is ordered adjudged and decreed that the Said Lydia Wilson be and is forever divorced from the Said Charles L. Wilson and that the Bonds of Matrimony heretofore existing between them be and they are hereby dissolved and forever annulled, and it is further adjudged ordered and decreed*

---

15. 1850 Census; Place: Division 14, Alachua, Florida; Roll: M432_58; Page: 18A.
16. James M. Denham and Cantor Brown, Jr, editors, Cracker times and pioneer lives : the Florida reminiscences of George Gillett Keen and Sarah Pamela Williams (SC: Univ. of South Carolina Press, 2000) , 38.

> *that the Said Charles L. Wilson do pay all the costs attending this application for Divorce.*[17]

That same day in December 1854 he also gave / sold for $5 slaves to Lydia "Emily a woman about twenty four years old, and her three Children, Hendry, John and Eliza." that he had bought for $1100 in 1851.[18] (This record also shows us the middle names of two of his children.[19])

Ten days later he was back in court with Mary Russell, who, "desirous to make provision" for the children, agreed for the sum of five dollars to put into trust "seven negro slaves of the following description to wit Silver fifty four years old, Rebecca sixteen years old, Malinda eleven years, Sarah six years old, Gabriel five years old, Edward five years old, and Elvira three years old[20]" for the maintenance and support of his Charles' minor children. These slaves were to be used to generate income to provide the money to support, maintenance and education of the children. Somehow I don't think this speculative solution would work for today's legal system but it does give a look at how slaves could be used and how valuable and concrete an investment they could be.

Mary Caroline Tison Russell was the wife of Samuel Russell, a former clerk of court and Charles' business partner, who had died in November of 1853 - about a year before the divorce. She had purchased those slaves from Jerome Jones, Charles' ward, on 7 Oct 1854 for $2500. Those slaves may have represented a substantial portion of Charles' total number of slaves at the time as there were only twelve in the 1850 census.[21]

On 28 Dec 1854[22] only days after the trust for the children agreement was recorded, Mary Russell and Charles married.

---

17. Alachua County, Judgment Record A:211. http://goo.gl/SQ7Gtx
18. Alachua County Mortgage Record A:60, http://goo.gl/hxWlWm
19. Alachua County Deed Book B:441, http://goo.gl/bgtO3O.
20. Alachua County Records, D:13, http://goo.gl/dMgULn, accessed 1 May 2014.
21. 1850 U.S. Federal Census - Slave Schedules [database on-line]. Ancestry.com.
22. "Florida, Marriages, 1837-1974," (https://goo.gl/At1Oep).

I think it is worth noting that Mary b.27 Oct 1827 d.18 Dec 1893[23] was also much younger than Charles - by nine years. Lydia had been about 12 years younger. That age spread is not unusual: men tended to marry much younger wives in order to take care of surviving children after their mother's death. Mary's first husband, Samuel, was ten years older than her as well. The Maine Wilsons seem to be more likely to marry someone close in age but perhaps this was normal for Florida? I do not know but it does make me wonder about Charles who seems to have needed that attention from or control of a younger spouse. Both wives were not able to read or write.

This may have been a case of businessman / friend who got too close to a surviving wife after the death of her husband. The firm was called Wilson & Russell and they took a mortgage on property in Newnansville from an Elijah Barrow, Merchant.[24] I found a record where both Charles and Samuel Russell were charged and convicted of "keeping open store on the Sabbath" which does sound like they were operating a store together in late 1851. They were fined $20 together. Four other indictments for the same offense were also handed down the same day.[25] 'Tis interesting since he was Sheriff at the time and had just acted as a juror as well.

So the divorce said he had deserted Lydia more than one year prior - as soon as Samuel Russell died? I can well imagine Charles wanting to help his business partner's wife (only 26 with four children, the youngest being barely a year old) after an unexpected death. Samuel had died on a trip to Savannah and was only 37.[26] I could not find any information about his death but I can't help but wonder if Charles had gone with him.

Jerome Jones' status and presence is quite intriguing. According to census information, he was born in South Carolina. There is no record of whose child he was but many of the early settlers of this area were from South Carolina. Charles gained guardianship of

23. Findagrave.com, http://goo.gl/JKODi6, accessed 1 Aug 2015.
24. Alachua County Clerk of Court, Mortgage Record A:63, http://goo.gl/8L0CQv
25. Alachua County Clerk of Court, Judgement Record A:69 - 70, http://goo.gl/fRtfjv.
26. Findagrave.com, gravestone photo, http://goo.gl/ziLUD5.

him in 1848;[27] he would have been between 13 and 16 at the time. In 1850 Jerome was listed with the Russell household as as 18 years old and also with Wilsons as 15 years old in Nov 11 days apart by the same census taker. He later sold those slaves to Mary Russell in 1854 - perhaps those slaves were provided or given to him for his support like Charles did later for his children? That sale could have taken place on his reaching his majority. Also, it could have been an effort to move Charles' assets to Mary as this happened in October before Lydia filed for divorce.

Those slaves were part of Charles' household based on the 1850 slave census. One of Charles' descendants, Debbie Rotstein, makes the case for this in a blog post comparing ages of the slaves that were sold to the census.[28]

So far what we have is a probably rather public divorce and remarriage of a sheriff in the most populated area of Florida at that time. Oh, but there is more.

The Alachua Clerk's office has been very proactive digitizing the old records so there is a fair amount of information available - just enough to make us want more details. But here is what is a matter of record. Right after Mary and Charles marry, he sells his portion of a business or real estate to his partner, T.K. Prevatt. He had bought a second plantation in May of 1854 for $2500 and then he sold it in March of 1855 at a loss for $2000. That December, lawyers still working on Samuel Russell's estate win a judgment for $64 in damages. No other collections in the record but it sound like there is money still coming in from his estate two years after his death.

That same court session in December sees indictments handed down for Charles on the charges of "Carrying Arms Secretly" and assault with intent to kill.[29] He pleaded guilty two days later on the arms charge and was fined $5 and agreed to a bond on the assault charge of $500 which he/his securities agreed was "to be levied

27. Alachua County Clerk of Court, Guardian Record, http://goo.gl/A0i9Jj
28. Ask Debbie, http://goo.gl/TV9ijB, accessed 4 April 2014.
29. Alachua County, Judgment Record A:329, http://goo.gl/cxQB2I.

upon of their respective good & chattels, slaves, lands and tenements if default be made".[30] It looks like two men posted bond for him and that he did not put up his assets.

In March the dismantling of Charles holdings continues when he and Mary sell 357 acres for $1295 and he also wins a judgment of $1500.98. A number of other legal actions arise during the May 1856 court session with debts and the court is also informed that Charles is ill and his trial for the assault is continued until December. We do find another debt collection attempt that month on the ninth but the case was taken under advisement. The next day Charles is indicted for slave stealing, along with a James J. Kennard, who is jailed on the next day.[31] There is no mention of Charles appearing in court at all but he is still under bond for the assault charge. It does not appear that anyone is worried about him. Kennard, on the other hand was a British citizen who had just been granted his US citizenship on 16 May 1856.[32]

Later that week Charles does not show in court for a debt proceeding against him and his assault trial is continued. "And now on this day came the Plaintiff by his Atty and the defendant being three times solemnly called came not but made default."[33]

Then on 11 May 1857, the assault charge is sent to dead docket - an acknowledgment by the court that it may never come to trial but the charges are not dismissed. It is "suggested" that Charles is dead.[34] Since they can't produce Charles on that slave stealing charge, Kennard is ordered to be brought to court for his trial. He had been jailed in neighboring Columbia County awaiting his trial due to lack of space or facilities there in Alachua County. Then the court learns that he has escaped from jail on March 15.[35]

Neither Charles or Kennard ever appears on the dockett again.

30. Alachua County, Judgement Record A:341, http://goo.gl/YJkNZr.
31. Alachua County, Judgement Record A:465, http://goo.gl/uz6EO6
32. Alachua County, Judgement Record A:402, http://goo.gl/ec4LxI
33. Alachua County, Judgement Record A:479, http://goo.gl/RhYytR.
34. Alachua County, Judgement Record A:504, http://goo.gl/3agpV7.
35. Alachua County, Judgement Record A:519, http://goo.gl/TKNwfu.

The rise and fall or retreat of a prominent figure? It does look as if Charles was dismantling his holdings - whether to get cash for living on or fleeing with. He is never actually seen as positively physically present in court documents after he sells that last acreage in March of 1856. His lawyers do appear in other cases but his physical presence is never confirmed. His "illness" is noted after that property sale.

Charles could have been alive in May of 1857 when his death was "suggested". There are only two possible scenarios: he did die, possibly even murdered, elsewhere and his body was never found or he fled the area and never returned. Imagine the rumors swirling around when he disappeared. After all, it appears that he was living in Newnansville when all this was taking place - all his property seems to have been sold off. Newnansville was not a large town and Charles would have been well known.

The 1870 census shows Mary also went on to have another child who was born in 1861, Edward Musco b.20 Jul 1861 d.15 Aug 1938[36] but there was a 50 year old man, James Petit, living with her one year prior according to the 1860 census. He was not listed as a boarder but as a day laborer so it appears they were cohabiting. Edward's death certificate lists her (as Carabele Tyson) as mother and no father. It has been suggested that he might be Charles' son and proof that Charles is still alive, "just laying low". I think it more likely that Edward was Petit's son. Based on that surmise, I am not including him in the Wilson family tree.

After combing through all the records available, I am not able to find where all of Samuel Russell's properties were sold. In 1860, however, Mary is left with no real estate and only $200 in assets. I can't find any further mentions, transactions, deeds or judgments against Charles or Mary after the suggestion of his death. I had access to only digital records - that does not mean I have access to all records.

36. "Florida, Deaths, 1877-1939," (https://goo.gl/TuIzZl)

She did stay in Newnansville initially but moved to Bradford, north of Newnansville, by 1870. Using Russell as her last name in that census, she has no assets of any kind and is living out amongst a number of farms, probably in some housing provided by her son's employer. Samuel Russell is obviously supporting her as a farm laborer. The census lists him as sixteen but he was born in July of 1852 making him closer to eighteen.

The time line on the next page is a graphic look at the events.

So here's the timeline:

'45 registers to vote
'47 marries Lyidia Gillette
'48 Jerrome guardianhip
'49 May, deed, 635 acres.
'50 Oct, Sheriff's election
'51 12 slaves in census
1st mortgage, 635 acres.
Jan. bought 4 slaves
bought business
slave as pymt on deed
'52 bought town lot
July, sold 465 acres
Oct, sold 160 acres
'53 bought 8 town lots
April, sold more acres
Jerome gets in trouble
Nov, Sam Russell dies
'54 town lots w/Prevatt
new plantation & slave
Oct Jerome sells slaves
Nov, town lots sold
Dec, divorce
slaves to Lydia
sold to Prevatt
Marries Mary
Mar '55 sold plantation at loss
'56 Dec, Russell collects
Dec, posts bond
March, sold 357 acres
May, ill not in court
Dec, Slave stealing
May '57 dead docket for assault

The Bradford area first got rail lines east to west in 1857 - leading to it becoming a major crossroad - and the county seat was moved from Newnansville to Gainesville, another proposed rail terminal, in 1854. Newnansville was definitely in decline by 1870 and this may have precipitated the move. Gainesville was not a good place for a single white mother and children nor for jobs for young Samuel. Due to the arrival of many freed blacks after the Civil War and a ruined cotton crop, blacks outnumbered the whites by 1870.[37]

Mary died in 1893 in Columbia County[38] but cannot be found in an 1880 census. Her tombstone lists her name as Mary C. Russell. All in all, this is more the picture of an ashamed / abandoned spouse than just a widow.

Charles' and Lydia's daughters are shown in the 1860 census, all with the last name of Ellis, their step-father's name, but he did not adopt them. That same year Mary is listed with all of her children under the Wilson name though most were Russells. I suspect that both instances were due to laziness or incompetence on the part of the census taker.

The children were Susan Elizabeth^6, Frances Elizabeth^6, Matilda Jane^6, and Martha J^6.

Frances Elizabeth^6 & Matilda Jane^6 (Charles^5, Hugh^4, Hugh^3, Hugh^2, James^1)

Francis Elizabeth^6 b.abt 1854 is last seen in the 1860 census while her twin sister, Matilda, is found residing with her sister, Susan, after her marriage to VanDyke Ellis in 1870. Though it is possible that Francis married after the 1860 census, I cannot find any records that can proven to be her for any marriage.

Matilda^6 may have married a much older man, Joseph Holt b.abt 1830 from Canada. There are two children, Susan and George, list-

37. Gainesville, Florida, https://goo.gl/VRKRnD, accessed 20 May 2014.
38. Findagrave.com, gravestone photograph: http://goo.gl/K0CiQm.

ed in the 1880 census but they are listed as step-children with the Holt surname.[39] That suggests that she might had been married before that. There is a record for a marriage to a Joseph Roth on 5 Feb 1882[40] but no other records for him afterwards. The Joseph Holt in the 1880 census looks to have married again by 1900 because there are other records for him. So it is possible that Matilda did marry Joseph Holt and may have died before 1900.

Susan Elizabeth^6 (Charles^5, Hugh^4, Hugh^3, Hugh^2, James^1)

Susan Elizabeth^6 b.30 Oct 1847 d.8 Oct 1933[41] married VanDyke Hoffman Ellis b.5 May 1839 d.15 Oct 1915,[42] who could have been a relative of her stepfather, in 1866 after he returned from a full four years of war. Interestingly, Susan's death certificate lists her father as Frank Wilson, a sign that Charles L was forgotten in later generations.

They had seven children: Washington Lee^7 b.11 May 1867 d.12 Apr 1937,[43] Regina Reed^7 b.13 Oct 1868 (unc) d.10 Aug 1933,[44] Anderson Mayo^7 b.13 Dec 1870 d.13 Dec 1910,[45] Francis Harrison^7 b.8 Feb 1873 (unc) d.14 Oct 1934[46] (salesman), Samuel Josephus^7 b.30 May 1875[47] d.18 Apr 1935,[48] Carrie Agnes^7 b.8 Jul 1879 (unc) d.19 Dec 1935,[49] and the late baby, Atlanta Gertrude^7, b.28 Jul 1889 d.16 Oct 1972.[50]

Regina never married and Samuel may have married but there are no children on record.

---

39. Year: 1880; Census Place: Precinct 6, Columbia, Florida; Roll: 126; FHL: 1254126; Page: 387A; District: 022; Image: 0364.
40. "Florida, Marriages, 1830-1993," (https://goo.gl/iB0A29).
41. "Florida, Deaths, 1877-1939," (https://familysearch.org/pal:/MM9.1.1/FPHP-FR6).
42. Historical Data Systems, comp. U.S., Civil War Soldier Records & Profiles, 1861-1865. Ancestry.com.
43. "Florida, Deaths, 1877-1939," (https://goo.gl/FjALvY)..
44. "Florida, Deaths, 1877-1939," (https://goo.gl/GdbWsM)
45. Findagrave tombstone photo: http://goo.gl/vNKjsJ.
46. "Florida, Deaths, 1877-1939," (https://familysearch.org/pal:/MM9.1.1/FPW1-VG9).
47. "United States World War I Draft Cards, 1917-1918," (https://goo.gl/hjwNRK).
48. Findagrave.com tombstone photo, http://goo.gl/8NFsnN.
49. "Florida, Deaths, 1877-1939," (https://goo.gl/V3YXvT).
50. Florida Death Index, 1877-1998 Ancestry.com.

Washington Lee[7] married Elizabeth Markey on 8 May 1890[51] and had two children, Osceola b.5 Dec 1891 d.10 Apr 1925 who served in WWI[52] but died before having children and Markey[8] b.July 1893 who possibly died in 1907.[53] Elizabeth died in 1901 and Washington Lee[7] remarried but had no more children.

Anderson Mayo[7] married Rhoda Ann Barry b.1873 d.1959[54] and they had five children. They are all buried in the Newnansville Cemetery. Francis[7] had one child in his marriage to a Mary (Austin?). Carrie Agnes[7] married George Louis Churchwell on 18 November 1898[55] and had six children. Atlanta Gertrude[7] also married (Russell Thomas Taylor b.26 Jul 1881[56] d.7 May 1960[57]) and had seven children.

Martha J[6] (Charles[5], Hugh[4], Hugh[3], Hugh[2], James[1])

It is believed that Martha[6] married Jacob Israel "Doc" Holbrook b.7 Oct 1841 d.1 Feb 1921.[58] Doc's mother and sister were also named Martha but the 1870 census has a young family with Martha who is four years younger than him - definitely not his sister. The first name is actually unreadable, scanned as Doet, which seems to be hastily inscribed with (if it is a T) the crossbar for the T next to the name and what looks to be a period underneath it. The first letter can easily be an I for the D does not match the D on a subsequent row of the record. He was listed in previous censuses as Israel. Also, if that is a D, that could actually be a bad rendition of Doc, his nickname.

I am sure that it is him as his parents are listed on the next page of

51. "Florida, Marriages, 1837-1974," (https://goo.gl/xMYTv3).
52. National Archives and Records Administration; Washington, D.C.; Applications for Headstones for U.S. military veterans, 1925-1941; National Archives Microfilm Publication: A1, 2110-C; Record Group Number: 92.
53. Florida Death Index, 1877-1998 [database on-line]. Provo, UT, USA: Ancestry.com.
54. Findagrave.com tombstone photo, http://goo.gl/RlfOMU.
55. "Florida, Marriages, 1837-1974," (https://goo.gl/n6twld).
56. WWI, Registration State: Florida; Registration County: Bradford; Roll: 1556879.
57. Florida Death Index, 1877-1998 [database on-line]. Ancestry.com.
58. Historical Data Systems, comp. U.S., Civil War Soldier Records & Profiles, 1861-1865 Ancestry.com.

the census - thus pretty close physically as well. The source for his birth and death dates is from the Biographical Rosters of Florida's Soldiers 1861-1865 incorporated into a database for listings of all soldiers. In this case, we even get a physical description: height: 5 ft. 8½ in., light complexion, grey eyes, auburn hair. They would have married after the Civil War and their first child, Emma[7], was born in 1866, followed by Lawrence[7] on 26 Aug 1867 (d.2 Apr 1933).[59] They had three more children, Elizabeth[7] b.abt 1871, Laura[7] b.abt 1873 and George[7] b.abt 1875.[60]

Martha[6] may have died in or about childbirth: Doc had remarried by 1880 and has all of the children with him. Someone has placed a twentieth century style bronze marker for her (Martha W. Holbrook) in the Newsmanville cemetery with a date of 1849 only. It is in the Anderson Mayo Ellis burial plot and there is a matching marker for her mother, Lydia W. Ellis[5], with only a birth year as well, right next to Martha's.[61] Perhaps someone added in those markers after confirming these relationships or having family knowledge early last century. Anderson Mayo[7] was one of Susan's sons.

One other fact that is pertinent. Their son's (Lawrence Holbrook) death record in 1933 has his father listed as J.I. Halbrook and mother as Martha Ellis, another link to Martha's step-father and a name used in one census.

With no other confirmation, however, Martha's and Doc's relationship remains a bit tenuous.

59. "Florida, Deaths, 1877-1939," (https://goo.gl/PH1Nvj)..

60. Year: 1880; Census Place: Newnansville, Alachua, Florida; Roll: 125; Family History Film: 1254125; Page: 45A; Enumeration District: 002; Image: 0091.

61. Photograph and email description by J E Emery, Emery 1959, 3 May 2014.

The Purintons and the Wilsons

The Purintons of Topsham, Maine, are an integral part of the Wilson story but the reach of the Purintons is larger than just Topsham for the Wilson family. Some history is in order - only partially because it is necessary for the backstory. It is also a very interesting tale. Oh, and by the way, no matter how it's spelled, it is pronounced Purr (as in kitty cat) ington (only takes mispronouncing it once while in Maine to get that straightened out!)

John Purrington (son of George Puddington) came to York, Maine, prior to 1661 from Devonshire, England. His children were born in Maine but they nearly all scattered to other places such as Massachusetts and New Hampshire. One son, Hezekiah, moved to Truro, Massachusetts, the original Pilgrim landing choice on the cape (100 miles from Boston). Other branches of the Wilson tree also originate there.

One son stayed in Massachusetts, one moved to New Hampshire and the eldest, Humphrey I, moved back to Maine after his children were born. All of them married and died in Maine - in Georgetown, Bath, Harpswell and Topsham. Every generation spelled the surname differently or variously. Purinton is frequently the spelling adopted in later generations in this tree that intermarried with the Wilsons.

One of the reasons why I was able to find so many connections, and therefore additional Wilsons, was that I tracked down the trees and then tracked back up. In some cases I could verify their existence but with no birth dates. It was this Purinton tree that provided extra daughters for several Wilson families including three for John Wilson, my own fourth great-grandfather. So the excursion was well worth it.

Nearly all of these marriages only happened in William Wilson's family and not in any of Hugh's or Samuel's.

The marriages and the players are:

The first Humphrey's daughter, Abiel[2] (b.1738) married General

Samuel Thompson and they eventually settled in Topsham. It is their daughter, Rachel[3], who married my fourth great-grandfather, John[3] Wilson. Two of his children married Purintons from two different sons of Humphrey[1].

David Purinton's[2] (1730 - 1806) son, Rev. Elihu Purinton[3], married Isabella[3], daughter of William[2] Wilson and Isabella Larabee.

Humphrey's son, Humphrey II (1759 - 1789) had two sons, Humphrey III (1858 - 1832), and Nathaniel[3] (1756 - 1832) whose son Charles (b.1791) married Thankful[4] Wilson (1792 - 1885). Thankful is John Wilson's daughter. Their son, Charles W married Margaret Maxwell, another grand-daughter of John[3] Wilson.

Humphrey III[3] had two sons, Nathaniel[4] who married Priscilla[3] Wilson, the daughter of Samuel[2] and Humphrey[4] who married John[3] Wilson's daughter Rebecca[4]. Nathaniel's son, Joseph[5], married Priscilla[3], daughter of Samuel[3] and Priscilla Purinton.

Another of the first Humphrey's sons, James[2] (1742 - 1832), was the father of Priscilla[3], Samuel's[2] wife, and Ezekial[3] who married Isabella[4] Wilson, John's daughter.

The reason for including all of this is part of the research I did for the Mayflower Society membership. John[3] Wilson's son, Humphrey,[4] is the weak link in our tree with no birth certificate with parents' names. His name, however, is obviously a nod to Rachel[3]'s mother's Purinton family and helps cement the fact that Humphrey[4] Wilson is indeed John[3] and Rachel[3]'s child.

The chart on the next page took hours to figure out but makes the connections as clear as possible.

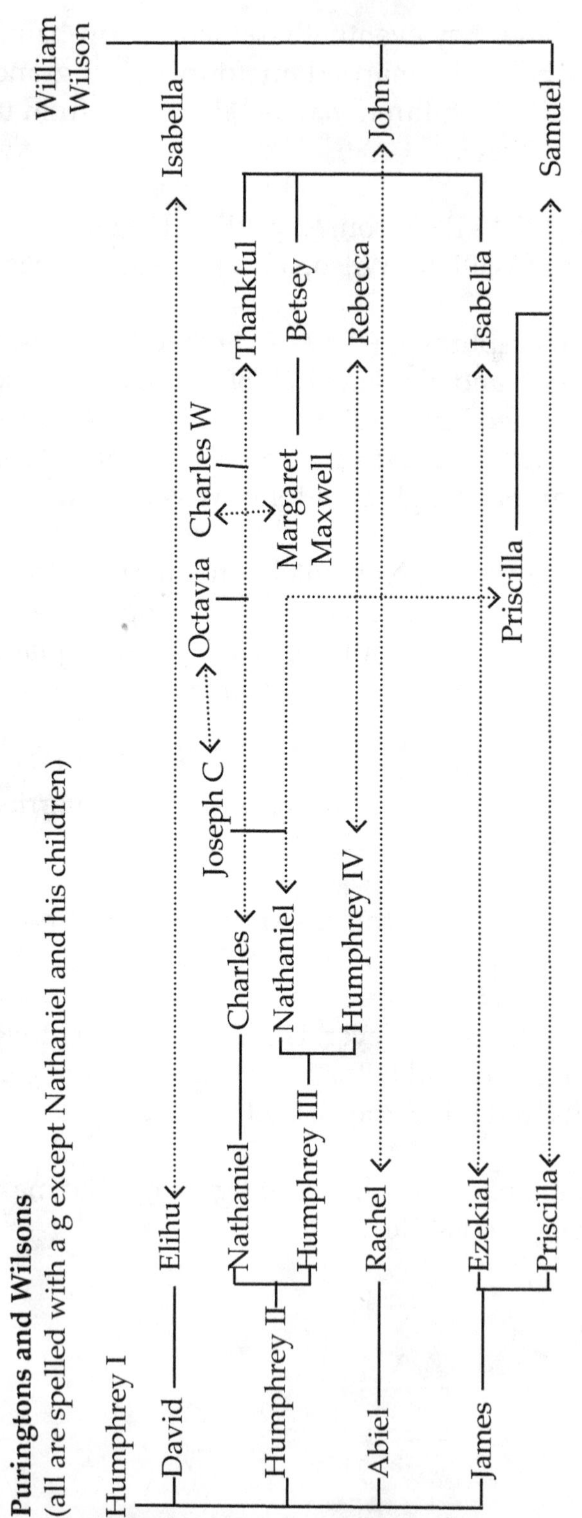

Note: Straight lines denote blood relationships and the dotted lines with arrows are marriages.

William's Children

William[3] (William[2], James[1])

William, Lieut., Nov. 12, 1786, a. 35 y., G.R.I. (Topsham II, 399)
Margret Owens Daughter to Gideon Owens and Jane his wife was born Octr 6 1751 (Brunswick, 26)

William Wilson's and Isabella Larrabee's oldest son, William[3], was born in 1751. He married Margaret Owen d.Aug 1840[1] on 30 Jan 1783. She was the daughter of Gideon Owen (1742-1792) and Jane White. Gideon acted as administrator of William's estate after his death

Owen, Margaret and William Wilson, Jr., Jan. 30, 1783. [int. adds both of T.] (Topsham II, 187)

William was the only male child of that generation in the Wilson family to be named William. He did join the Baptist Church Society in 1797 along with his brothers, John and Samuel.[2]

He fought in the Revolutionary War and ended up a Lieutenant.[3] I'm sure there is a story to be told there but it hasn't survived; he had no children.

He bought out his siblings after his father's death; he is listed as "Gentleman" in the deeds. (20:104) Essentially, that means he didn't work because he didn't need to. The homestead and sawmill part was sold to Samuel Thompson who agreed to allow Margaret to live there til death. (Lincoln County Probate, 34:194) She did remarry, however, and died in Richmond. The part of the land that Isabella was living on was sold to Benjamin Thompson allowing her to live there until her death. (26:107)

Both John and Samuel kept the mill privileges and bit of land at the point southward of the Mill Pond and the Drain (so called)

His grave is near his uncle Hugh's in the First Parish Cemetery in Topsham; his gravestone reads "Halt Passengers as you go Remember you are born to Die."[4] He left no will.

---

1. "Maine, Vital Records, 1670-1907 ," https://goo.gl/bPZomf.
2. Wheeler, 420.
3. Abstract of Graves of Revolutionary Patriots; Volume: 4; Serial: 8542; Volume: 4, Hatcher, Patricia Law. Abstract of Graves of Revolutionary Patriots Ancestry.com.
4. Findagrave.com, gravestone and personal photograph http://goo.gl/btAajl.

"William Wilson, late of Topsham. Gideon Owen, of Topsham, Adm'r, 4 Dec., 1786; Nicholas Gaubert, of Bowdoinham, and Nymphas Bodfish, of Pownalborough, sureties. [III, 160.] Account filed 1 Sep., 1789. [IV, 57.] Philip Hoyt and John Fulton, commissioners to examine claims. [IV, 57.] Distribution ordered 29 Sep., 1789. [IV, 58.] Inventory by William Randall, John Rogers and Philip Hoyt, all of Topsham, 6 Nov., 1787. [V, 173.]"[5]

Samuel³ (William², James¹)

Samuel was born about 1755 in Topsham and married Priscilla Purinton, daughter of James Purinton and Priscilla Harding.

Preselah [Priscilla, d. of James and Priscilla (Harding), p.R.22] and Samuel Wilson, July 12, 1784. [Samuel s. of William, p.R.80. (Topsham II, 211)
Purinton, Prissiller, d. James and Prissiller, Oct. 6, 1764, in G. (Georgetown I, 127)
Priscilla, w. Sam[ue]l W., consumption, Feb. 3, 1818. [d. James and Priscilla (Harding) Purinton, P.R.22.] (Topsham II, 399)

They are buried together in Haley cemetery with a small marker for each on either side of the large gravestone that reads Families of Samuel and James Wilson 2. A death record does not seem to exist for Samuel. There is a Samuel and a James mentioned together, which appears to be them, in the church section of Wheelers' history dated 1824.

On January 19, 1824, Henry Kendall, Jabez Perkins, James Cook, Richard Orr, Samuel Wilson, James Wilson, Elijah White, George Howland, and Daniel Welch petitioned the legislature for incorporation as a religious society.[6]

That was for the Baptist Church Society, one of the church societies whose church records no longer exist. And that might be one of the reasons we are lacking so many birth and death dates for this family.

Before that, in March of 1804, John Merrill sold his pew in the Baptist Meeting House for $30 to Samuel. That pew was located in the southeast corner on the lower floor numbered three.[7]

The location for the First Baptist Meeting House was the present day Haley cemetery where they are buried. Also, according to an article pasted into Cyrus Woodman's History of Topsham, Samuel

5. Lincoln Probate Records, 160.
6. Wheeler, 423.
7. Microfilm roll II, town records, Topsham.

lived very close to the Meeting House.

Samuel did purchase 100 acres of the 200 acre Joseph Dennison lot on the Androscoggin River in 1796 but that does not look any closer to the meeting house than any of the other properties owned by the Wilson family. He then sold that property to James in 1815. That last transaction was recorded after Priscilla's death in 1819. (47:209, 107:66)

Samuel does not appear in the 1830 census so he died between 1824 and 1830.

The other small markers (about 6 inches wide) in Haley read Elizabeth, James M, William, Josphine and at the end is Hannah Linscott, Samuel's sister. It does look like at least one marker is missing. Hill also mentions markers for Madison J, Mary, and Rachel. One marker has probably the remnants of Madison left on it.

Their children took some real digging but seeing the graves there in Haley made me realize who was who.

In the vaccination list from April of 1810[8] there is an Esther 4 years old, Hannah twelve years old, Josephine, eight years old, Mary six years old, and William nine years old. After each name, there is a notation for perfect but Mary's says doubtful. I don't know how one could tell what was a good vaccination but the neat thing about this was that is happened in 1810 in Maine. The American push for vaccination was headed up by a Harvard medical professor named James Waterhouse who had started testing inoculations in 1800.[9] All told, 168 Topsham citizens were vaccinated in 1810.

There those who refused the vaccinations - perhaps James and Betsey were among them. They were living at home that year as the census attests yet neither name was on the list.

8. Microfilm roll II, town records, Topsham.
9. The Beginning of the End of Smallpox, http://goo.gl/yKodY9 accessed 12 May 2015.

There was two more pertinent records:

[----], s. Samuel, May 23, 1792, C.R. (volume I, 211)
Betsey, ch. Sam[ue]l, drowned, July 2, 1820, a. 26. (volume II, 397)

Between these records and the gravestones, I began to get a clearer picture. The section does say families of Samuel and James 2. The 2 was not a senior or junior thing denoting his place in the family. It is how they distinguished between like named individuals back then. Many didn't have a middle name and frequently same named individuals were not immediate family. Samuel was the second Samuel - to his uncle. James 2 was the second James in Topsham; the first was not related, James, son of James and Ann Henry Wilson. So by the time James 2 married and appeared in the census, he was the second living James, with a birth date of 13 May 1790.

Then the census records started making sense: in 1790, there was one boy and one girl, James and Priscilla.[10] In 1800 there were two boys under 10 (William and the unnamed boy born 1792), one boy 10 to 15 (James), three girls under 10 (Betsey or Elizabeth b. 1794, Hannah b.1798, Rebecca b.1797).[11] In 1810, there is one boy under 10 (William), one boy 16 to 25 (James), three girls under 10 (Esther, Josphine and Mary), 2 10 to 16 (Betsey and Hannah), and one 10 to 15 (Rebecca)[12]. Mother Priscilla is not noted in the census.

Priscilla didn't marry until September of that year so I would expect her to be living there as well and she isn't. She also is not in the vaccination list that same year. The first unnamed boy is gone. This might be his death even though it was recorded in 1800 supposedly just before the census in the summer:

[----], ch. Samuel, — —, —, [rec. between Jan. 17, and June 4.] 1800, a. abt. 10 y., C.R.I. (Topsham II, 400)

There's a marker for a Madison according to Hill and there is an existing marker that has visible on it -lison. that l must be a truncated d. That might be the missing boy. Madison was an unusual

10. Census, 1790, p. 260, NARA microfilm pub M637, roll 2; FHL microfilm 568,142.
11. Census Year: 1800; Topsham, Lincoln, Maine; Series: M32; Roll: 6; Page: 488; Image: 458; Family History Library Film: 218676.
12. Census Year: 1810; Topsham, Lincoln, Maine; Roll: 12; Page: 14; Image: 00022; Family History Library Film: 0218683.

name for the family. James Madison served as president from 1809 to 1817 but came to prominence before 1790 so that could be the reason for the name. Since there were also an Esther and Josephine, obviously Samuel reached out beyond the usual family names.

The 1820 census dated 7 Aug[13] was just after Betsey's death and before James' marriage and William's death. There was one boy 10 to 15 (William), one 26 to 44 (James), three girls, 16 to 25 (Hannah, Mary, and Esther). We know Josphine is buried in Haley and as she would have been 14 in 1820, there is no tick mark for that age group; Esther remains untraced so she may have lived and married but there seems to be no trace of her.

William L., s. Samuel of T., Nov.—, 1820, a. 20 y., N.P.8. (Topsham II, 400)

That was taken from the deaths section of the newspaper dated 24 Nov 1820:

"In this town William L, son of Samuel Wilson of Topsham, aged 20."[14]

Since the vaccination record said he was nine in April of 1810, his birthday probably fell after April so that he was twenty in November when he died.

I realized later that both he and his sister, Betsey drowned in 1820. Did they die together? Her record is dated July and the newspaper item is in November. Looking at the arrangement of the markers in Haley, I don't find a correlation between when they died or their ages and the arrangement of the markers. The first marker after Samuel's is William's; the second is Betsey's. It does not appear that he died first and Betsey was older than him.

I can find no birth record for a Mary but the Mary marker present when Hill was doing her inventory is definitely not Samuel's daughter Mary who died in Fairfield and is buried with her husband. Though once again, there could have been an earlier child for Samuel named Mary who died as an infant. She also could have been James' child but the markers that do remain intact are main-

13. 1820 U S Census; Census Place: Topsham, Lincoln, Maine; Page: 163; NARA Roll: M33_36; Image: 95.

14. Maine Intelligencer (Brunswick, ME), Friday, Nov 24, 1820,Volume: I :10, 79.

ly the markers for James and not Samuel. We will probably never know for sure. What we do know is that there were a lot of deaths around the time of Priscilla's death from tuberculosis in 1818.

I started thinking about why there would be such a marker. What would spur two men to create such an odd grouping? The answer might be multiple deaths coming close to each other. I have seen it in other families where family members die within days of each of tuberculosis and I've also seen various reasons for dying in a close grouping as well. I do believe there must of been a number of deaths very close together to put up a marker for them all.

James[4] (Samuel[3], William[2], James[1])

James repeatedly appears as James 2 in Hill's records with one exception - his marriage where he is referred to as junior.

> *James 2d., h. Rebecca, May 13, 1790, in T. (Topsham I, 210)*
> *James, Jr., of T. and Rebekah Linscott of Harpswell, int. Oct. 14, 1820. [cert. Oct. 29.] (Topsham II, 285)*

James' wife was the daughter of Moses and Hannah Linscott of Harpswell. This is significant for two reasons. I had wondered why Samuel's sister, Hannah[4], was buried in Haley with this family. It turns out that it was because she was the mother of James' wife. He married his first cousin Rebecca Linscott.

> *Rebecca [— — —], w. James 2d, June 15, 1790, in T. (Topsham I, 211)*

Rebecca[4] and James[4] had four children (one adopted): at least two may be buried with them in Haley, William[5], and James M.[5]

> *William L., ch. James 2d and Rebecca, Jan. 13, 1823, in T. (Topsham I, 211)*
> *William, Mar. 11, 1849, in T. (II, 399)*
> *James M., ch. James 2d and Rebecca, Oct. 5, 1829, in T. (210)*
> *James M., Mar. 3, 1847, in T. (II, 398)*
> *Rachel H., ch. James 2d and Rebecca, Sept. 1, 1832, in T. (211)*
> *Frances Allen, [adopted] ch. James 2d and Rebecca, [ ] in Brunswick. (209)*

The census bears out this scenario:

In 1830[15] James[4] has one son under five (James M) and one 5 to 10

15. Census 1830; Topsham, Lincoln, Maine; Series: M19; Roll: 49; Page: 304; Family

(William). There is also an extra female, age 10 to 15, which might be the adopted daughter, Frances. Both James and Rebecca's ages are correct.

1840[16] there is one boy 10 to 15 (James M), one 15 to 20 (William), one girl 5 to 10 (Rachel), one 10 to 14 (Francis Allen?). The adult female is 40 to 50 which is not correct for Rebecca, one decade off.

Assuming that Rebecca outlived James and was buried years later, I did a digital search and turned up a Rebecca who died in 1856 in Cape Elizabeth who was buried in Portland.[17] That same search turned up a census record from 1850 with a James and Rebecca, both 60 years old in Portland with a child, Rachel, born about 1833. The coincidence was intriguing and I followed that path for a long time until finally I found death record for a child of Rachel's in Massachusetts which lists her birthplace as Topsham.

Towards the end of collecting the information about her family, I ran across a census record from 1860 for James where he was living with Rachel's family in Cape Elizabeth. By 1865 Rachel had moved to Massachusetts and James was no longer with her.

I found several records of a death for a James Wilson, one specifically looks to be his: 25 Mar 1862 in Portland where he was listed as 71 years old.[18] The birth date was May of 1790 so he would have been 71 years, almost 72. The cause of death was consumption.

And on that note, I formed a theory for the deaths in this family. Mother Priscilla died of consumption. My grandfather Vance had tuberculosis in the late '30s and/or the early 40's. I had not thought much of it until my aunt started having back issues late in life and the doctors speculated that she might have TB of the spine.

One can carry dormant TB for a lifetime and it can manifest itself

---

History Library Film: 0497945.

16. Year: 1840; Census Place: Topsham, Lincoln, Maine; Roll: 144; Page: 22; Image: 49; Family History Library Film: 0009705.

17. Findagrave.com, http://goo.gl/TI3Qk5, accessed 4 May 2015.

18. "Maine, Vital Records, 1670-1907 ," (https://goo.gl/dGuqox).

many years later. Tuberculosis is highly contagious, spread through the air. It was called the Great White Plague starting in the 17th century and lasting 200 years. It was spurred on by the Industrial Revolution when unsanitary conditions and crowding proved to be the perfect environment for propagation of the disease.

It's entirely possible that though James[4] may have lost half of his siblings early (and some to TB) he may have emerged from his childhood infected with dormant TB, showing no signs until many years later.[19] Could his father have been infected as well? Could James' children have died from TB? We'll never know but I believe that TB played a role in more than just Priscilla[3] and James' deaths in this family.

If the boys', William and James M, death dates are correct for them, then James and Rebecca left Topsham for Portland right afterwards.

I believe Frances[5] was born about 1822.[20] It looks like she is listed in the 1850 census in Hugh Wilson's household but I was not able to find any trace of her after that. There were some reported cases of small pox in the area in 1851[21] and she could have married as well.

Rachel H[5] (James[4], Samuel[3], William[2], James[1]) - The Hunts

Rachel H., ch. James 2d & Rebecca, Sept. 1,1832, in T. (Topsham I, 211)

Rachel H[5] d.1 Apr 1885[22] married William Henry Hunt b.5 Nov 1829[23] of Lubec on 30 Dec 1852.[24] They moved to Boston in 1863 after her father died: son William's birth record says he was born in Portland but died that same year in Boston. They had seven children, three who died young, Ida M[6] b.28 Oct 1872[25] d.9 Aug 1873 (consumption),[26] William H[6], b.Dec or Jan 1862 d.27 Aug 1863,[27]

---

19. History of Tuberculosis, https://goo.gl/n5LE4F, accessed 9 May 2015.
20. Census Year: 1850; Topsham, Lincoln, Maine; Roll: M432_261; Page: 346B:480
21. Wheeler, 315.
22. Massachusetts, Death Records, 1841-1915 Ancestry.com Operations, Inc., 2013.
23. Maine, Births and Christenings, 1739-1900," (https://goo.gl/pdrMFk)..
24. "Maine Marriages, 1771-1907," (https://goo.gl/tGSTz1)
25. "Massachusetts, Births, 1841-1915," (https://goo.gl/HZXhKQ) .
26. "Massachusetts, Deaths, 1841-1915," (https://goo.gl/nsA62n).
27. "Massachusetts, Deaths and Burials, 1795-1910," (https://goo.gl/wVBhet).

Ella J[6] b.1857 d.22 Sep 1871[28] and Laura Etta[6] b.11 Nov 1865[29]d.7 Oct 1871.[30] Both Ella and Laura died of typhoid fever.

The other three children all married and had children of their own. Amanda M[6] b.1854 d.1 Dec 1903[31] married William H Ford b.9 Feb 1858[32] on 9 May 1878.[33] They had Annie Ella[7] b.19 Jun 1878,[34] Sadie Bell[7] b.Jan 1880 d.8 Jun 1880,[35] Cora Elizabeth[7] b.17 Oct 1893,[36] Hattie Rachel[7] b.abt 1888[37] and William Henry[7] b.1 Apr 1891[38] d.2 Apr 1912.[39]

Cora Elizabeth[6] b.17 Mar 1868[40] married twice; the first time to Frank E Bayles b.1850 d.26 Nov 1901.[41] They had three children: Edna Elizabeth[7] b.3 Jun 1890[42] d.26 Mar 1903,[43] Harold Earle[7] b.23 Aug 1898[44] and Charles Arthur[7] b.3 Aug 1892.[45] Cora then married Eugene Ceymont Parker b.5 Nov 1877[46] d.3 May 1938[47] but the wedding date (5 Oct 1901[48]) I found was one month before Frank Bayles death. They had Mildred E[7] b.14 Feb 1903 d.13 May 1988[49] and Eugene Ceymont[7] b.28 Jul 1905.[50]

James T[6] was born about 1855. He married Annie Elizabeth Honey

---

28. Massachusetts, Death Records, 1841-1915 Ancestry.com Operations, Inc., 2013.
29. "Massachusetts, Births, 1841-1915," (https://goo.gl/T1D9n3).
30. "Massachusetts, Deaths, 1841-1915," (https://goo.gl/WL8qYU).
31. "Massachusetts, Deaths, 1841-1915," (https://goo.gl/IxQC4I).
32. "Massachusetts, Births and Christenings, 1639-1915," (https://goo.gl/nyLdpL).
33. "Massachusetts, Marriages, 1841-1915," (https://goo.gl/gvDLt9).
34. "Massachusetts, Births, 1841-1915," (https://goo.gl/3XNyWQ).
35. Massachusetts, Death Records, 1841-1915 Ancestry.com Operations, Inc., 2013.
36. "Massachusetts, Births and Christenings, 1639-1915," (https://goo.gl/uKPZuH).
37. "United States Census, 1940," (https://goo.gl/DXKPl6).
38. "Massachusetts, Births, 1841-1915," (https://goo.gl/JLJl5D).
39. "Massachusetts, Deaths, 1841-1915," (https://goo.gl/Vp46Ds).
40. "Massachusetts, Births, 1841-1915," (https://goo.gl/IdGEUJ).
41. "Maine, Vital Records, 1670-1907 ," (https://goo.gl/b3MB5Z).
42. "Massachusetts, Births and Christenings, 1639-1915," (https://goo.gl/xL6g8P).
43. "Maine, Vital Records, 1670-1907 ," (https://goo.gl/3ljikD).
44. "Maine, Vital Records, 1670-1907 ," (https://goo.gl/CDeM6b).
45. "Massachusetts, Births, 1841-1915," (https://goo.gl/FdYRjd).
46. "United States World War I Draft Registration Cards, 1917-1918," (https://goo.gl/oae46J), NARA microfilm pub M1509; FHL microfilm 1,685,008.
47. "New Hampshire, Deaths and Burials, 1784-1949," (https://goo.gl/1p1jnn).
48. "Maine, Marriage Index, 1892-1966, 1977-1996," (https://goo.gl/EuFDkt).
49. Massachusetts Death Index, 1970-2003 Ancestry.com Operations Inc, 2005.
50. "Massachusetts, Births and Christenings, 1639-1915," (https://goo.gl/SD6jFf).

b.1858 d.1925 on 3 May 1877[51] and supposedly moved to California where he died in 1900. Annie is listed in the California 1900 census with her parents and her son Frank as widowed.[52]

Hannah[4] (Samuel[3], William[2], James[1]) - The Whittemores

Hannah, under, "Head of family, Samuel," a. 12 y. in 1810, L.v. (Topsham I, 209)
Hannah of T. and John Whitmore of Lisbon, int. Mar. 10, 1825. [cert, issued Mar. 25, "Wilson."] (Topsham II, 285)
John was born Feb the 22[d] AD 1798 (Lisbon, 154) d.21 Oct 1879

Deacon John Whittemore, a farmer took Hannah b.3 June 1798[53] back to Lisbon and they had four children. She died 11 Jan 1880 of "softening of the brain".[54]

Rebecca Crooker Whittemore was born September the 6th AD 1828 (Lisbon, 111) d.10 Jan 1910[55] unmarried
Albert P Whittemore was born Oct 23 AD 1836 (111)
Albert P Whittemore d. in Hospital, Jefferson Barracks Mo Oct 10th AD 1863 (111)
Charita Ellen Whittemore was born Oct 9 AD 1840 (111) d.1934[56] unmarried
Charles Augustus Whittemore was born August the 2nd AD 1826 (111) unmarried
Charles A Whittemore Died Sept[r] the 11th AD 1848 (111)

Priscilla Purinton Whittemore was born May the 14th AD 1831
Mr John Q Adams & Miss Priscilla P Whittemore both of Lisbon Intend Marriage Lisbon April 20th 1869 (Lisbon, 263)
Nellie Mabel Adams was born Dec 27th 1870 (182)

The only child that had children, Priscilla Purinton[5] d.12 Jan 1914,[57] married John Quincy Adams b.16 Dec 1827[58] d.16 May 1908[59] (his second marriage) and had one daughter Ellen (Nellie Mabel) d.21 Feb 1950 who married Frederick Clarence Strout b.20 Oct 1873 d.16 Oct 1946.[60] They had 9 children and at least 14 grandchildren.

---

51. "Massachusetts, Marriages, 1841-1915," (https://goo.gl/ez01sT),.
52. Census 1900; Place: Orange, California; Roll: 95; Page: 5B; District: 0144; FHL microfilm: 1240095.
53. Findagrave.com, gravestone photograph, http://goo.gl/yX46SY
54. Maine State Archives; U.S. Census Mortality Schedules, Maine, 1850-1880; Archive Collection: 4; Census Year: 1880; Census Place: Lisbon, Androscoggin, Maine; Page: 1.
55. Maine State Archives; 1908-1922 Vital Records; Roll #: 60.
56. Findagrave.com, http://goo.gl/Dwa4i9, accessed 18 May 2015.
57. Maine State Archives; 1908-1922 Vital Records; Roll #: 1.
58. "Maine, Births and Christenings, 1739-1900," (https://goo.gl/2w9hKG).
59. Maine State Archives; 1908-1922 Vital Records; Roll #: 1.
60. Findagrave.com, http://goo.gl/js1oiY, accessed 18 May 2015.

Rebecca[4] & Mary[4] (Samuel[3], William[2], James[1]) & David Pearson

Mary, under, "Head of family, Samuel," a. 6 y. in 1810, L.V. (Topsham I, 211)
Mary of T. and Capt. David Persons of Fairfield, June 3,1829 (Topsham II, 287)
Mary, 26 Nov. 1852, ae 47 yrs., w. of David. G.R. 5 (Fairfield I, 519)
Rebecca, 31 Jan. 1825, ae 28 yrs., da of Daniel Wilson; consort of David. G.R. 5 (Fairfield I, 519)
Rebecka of T. and David Parsons of Fairfield, Feb. 23, 1820 [int. Persons of Litchfield.] (Topsham II, 287)
Pearson.David. Junr-. 28 May 1789. so of David and Thankful (I, 155)
David, 22 Feb. 1852, ae 63 yrs., G.R. 5 (I, 519)

Rebecca's grave states that she was the daughter of Samuel, not Daniel as the above record shows.[61] She and David had one child that lived, Thankful C[5], and two young ones that died after her death on 1 Jan 1825, Mary Ann b.1823 d.3 Mar 1825 and William b.Aug 1825 d.16 Dec 1825.[62] Note, too, that William was supposedly 4 months old at his death but that makes his birth after his mother's death so there is something wrong. This information comes from a photograph of the gravestone that states the parents names. The children's marker is located with their parents in the Emery Hill Cemetery.

Mary[4] was the youngest child of Samuel and Priscilla. She and David Pearson had six children all born in Fairfield where she died 26 Nov 1852 just months after David's death on 22 Feb 1852.[63]

Isabel. 16 May 1834. G.R. 10 (I, 155, birth)
Isabel, 18 July 1893. G.R. 10; sister of David (I, 519, death)
Mary F. of Fair., and Shepherd Low of Clinton int. 29 May 1857 at Clinton, Md. 14 June 1857 (I, 321)

There is a grave in Riverview Cemetery in Clinton with both Shepard and Mary's names. It has only his birth date and a death date of 27 Oct 1859 in California.

The children who married were Thankful C[5] b.5 Feb 1921 d.13 Dec 1884[64], David[5], Celestia[5], Esther Helen[5] and William Henry[5].

---

61. Findagrave.com, gravestone photograph, http://goo.gl/GWKqx7
62. Gravestone photograph posted on ancestry.com with parents names, confirmed by photographer Lloyd Magnuson that the graves are in the Emery Hill Cemetery near their parents, 25 Aug 2015.
63. "Maine, Nathan Hale Cemetery Collection, ca. 1780-1980," (https://goo.gl/1F0ZdX).
64. Findagrave.com, gravestone photograph for both, http://goo.gl/l6v0tc.

Thankful C[5] Pearson (Rebecca[4], Samuel[3], William[2], James[1]) - The Lows

Thankful C. & Ivory C. Low, both of Fair., int. 4 Sept.1850: md. 26 Sept 1850 (Fairfield I, 321)

Low, Ivory H d.20 Dec 1896 Watrv, ae 78 yrs, 11 mos, 11 das b Fair., so of Ivory C. and Fannie (Colcord b. Fair) (II, 139)

Ivory Low's grave does state that he died on 4 Nov 1883 which makes his birth year still 1816 so the death record is partially incorrect. He had two children by a previous marriage and he and Thankful did not have one of their own.

David[5] Pearson (Mary[4], Samuel[3], William[2], James[1])

David, 1830. hus of Mary J. (Woodman). G.R. 10 (Fairfield I, 155)
David, 28 Dec. 1905, hus. of Mary J. (Woodman). G.R. 10 (I, 519)
David of Fair., and Mary Jane Woodman of East Sanbomton, N. H. int. 7 Jan 1861; Cert. issued 12 Jan 1861 (I, 321)
Mary J (Woodman) 28 June 1843. w. of David G.R. 10 (I, 155)
Mary J. 4 May 1927, ae 83 yrs., 10 mos., 6 das., w. of David. G.R. 10 (I, 519)

Chancey P., 4 June 1873/4, ae 2 (I, 519)
Maria Jane, 6 Oct. 1850, ae 13 yrs., l0 mos., 9 das., da of David and Mary. G.R. (I, 519)

David and Mary Jane Woodman had two children that survived and married: Josephine[6] and Louisa B.[6]

Josephine, 29 Aug 1866, da of David and Mary J (I, 155)
Josephine (Pearson), 12 Jan. 1896, ae 30 yrs., 4 mos., 14 das. (I, 483)
Knowles, Male ch., 30 Dec. 1895, of Elmer E. and Josephine (Pearson) . (I, 120)
Joseph, 2 Mar. 1897, ae 14 Mos., so of Elmer E. and Josephine (Pearson). LB. "and son Joseph"; w. of Elmer. G.R. lO (I, 483)
Edmund E., 17 Feb. 1892, so of Elmer E. and Josephine (Pearson) G.R. 10 (I, 120)
Knowles, Edmund E., 7 Aug. 1920. G.R. 10 (I, 483)

Josephine[6] married Elmer E Knowles b.1865 on 6 Jul 1889[65] and had two children before she died at age 30 from tuberculosis. Their son, Joseph[7] also died from tuberculosis less than a year later on 12 Mar 1897.[66] Edmund Ellsworth[7] died young as well without marrying. I was not able to find his actual death record with cause of death.

McClintock, Lou B. (Pearson), 20 Feb. 1903, ae 25 yrs., 3 mos., 17 das. w. of William F. G.R. 10 (I, 495)

David's daughter Louisa[6] died after marrying William F McClin-

65. Maine State Archives; Augusta, Maine, USA; Pre 1892 Delayed Returns; Roll #: 62.
66. "Maine, Vital Records, 1670-1907 ," (https://goo.gl/2joIFr).

tock. Her death was also due to tuberculosis.[67]

Twins William Henry[6] and Esther Helen[6] were born 25 Dec 1842.[68]

Esther Helen[5] Pearson (Mary[4], Samuel[3], William[2], James[1]) - The Millers

Esther H. of Fair., and William Miller of Clinton int. 2 Dec 1865; Cert. issued 7 Dec 1865

Esther[6] married farmer William Miller b.1839 d. on 7 Dec 1865.[69] Their daughter, Mae[6], b.abt 1871 died at age 24 of consumption in Lowell, Massachusetts, on 26 Mar 1895.[70] The family moved to Lowell from Benton between 1870 and 1880[71] and then to California between 1883 and 1900. Daughters, Florence Elizabeth[7] b.28 Aug 1879[72] d.30 Aug 1917[73] and June E[7] b.17 Jun 1883[74] d.bef 1930, appear in the 1900 census[75] but Beth P[7] b.abt 1867 does not. I can find no records for her after 1880. Son Merton Leland[7] b.3 Oct 1868 d.25 Jan 1953[76] married a Georgia Mae b.abt 1971.[77] He may have been a sailor based on his travels. June E[7] did marry Ralph John Reed and had two children in California.

William Henry[5] Pearson (Mary[4], Samuel[3], William[2], James[1])

W. H. of Fair., and Mahala R. Tufts of Farmington 22 June 1871 (I, 321)

William Henry[6] was a Civil War veteran. He married Mahala Ramsdell Tufts b.12 Apr 1848 d.1 Apr 1927[78] in Farmington, Maine, where he died 16 Sep 1923.[79] They had six children, one that died as a young child, Peter Parker Tufts[7] b.7 Nov 1877 d.20 May 1878. All the others married and had children: Raymon E[7] b.5 Apr 1872 d.8

67. Maine State Archives; 1892-1907 Vital Records; Roll #: 37
68. "Maine, Veterans Cemetery Records, 1676-1918," (https://goo.gl/MpTdDP)
69. "Maine, Marriages, 1771-1907," (https://goo.gl/WHWQM0).
70. "Massachusetts, Deaths, 1841-1915," (https://goo.gl/iL1Slb).
71. Year: 1880; Census Place: Lowell, Middlesex, Massachusetts.
72. Massachusetts, Birth Records, 1840-1915 [database on-line]. Ancestry.com.
73. California, Death Index, 1905-1939 [database on-line]. Ancestry.com.
74. Ancestry.com. Massachusetts, Birth Records, 1840-191. Ancestry.com
75. Year: 1900; Census Place: Los Angeles Ward 4, Los Angeles, California; Roll: 89; Page: 3B; Enumeration District: 0040; FHL microfilm: 1240089.
76. California, Death Index, 1940-1997 Ancestry.com Operations Inc, 2000.
77. Year: 1940; Census Place: Los Angeles, Los Angeles, California; Roll: T627_407; Page: 14A; Enumeration District: 60-217
78. Findagrave.com, gravestone for year only, http://goo.gl/mQBEQn)
79. "Maine, Veterans Cemetery Records, 1676-1918," (https://goo.gl/MpTdDP)

Mar 1849, Flora Alice[7] b.7 Aug 1875 d.17 May 1964, Parker Tufts[7] b.8 Jun 1879[80] d.17 Sept 1943, Harland Curtis[7] b.25 May 1882[81] d.2 Oct 1958 and Edwina Lowe[7] b.15 Sep 1884 d.23 Sept 1934.[82]

Celestia[5] Pearson (Mary[4], Samuel[3], William[2], James[1]) - The Giffords

Pearson, Celestea of Fair., and John A. Gifford of Clinton, Iowa int. 16 Oct 1866; Cert. issued 21 Oct 1866 (I, 321)

Celestia b.9 Apr 1840 d.22 Oct 1912[83] married John Alfred Gifford b.29 Oct 1835 d.27 Oct 1929[84] and promptly began moving, first to Iowa, then Kansas for several decades. John moved on to Idaho after Celestia's death where he died. There was one daughter, Gertrude, that died young but both of his surviving children went with him to Idaho. Florence Belle b.24 May 1881 d.14 Feb 1962[85] married Charles C Stevens there in 1922.[86] He was much older widower and they had no children. Celestia's son, Ernest Pearson b.26 Apr 1876 d.5 Oct 1950[87] married Susan Lavola Sewell b.19 Jun 1876 d.12 Jun 1961;[88] they had four children including one killed in the Philippines in WWII.

Priscilla[4] (Samuel[3], William[2], James[1]) and her Purintons

Priscilla[4] b.28 Jan 1788[89] married her second cousin, Rev. Nathaniel Purinton, son of Rev. Humphrey Purinton III and Thankful Harding, first cousin of her mother, Priscilla, on 20 Sep 1810.

Priscilla, w. Nathaniel, Aug. 14, 1864, a. 72 y., G.R.l. (Bowdoin, II, 104) Gravestone death year is 1860 not 1864.[90]
Purington Nathaniel of B. & Priscilla Wilson, Sept. 20, 1810, in Topsham, by James Purinton, Esq., P.R.141. (Bowdoin III, 140)
Purington, Nathaniel, ch. Humphrey and Thankful, Aug. 20, 1787.
Purington, Nathaniel, h.Priscilla, June 12, 1862, a. 74 y., G.R.1. (Bowdoin, II, 104)

---

80. "United States World War I Draft Cards, 1917-1918," (https://goo.gl/8N574F).
81. World War I Draft Registration Cards, 1917-1918 USA: Ancestry.com.
82. Findagrave.com, gravestone, http://goo.gl/xivLmw, accessed 10 May 2015.
83. Findagrave.com, gravestone photograph, http://goo.gl/t2gPft.
84. Ancestry.com. Idaho, Death Index, 1890-1963 Ancestry.com Operations Inc, 2003.
85. Ancestry.com. Idaho, Death Index, 1890-1963 Ancestry.com Operations Inc, 2003.
86. Idaho, Marriage Index, 1842-1962, 1975-1996 Ancestry.com Operations, Inc., 2005.
87. Findagrave.com, http://goo.gl/3a25MC, accessed 3 August 2015.
88. Idaho, Death Index, 1890-1963 Ancestry.com Operations Inc, 2003.
89. Sinnett, William Wilson's Descendants, 4.
90. Findagrave.com, gravestone, http://goo.gl/RKFQGs, accessed 29 March 2015.

The Wilsons and the Purintons are tightly entwined which has helped to keep the daughters in the family tree. A more extensive look at this entanglement with the Purintons can be found in the previous chapter, "The Purintons and the Wilsons".

Priscilla and Reverend Nathaniel had four girls and five boys in Bowdoin. Four died young or never married:

Israel B., ch. Nathaniel and Priscilla, Apr. 16, 1831, P.R.141. (Bowdoin, II, 19)
Israel B., ch. Nathaniel and Priscilla, July 15, 1831, a. 3 m., in B., P.R.141. (II, 104)
Samuel, ch. Nathaniel Jr. and Priscilla, Dec. 24, 1816. (I, 163)
Samuel, ch. Nathaniel & Priscilla, Dec. 5, 1836 a. 20 y. G.R.1. [At sea] (II, 104)
Mary Ann, ch. Nathaniel and Priscilla, Feb. 24, 1827, P.R.141. (II, 20)
Mary Ann, ch. Nathaniel and Priscilla, Sept. 22, 1868, a. 41 y., G.R.l. (II, 104)
Hannah, ch. Nathaniel and Priscilla, Oct. 10, 1820, P.R.141. (II, 19)
Hannah, ch. Nathaniel and Priscilla, Dec. 11, 1838, a. 18 y., G.R.1. (II, 103)

The others did marry and have families: Albert W^5, Thankful^5, Joseph^5, Nathaniel Larrabee^5 and Priscilla^5.

Rev Albert W^5 Purinton (Priscilla^4, Samuel^3, William^2, James^1)

Albert W, ch. Nathaniel Jr. and Priscilla, July 2, 1811. (Bowdoin I, 161)
Albert W., Rev., h. Sally, May 10, 1878, a. 66 y. 10 m., G.R.1. (II, 103)
Sally w. Rev. Albert W., Jan. 22, 1866, a. 53 y. 9 m., G.R.1. (II, 104)

Their oldest was Rev Albert W^5 a Baptist minister like his father. According to the memorial on findagrave.com, he was a carpenter who did all the woodwork in the first West Bowdoin Freewill Baptist Church building. He married Sally R Jamison b.10 Apr 1812[91] and they had seven children, one of whom, Lucinda J^6 b.12 Nov 1838 d.22 Sept 1839[92] lived less than a year. Another, Rebecca E,^{7} b.22 Feb 1848[93] died at age 18 on 20 Feb 1866.[94]

The others were Melissa Ann^6 b.20 Feb 1837[95] who married Isaac Emery Mallet. She was his second wife, the first having died in 1852. They had four children but she died a year after the birth of the last one. Isaac was another grandchild of Humphrey Purinton III making them first cousins. Isaac was a Topsham resident and

91. "Maine, Births and Christenings, 1739-1900," (https://goo.gl/Pu8FnT)
92. Findagrave.com, gravestone, http://goo.gl/dqJgbK, accessed 29 Mar 2015.
93. "Maine, Births and Christenings, 1739-1900," (https://goo.gl/VIyLCK.
94. "Find A Grave Index," (https://goo.gl/S7FSeo).
95. "Maine, Births and Christenings, 1739-1900," (https://goo.gl/GQBd8y).

she moved there.

Melissia Ann, [Purinton, G.R.3], second w. Isaac E., Feb. 20, 1837, in Bowdoin. (Topsham I, 122)
Melissa Ann Purinton, second w. Isaac E., Jan. 1, 1866, a. 28 y. 11 m., G.R.3. [d. Rev. A. W. and Sarah J. Purinton, N.P.6.] (II, 349)
Isaac E. and Melissa A. Purinton, both of T., July 23, 1854. (II, 349)
Isaac E., ch. William, Jr., & Betsey, Oct. 5, 1829, in T. (Topsham I, 120)
Isaac E., h. Frances, A. Baker, Mellissa A. Purinton, and Mary Purinton, Dec. 21, 1890, G.R.3. [a. 61 y., N.P.6.] (II, 349)

All of their children married but had no children:

Emma F., ch. Isaac E. & Melissia Ann, Oct. 5, 1855, in T. (II, 121)
Emma F, d. Isaac E. & Melissa, Apr. 19, 1882, in Bowdoinham, p.R.15. (II, 349)
Walter M., ch. Isaac E. & Melissia Ann, July 25, 1859, in T. (II, 122) d.1931[96]
Edwin W, ch. Isaac E. & Melissia Ann, July 1, 1861, in T. (II, 121) d.11 Jun 1946[97]
Sarah Melissa (called Lillian), d. Isaac E. & Melissa Anne (Purinton), Feb. 15, 1865, in T., p.R.15. (II, 122) d.6 Mar 1945[98]

Purington, Mary Ann, ch. Nathaniel & Priscilla, Feb. 24, 1827, P.R.141. (Bowdoin II, 20)
Isaac E. and Mary P. Purinton, both of T., Jan. 13, 1867. (II, 349)
Mary P., 3d w. Isaac E., Dec. 25, 1892, G.R.3. [P.R.15.] (II, 349)

Emma F7 married William Walton Thomas. A year after Melissa6 died, Isaac married her sister, Mary Ann6 and they had three boys, Wilber Grant7, John Purington7, and Harry Despain7.

Wilbert Grant7 Mallet b.10 Apr 1867[99] d.1942[100] married Ella Jane Longfellow b.Apr 1867[101] d.1942[102] on 28 Nov 1893[103] and they had three children. John Purington Mallet7 b.20 Jan 1868 d.11 Jul 1945[104] married Charlotte Ballou b.25 Jul 1870[105] in Massachusetts on 13 Sep 1899.[106] He was a consulting engineer and he and his family of wife and four children lived in New Jersey, Wisconsin and Rhode Island

96. Gravestone, http://goo.gl/1Gxaxd, accessed 29 Mar 2015.
97. Nathan Hale Cemetery Collection, https://goo.gl/jeP7xW, accessed 29 Mar 2015.
98. "Nathan Hale Cemetery Collection, ca. 1780-1980," (https://goo.gl/814FX4).
99. "Maine, Births and Christenings, 1739-1900," (https://goo.gl/rJK4R7).
100. "Find A Grave Index," (http://goo.gl/B3V5CG).
101. Year: 1900; Census Place: Farmington, Franklin, Maine; Roll: 592; Page: 19B; Enumeration District: 0091; FHL microfilm: 1240592
102. Findagrave.com, gravestone, http://goo.gl/reOHhV) accessed 29 March 2015.
103. Maine State Archives; Augusta, Maine, USA; 1892-1907 Vital Records; Roll #: 36
104. "Rhode Island, Deaths and Burials, 1802-1950," (https://goo.gl/ehlRHv).
105. Massachusetts, Birth Records, 1840-1915 Ancestry.com Operations, Inc., 2013.
106. Massachusetts, Marriage Records, 1840-1915 Ancestry.com Operations, Inc., 2013.

but he is buried in Topsham. Harry Despain[7] Mallet b.21 Jan 1871[107] d.aft 1940 had two boys that survived. He and his wife, Fannie Louise Hawes b.31 Aug 1875,[108] raised their children in Massachusetts where he died but they did live in Washington D.C. where two of his children were born.

Sarah[6] Purinton was born in 1840[109] and was alive in 1860[110] but I can find no record after that.

Nathaniel Snow[6] Purinton was a Civil War veteran who married Jane "Jennie" E Williams.

> *Nathaniel S, h. Jennie (Williams), Feb. 4, 1844, G.R.1. [ch. Albert W. & Sally R. (Jameson).] (Bowdoin I, 163)*
> *Nathaniel S., h. Jennie (Williams), June 1, 1908, G.R.1. [Col., Private secretary under Governor Powers, Cleaves & Hill. Co. E. 21 Maine Infantry in the Civil War. N.P.2.] (II, 104)*
> *Nathaniel S. of B. & Jennie E. Williams of Woolwich, int. Nov. 20, 1865. (III, 140)*
> *Jennie (Williams), w. Nathaniel, May 12, 1843, G.R.I. (I, 163)*

They had six children but all but one never married or had children. Henry T[7], owner of a plumbing company in Pittsburg, PA,[111] Royce Davis[7], a school teacher and young Newman Albert never married. Lester Given[7] was a doctor but died at 30 from tubercular meningitis having married only a month before. His sister, Frances "Fannie" Elizabeth[7] also married and died of tuberculosis.

> *Henry T, ch. Nathaniel S. & Jennie E, July 17, 1869. (Cox, I, 162) d.11 Mar 1936*[112]
> *Royce D , ch. Nathaniel S. and Jennie E , Oct. 27, 1877. (I, 163) d.25 Mar 1919*[113]
> *Newman Albert, Nov. 2, 1882, G.R.I. (I, 163) d.10 Apr 1901*[114]
> *Lester Given, M.D, ch. Nathaniel & Jennie (Williams), Mar. 28, 1873, G.R.I. (I, 163) 13 Nov 1903*[115]
> *Fannie E, ch. Nathaniel S. & Jennie E , Aug. 21, 1875. (I, 162) d.1 May 1907*[116]
> *Sarah L, ch. Nathaniel S. & Jennie E , May 6, 1886. (I, 163) d.1970 (unc)*

---

107. "Maine, Births and Christenings, 1739-1900," (https://goo.gl/4f0sqK) .
108. Massachusetts, Birth Records, 1840-1915 Ancestry.com Operations, Inc., 2013.
109. Maine, Births and Christenings, 1739-1900," (https://goo.gl/JfeaHy).
110. Year: 1860; Census Place: Bowdoin, Sagadahoc, Maine; Roll: M653_448; Page: 78; Image: 78; Family History Library Film: 803448
111. Year: 1920; Census Place: Pittsburgh Ward 7, Allegheny, Pennsylvania; Roll: T625_1520; Page: 5B; Enumeration District: 430; Image: 818
112. Pennsylvania (State). Death certificates, 1906–1963. Series 11.90. Ancestry.com.
113. Maine State Archives; 1908-1922 Vital Records; Roll #: 46
114. Maine State Archives; 1892-1907 Vital Records; Roll #: 46.
115. Maine State Archives; 1892-1907 Vital Records; Roll #: 46.
116. Maine State Archives; 1892-1907 Vital Records; Roll #: 53.

The only one who had children was Sarah Louise[7]. She was a nurse who married Charles Emerson Lord b.23 May 1887[117] d.28 Feb 1953,[118] a teacher, on 30 Sep 1911[119] and they had three children.

John Albert[6] b.19 Feb 1846 d.18 Dec 1919[120] married Emma Page b.1846 d.1926 on 20 Oct 1875[121] and they had three daughters: Mabel Rebecca[7] b.9 Sept 1877[122] d.1954, Angie Lois[7] b.1879 d.1958 and Stella Francis[7] b.Oct 1888[123] d.11 Apr 1970.[124] Only Stella married and had children. John, Emma, Mabel and Angie are all buried together in Riverview Cemetery.[125]

Thankful[5] Purinton (Priscilla[4], Samuel[3], William[2], James[1]) & Stephen Snow

Thankful, ch. Nathaniel Jr, and Priscilla, Dec. 6, 1814. (Bowdoin I, 164)
Mr Stephen Snow of Brunswick to Miss Thankful S. Purington of Bowdoin Octo 25. 1841 (Brunswick, 279)
Stephen Snow was born July 25th 1795 in Brunswick (190)
Stephen Snow & Thankful S. Purrington his wife
Priscilla Antoinette Snow born Sept 5th 1842 (368)
Francenor Aarabine born Decr 12. 1844 (368)

COX, F. J., May 26, 1875, c.R.5. [Mrs. Fannie E., a. 30 y., N.P.6.] [Fannie Arabine, w. F. J., data given me by a relative..] (Topsham, 308)

Thankful[5] d.17 Mar 1850 and Stephen Snow d.10 Oct 1853[126] had two children: Antoinette[6] d.12 Dec 1913 was a nurse who never married.[127] Francina Arabine[6] and James Franklin Cox b.7 Jun 1844 d.8 Apr 1916[128] had one child a few years before she died.

Cox, James F. and Fannie A. Snow, both of T., Jan. 23, 1869, in T. [Francena, of Bath, N.P.6.] (Topsham II, 72)
Gilbert Gowell, ch. J. Frank and Francena Arabine Snow, Jan. 9, 1871, in T . (Top-

117. Maine State Archives; Pre 1892 Delayed Returns; Roll #: 68.
118. "Find A Grave Index," http://goo.gl/0Ei0e0, accessed 29 March 2015.
119. Maine State Archives; Augusta, Maine, USA; 1908-1922 Vital Records; Roll #: 34.
120. Maine State Archives; Cultural Building, 84 State House Station, Augusta, ME 04333-0084; 1908-1922 Vital Records; Roll #: 46.
121. "Maine, Marriages, 1771-1907," (https://goo.gl/7VtRB3).
122. "Maine, Births and Christenings, 1739-1900," (https://goo.gl/PyWhCz).
123. "United States Census, 1900," (https://goo.gl/Oj2olk).
124. "Maine, Death Index, 1960-1996," (https://goo.gl/6TLSLh).
125. "Nathan Hale Cemetery Collection, ca. 1780-1980," (https://goo.gl/VzWZWk).
126. Findagrave.com, year only, https://goo.gl/5LlLXn
127. Maine State Archives; 1908-1922 Vital Records; Roll #: 52.
128. Maine State Archives; 1908-1922 Vital Records; Roll #: 13.

sham I, 45) d.12 May 1919[129]

James was a first cousin of Fannie's, son of Priscilla Purinton and James C Cox. Their son, Gilbert Gowell[7], was a brick mason who married Justine Copeland French b.1879 d.1966[130] and had two boys. James married again after Priscilla's death and that family is later in this chapter.

Deacon Joseph[5] Purinton (Priscilla[4], Samuel[3], William[2], James[1])

Deacon Joseph[5] C married a double cousin, Octavia, daughter of Charles Purington and Priscilla Wilson.

Joseph C, ch. Nathaniel Jr. and Priscilla, Dec. 9, 1818. (Bowdoin, I, 163)
Joseph C., Dec. 18, 1882. [Joseph, "Dea.", h. Octavia (Purinton), a. 64 y., G.R.l.] (II, 104)
Octavia, d. Charles W. and Thankful, Nov. 7, 1822, in B, T.R.3. (I, 163)
Octavia (Purinton), w. Dea. Joseph, June 25, 1903, a. 80 y., G.R.1. (II, 104)
Octavia and Joseph C. Purinton, both of B., Oct. 21, 1845, in Topsham by "Elder" David Jackson, P.R.59. [He s. Nathaniel and Priscilla, P.R.141.] (III, 139)

James F., ch. Joseph C. and Octavia, May 21, 1857, in B., P.R.59. (II, 19)
Frank, 1857,,G.R.1,s. Joseph C. and Octavia, P.R.59. (II, 19) d.6 Jun 1909[131]
Clara, ch. Joseph C. and Octavia, June 29. 1852, in B., P.R.59. (II, 19)
Clara, ch. Dec. Joseph and Octavia (Purinton), Apr. 29, 1924, a. 71 y., G.R.1. (II, 103)

Clara[6] never married but Alonzo[6] and Charles[6] did though Alonzo[6] had no children. Married to Emma Adelaide Healy b.16 Mar 1852,[132] Alonzo[6] was a Civil War veteran and the postmaster in Bowdoin for many years. He also served as Town Clerk and Treasurer[133] as well as running a general store.[134]

Alonzo, h. Emma A. (Healy), Aug. 24, 1916, G.R.1. (II, 103)
Emma A. (Healy), w. Alonzo, Dec. 2. 1920, in B., G.R.l. (Bowdoin, II, 103)
Alonzo & Emma A. Healy, both of B., int. Dec. 13, 1872. [cert. Dec. 25, P.R.17.] [He s. Joseph C. & Octavia, P.R.59.] (III, 138)
Alonzo, h. Emma A. (Healy), Sept. 20, 1847, in B , G.R.I. [Union Soldier, Civil War.] [s. Nathaniel and Priscilla.] (I, 161)

---

129. Maine State Archives; 1908-1922 Vital Records; Roll #: 13.
130. Findagrave.com, gravestone, http://goo.gl/FRDn06, accessed 29 March 2015.
131. Maine State Archives; 1908-1922 Vital Records; Roll #: 45.
132. "Maine, Births and Christenings, 1739-1900," (https://goo.gl/a7AQc3).
133. Hoyt, Edmund S, Maine State Year-book, and Legislative Manual, for the Year ... (Hoyt & Fogg, 1885), 580. Digitally available at https://goo.gl/fCQoa6.
134. Bowdoin Historical Society, http://goo.gl/L6tIaq, accessed 20 March 2015.

Charles W[6] married Hattie May Newman b.4 Mar 1860[135] d.1942[136] and they had three children: Ray[7] (married and had four children), Granville[7] (married and one child) and Clara May[7] who did marry as well.

Charles W., Rev, , —, 1849, G.R.I. [S. Nathaniel and Priscilla, h. Hattie E. (Newman).] (Bowdoin II, 19) 28 Feb 1849 (unc)
Charles W., Rev., h. Hattie, , —, 1910, G.R.1 (II, 103) d.21 Oct 1910[137]
Charles W. of B. and Hattie M. Newman of Weld, int. Sept. 25, 1882. (III, 138)
Ray, ch. Rev. Charles W. and Hattie (Newman), Aug. 13, 1885, in Weld, Me., P.R.59. (Cox, II, 19) d.1954[138]
Granville, ch. Rev. Charles and Hattie (Newman), Jan. 14, 1888, in Durham, N. H., P.R.59. (19) d.9 Jan 1966[139]
Clara May, ch. Rev. Charles W. and Hattie (Newman), Nov. 2, 1890, in Boston, Mass., P.R.59. (20)

Nathaniel L[5] Purinton (Priscilla[4], Samuel[3], William[2], James[1])

Nathaniel L, ch. Nathaniel Jr & Priscilla, Feb. 24, 1813 (Cox, I, 163) d.5 Apr 1870[140]

Nathaniel Larrabee[5] married another Purinton, Melinda P b.24 May 1812 d.29 Jan 1895,[141] the daughter of Hezekiah of Massachusetts. They married in Portland on 4 Mar 1837[142] where they lived the rest of their lives.

Their son, Alonzo[6] b.31 Oct 1841[143] d.12 Jun 1844[144] died at age 2 and two of their daughters never married, Susanna Priscilla[7] b.11 Mar 1838[145] d.1927[146] and Frances Ellen[7] b.23 Mar 1843 d.23 May 1916.[147] One daughter did marry, Louisa Josephine[7] b.7 Aug 1840[148] d.5 Jun 1915.[149] Her husband was Israel P Butler b.8 Aug 1830 d.15 Nov

135. Maine, Births and Christenings, 1739-1900," (https://goo.gl/LKaXvf).
136. Findagrave.com, gravestone photograph (http://goo.gl/1ahpDn).
137. Maine State Archives; 1908-1922 Vital Records; Roll #: 45.
138. Findagrave.com, gravestone photograph (http://goo.gl/CmZdhq).
139. California, Death Index, 1940-1997 [database on-line]. Ancestry.com.
140. Maine State Archives; Pre 1892 Delayed Returns; Roll #: 86.
141. Findagrave.com, gravestone, http://goo.gl/XmpMmS, accessed 22 May 2015.
142. "Maine, Vital Records, 1670-1907 ," (https://goo.gl/mI8cTt).
143. Maine State Archives; Pre 1892 Delayed Returns; Roll #: 86.
144. Maine State Archives; Pre 1892 Delayed Returns; Roll #: 86.
145. Maine State Archives; Pre 1892 Delayed Returns; Roll #: 86.
146. Findagrave.com, gravestone photograph, http://goo.gl/8hCvd9.
147. Maine State Archives; 1908-1922 Vital Records; Roll #: 45.
148. Maine State Archives; Pre 1892 Delayed Returns; Roll #: 86.
149. Maine State Archives; 1908-1922 Vital Records; Roll #: 8.

1922,[150] a blacksmith from South Thomaston.[151]

Louisa[7] and Israel had Dr. Nathaniel Purinton[8] b.26 Sep 1866 d.22 Nov 1918,[152] Cora Louisa[8] b.Aug 1868 d.28 Aug 1954[153] and Edward H[8] b.abt 1872[154] d.9 Oct 1962.[155] Arthur Robinson[8] b.1863 d.5 Aug 1908[156] married Mabel S Lewis b.abt 1868 on 27 Dec 1894[157] in Cazenovia, NY. He can be found in the 1900 census at the Cazenovia Seminary as a teacher with his wife and year old son.[158]

Priscilla[5] Purinton (Priscilla[4], Samuel[3], William[2], James[1]) - The Coxes

Priscilla, ch. Rev. Nathaniel and Priscilla (Wilson), Oct. 3, 1825, at West B , N.P. (Bowdoin I, 161) d.1897
Priscilla & James C. Cox, both of B., Sept. 3, 1843, P.R.92. [He s. Isaac and Desire (Estes) ; she d. Nathaniel & Priscilla (Wilson), P.R.141.] (III, 138)
James, ch. Isaac and Disiere (Estes), Mar. 14, 1820, in B., P.R.92. (I, 73) d.29 Nov 1910[159]

Ann L., ch. James C. & Priscilla, Dec. 20, 1852, in Bath. (44) Ann Louise d.1930[160]

All of the children recorded in the Topsham records lived into the 20th century but there was another child, Susan[6], who died young. Ann Louise[6] never married but the others did. They were James Frank[6], Katherine Maria[6], Lizzie Eveline[6] and Mary E[6].

J. Frank, ch. James C. and Priscilla, June 7, 1844, in Bath. (Topsham I, 45)
James F. and Fannie A. Snow, both of T., Jan. 23, 1869, in T. [Francena, of Bath, N.P.6.] (Topsham II, 72)

F. J., May 26, 1875, c.R.5. [Mrs. Fannie E., a. 30 y., N.P.6.] [Fannie Arabine, w. F. J., data given me by a relative..] (II, 308)

150. Maine State Archives; 1908-1922 Vital Records; Roll #: 8.
151. Year: 1860; Census Place: South Thomaston, Knox, Maine; Roll: M653_443; Page: 361; Image: 361; Family History Library Film: 803443.
152. Maine State Archives; 1908-1922 Vital Records; Roll #: 8.
153. Findagrave.com, gravestone photograph, http://goo.gl/47IuGI
154. Year: 1920; Census Place: Portland Ward 8, Cumberland, Maine; Roll: T625_640; Page: 16B; Enumeration District: 55; Image: 512
155. "Maine, Death Index, 1960-1996," (https://goo.gl/OtKzJH).
156. "Maine, Deaths and Burials, 1841-1910," (https://goo.gl/kDZ0pE).
157. "Maine, Marriages, 1771-1907," (https://goo.gl/lWn1xP).
158. Year: 1900; Census Place: Cazenovia, Madison, New York; Roll: 1071; Page: 14B; Enumeration District: 0006; FHL microfilm: 1241071.
159. Maine State Archives; 1908-1922 Vital Records; Roll #: 13.
160. Findagrave.com, gravestone photograph, http://goo.gl/sJFcw4.

James Frank's first wife, Fannie was living with the household in 1860 when they were 15.[161] They had that one child, Gilbert Gowell[7] d.12 May 1919.[162]

James F. of T. & Mary J. Day of Durham, int. June 26, 1877. [cert, issued July 2.] (II, 72)
Mary Jane Day, (second w) J. Frank, July 7, 1844, in Durham. (I, 45)

Perley Merriman, ch. J. Frank & Mary Jane Day, Dec. 24, 1882, in T . (I, 45) d.1957[163]
Fannie May, ch. J. Frank & Mary Jane Day, Apr. 13, 1886,in T. (I, 45) d.5 Feb 1988[164]
Walter Merriman, ch. J. Frank & Mary Jane Day, Nov. 6, 1888, in T. (I, 45) d.1992[165]
Wilbur Ernest, ch. J. Frank & Mary Jane Day, June 5, 1881,in T. (I, 45) d.1961[166]

All four children lived to adulthood; Fannie[7] never married but the three boys did.

Mary E., ch. James C. and Priscilla, Sept. 25, 1850, in Bath. (I, 45) d.1926
Mary E. of T. and Capt. Jacob Merryman of Harpswell, int. Mar. 20, 1869. [Mary Ella, m. Mar. 21, in T., N.P.6.] (II, 72)
Merriman, Jacob, Capt., h. Mary Ella Cox, Aug. 29, 1843, in Harpswell. (I, 125) d.7 Sep 1918[167]

Clara Belle, ch. Capt. Jacob and Mary Ella Cox, Sept. 5, 1874, in T. .
Clara, d. Capt. Jacob & Mary E., Oct, 1882, a. 8 y., G.R.3. [Clara B., Oct. 21, N.P.6.]
Florence Priscilla, ch. Capt Jacob and Mary Ella Cox, Aug. 1, 1876, in T. d.1949
Henry Failing, ch. Capt. Jacob and Mary Ella Cox, Oct. 23, 1878, in Portland Oregon. d.5 Dec 1954
James Guy, ch. Capt. Jacob and Mary Ella Cox, Mar. 17, 1880, on the Indian Ocean. d.5 May 1905[168] *(electrical shock, railroad accident)*
Ralph, [twin] ch. Capt. Jacob and Mary Ella Cox, Feb. 16, 1883, in T. d.23 Feb 1883
Ray Sawyer, [twin] ch. Capt. Jacob & Mary Ella Cox, Feb. 16, 1883, in T. d.9 Feb 1961

Mary Ella[6] obviously traveled with Jacob Merriman with one child born on the ocean and another in Portland, Oregon. Two did not

161. Census Year: 1850; Bath, Lincoln, Maine; Roll: M432_261; Page: 149A; Image: 87.
162. Maine State Archives; 1908-1922 Vital Records; Roll #: 13.
163. Findagrave.com, http://goo.gl/LNiZUU, accessed 24 Aug 2015.
164. Social Security Death Index, 1935-Current, Number: 006-32-6310; Maine; 1951.
165. Findagrave.com, http://goo.gl/KRdQWy, accessed 24 Aug 2015.
166. Findagrave.com, http://goo.gl/9y7Wnr, accessed 24 Aug 2015.
167. Maine State Archives; 1908-1922 Vital Records; Roll #: 38.
168. Maine State Archives; 1892-1907 Vital Records; Roll #: 39.

survive childhood; Florence Priscilla[7] never married and even though the others married, not one had children. All death dates are from findagrave.com: they are all buried together in Brunswick's Riverview Cemetery.

Lizzie E., ch. James C. and Priscilla, Apr. 13, 1856, in Bath. (I, 45) d.28 Jun 1927[169]
Lizzie E. and William Dunning, both of T., Nov. 26, 1879, in T . (II, 72)
William, ch. Elisha and Lydia, Jan. 8, 1847, in Brunswick, [dup. h. Lizzie Eveline Cox.] (I, 59) d.1929

Bernice Parker, ch. William and Lizzie Eveline Cox, Sept. 4, 1882, in T. (I, 58) d.1955[170]
Ella Frances, ch. William and Lizzie Eveline Cox, Apr. 10, 1889, in T. (I, 58)
Henry James, ch. William and Lizzie Eveline Cox, Mar. 19, 1885, in T. (I, 58) d.16 Apr 1909[171]

Lizzie's husband, William Dunning, was a farmer and the family lived in Topsham. Bernice[7] Parker Cox did not have children nor could I find a death for Ella Francis[7] Cox who may have married after 1930.

Kattie Maria, ch. James C. and Priscilla, Aug. 19, 1859, in Bath. (I, 45) d.1953[172]
Kate Maria & Capt. Walter M. Mallett, both of T., May 27, 1886, in T. (II, 72)
Walter M., ch. Isaac E. and Melissia Ann, July 25, 1859, in T. d.1931

Katherine Maria[7] and Captain Walter Mallet had no children and are buried with her parents and sister.

Mary[3] (William[2], James[1]) - The Hinkleys

Mary married Elnathan Hinkley. Her story is told in "Mary Wilson & The Hinkleys".

Hannah[3] (William[2], James[1]) - The Linscotts

Linscott[ ], a widower and Hannah, d. of William Wilson the eldest, the Innholder, and [ ] Larrabee, [— —], P.R.80. (Hill II, 285)
Linscott, Hannah, Dec. —, 1838, C.R.2. ["Families of Samuel and James Wilson," G.R.2.]" Church Record from First Congregational Church and grave record, Haley Cemetery. (Topsham II, 400)

169. U.S. City Directories, 1822-1989 Ancestry.com, Brunswick, Maine, 1928.
170. Findagrave.com, http://goo.gl/wdj6PD, accessed 24 Aug 2015.
171. Maine State Archives; 1908-1922 Vital Records; Roll #: 17.
172. Findagrave.com, gravestone photograph, http://goo.gl/BExW5G..

Her birth year is unknown; looking at the censuses I get conflicting math. Since she wasn't in William's will, just like Elizabeth, she might have been born as late as 1766 but that would make her nineteen when her first child was born - awfully early for this family. I think closer to 1762 would be more probable.

I don't think anyone had delved into what widower Hannah could have married. I didn't think there could be too many Linscotts in that time frame but found none for Topsham. Casting further afield I found a Moses Linscott b.1758 d.24 Feb 1814[173] in Harpswell. Moses is not known to have been married twice though so I was really cautious. Family histories say that he married a Hannah Wilson in 1785. So looking further, I found that he is buried in Cranberry Horn Cemetery in East Harpswell without a wife.

Moses and the other Harpswell Linscotts are descendants of a John Linscott who came directly to York, Maine, in the 1600s from England. Moses' father was an original settler of Harpswell.

I was sure this was correct but it really was circumstantial but I found a DNA match on ancestry.com to someone who is a Linscott descendant but not from James and Rebecca Linscott. DNA matching can be useful sometimes - to confirm what you already know is the truth.

The problem arose when I realized how many descendants there were in the Linscott tree - enough to have a chapter all their own, in fact. In the interest of conserving space, I have decided to describe only the children and grandchildren of Hannah and Moses. The Linscott clan was a fertile one and the number of descendants are staggering.

The children who may not have lived long enough to have children were William[4] b.3 Nov 1787,[174] Rachel[4] b.13 May 1792[175] and Horace[4] b.1800. The others were Rebecca[4], Stephen[4], Isaac[4], Moses[4], Lacro-

173. "Maine, Nathan Hale Cemetery Collection, ca. 1780-1980," https://goo.gl/a99PZT.
174. Harpswell Family History by DAR, Maine Historical Society, call no. H 236.5.
175. Harpswell Family History

nia[4] and Joseph[4].

Rebecca[4] Linscott (Hannah[3], William[2], James[1]) - wife of James Wilson II

Rebecca and James[4] (Samuel[3], William[2], James[1]) are delineated earlier in this chapter.

Moses[4] Linscott (Hannah[3], William[2], James[1])

The eldest son, Captain Moses[4] b.20 May 1785,[176] died in 1809 and was noted as lost at sea after marrying Mary Ridley and having one child, James A[5] b.1808 d.12 Oct 1866.[177] Mary remarried after her husband's death and moved to Durham.

I found a story that said James was adopted by Captain Stephen Sinnet of Orr's Island.[178] He did live and die on Orr's Island. In the tradition of island families, he and Mary Black b.23 May 1816 d.19 Sept 1889[179] had eleven children and only one of those died young. Nearly all of them had children. They were Harriett Lucinda[6], Moses Black[6], Mary Ellen[6], John Black[6], Martha Jane[6], Isaac[6], William Henry[6], Charles A[6], Isaac Orrin[6], and Hugh Sinnett[6]. Moses[6] and John[6] married Doughty sisters, one of whom died early and the other raised her children.

Lacronia[4] Linscott (Hannah[3], William[2], James[1])

Lacronia[4] b.1803 married Eveline and they had at least five children: Joseph[5], Martha[5], Benjamin[5], Eveline[5] and Harriet[5]. Eveline[5] was the only one I found children for. She was married twice and there were three children.

Isaac[4] Linscott (Hannah[3], William[2], James[1])

---

176. Harpswell Family History
177. Findagrave.com, gravestone, http://goo.gl/ONIfHY, accessed 18 May 2015.
178. Little, George Thomas, Genealogical and Family History of the State of Maine, 4 volumes (New York: Lewis Historical Publishing Company, 1909), II: 966.
179. Findagrave.com, http://goo.gl/CPQLTm, accessed 2 Aug 2015.

I was meticulously documenting all descendants and towards the end of the project, I met up with and bought Jeffrey Linscott's genealogy on CD.[180] That started a number of days of plowing through big families after big families. Isaac was my downfall. I found one really great descendant and knew I had to add her into the book so I'll start with Rattlesnake Kate McHale. Her house is actually been moved, piece by piece to a museum in Colorado. The story of how she got her name is pretty cool but there was more to her than that so be sure to read all about it here:
http://goo.gl/WfJBSF.

Not all of the descendants of Isaac[4] are that colorful but there are more pioneers and by the way, I do think that family was trying to populate the entire state of Maine! This is more like my southern families.

Isaac[4] went west to Parsonfield and they clustered in the area in towns like Cornish. The names - there are Days, Hubbards, Tripps, and Littlefields. Eventually I will add them all to the ancestry tree but it is going to take a while and I need to finish this book first.

Isaac[4] b.17 Oct 1795 d.1840 married Meribah Stuart b.1 Jun 1777 d.1870 had at least ten children: Sally[5], Noah[5] (4 children), Abram[5] (6), Meribah[5], Isaac[5], Mary Ann[5] (13), Susan[5] (11), Stephen[5] (6), Ballad[5] and Harriet[5] (8).

Joseph[4] Linscott (Hannah[3], William[2], James[1])

Joseph Linscott	*Mar 28 1805*	*Jan. 16 1870 (Brunswick, 484)*
Rebecca H. Gardner	*April 4 1810*	*Novr 21. 1842*
Frances A. Linscott	*May 13 1829*	
Charles C. "	*Decr 16 1831*	*Feby 6 1852*
Joseph O. "	*Oct 12 1833*	*Feby 13 1851*
William H "	*July 31 1838*	*June 26 1857*
Robert "	*Novr 18 1841*	*(d.17 June 1930 unc)*
Susan Foss 2nd Wife	*July 13 1803*	
James E. Linscott	*Novr 25 1847*	*April 30 1864*
Hiram H "	*April 6 1851*	*Sept 12 1851*
Esther B. Doughty 3rd Wife	*Augt 18 1807*	

180. Linscott, Jeffrey, The Linscott Family, Sam Teddy Publishing, http://goo.gl/bmphnR

Joseph's story is neatly told in the Brunswick records. He married three times and had children by two wives. I looked for a cause for all those young deaths and the only one I could pinpoint was Joseph O who burned to death in Portland. He was a seaman. Only one child lived to marry and have children, Frances A5, who had 6 children but possibly only one that married.

Elizabeth3 (William2, James1) - The Owens

Elizabeth [d. of William the eldest, the Innholder, and [ ] Larrabee, P.R.80.] and Thomas Owen, both of T., Sept. 22, 1789 (Topsham II, 284)
Thos Owens was born to them Sept 1st 1766 (Brunswick, 26)

Elizabeth married Thomas Owen who was the younger brother of Margaret Owen, her sister-in-law, William's wife. Elizabeth's birth date is unknown and she is one of two daughters not mentioned in William's will. Since Thomas was born in 1766, I doubt her birth was much before that. Her father died in August of that year so it is conceivable she could have been born as late as 1767. No death dates are known for either Elizabeth or Thomas. I cannot find any censuses for them at all. All of their children's birthdays (christening records actually) and marriages are recorded in Topsham.

The children were Jane4, Isabella4 and Gideon4.

Jane4 Owen (Elizabeth3, William2, James1) - The Staples

Jenny, ch. Thomas, bp. July 24, 1791, C.R.I. (Topsham I, 135)
Jane and Robert Stapel, Dec. 1,1811. [int. adds both of T.] (II, 187)
Robert, ch. Stephen and Susanna, May 6, 1788. (I, 174)

Robert Staples and Jane3 had five daughters and one son, Solon b.13 Mar 1812[181] d.9 March 1889.[182]

Though Solon married twice, he had no children that lived past infancy. Robert and Jane's daughters were Susan A3 b.10 May 1824[183] d.8 July 1831[184] and Isabell5 b.11 Aug 1829,[185] Elizabeth5 b.26 May

181. "Maine, Births and Christenings, 1739-1900," (https://goo.gl/CQynAT).
182. Findagrave.com, gravestone, http://goo.gl/RGB76V, accessed 19 May 2015.
183. "Maine, Births and Christenings, 1739-1900," (https://goo.gl/ebTFXG)
184. Findagrave.com, http://goo.gl/4ae0YG, accessed 2 Aug 2015.
185. "Maine, Births and Christenings, 1739-1900," (https://goo.gl/Dga4Cq).

1821,[186] Mary Eaton[5] and Margaret[5].

Margaret[5] Staples (Elizabeth[3], William[2], James[1]) - The Graves

Margaret[5] married Jacob Graves of Topsham.

Margaret [— — —], w. Jacob, Jr., Aug. 10,1815, in Bowdoinham. (Topsham I, 80)
Margaret M., w. Jacob, Oct. 18, 1890, G.R.I. [a. 76 y. 2 m., N.P.6.] (II, 327)
[Margaret M., 1814, G.R.I.] Jacob, Jr., of T. & Margarett Staple of Bowdnhm, int. Oct. 26, 1839. [cert, issued Nov. 18.] (II, 112)
Jacob, Jr., ch. Jacob and Fanny, Sept. 13, 1805, in T. [dup. h. Margaret.] (I, 79)
Jacob, July 8, 1884, a. 77 y. 10 m., G.R.I. (II, 326)

Almira R., ch. Jacob, Jr., and Margaret, Sept. 5, 1841, in T. (I, 78)
Almira R., June 29, 1843, in T. [d. Jacob and Margaret, June 29, 1842, a. 1 y. 10 m., G.R.I.] (II, 325)
Wilbur, [Wilson, in u.s.c] ch. Jacob, Jr., and Margaret, June 17, 1848, in T. (I, 81)
Wilbur F., s. Jacob and Margaret, Aug. 14, 1864, a. 16 y. 1 m., G.R.I. (II, 327)
Jane S., ch. Jacob, Jr., and Margaret, Sept. 6, 1845, in T. (I, 79)

In 1880 Jane was living at home with her mother and Ellen's family.[187] There is a grave in First Parish for a Jennie S Graves but the birth date is Sept 5, 1846.[188]

Ellen, ch. Jacob, Jr., and Margaret, Apr. 26, 1843, in T. (I, 79)
George M. & Ellen Graves, both of T., int. [cert, issued in 5 d. on Oct. 8, 1865.] (II, 112)
George M., ch. Andrew and Roxana, Aug. 8,1839, in T. (I, 79)

Ellen[6] and her first cousin, George M Graves, had one child, Carrie or Clara B b.abt 1868. The last time the three are found together is in 1900 in Topsham.[189] George died 18 Apr 1902 - he hung himself.[190] I simply was not able to find any other records for Ellen or Carrie/Clara. It's one of those mysteries I wish I could solve. I can see a suicide if both Ellen and Carrie had died first.

186. "Maine, Births and Christenings, 1739-1900," (https://goo.gl/SymO9P).
187. Year: 1880; Census Place: Topsham, Sagadahoc, Maine; Roll: 488; FHL Film: 1254488; Page: 193B; District: 151; Image: 0397.
188. Findagrave.com, http://goo.gl/e5A2u5.
189. Year: 1900; Census Place: Topsham, Sagadahoc, Maine; Roll: 599; Page: 4A; Enumeration District: 0217; FHL microfilm: 1240599
190. Maine State Archives; 1892-1907 Vital Records; Roll #: 23.

Mary Eaton[5] Staples (Jenny, Elizabeth[3], William[2], James[1]) - The Cahills

CAHILL, Andrew and Mary Staples, both of T., int. Oct. 8, 1849. [cert. Oct. 23.] (Topsham II, 59)

Mary Eaton[5] b.20 Jan 1826 d.18 Apr 1915[191] and Andrew b.11 Dec 1825 (Nova Scotia) d.31 Mar 1894 had their family in Bath. Three of their children married but had no children: Solon Staples b.1850 d.15 Dec 1912,[192] William A b.1854 d.1938[193] and Wilbur Graves b.1865 d.1944.[194] Those who married were Frances E[6], George Albion[6], Oceola[6], Jennie[6] and Frederick R[6].

Frances E[6] Cahill b.1852 married Charles Wholston b.abt 1845 d.aft 1925 and ended up dying in New York on 19 Jul 1926[195] where they had lived since at least 1892. They had two daughters, Clara Cora[7] b.22 Jun 1884 d.10 Aug 1965[196] and Elizabeth Blanche[7] b.1876 d.22 April 1964.[197] Both married and Elizabeth had three sons.

George Albion[6] Cahill b.abt 1858 married Eva Jane Duley b.1867 d.19 Dec 1941[198] and had four children, Elizabeth "Lizzie" M[7] b.6 Sep 1885 d.1 Aug 1969,[199] Eleanor D[7] b.abt 1888 d.aft 1940, Silie Mason[7] b.8 Oct 1890 d.23 Apr 1988[200] and George Albion[7] b.21 Feb 1903 d.4 Sep 1987.[201]

Oceola[6] Cahill b.abt 1860 d.23 Aug 1908[202] married Lucy Morse b.1860 d.1946[203] and had Charlotte E[7] b.1893 d.1979.[204]

Jennie[6] Cahill b.abt 1864 d.aft 1930 married John S Jackson b.abt

---

191. Findagrave.com, gravestone photograph, http://goo.gl/8W4RD3.
192. Maine State Archives; 1908-1922 Vital Records; Roll #: 8.
193. "Maine, Nathan Hale Cemetery Collection, ca. 1780-1980," (https://goo.gl/5hti0E).
194. Findagrave.com, gravestone, http://goo.gl/UlPxF0.
195. New York, New York, Death Index, 1862-1948 Ancestry.com.
196. Vermont State Archives & Records Administration; Montpelier, Vermont; Vermont Death Records, 1909-2008; User Box: PR-01776; Roll Number: S-31322; Archive Number: PR-1250-1251.
197. Maine Death Index, 1960-1997 Ancestry.com Operations Inc, 2002.
198. Bath, Maine, City Directory, 1949, Ancestry.com. U.S. City Directories, 1821-1989.
199. California, Death Index, 1940-1997 Ancestry.com Operations Inc, 2000.
200. Social Security Administration, Number: 004-07-3571; Maine; Before 1951.
201. Social Security Administration, Number: 141-07-4175; New Jersey; Before 1951.
202. Boston, 1909, U.S. City Directories, 1821-1989 Ancestry.com Operations, Inc., 2011.
203. Findagrave.com, http://goo.gl/tA69iZ.
204. Findagrave.com, gravestone, http://goo.gl/y28gsF.

1859 d.aft 1930 and had Corrine C[7] b.21 Oct 1894 d.9 Feb 1971.[205]

Frederick R[6] Cahill b.1868 d.1913[206] married Minnie Louise Hicks b.1869 d.4 Jun 1946[207] and they had three children, Ruth Marion[7] b.23 Dec 1892 d.4 Dec 1917[208] (TB), Andrew Russell[7] b.5 Mar 1898[209] d.aft 1950, and Charles Herbert[7] b.6 Jul 1870 d.4 Apr 1945.[210]

Isabella[4] Owen (Elizabeth[3], William[2], James[1]) - The Rogers

Isabel [ ], w. Hugh, May 30,1793, in Lisbon. (Topsham I, 161)
Isabella, ch. Thomas, bp. Nov. 24, 1793, C.R.I. (I, 134) christening record
Isabella, June 21, 1875, in T. [w. Hugh, a. 82 y., G.R.I.] (II, 374)

Isabella and Hugh Rogers, both of T., int. July 24, 1814. [cert, issued Aug. 11.] [Hugh, s. of Capt John & Jane (Potter), p.R.80.] [m. Aug. 18, in T.] (II, 187)

Hugh, ch. John and Jane Potter, Feb. 9, 1783. (I, 161) original record?
Hugh, h. Isabel, Feb. 9, 1785, in T. (I, 161) declared as an adult?

Hugh, Apr. 30, 1867, a. 82 y., G.R.I. [a. 82 y. 2 m., N.P.6.] (II, 374)

Julia H., ch. Hugh and Isabel, Apr. 5, 1815, in T. (I, 161) d.14 Nov 1885[211] buried with Hugh

Isabella[4] Owen and Hugh Rogers had eight children; only one, Julia Henry[5], never married. They were Almira[5], Martha F[5], Lucy Hunter[5], Eliza[5], Thomas,[5] Isabella[5] and Lucinda[5].

Lucinda Priscilla[5] Rogers (Isabella[4], Elizabeth[3], William[2], James[1]) - The Umberhines

Lucinda, ch. Hugh and Isabel, Feb. 19,1834, in T. (Topsham I, 161)
Lucinda P. of T. and Gorham Umberhine of Richmond, May 6, 1857, in Buffalo, N. Y., N.P.6. (II, 225)
Umberhind, Gorham, h. Lucinda R., May 6, 1831, G.R.4. (II, 192)

Charles A., s. Gorham and Lucinda P., Mar. 5, 1867, a. 8 y., G.R.4.

Lucinda and Gorham had eight children in Bowdoinham: Charles died in childhood and these either did not marry or have children:

---

205. Florida Death Index, 1877-1998 Ancestry.com Operations Inc, 2004.
206. Findagrave.com, gravestone, http://goo.gl/e1rhfp.
207. Bath, Maine, City Directory, 1949, U.S. City Directories, 1821-1989 Ancestry.com.
208. Maine State Archives; 1908-1922 Vital Records; Roll #: 25.
209. WWI, Registration State: Maine; Registration County: Sagadahoc; Roll: 1654016.
210. Findagrave.com, gravestone, http://goo.gl/pP0gIl.
211. Nathan Hale Cemetery Collection, ca. 1780-1980," (https://goo.gl/4Hg483).

Mary Belle[6] b.11 Mar 1861[212] d.1927,[213] Fred G[6] b.20 Mar 1864,[214] Merton[6] b.9 Apr 1869[215] d.1936[216] and Cleora Alice[6] b.31 Jul 1876[217] d.5 Dec 1941 (unc).

Carrie Minta[6] b.5 Mar 1871[218] d.1 Aug 1954[219] married Edward Elmer Wilson of Massachusetts; they had two children, Edward and Lauris. Virginia "Jennie" A[6] b.5 Mar 1873[220] married Walter Osband Gates and had three children (Betrina[7], Merton[7], Elmer[7]) and Cinda Eliza[6] b.29 Jul 1878 d.1 Nov 1947[221] had one child with Ralph Corydon Cutler, Frances Rogers[7] who never married.

Isabella[5] Rogers (Isabella[4], Elizabeth[3], William[2], James[1]) - The Douglasses

Isabella, ch. Hugh and Isabel, July 29, 1830, in T. (Topsham I, 161)
Isabella and Samuel Douglass, both of T., Dec. 25, 1865. [int. Samuel, Jr.] (II, 225)
Douglass, Samuel Jr., ch. Samuel & Esther, Oct. 14, 1819, in T. (I, 55)

Isabella[5] d.20 Oct 1910[222] and Samuel Douglas raised their daughter, Mary Belle, in Topsham but Isabella[5] moved to Brunswick after his death in 1888. They are buried together with Mary Belle[6] in the Rogers Cemetery in Topsham.[223] Mary Belle[6] b.26 Oct 1866[224] d.20 Oct 1893[225] married William Henry Cates (died WWII) but died of consumption at 26. They had one son, Archie[7] b.abt 1889.[226]

Eliza[5] & Almira[5] Rogers (Isabella[4], Elizabeth[3], William[2], James[1]) & Capt. Hardie

Almira, ch. Hugh and Isabel, Dec. 23, 1816, in T. (Topsham I, 160)

---

212. "Maine, Births and Christenings, 1739-1900," (https://goo.gl/24kcXe).
213. "Nathan Hale Cemetery Collection, ca. 1780-1980," (https://goo.gl/8uPe7T)
214. "Maine, Births and Christenings, 1739-1900," (https://goo.gl/tosErd).
215. "Maine, Births and Christenings, 1739-1900," (https://goo.gl/lqkOnU).
216. Findagrave.com, gravestone, http://goo.gl/oEFLvh, accessed 5 July 2015.
217. "Maine, Births and Christenings, 1739-1900," (https://goo.gl/ohC2i8).
218. "Maine, Births and Christenings, 1739-1900," (https://goo.gl/gfXB6G).
219. Connecticut Death Index, 1949-2012 Ancestry.com, # 12385.
220. "Maine, Births and Christenings, 1739-1900," (https://goo.gl/BbAHFy).
221. Gravestone, http://goo.gl/vd6uWf, accessed 5 July 2015.
222. Maine State Archives; 1908-1922 Vital Records; Roll #: 16
223. Findagrave.com, gravestone, http://www.findagrave.com/cgi-bin/fg.cgi?page=gr&GRid=35943734, accessed 5 July 2015.
224. Findagrave.com, http://goo.gl/v4Q9d3, accessed 23 Nov 2015.
225. Maine State Archives; 1892-1907 Vital Records; Roll #: 9
226. Year: 1900; Census Place: Brunswick, Cumberland, Maine; Roll: 589; Page: 2B; Enumeration District: 0037; FHL microfilm: 1240589.

Almira E., June 21, 1851, in T. [w. Capt. Charles F., G.R.4.] (II, 332)
Eliza, ch. Hugh and Isabel, July 6,1823, in T. (I, 160)
Almira E. of T. & Charles F. Hardie of Virginia, N.P.7. [Feb. 1, 1845.] (II, 124)
Eliza and Capt. Charles F. Hardie, both of T., Aug. 26, 1852. (II, 124)
Charles F., Capt., h. Almira E., Feb. 19, 1822, in Richmond, Va. (I, 90)
Charles F., 1855, [Capt. Hardie, h. Almira E., lost at sea 1856, G.R.4.] (II, 332)

Sea captain Charles Hardie married Almira[5] and then her sister, Eliza, after her death in 1851. Eliza never remarried after Charles was lost at sea six years later and died at age 93 on 3 Feb 1917.[227] Eliza and Charles did have one child, William Thomas d.1948 (unc) who did marry.

Thomas William, ch. Capt. Charles F. and Eliza, June 15, 1855,in T.

He, his wife, Clara Kimball b.15 Nov 1855 d.1945, and two children, Mary b.1 Dec 1886 d.Aug 1969[228] and George W b.May 1885 d.18 July 1887 were buried in the Topsham Rogers cemetery after residing in Bowdoinham.[229]

Martha[5] Rogers (Isabella[4], Elizabeth[3], William[2], James[1]) - The Adams

Martha, ch. Hugh and Isabel, Jan. 23, 1819, in T. (I, 162)
Martha F., w. Richard, Dec. 25, 1885, a. 66 y. 11 m., G.R.4. [a. 67 y. 11 m., N.P.6.] (II, 295)
Martha and Richard Adams, both of T., Dec. 17, 1848. (Topsham II, 226)
Richard, Jr., ch. Richard and Silence (Hunter), Nov. 28, 1818, in Charlestown, Mass. [dup. h. Martha F.] (I, 16)

Carrie, ch. Richard and Martha F., Feb. 19,1856, in T. (I, 14)
Carrie B., Oct. 11, 1891, a. 35, G.R.4. [in Augusta, of T., N.P. 6.] (295)
Lucinda R., ch. Richard and Martha F., May 7, 1854, in T. (Topsham I, 16) (15)
Lucinda R., Oct. 6, 1855, in T. [a. 1 y. 5 m., G.R.4.] [ch. Richard and Martha, P.R. I.] (295)

Three other children had children of their own, George S[6], Julia Maria[6] and Martha[6].

George S., ch. Richard and Martha F., July 14,1851, in T. (I, 15)

George S[6] Adams d.24 Apr 1898[230] had five children who did not marry with Marcia Ellen Thomas: Ellen Thomas[7] b.1858 d.1937,[231]

227. Maine State Archives; 1908-1922 Vital Records; Roll #: 25.
228. Social Security Administration, Number: 007-42-2859; Maine; 1960-1961.
229. "Nathan Hale Cemetery Collection, ca. 1780-1980," https://goo.gl/0a3UDd..
230. "Maine, Vital Records, 1670-1907 ," (https://goo.gl/8PWxnS).
231. Findagrave.com, gravestone, http://goo.gl/7FCCUG, accessed 23 May 2015.

Mary M b.Sept 1883,[232] Eunice[7] b.7 Apr 1891 d.Mar 1983,[233] Parker S[7] b.29 Sept 1895 d.2 Aug 1968[234] and Marcia[7] b.1 Sep 1889 d.aft 1940.

Julia Maria, ch. Richard and Martha F., Oct. 23, 1849, in T. (I, 15)
Julia M. [int. adds Miss] and William R. Hildreth, both of T., Nov. 7, 1872. (II, 35)

Julia Maria[6] Adams d.16 Mar 1925 and William Randall Hildreth b.21 Mar 1850 d.12 Jun 1931[235] had two boys, Edwin Randall[7] b.1 Mar 1879[236] d.28 Feb 1961[237] and George William[7] b.5 Jan 1875 d.Sep 1964.[238]

Martha R., ch. Richard & Martha F., June 10, 1858, in T. P.R.I. (II, 15)
Isaac A. of Brunswick and Martha R. Adams of T., int. June 19, 1882. [cert, issued June 24.] [d. Richard and Martha, P.R.I.] [m. June 27, T.R.4.] (II, 195)
Isaac A Pennell Augt 3 1852 (Brunswick, 540)

Martha[6] d.1943 and her husband, Isaac A Pennell d.1927[239] had two children, Elizabeth[7] b.2 Jul 1883 d.11 Feb 1966[240] and Harold[7] b.10 Mar 1891 d.8 Nov 1980.[241]

Lucy Hunter[5] Rogers (Isabella[4], Elizabeth[3], William[2], James[1]) - The Footes

Lucy H., ch. Hugh and Isabel, June 25, 1821, in T. (I, 162) d.6 May 1906[242]
Lucy H. of T. and Samuel W. Foote of New Orleans, La., May 28, 1844. (Topsham II, 225)

Parents	*Samuel W Foote*	*May 3 1889*		
	Lucy Rogers	*June 25 1821*		
Children	*Augusta J Foote*	*July 7 1844*	*d.14 Dec 1912[243]*	*unmarried*
	Hugh R	*May 17 1846*	*d.9 Feb 1847[244]*	*unmarried*
	Virginia M	*Jan[y] 4 1848*	*d.20 Sep 1922[245]*	*unmarried*
	Charles	*Jan 24 1850*		

232. Year: 1900; Census Place: Topsham, Sagadahoc, Maine; Roll: 599; Page: 3A; Enumeration District: 0217; FHL microfilm: 1240599.
233. Social Security Administration, Number: 004-20-4614; Maine; Before 1951.
234. Findagrave.com, gravestone photograph, http://goo.gl/NBdg1X.
235. Findagrave.com, gravestone, http://goo.gl/R9cpA5, accessed 23 May 2015.
236. WWI registration: Maine; Registration County: Sagadahoc; Roll: 1654016.
237. Maine Death Index, 1960-1997 Ancestry.com Operations Inc, 2002.
238. Social Security Adminstration, Number: 004-40-1298; Maine; 1956-1958.
239. Gravestone, http://goo.gl/D2xagw, accessed 23 May 2015.
240. "Maine Death Index, 1960-1996," (https://goo.gl/m1JVBp).
241. Findagrave.com, gravestone photograph, http://goo.gl/qmyfGJ.
242. "Maine, Vital Records, 1670-1907 ," (https://goo.gl/JE4Fms).
243. Maine State Archives; 1908-1922 Vital Records; Roll #: 19
244. "Maine, Deaths and Burials, 1841-1910," (https://goo.gl/xwbZK2).
245. Maine State Archives; 1908-1922 Vital Records; Roll #: 19.

Samuel	*Sept 1 1851*	
John A	*Jany 18 1854*	
Fred E	*April 14 1861*	*d.10 Jan 1917*[246]
Kattie	*Jany 30 1863*	*(Brunswick, 485)*

Samuel[6] Foote b.3 May 1818 d.29 Jul 1900[247] was a Bath native and not from New Orleans as the record states. They had seven children all born in Brunswick but they moved to Bath between 1870[248] and 1880.[249] The children who did marry and have children were Charles R[6], Samuel W[6] and John Alden[6].

Charles R[6] Foote d.11 Jan 1920[250] married Clara M Rowell b.Aug 1857.[251] They divorced prior to the 1900 census[252] in which are found their four children, Harry Samuel[7] b.Oct 1882[253] d.20 Jun 1908 of consumption,[254] Charles[7] b.21 Jun 1886[255] (1885?) d.12 Nov 1970,[256] Cora[7] b.2 Feb 1886 d.7 Apr 1974[257] and Edward Mallet[7] b.8 Oct 1891 d.Jul 1969.[258]

Samuel[6] Foote d.22 Feb 1928[259] married a Catherine and they had one son Fred b.6 Apr 1889 d.3 Jan 1965, a World War I veteran.[260] He was born in Washington State and was buried in Nashville, Tennessee.

---

246. Maine State Archives; 1908-1922 Vital Records; Roll #: 19.
247. Maine State Archives; 1892-1907 Vital Records; Roll #: 20
248. Year: 1870; Census Place: Brunswick, Cumberland, Maine; Roll: M593_539; Page: 106A; Image: 216; Family History Library Film: 552038
249. Year: 1880; Census Place: Bath, Sagadahoc, Maine; Roll: 488; Family History Film: 1254488; Page: 82B; Enumeration District: 145; Image: 0175
250. Maine State Archives; 1908-1922 Vital Records; Roll #: 19.
251. Year: 1900; Census Place: Bath, Sagadahoc, Maine; Roll: 599; Page: 14A; Enumeration District: 0211; FHL microfilm: 1240599.
252. Year: 1900; Census Place: Bath, Sagadahoc, Maine; Roll: 599; Page: 14A; Enumeration District: 0211; FHL microfilm: 1240599.
253. Year: 1900; Census Place: Bath, Sagadahoc, Maine; Roll: 599; Page: 14A; Enumeration District: 0211; FHL microfilm: 1240599.
254. Massachusetts, Death Records, 1841-1915 [database on-line]. Ancestry.com.
255. Social Security Administration, Number: 533-32-5513; Washington; 1951-1952.
256. Washington Death Index, 1940-1996 [database on-line]. Ancestry.com.
257. Social Security Administration, Number: 004-64-0414; Issue State:
258. Social Security Administration, Number: 003-30-1828; New Hampshire; Issue Date: 1956-1958.
259. "Washington, Death Certificates, 1907-1960," (https://goo.gl/MLVMPz).
260. National Cemetery Admin. US Veterans Gravesites, ca.1775-2006 Ancestry.com

John Alden[6] Foote b.18 Jan 1854[261] d.21 Jan 1933 (unc) married Anne Eleanor Tallman b.14 May 1865 d.21 Aug 1909.[262] They had Elmira Percy "Myra" b.28 Feb 1891 d.20 Dec 1990[263] and Eleanor Tallman b.11 Nov 1887 d.29 Sept 1965.[264]

Thomas[5] Rogers (Isabella[4], Elizabeth[3], William[2], James[1])

Thomas, ch. Hugh and Isabel, July 31, 1826, in T. [dup. h. Susan P.] (I, 162)
Thomas of T. and Susan P. Fisher of Winterport, Me., int. Jan. 22, 1866. (Topsham II, 226)

Thomas[5] Rogers d.19 Jun 1903 and Susan b.30 Nov 1840 d.18 Apr 1916[265] had five children.

Henry H., ch. Thomas and Susan P., Mar. 16, 1876, in T. (Topsham I, 161)
Cornelia M., ch. Thomas and Susan P., July 31, 1868, in T. (160)
Eugene, ch. Thomas and Susan P., Feb. 23, 1872, in T. (160)
Elmer, ch. Thomas and Susan P., June 3, 1879, in T. (160)
Robert, ch. Thomas and Susan P., May 11, 1882, in T. (162)

Robert F[6] Rogers died 25 Jun 1965 in Los Angeles.[266] He did marry but seems to have had no children just like his brother, Eugene[6] d.19 Aug 1922.[267] Cornelia[6] (George W Cothran) and Elmer George[6] d.1 Dec 1954 in Los Angeles[268] (Grace Phebe Salisbury) did marry and have children.

Gideon[4] (Elizabeth[3], William[2], James[1])

Gideon, ch. Thomas, bp. Aug. 2, 1795, C.R.I. (Topsham I, 134)

Gideon[4] Owen d.25 May 1876[269] and Amelia Emily Hood b.abt 1798 d.24 Jan 1870[270] raised their family in Leeds. Thomas Albion[5] b.3 Aug 1824 d.2 Oct 1834[271] was only ten when he died. The other three children, Jefferson Billings[5], Almeda[5], Roxana[5], and Ellen Eliza[5], lived to marry and have their own children.

---

261. "Maine, Births and Christenings, 1739-1900," (https://goo.gl/eBfBdu).
262. Findagrave.com, http://goo.gl/Y3IyHm, accessed 23 May 2015.
263. Social Security Administration, Number: 004-22-1744; Maine; Before 1951.
264. Findagrave.com, http://goo.gl/9JmorX, accessed 28 Oct 2015.
265. Findagrave.com, gravestone photograph, http://goo.gl/OwcAuZ.
266. California, Death Index, 1940-1997 Ancestry.com.
267. Maine State Archives; 1908-1922 Vital Records; Roll #: 48.
268. California, Death Index, 1940-1997 Ancestry.com Operations Inc, 2000.
269. Findagrave.com, gravestone: http://goo.gl/HCNFpj, accessed 19 April 2015.
270. Maine State Archives; Pre 1892 Delayed Returns; Roll #: 82.
271. Maine State Archives; Pre 1892 Delayed Returns; Roll #: 82.

Jefferson Billings[5] Owen (Gideon[4], Elizabeth[3], William[2], James[1])

Jefferson Billings[5] Owen b.12 Nov 1818 d.17 Sep 1866 was a carpenter and carriage builder.[272] He and his wife, Mary Hobbs Brown b.27 Feb 1824[273] d.12 Aug 1899,[274] had four children: Mary Ella[6] b.1848 d.28 Oct 1850,[275] Ella L[6] b.7 Sep 1851 d.5 May 1881[276] who married Francis Lang White from Candia, NH, but died at age 30, Georgia Jennie[6] b.19 Aug 1855 who also married Francis in 1894,[277] and Thomas Jefferson[6] b.27 Jan 1845 d.10 Sep 1908.[278]

Ella[6] and Francis produced one son, Frank Owen[7] b.24 Jul 1876[279] who married and had three children in Brookline, Massachusetts. Thomas Jefferson[6] married Julia F Boothby b.abt 1849 d.20 May 1903[280] and had three children also.

Almeda[5] Owen (Gideon[4], Elizabeth[3], William[2], James[1]) - The Jones

Almeda[5] Owen b.11 Jun 1821[281] d.11 Dec 1892[282] married James Niles Jones b.19 Feb 1818[283] d.1897.[284] They had Jeanette E[6], Loduscа Ellen[6], Ida Eldora[6] and Florence Eva[6].

Jeanette[6] Jones b.1842 d.1916[285] married twice; her first husband, Alonzo Brett, died three years after his youngest child's birth on 9 Aug 1868.[286] She then married Hannibal Thompson b.6 Jul 1823[287] d.4 Aug 1901[288] and had two more children. The Brett children

272. Maine State Archives; Pre 1892 Delayed Returns; Roll #: 82.
273. Maine State Archives; Pre 1892 Delayed Returns; Roll #: 13.
274. Findagrave.com, gravestone, http://goo.gl/heVXIy, accessed 5 July 2015.
275. "Nathan Hale Cemetery Collection, ca. 1780-1980," (https://goo.gl/24e3rn .
276. Maine State Archives; Pre 1892 Delayed Returns; Roll #:103.
277. Massachusetts, Marriage Records, 1840-1915 Ancestry.com Operations, Inc., 2013.
278. Findagrave.com, years only, http://goo.gl/7AsRxp
279. Massachusetts, Birth Records, 1840-1915 Ancestry.com Operations, Inc., 2013.
280. "Massachusetts, Deaths, 1841-1915," (https://goo.gl/MRu5xB).
281. "Maine Vital Records, 1670-1907 ", (https://goo.gl/184JIU)
282. Maine State Archives; 1892-1907 Vital Records; Roll #: 30.
283. Maine State Archives; Pre 1892 Delayed Returns; Roll #: 58.
284. Findagrave.com, http://goo.gl/kfaUsU, accessed 24 Aug 2015.
285. Findagrave.com, gravestone photograph, http://goo.gl/939ydp.
286. Maine State Archives; Pre 1892 Delayed Returns; Roll #: 12.
287. Maine State Archives; Pre 1892 Delayed Returns; Roll #: 97.
288. Maine State Archives; 1892-1907 Vital Records; Roll #: 56.

were Simeon James Brett[7] b.1863 d.1940[289] who had one child, Hazel Mary[8], with Caroline E Lamb b.1863 d.1916 and Etta May[7] Brett b.19 Nov 1865 (unc) d.28 April 1932[290] who married Virgil Greenleaf Verrill b.8 Apr 1878[291] buried 14 Oct 1932 and had one child. The Thompson children were William H[7] Thompson b.10 Oct 1871 d.1 Nov 1949[292] (3 children) and Ida Florence[7] Thompson b.4 June 1876 d.26 Jan 1955[293] who married Edward A Packard and had two children.

Ida Eldora[6] Jones b.1850 d.1935 married George W Moore and had two children, Vertie and George, Jr, but neither had children of their own. All worked in the shoe industry in Auburn.

Lodusca Ellen[6] Jones b.25 Aug 1844 d.8 Nov 1897[294] married Marcus Martin Keith b.16 June 1843 d.27 Apr 1917. They had three children, Martin Lee b.1864 d.1948,[295] Almanda "Medie" May b.abt 1869 and Linnie Elle b.abt 1878. All three married and had children.

Florence Eva Jones b.27 Nov 1856 d.10 Oct 1910 married Erlon Jerrus Mower b.27 Jun 1851 d.12 Sep 1918[296] and had seven children who in turn did have as many as sixteen children.

Roxanna[5] Owen (Gideon[4], Elizabeth[3], William[2], James[1]) & Alphonso Palmer Richmond

Roxanna[5] Owen b.17 Feb 1830[297] d.18 Feb 1911[298] married Alphonso Palmer Richmond b.1 Apr 1825 (unc) d.23 Dec 1891 (unc) and they had six children, Elva[6], James E[6], Sylvia E[6], William P[6], Dana Alphonse[6] and Belle G[6].

---

289. Findagrave.com, gravestone photograph, http://goo.gl/S47OUG.
290. "Faylene Hutton Cemetery Collection, ca. 1780-1990," (https://goo.gl/BVpYeO).
291. U.S., World War I Draft Registration Cards, 1917-1918, Maine.
292. Findagrave.com, gravestone photograph, http://goo.gl/8HLc7x.
293. Findagrave.com, gravestone photograph, http://goo.gl/wDM8yy.
294. Findagrave.com, gravestone photograph, http://goo.gl/iaQqZP
295. Findagrave.com, gravestone photograph, http://goo.gl/mMepQD
296. Findagrave.com, gravestone photograph, http://goo.gl/DfYYVt
297. Maine State Archives; Pre 1892 Delayed Returns; Roll #: 82.
298. Maine State Archives; 1908-1922 Vital Records; Roll #: 47.

Elva^{6} Richmond b.25 Jul 1848 (unc) d.27 Nov 1898[299] married Walter Herbert Snow and had one child, Eddie Elbridge^{7} Snow b.1 Jun 1883.[300] They lived in Somerset, Massachusetts. Eddie^{7} did marry and had two daughters.

James E^{6} Richmond b.12 May 1850 (unc) d.bef 1930 married Julia Rebecca Pettengill b.10 Dec 1855[301] d.bef 1940 and had three children, Harry E^{7} b.abt 1877, Leslie Abial^{7} b.7 Jul 1879,[302] Archie P^{7} b.14 May 1883 d.26 Sep 1966[303] and Alta Gertrude^{7} b.abt 1891. All of them lived past 1940.

Sylvia E^{6} Richmond b.14 Sep 1852 (unc) d.16 Nov 1909[304] married Herbert Lee Foster and had five children. They were Blanche Goodwin^{7} b.abt 1879, Henry Palmer^{7} b.29 Apr 1881,[305] Clifford F^{7} b.abt 1887, Myra Hood^{7} b.4 Sep 1890[306] d.18 Mar 1943[307] and Belle Richmond^{7} b.8 Jan 1896.[308]

William P^{6} Richmond b.12 Nov 1854 (unc) d.8 Jun 1908[309] married Ella Jane Norton b.abt 1854 d.11 Sep 1911[310] They had John Henry b.28 Nov 1875,[311] Samuel Sylvester b.14 Dec 1879,[312] Elva or Elvira A b.1879 d.1 Feb 1896 (consumption),[313] Owen b.30 May 1884[314] d.1940,[315] Guy b.25 Feb 1896[316] and Elsie b.abt 1881 d.6 May 1895.[317]

---

299. Massachusetts, Death Records, 1841-1915 Ancestry.com Operations, Inc., 2013.
300. WWI, Registration State: Mass; County: Middlesex; Roll: 1684686; Draft Board: 30.
301. Massachusetts, Birth Records, 1840-1915, Ancestry.com
302. WWI, U.S., World War I Draft Registration Cards, 1917-1918.
303. Findagrave.com, http://goo.gl/BDYoS9, accessed 25 Aug 2015.
304. Massachusetts, Death Records, 1841-1915 Ancestry.com Operations, Inc.
305. Maine State Archives; Pre 1892 Delayed Returns; Roll #: 39.
306. Massachusetts, Birth Records, 1840-1915, Ancestry.com.
307. Findagrave.com, http://goo.gl/WBy9EJ, accessed 25 Aug 2015.
308. Massachusetts, Birth Records, 1840-1915 Ancestry.com Operations, Inc.
309. Maine State Archives; 1908-1922 Vital Records; Roll #: 47.
310. Maine, Death Records, 1617-1922, Ancestry.com
311. "Maine Vital Records, 1670-1907 ", (https://goo.gl/1MYUTr).
312. "Maine Vital Records, 1670-1907 ", (https://goo.gl/xubjl0).
313. Maine State Archives; 1892-1907 Vital Records; Roll #: 48.
314. WWI, U.S., World War I Draft Registration Cards, 1917-1918.
315. Findagrave.com, http://goo.gl/D2YHLm, accessed 12 Oct 2015.
316. "Maine Vital Records, 1670-1907 ", (https://goo.gl/70Lqkq).
317. "Maine Vital Records, 1670-1907 ", (https://goo.gl/VnoZBH)5.

Dana Alphonse[6] Richmond b.11 Mar 1863 (unc) d.15 Mar 1915[318] married Corietta Francis "Etta" Timberlake b.8 Jan 1865 (unc) d.13 Jan 1939 (unc) had three: Linna Ellen b.4 Jan 1888 d.1 Jun 1952,[319] Walter Maynard b.27 Oct 1890[320] d.17 Jan 1947[321] and Floyd Marlon b.27 Jun 1897[322] d.1937.[323]

Belle Gertrude[6] Richmond b.22 Oct 1866 d.26 June 1943[324] married George Hinds b.29 Jul 1860 d.6 Sep 1941 and they had nine children.

Ellen Eliza[5] Owen (Gideon[4], Elizabeth[3], William[2], James[1]) & Granville Richmond

Ellen Eliza Owen b.20 Jan 1834 d.6 Sep 1866 married Granville Richmond b.19 May 1827 d.3 Apr 1889,[325] brother to Roxanna's husband. They had four children, Charles Granville b.29 Mar or Apr 1856 d.1 Aug 1923,[326] Frank Owen b.16 Apr 1854 d.25 Dec 1928,[327] Lucy Edna b.27 July 1852[328] d.13 Mar 1899[329] and Nellie b.abt 1858 d.30 Sept 1909.[330]

Isabella[3] (William[2], James[1]) & Elihu Purington

Isabella,w.Elder Elihu,d.Oct.13,1833 ae 76 y.g. r.20 (Bowdoinham, 94)
Isabella, d. William, the eldest, the innholder, & [-] Larrabee & w. of Rev. Elihu Purington of Bowdoinham, P.R.80. (Topsham II, 31)
Bellah of T. and Elihu Purintin of Bowdoinham, int. Nov. 30, 1788. (II, 283)
Elihu, Elder, h. Isabella d. July 20, 1846 a.e. 79 y. g. r. 20 (Bowdoinham, 94)

Isabella Wilson married a Purington just like her brother, Samuel, and her nieces.

---

318. Maine State Archives; 1908-1922 Vital Records; Roll #: 47.
319. Findagrave.com, gravestone photograph, http://goo.gl/kvDRLA.
320. WWI: Maine; Registration County: Androscoggin; Roll: 1653901; Draft Board: 2.
321. New Hampshire, Death & Burial Records Index, 1654-1949 Ancestry.com.
322. Maine State Archives; 1892-1907 Vital Records; Roll #: 48.
323. "Nathan Hale Cemetery Collection, ca. 1780-1980," (https://goo.gl/Db9wd8).
324. Findagrave.com, gravestone for both, http://goo.gl/rkoc81.
325. Findagrave.com, http://goo.gl/9miA1N, accessed 25 Aug 2015.
326. Findagrave.com, http://goo.gl/nJSvtD, 25 Aug 2015.
327. Findagrave.com, http://goo.gl/2qEv8s, accessed 25 Aug 2015.
328. "Maine Vital Records, 1670-1907 ", (https://goo.gl/931Sgi)
329. Massachusetts, Death Records, 1841-1915 Ancestry.com Operations, Inc.
330. "Massachusetts Deaths, 1841-1915," (https://goo.gl/7kaymM).

James, s. Elder Elihu and Isabella,d.Nov.20,1821 ae 21 y.g.r.20 (Bowdoinham, 94)

In addition to James, this Bowdoinham family supposedly included William b.19 Mar 1790,[331] Hannah b.1 Jan 1793 and Elizabeth b.24 Jul 1796. Isabella's tombstone listed her age as 76 making her birth year about 1757 and years younger than Elihu b.1767.[332] She, Elihu and son James are all buried in a family cemetery along with Humphrey and Rebecca Wilson, her niece and husband.[333] More on the Purintons and how that family is entwined with the Wilsons can be found in the previous chapter.

Hannah may have married a John Sedgely[334] though I have only a marriage record and no confirming data. I simply cannot find any other information on the other siblings and they are not buried with their parents but their son, Isaac[4], did marry and was buried with them.

Isaac[4] Purington (Isabella[3], William[2], James[1])

Isaac[4] Purington b.9 Jan 1794[335] married Rachel Pennell of Topsham on 16 Mar 1822.[336]

Isaac, h.Rachel, d.June 6, 1871 g.r.20 (Bowdoinham, 94)
[ ], d. Stephen, Mar. 7, 1794, C.R.I. (140) Rachel's birth?
Rachel, w.Isaac, d.Nov,26,1846 g.r.20 (94)
Rachel of T. & Isaac Purinton of Bowdoinham, Apr. 4, 1822. (Topsham II, 194)

They had Humphrey[5] b.12 May 1831[337] d.1832 and Clarissa[5] b.2 Jul 1826[338] who last appears in the 1850 census at age 22 and two other children who married, William James[5] and Esther Chamberlain[5].

Isaac[4] appears to have remarried after Rachel's death in 1846 as there is a Betsey b.abt 1804 with him in the census of 1850[339] but she

331. "Maine, Births and Christenings, 1739-1900," (https://goo.gl/EIzsDp)
332. Maine Cemetery Association, Sagadahoc County, Purinton Cemetery.
333. Bowdoinham Historical Society, http://goo.gl/1cBgLC, accessed 7 Feb 2015.
334. "Maine, Marriages, 1771-1907," (https://goo.gl/TChHcG)
335. "Maine, Births and Christenings, 1739-1900," (https://goo.gl/cyFjs8).
336. "Maine, Marriages, 1771-1907," (https://goo.gl/M6qA2z)
337. "Maine, Births and Christenings, 1739-1900," (https://goo.gl/AS2oJC).
338. "Maine, Births and Christenings, 1739-1900," (https://goo.gl/bvQE9g).
339. Year: 1850; Census Place: Bowdoinham, Lincoln, Maine; Roll: M432_261; Page: 315A; Image: 418

is not in the 1860 census.[340]

William James[5] Purington (Isaac[4], Isabella[3], William[2], James[1])

As a post office employee, William[5] Purington b.16 Apr 1823 d.13 Jul 1894[341] was one of those few who left Maine in the 1800s. He married Mary Quint b.7 Sept 1820 d.19 Sept 1908[342] on 12 October 1848[343] in Somerset County. In 1860 he and his wife are living in Washington, D.C., and his profession is listed as clergyman.[344] In 1870 he's in Southampton, PA,[345] and in 1880 he's moved to Hopewell, NJ,[346] where he died in 1894. They had no children.

Esther Chamberlain[5] Purington (Isaac[4], Isabella[3], William[2], James[1]) & Carlton Lancaster

Esther C , a. 30 y., of Brunswick, 1st. m., d. of Isaac, b. Bowdoinham, farmer; mother, Rachel Purinton, b. Bowdoinham; and Carleton Lancaster, a. 28 y., soldier, 1st m., Bowdoinham; mother, Maria Lancaster, b. Bowdoinham; father, Ebenezer, farmer, b. Bowdoinham, int. Sept. n , 1864-5. [m. Sept. 11, 1864, in T., N.P.6.] (Topsham II, 208)

Esther[5] Purington b.17 May 1834 (unc) married Carlton Lancaster b.10 May 1836[347] d.3 Feb 1917[348] but unfortunately their only child did not survive, dying on 4 Apr 1880 and her mother then dying less than a week later on 10 Apr 1880.[349]

Mary Isabella[5] Purington (Isaac[4], Isabella[3], William[2], James[1]) - The Cummings

Parents	*Amaza Cumming*	*Decr 27 1822 (Brunswick, 411)*
	Mary I Purrington his wife	*April 18 1837*

340. Year: 1860; Census Place: Brunswick, Cumberland, Maine; Roll: M653_437; Page: 112; Image: 949; Family History Library Film: 803437

341. Findagrave.com, gravestone photograph, http://goo.gl/U10UdK.

342. Findagrave.com, gravestone, http://goo.gl/51lPJo, accessed 23 May 2015.

343. "Maine, Marriages, 1771-1907," (https://goo.gl/hyqqUe).

344. Year: 1860; Census Place: Washington Ward 3, Washington, District of Columbia; Roll: M653_102; Page: 747; Image: 538; Family History Library Film: 803102.

345. Year: 1870; Census Place: Southampton, Bucks, Pennsylvania; Roll: M593_1314; Page: 694B; Image: 522; Family History Library Film: 552813.

346. Year: 1880; Census Place: Hopewell, Mercer, New Jersey; Roll: 788; Family History Film: 1254788; Page: 61D; Enumeration District: 092; Image: 0124.

347. "Maine, Births and Christenings, 1739-1900," (https://goo.gl/p85v2i).

348. Findagrave.com, gravestone photograph, http://goo.gl/4k0JMv.

349. Findagrave.com, gravestone photograph, http://goo.gl/LFUdZy.

Levoy Cummings	*Feby 13 1860*
Francis	*March 3 1862*

Mary[5] Purington d.20 Dec 1914[350] married Amasa F Cummings of Brunswick, a Civil War veteran. They had two children born in Maine, Leroy[6] d.9 Mar 1944[351] and Francis F[6], and then they moved to California after 1880. He was farming in 1880 so it is a curiosity why he moved his family to California. Neither son seems to have married, having lived with their mother until her death and together after that.[352] That 1930 census is the last trace of Francis.

John[3] (William[2], James[1])

John was the youngest son and as my fourth great grandfather, he gets special treatment in "John Wilson, Such a Common Name".

---

350. Member & Institutional Collections Ancestry.com Operations, Inc., 2011.
351. California, Death Index, 1940-1997 Ancestry.com Operations Inc, 2000.
352. Year: 1930; Census Place: National City, San Diego, California; Roll: 190; Page: 6A; Enumeration District: 0045; Image: 1024.0; FHL microfilm: 2339925.

Mary Wilson & The Hinkleys

Mayflower Descendants

The Hinkleys from Mary Wilson's family at least left the state and even New England - a not common occurrence for the Scotch Irish families - but that looks more like my English descendant families who arrived in Virginia at about the same time.

It is through the Hinkley line (though not through Mary's husband, Elnathan) that my family are Mayflower descendants as my sixth great-grandmother, Reliance Hinkley, was a William Brewster descendant.

The original Hinkley ancestor was Thomas Hinckley, born in Kent, England, the last Governor of the united Plymouth colony.[1] Note the spelling of the name; I believe that the children of Reliance and Edmund only used Hinkley as I actually find no instances of their using the c. Other Hinckleys that moved into Maine seemed to have used the c and one can find references in Maine today with it.

Elnathan Hinkley's father was Edmund Hinkley of Massachusetts, a prominent family in that state.[2] Edmund was the great grandson of Thomas Hinckley and sister to Reliance. That makes Elnathan and Mary distant cousins - and makes me related to both of them!

Other Hinkleys in the Wilson family

Descendants of two of Elnathan's brothers, Lemuel and Samuel, also married into the Wilson family in later generations. Harriet Stover (Lois[3], Lemuel[2], Edmund[1]) married Captain Edmund Wilson b. 1822 (David[4], James[3], Alexander[2], James[1]). Bethia Hinkley b.1800 (Samuel[2], Edmund[1]) married Charles Alexander b.1797 (William[4], James[3], William[2], James Wilson[1]).

Last but definitely not least is a marriage of major consequence to my family is the marriage of Reliance Hinkley b.21 Nov 1714 who

1. Thomas Hinkley, https://goo.gl/Bt2CF0, accessed 22 April 2014.
2. Roser, Susan E. Mayflower Births and Deaths: From the Files of George Ernest Bowman at the Massachusetts Society of Mayflower Descendants. Volumes 1 & 2. Baltimore, MD: Genealogical Publishing Company, Inc., 1992, 227.

married James Thompson b.22 Feb 1707. Their son, General Samuel Thompson, is the father of Rachel Thompson who married John Wilson (William[2], James[1]), my fourth great grandfather.

Mary[3] (William[2], James[1])

William's daughter Mary's birth date has to be before Oct 1762 because she is mentioned in her father's will of that date. The 1800 census says she could have been born as early as 1755[3] but her siblings were born Jan of '55, Jan of '57, and one possibly later in '57 making a birth year of after 1758 be more likely.

Mary and Elnathan Hinkley, Mar. 25, 1782. [int. adds he of Brunswick, she of T.] (Hill II, 287)

Elnathan Hinkly born to them January 19th 1749 (Brunswick, 25)

The census records tell the story of another family who raised their children in Topsham, Maine. Elnathan appears in every census from 1790 to 1810. In both 1790 and 1800 he was the head of the only Hinkley family. In 1810, his son, William[4] b.1 Aug 1782[4], also appears alongside his father. Elnathan Hinkley is gone from Topsham census data by 1820 as is William[4] who had moved away.

In 1794 he was one of the founders of the Baptist Religious Society in Topsham. He and several of his wife's family were designated by the Massachusetts General Court as part of this society along with Ebenezer Farrin (Hugh Wilson's son-in-law), John Wilson[3] (brother-in-law), Humphrey Thompson (John Wilson's brother-in-law) and James Purinton (father of two children who married into the Wilsons) and Hugh Wilson[3] (cousin). That same church invited Elihu Purington (John Wilson's brother-in-law) to preach in 1797.[5]

The 1790 census lists one adult male, three boys under 16 and two girls. One boy died soon after:

"[----], s. Elnathan, Jan. 20, 1792, a. 16 m., C.R.I." (Hill II, 335)

By 1800 there are two boys, William[4] and Samuel[4], and two girls,

3. Year: 1800; Census Place: Topsham, Lincoln, Maine; Series: M32; Roll: 6; Page: 489; Image: 459; FHL Film: 218676

4. Rootsweb, documented work by Frederick R. Boyle, Springville, ME, http://goo.gl/3HjBSN accessed 17 March 2014.

5. Wheeler, 420.

one 10 to 15, Betsey[4], and one 16 to 25.[6] The grown woman is listed as being born between 1755 and 1775, making Mary's birth year between 1755 and 1762 (date of her father's will). The 1810 census has an additional Hinkley, Ezekial, but Elnathan's family does not have an older woman, only 2 women between 16 and 45 which would be the two daughters and Mary is not there. I don't know whether the other daughter has died (there's no record of her after this) and Mary's age is wrong or if Mary wasn't there to be counted. There is one son still at home under 26, Samuel[4], and one girl under 16, Betsey[4].

There is a Lincoln County deed 131:354 that names William[4] and Elnathan as father and son:

> *William Hinkley of Sangerville, with wife Rachel Hinkley, conveyed to Benjamin Thompson of Topsham, 26 February 1825, all his right to land in Topsham "at the northerly end of the bridge in the highway on the western branch of the Cathance River ... formerly owned by my father Elnathan Hinkley, late of Topsham, deceased*

Another deed exists 6 April 1824 from Samuel but that does not list his father. (15:224)

Elnathan died prior to January 1812[7] but the location of either his or Mary's grave is unknown. Mary died between February 1812 and February 1813 when their son, Samuel[4], was appointed administrator of Elnathan's will. (Lincoln County Probate 16:53)

The inventory of his estate includes a homestead farm with 100 ($1633) and another 110 acres "commonly called William's Farm ($500). I want to assume that means that was on William the Eldest's original farm. He had oxen, a steer, 4 yearlings, 14 sheep, 2 lambs, a goat and 3 pigs. There were 5 beds, 4 spinning wheels, dining room table, 3 common tables and 2 chests. (19:136)

The distribution of the monies from his estate totaling $493.64 were divided equally between Samuel[4], William[4] and Elizabeth[4] (Betsey). (19:236)

6. Year: 1800; Census Place: Topsham, Lincoln, Maine; Series: M32; Roll: 6; Page: 489; Image: 459; FHL Film: 218676.
7. Lincoln County Probate, vol 15, page 415-416.

What I also found interesting was who Elnathan owed at his death: David Douty $3.25, Dr. Isaac Lincoln $13.50, Moses Plummer $17.75, Moses Waymouth $17.12, Robert Sayer $7.72, James Purrinton Jr for taxes $2.90, James Purrinton Jr note $20.00, James Jameson $8.50. I believe James Purrinton was the town clerk and of course Dr. Lincoln is a recognizable name but none of the other names show up in the family tree or in my research. I haven't looked for them specifically.

Samuel Hinkley[4] (Mary[3], William[2], James[1])

Samuel[4] was born about 1788. The deed from 1824 does not mention his relationship with Elnathan so the Hill notation below is the only indication that he is Elnathan's other son. But coupled with being the administrator of Elnathan's will and getting part of the estate, the connection is firm.

Samuel, under "head of family of Elnathan," a. 22 y., in 1810, L.V. (Hill I, 96)

Unfortunately, Samuel is a common Hinkley first name and though I can find several possible marriages, there seems to be no way to know who or even if he married. There is, however, a Samuel Hinkley in the 1820[8] census with a teenage son and two females. A deed from 1822 shows that he is still living in Topsham (Lincoln County 120:71 - his sister, Betsey[4], sells to Samuel[4]). That is, however, the last trace of him that I found that had his location but there missing deeds.

Elizabeth "Betsey" Hinkley[4] (Mary[3], William[2,] James[1]) & James Alexander

Betsy, under "head of family of Elnathan," [----], L.V. (Hill I, 96)
Betsey of T. and James Alexander of Bowdoin, int. Sept. 1, 1821. [cert. Sept. 16.] (Hill II, 133)

Betsey[4] b.1783 d.21 July 1857[9] married sea captain James Alexander b.1787 d.27 Oct 1856[10] on 16 Sept 1821[11] and raised her family in Bowdoin. He was actually a cousin of hers, a great-grandchild of

8. 1820 U S Census; Census Place: Topsham, Lincoln, Maine; Page: 156; NARA Roll: M33_36; Image: 92.
9. Findagrave.com, gravestone photograph, http://goo.gl/T1F0GE.
10. Findagrave.com, gravestone photograph, http://goo.gl/TJY45D.
11. "Maine, Marriages, 1771-1907," (https://goo.gl/HKW25h)

Jennet Wilson Alexander[2]. They had one daughter, Mary E[5] b.1824 d. 2 Sep 1891.[12] There's more on the Alexanders in "William & Jennet Alexander in Harpswell" on page 335.

Mary E[5] married her cousin, son of William[4], Thatcher Thomas Hinkley[5]. Her family is delineated in the next section below.

William Hinkley[4] Hinkley (Mary[3], William[2], James[1])

William b.1 Aug 1782[13] d.16 Mar 1846[14] married Rachel Patten b.12 Jun 1787.[15] Rachel was the daughter of John Patten and Sarah Wiswell of York and not a Topsham Patten.[16] They were in Topsham for the 1810 census but the oldest child, Sally, was born in Sangerville the year before.[17]

William and Rachel Patten, both of T., int. Dec. 3, 1808. [cert. Dec. 31.] (Hill II, 134)

They had nine children, Sarah "Sally" Wiswell[5], John Patten[5], Mary Wilson[5], Henry William Smith[5], Increase Sumner[5], Thatcher Thomas[5], Betsey[5], Roxana[5], Rachel Ann[5], Betsey A[5], and Eunice D[5].

William is buried in Parkman; his gravestone spells his name as Hinckley.

Thatcher Thomas[5] Hinkley (William[4], Mary[3], William[2], James[1])

Thatcher Thomas[5] b.4 Aug 1818[18] or Thomas T, married Mary E. Alexander (Betsey[4], Mary[3], William[2], James[1]), his first cousin. They were living with James and Elizabeth Alexander at the time of the census in 1850.[19]

12. Findagrave.com, gravestone, http://goo.gl/IaRSAl, accessed 25 April 2015.
13. Spragues Journal of Maine History, vol 2 # 3 pages 164-170, July 1914, Sangerville, Maine Vital Records.
14. "Maine, Deaths and Burials, 1841-1910," (https://goo.gl/keAm4h).
15. "Maine, Births and Christenings, 1739-1900," (https://goo.gl/ENF4QB)
16. Boyle, rootwebs, http://goo.gl/3HjBSN accessed 17 March 2014.
17. Year: 1810; Census Place: Topsham, Lincoln, Maine; Roll: 12; Page: 8; Image: 00016; Family History Library Film: 0218683
18. "Maine, Births and Christenings, 1739-1900," (https://goo.gl/Xeujtw).
19. Year: 1850; Census: Bowdoin, Lincoln, Maine; Roll: M432_261; Page: 328B: 445.

Thomas died three years after Mary on 31 July 1884.[20] The death certificate and the 1880 Bowdoin census lists farmer as his occupation.[21] They had two daughters.

Isabella S., w. Ivory, Aug. 14, 1846, G.R.3. (Bowdoin I, 21)
Ivery T. and Sarah Isabell Hinkley, both of B., int. Oct. 26, 1863. (Bowdoin III, 12)
Ivory, h. Isabella S., Feb. 4, 1836, G.R.3. (I, 21)

Their oldest daughter, Isabella Sarah[6] d.1 May 1914, married Ivory Temple Allen d.26 May 1900.[22] Ivory was a civil war veteran who had only been in the service for a few months when he was mustered out on 23 Sep 1861.[23] He died at the disabled soldiers home in Togus so he was probably wounded in the war. They had four children: Everett L[7] b.1865 d.1940, Eben T[7] b.1872 d.17 Mar 1930, Mary Belle[7] b.3 Jan 1893[24] and Edwin T[7] b.1893 d.1893. All three of the boys are memorialized together in the same cemetery where their parents are buried.

I found records for what I believe is Everett's marriage and children but I don't have proof they are correct. He settled in Litchfield and had a number of children. Eben[7] seems to have not married. Mary Bell[7] did marry and had at least one child.

Ella, Aug. 15, 1852, P.R.17. (Bowdoin I, 22)
Ella A., w. Daniel A., Oct. 31, 1899, a. 47 y., G.R.3. (II, 48)
Combs, Daniel A. & Ella Hinkley, of B., Feb. 9, 1870, P.R.17. (Bowdoin III, 42)
Daniel A., ch. Daniel and Emily (Allen), Aug. 15, 1850, P.R.17. (I, 53)

Verson D., ch. Daniel A. & Ella A. (Hinkley), May 18, 1871. [ch. Daniel A. and first w. Ella A. (Hinkley), in B., P.R.17.] (I, 63)

Ella A[6] Hinkley married Daniel Allen Coombs d.29 Nov 1938[25] and had two children, Verson D[7] b.1870 d.1941[26] who married Lillian B Hogan on 31 May 1891[27] and had one child, Mary Emily[7] b.1878

20. Maine State Archives; 1892-1907 Vital Records; Roll #: 27.
21. Year: 1880; Census Place: Bowdoin, Sagadahoc, Maine; Roll: 488; FHL: 1254488; Page: 98B; Enumeration District: 146; Image: 0206.
22. Findagrave.com, gravestone, http://goo.gl/o5Fa2J, accessed 25 March 2015.
23. Historical Data Systems, comp. U.S., Civil War Soldier Records and Profiles, 1861-1865 Ancestry.com.
24. "Maine, Vital Records, 1670-1907," (https://goo.gl/2gDk7h).
25. Findagrave.com, gravestone for year, http://goo.gl/IQDqN5, accessed 25 Mar 2015.
26. Findagrave.com, gravestone, http://goo.gl/Zw41ML, accessed 25 March 2015.
27. "Maine, Marriages, 1771-1907," (https://goo.gl/CT1NZ4).

d.1942[28] who married Everett E Rogers b.1868 d.1930[29] and had at least five children.

John Patten[5] Hinkley (William[4], Mary[3], William[2], James[1])

John[5] b.11 Mar 1811[30] married Eunice Libbey b.abt 1813 on 2 Dec 1835[31] and they had three children according to censuses of 1850 and 1860: Sarah[6] b.abt 1838, Thomas P[6], and George F[6]. He married again on 10 July 1869[32] to Joann Savage Williams b.1811 d.11 March 1890.[33] He was a ship carpenter. Joann's gravestone has Hinkley spelled with a c. I do not know his death date or where he is buried.

His son, George F[6] b.26 Dec 1835,[34] lists an occupation of sailor in that same 1860 census.[35] He married an Eliza Luce from New Brunswick, Canada, on 30 Aug 1863.[36] She had a daughter (so Luce may have been her married name). They had no other children. They last appeared in the 1880 census.[37]

Thomas P[5] b.abt 1841 d.30 Dec 1908[38] also married. He was a Civil War veteran, having served from 1861 to 1865[39] who may not have had children. There are no records between 1870 with his wife and his entry into Togus in 1906. His wife had remarried by 1880 so I assume they divorced. I did find a record for a Thomas Hinkley in Boston - in jail - in 1900 but I cannot be sure it's him. The information matches well enough so that I believe it is him. He is buried in the Togus Cemetery.

---

28. Findagrave.com, gravestone, http://goo.gl/OTEUWN
29. Findagrave.com, gravestone, http://goo.gl/GjoEPH, accessed 25 March 2015.
30. "Maine, Births and Christenings, 1739-1900," (https://goo.gl/EQRk2K).
31. "Maine, Marriages, 1771-1907," (https://goo.gl/XaC37K).
32. "Maine, Marriages, 1771-1907," (https://goo.gl/D5Stke) .
33. Findagrave.com gravestone, http://goo.gl/2m9Wto, accessed 25 March 2015.
34. "Maine, Births and Christenings, 1739-1900," (https://goo.gl/XryUJq).
35. Year: 1860; Census Place: Hampden, Penobscot, Maine; Roll: M653_447; Page: 1; Image: 308; Family History Library Film: 803447
36. "Maine, Marriages, 1771-1907," (https://goo.gl/G7KIRl).
37. Year: 1880; Census Place: Hampden, Penobscot, Maine; Roll: 486; FHF: 1254486; Page: 317C; District: 035; Image: 0235.
38. National Cemetery Admin. U.S. Veterans Gravesites, ca.1775-2006 Ancestry.com.
39. Historical Data Systems, comp. Civil War Soldier Records, 1861-1865 Ancestry.com

Henry William Smith[5] Hinkley (William[4], Mary[3], William[2], James[1])

Henry[5] b.30 Aug 1814 d.16 Aug 1893 married Laura E Webster b.30 Apr 1834 d.7 Apr 1909[40] on 22 June 1847[41] and later moved to Minnesota before dying in South Dakota. He moved to Wisconsin in between the births of two of his children around 1850. His children were Adrienne[6], Augustus Henry[6], Matilda[6], Charles[6] b.abt 1856, Clara Roxana[6] b.Nov 1857, Betsey Alice[6], William L[6] b.abt 1862 and Frank[6] b.abt 1867. The children's children did not stay put, moving on to other western states such as Washington, Idaho, Iowa, and California.

Adrienne[6] b.1849 d.30 Nov 1930[42] was born in Maine. She and her husband, William Leo, had moved to Idaho by 1900[43] and to Oregon by 1910.[44] They had six children, Cora May[7] b.abt 1869, William "Willie" Bradley[7] b.25 Feb 1873[45] d.12 Apr 1928,[46] Bert L[7] b.abt 1872 d.29 May 1942,[47] Maud[7] b.3 May 1876,[48] Dolly[7] b.1880 and Edna[7] b.7 May 1891.[49] William[7] is the only one that I could find a marriage and children for.

Henry Augustus[6] b.12 Jan 1850 (Wisconsin) d.8 Dec 1904 (South Dakota) married Harriet L Davis b.28 Jul 1857 d.1943 and had two children, Blanche L[7] b.11 Jun 1882 d.28 Jul 1951[50] and James Ray[7] b.25 Dec 1888 d.10 Sep 1952.[51] Some dates were supplied and cannot be confirmed if no footnote exists.

---

40. Findagrave.com, gravestone photograph, http://goo.gl/l26c8t.
41. Maine Marriages, 1771-1907," (https://goo.gl/znj8NE).
42. Oregon State Library; Death Index 1921-1930 Begin-A; .
43. Year: 1900; Census Place: Boise Ward 1, Ada, Idaho; Roll: 231; Page: 5A; Enumeration District: 0001; FHL microfilm: 1240231.
44. Year: 1910; Census Place: Portland Ward 10, Multnomah, Oregon; Roll: T624_1287; Page: 9B; Enumeration District: 0232; FHL microfilm: 1375300.
45. Minnesota, Marriages Index, 1849-1950 Ancestry.com Operations, Inc., 2011.
46. Minnesota, Death Index, 1908-2002 Ancestry.com Operations Inc, 2001.
47. Oregon State Library; Oregon Death Index Km-Z; Year Range: 1942-1950.
48. Minnesota, Births and Christenings Index, 1840-1980 Ancestry.com.
49. Washington State Archives; Olympia, Washington; Washington Births, 1891-1919; Film Info: Various county birth registers.
50. Minnesota, Death Index, 1908-2002 Ancestry.com Operations Inc, 2001.
51. California, Death Index, 1940-1997 Ancestry.com Operations Inc, 2000.

Matilda "Till" L^{6} b.abt 1853 d.10 Nov 1899[52] married Richard Wilkins b.abt 1851 on 30 Nov 1877[53] and adopted a son, George Borst^{7}, b.abt 1872. Clara Roxana^{6} b.abt 1857 d.aft 1915 married David Davis and had two children, May^{7} b.26 Dec 1879[54] and Lester Myron^{7} b.23 Dec 1881 d. 23 Dec 1969.[55]

Betsey Alice^{6} b.26 Aug 1859[56] d.5 Jan 1922 married Adelbert Davis b.2 July 1860 d.17 Jul 1926.[57] They had four children, Ray James^{7} b.19 Feb 1890 d.9 Aug 1951,[58] Frank^{7} b.5 Jan 1885 d.2 Nov 1931, Olive^{7} b.6 Nov 1895 d.28 May 1986[59] and William McKinley^{7} b.20 Sep 1897[60] d.20 May 1920.

William L^{6} b.abt 1862 who married Grace Leona Patterson b.abt 1863 had one daughter, Verna^{7} b.13 Apr 1890 d.13 Jul 1981.[61] Frank^{6} b.abt 1867 married Mary Winser b.abt 1866 in 1895[62] and had seven children in South Dakota: Henry H^{7}, Fred^{7}, Ross^{7}, Frank^{7}, Alice^{7}, Lora^{7} and Mary^{7}.

Increase Sumner Hinkley^{5} (William^{4}, Mary^{3}, William^{2}, James^{1})

Sumner^{5} b.19 Aug 1816[63] d.11 Mar 1902[64] married an Elizabeth Curtis, b.abt 1818. They had two children, Elenora, Elnora or Nora^{6} b.31 Jul 1862[65] and Frank Edgar^{6} b.17 Jan 1864.[66] Frank^{6} married twice: to Minnie Emily Kendall on 3 Sep 1889[67] and to Anna Meddieux Hast-

52. Findagrave.com, http://goo.gl/vv7h3M, accessed 4 Aug 2015.
53. Minnesota, Marriages Index, 1849-1950 Ancestry.com Operations, Inc., 2011.
54. "Minnesota, Births and Christenings, 1840-1980," (https://goo.gl/h9p3LN).
55. Social Security Administration, Number: 333-20-1602; Illinois; Before 1951.
56. Wisconsin Vital Record Index, pre-1907. Madison, WI..
57. South Dakota Death Index, 1905-1955 Ancestry.com.
58. U.S., Social Security Applications and Claims Index, 1936-2007 Ancestry.com.
59. Social Security Administration, Number: 519-18-2613; Idaho; Before 1951.
60. "United States World War I Draft Cards, 1917-1918," (https://goo.gl/t0UL69).
61. California, Death Index, 1940-1997 Ancestry.com Operations Inc, 2000.
62. South Dakota, State Census, 1935: Ancestry.com Operations, Inc., 2014.
63. "Maine, Births and Christenings, 1739-1900," (https://goo.gl/wKcenN).
64. Massachusetts, Death Records, 1841-1915 Ancestry.com Operations, Inc., 2013.
65. "Maine, Births and Christenings, 1739-1900," (https://goo.gl/Oycwo9)
66. National Archives and Records Administration (NARA); Washington D.C.; Emergency Passport Applications, Argentina thru Venezuela, 1906-1925; Collection Number: ARC Identifier 1244183 / MLR Number A1 544; Box #: 4728; Volume #: 2.
67. Massachusetts, Marriage Records, 1840-1915 Ancestry.com Operations, Inc., 2013.

ings b.abt 1862.[68] Elnora[6] married a Canadian, Donald M. Martin, b.1876 on 1 Mar 1909.[69]

Mary Wilson[5] Hinkley (William[4], Mary[3], William[2], James[1]) - The Goodwins

Mary[5] b.19 Sept 1812[70] married Woodbury Goodwin b.7 Nov 1816 d.1 Nov 1899 and had four children, Eliphalet Perkins[6] b.23 Dec 1842 d.12 May 1929,[71] William Woodbury[6], George M[6] born and died 1848 and Julia A[6] b.7 Sep 1849 d.27 Nov 1927.

William Woodbury[6] Goodwin b.9 Oct 1844 d.5 Jun 1926 (unc) married Ella A Berry on 3 June 1873 in Carthage.[72] They had one son, Burton Woodbury[7] b.31 Dec 1879 d.1975.[73]

Rachel Anne[5] Hinkley (William[4], Mary[3], William[2], James[1]) - The Malings

After marrying John Burnham Maling, Rachel[5] b.12 Oct 1824[74] moved to Kennebunkport and had four children, William Hinckley[6], Catherine E[6] b.Jan 1854 d.1936, George[6] and Frank Wilson[6] b.May 1868 d. 19 Dec 1903.[75]

William Hinckley[6] Maling b.10 Dec 1849 d.16 June 1929[76] married Ella Isabella Wells b.29 June 1857 d.16 Sept 1932.[77] They had three children, Howard Gilman[7] b.13 Jul 1878[78] d.18 Sep 1932[79], Ann[7] b.abt 1881 d.aft 1940 and Ethel[7] b.30 Jul 1890 d.Mar 1975.[80]

---

68. "Massachusetts, Marriages, 1841-1915," (https://goo.gl/XnSRoI).
69. "Massachusetts, Marriages, 1841-1915," (https://goo.gl/LGHcI4).
70. "Maine, Births and Christenings, 1739-1900," (https://goo.gl/gvy24o).
71. North Carolina Death Certificates. Microfilm S.123. Rolls 19-242, 280, 313-682, 1040-1297. North Carolina State Archives, Raleigh, North Carolina.
72. "Maine Marriages, 1771-1907," (https://goo.gl/dyazXa).
73. Social Security Applications and Claims Index, 1936-2007 Ancestry.com.
74. "Maine, Births and Christenings, 1739-1900," (https://goo.gl/BNtoQY).
75. Massachusetts Vital Records, 1911–1915. NEHGS, Boston, Massachusetts.
76. Findagrave.com, http://goo.gl/UFzVzH, accessed 5 Aug 2015.
77. Findagrave.com, http://goo.gl/4f0aNh, accessed 5 Aug 2015.
78. WWI, Michigan; Registration County: Wayne; Roll: 2024030; Draft Board: 07.
79. Ancestry.com. California, Death Index, 1905-1939 Ancestry.com.
80. Social Security Adminstration, Number: 004-22-7242; Maine; Before 1951.

George Maling[6] b.1858 d.1936 and Abigail F Grant b.1858 d.1936 had two children, Susan Catherine[7] b.9 Apr 1893[81] d.1943 and Burton Ward[7] b.19 Jan 1897 d.22 May 1955.[82]

Sarah Wiswell[5] Hinkley (William[4], Mary[3], William[2], James[1]) - The Fosters

Sarah[5] b.26 Dec 1809[83] d.1891[84] married George R Foster b.1808 d.1884 and they had at least eight children in Topsham. Several of those children also had large families. The 1850 census[85] is the source for many of the birth dates: Mary E[6] (Bisbee) b.1834 d.27 Jan 1912,[86] Joseph[6] b.1843, Rachel Patten[6] b.1 Nov 1845 d.16 Mar 1918,[87] Eliza[6] b.1850, Annie E[6], Heatherly[6], George[6] and William H[6]. They moved to Bowdoinham by 1860[88] and then on to Lisbon during the next decade. George was a Civil War veteran with the 24th Maine as a fife major.[89]

George[6] Foster b.1841/42 d.20 Sep 1924 married Martha Newall b.1849 d.1934[90] and had three children, George Edward[7] b.1869 d.1915,[91] James Albert[7] b.1873 and Benjamin Harrison[7] b.24 Oct 1888 d.aft 1940. He was a sailor, farmer, shoe store owner and Lisbon Falls postmaster.

Heatherly[6] Foster b.1838 d.21 Feb 1901[92] married Irene Woodward b.26 Aug 1841[93] d.aft 1920. They had seven children in Cape Elizabeth but only three of them had children of their own.

Heatherly's children that either did not marry or have children

81. Maine State Archives; 1892-1907 Vital Records; Roll #: 36.
82. U.S., Headstone Applications for Military Veterans, 1925-1963 Ancestry.com.
83. "Maine, Births and Christenings, 1739-1900," (https://goo.gl/eUH9C7).
84. Findagrave.com, gravestone, http://goo.gl/U084jj, accessed 5 April 2015
85. Year: 1850; Census: Topsham, Lincoln, Maine; Roll: M432_261; Page: 358B:504.
86. Maine State Archives; 1908-1922 Vital Records; Roll #: 5.
87. Maine State Archives; 1908-1922 Vital Records; Roll #: 53.
88. "United States Census, 1860," (https://goo.gl/BTDRNH:).
89. Records of Soldiers Who Served in Volunteer Organizations During the Civil War, 1899 - 1927, for 1861 - 1866, roll 0007.
90. Findagrave.com, http://goo.gl/qgW1Zx, accessed 5 July 2015.
91. Findagrave.com, gravestone photograph, http://goo.gl/5tXads
92. Massachusetts, Death Records, 1841-1915 Ancestry.com Operations, Inc., 2013.
93. "Maine, Births and Christenings, 1739-1900," (https://goo.gl/xK4ZaU)

were Georgiana Elizabeth[7] b.18 Dec 1866 d.23 Dec 1872,[94] Mary J[7] b.16 Dec 1871,[95] Hellena C[7] b.27 Nov 1873,[96] and Fostina Mabel[7] b.1876.[97] The others who did marry were Lincoln[7] b.20 Mar 1865[98] d.6 Jan 1940,[99] Joseph Woodward[7] b.11 Jul 1869[100] d.1917[101] and Everett Whittier[7] b.6 Apr 1879 d.Jan 1968.[102]

Annie E[6] Foster b.8 May 1837 d.18 Sep 1913[103] married Solon Temple b.14 Oct 1830 d.14 Oct 1899[104] and they had Maria I,[7] Annie E[7], Lucy E[7], John M[7], Charles H[7], Margaret[7], George Files[7], Adelbert Solon[7], Alice Graves[7], and Lysle Leonard[7]. Those ten children had 28 children.

William H[6] Foster b.1850 d.1919[105] married Mary T Jones. They had one child, George W[7] b.abt 1878 d.aft 1930.[106]

Eunice D[5] Hinkley (William[4], Mary[3], William[2], James[1]) - The Wakefields

Eunice[5] b.14 June 1827 d.24 Nov 1904[107] married William H Wakefield b.21 Apr 1823[108] d.9 July 1886.[109] They moved to Garland between 1850 and 1860. Their first child was William W[6] who died 18 Dec 1857[110] and there was another William[6] b.abt 1863.[111]

94. Maine State Archives; Pre 1892 Delayed Returns; Roll #: 107.
95. "Maine, Births and Christenings, 1739-1900," (https://goo.gl/zJy7KY).
96. "Maine, Births and Christenings, 1739-1900," (https://goo.gl/KwuyOW.
97. Year: 1910; Census Place: Eastport Ward 2, Washington, Maine; Roll: T624_547; Page: 1B; District: 0286; FHL microfilm: 1374560.
98. Maine State Archives; Pre 1892 Delayed Returns; Roll #: 107.
99. New Hampshire, Death and Disinterment Records, 1754-1947 Ancestry.com.
100. Maine State Archives; Pre 1892 Delayed Returns; Roll #: 107
101. Massachusetts, Death Index, 1901-1980 Ancestry.com Operations, Inc., 2013.
102. Social Security Death Index, Number: 010-14-8025; Massachusetts; Before 1951.
103. Findagrave.com, gravestone, http://goo.gl/zRpzsp, accessed 7 July 2015.
104. Findagrave.com, gravestone, http://goo.gl/1EMGXf, accessed 7 July 2015.
105. Findagrave.com, http://goo.gl/XgdE45, accessed 7 July 2015.
106. Year: 1930; Census Place: Corinna, Penobscot, Maine; Roll: 837; Page: 11A; Enumeration District: 0034; Image: 373.0; FHL microfilm: 2340572.
107. Findagrave.com, gravestone, http://goo.gl/vp2ZjS, accessed 25 April 2015.
108. "Maine, Births and Christenings, 1739-1900," (https://goo.gl/qNHAr5).
109. Findagrave.com, http://goo.gl/k7b389, accessed 25 May 2015.
110. Findagrave.com, gravestone, http://goo.gl/ZiwPYA, accessed 21 May 2015.
111. "United States Census, 1870," (https://goo.gl/2nKrGP:).

Charles Albert[6] Wakefield b.14 Dec 1853 d.19 Feb 1921[112] married Maria Josefa Littlejohn in California. They had George Theodore[7] b.22 Feb 1881 d.15 Mar 1969[113] and Charles Peck[7] b.5 Jun 1901 d.1 Dec 1966.[114]

Julia C[6] Wakefield b.28 Feb 1861[115] married Fred Clark b.1858. d.1946 and had two children Mary E[7] b.1890 d.21 Apr 1891[116] and James William[7] b.17 Jan 1893.[117]

Marcia S[6] Wakefield b.abt 1859 married Fred's brother, Howard, and several others but never had any children.

Roxana[5] Hinkley (William[4], Mary[3], William[2], James[1]) - The Hutchins

Roxana[5] b.22 Oct 1822[118] d.3 May 1898[119] married Moses Hutchins b.Apr 1804 d.6 Apr.1888[120] on 19 Apr 1860.[121] She was his second wife and they had a son, George Henry[6] b.abt 1861. I can find no trace of him after the 1880 census.[122]

Betsey A[5] Hinkley (William[4], Mary[3], William[2], James[1]) - The Harlows

Betsey A[5] b.16 June 1820[123] d.18 Nov 1890[124] married Hosea Harlow b.1820 d.5 Oct 1864.[125] As there were a number of Betsey Hinkleys who married in the correct date range, I was unsure about this relationship. Yes, she was listed as Betsey A in the marriage record but it wasn't until I tracked down her grave that I was sure. The grave

---

112. California, Death Index, 1905-1939 Ancestry.com Operations, Inc., 2013.
113. California, Death Index, 1940-1997 Ancestry.com.
114. California, Death Index, 1940-1997 Ancestry.com Operations Inc, 2000.
115. "Maine, Births and Christenings, 1739-1900," (https://goo.gl/BmZq6O).
116. Findagrave.com, gravestone, http://goo.gl/73abnb, accessed 25 May 2015
117. WWII (Fourth Registration) New Hampshire: M1963; Microfilm Roll: 4.
118. "Maine Births and Christenings, 1739-1900," (https://goo.gl/o17gsv)
119. Maine State Archives; 1892-1907 Vital Records; Roll #: 29.
120. Findagrave.com, gravestone photograph, http://goo.gl/SDkBI0.
121. "Maine Marriages, 1771-1907," (https://goo.gl/R3CKTJ).
122. Year: 1880; Census Place: Kennebunkport, York, Maine; Roll: 491; Family History Film: 1254491; Page: 320C; Enumeration District: 193; Image: 0381
123. "Maine, Births and Christenings, 1739-1900," (https://goo.gl/BWTIXM).
124. Findagrave.com, gravestone photograph, http://goo.gl/IJrly1.
125. U.S. National Cemetery Interment Control Forms, 1928-1962, ancestry.com.

marker says she was 70 and five months. That's not much to go on but that marriage took place in the same county where the family lived, in Guilford, Piscataquis county. Same age, same area and the exact same name. That is not as strong a proof as I would want but enough to follow that line.

Betsey[5] and Hosea had four children before the Civil War: Evalyn[6], Frederick A[6], Anna W[6] and Julia Etta[6]. Hosea enlisted on 2 Dec 1863 and was a private in company I, 2 Maine calvary. He is buried in the Barrancas National Cemetery in Pensacola, Florida, after dying from illness.[126]

Evalyn[6] Harlow b.1851 d. 31 Oct 1926[127] married Stephen R Came b.Oct 1840 d.1 Nov 1921 and had six children, Bertha[7], Rachel[7], Paul W[7], Frank Stephen[7], Ralph R[7] and Ruth[7]. Bertha[7] and Ruth died as teenagers and only two of the others had children.

Anna W[6] Harlow b.3 May 1854 d.22 Oct 1939 married Almon Brown b.17 Apr 1858 d.29 Dec 1940 and had two children, Amy Gertrude[7] who married three times and had two children and Mildred[7] who never married but had one child.

Frederick[6] Harlow b.abt 1854 d.after 1940 may have married twice but I could find no children.

The youngest child, Julia Etta "Letty"[6] Harlow b.abt 1859, I cannot find after 1880. Her name is iffy; I found her as Letty, Lettie and Julia E.

126. Findagrave.com,http://goo.gl/1cSZZd, accessed 26 Aug 2015.
127. Findagrave.com, gravestone photographs, http://goo.gl/2htL3n.

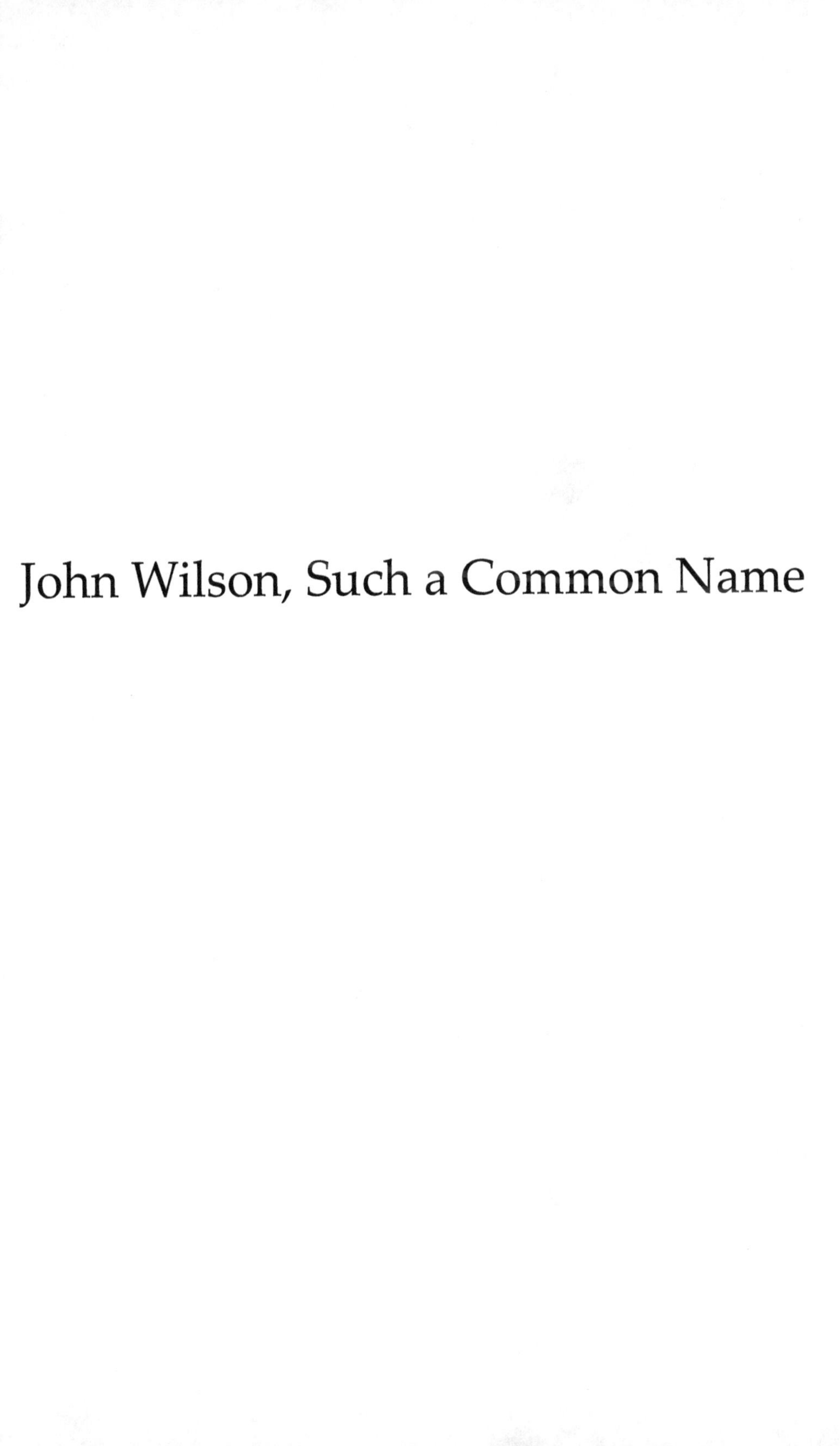

John Wilson, Such a Common Name

John's marriage to Rachel Thompson on 10 March 1783 is documented in various places because she was the daughter of Brigadier General Samuel Thompson, a well-known figure during the Revolutionary War and in Maine politics after the war. He is a Mayflower descendant and his family, including Rachel with a birth date of 9 July 1763, are listed in the Mayflower Births and Deaths, Vol. 1 and 2.[1] General Thompson was the son of James Thompson and Reliance Hinkley, another descendant of Edmund Hinkley as described in the previous chapter. This is a Brewster line, descending from Patience Brewster and her father, William Brewster. I have found a DNA match for me with another Brewster descendant (and certified Mayflower member) on Ancestry.com - further proof of this lineage.

John's father-in-law is well-known for his role in what is called Thompson's War[2] early in the Revolution. He was the tavern owner in nearby Brunswick and served on the Board of Selectmen there but moved to Topsham the year Rachel and John married. He served in the Massachusetts legislature until his death in 1798. He amassed great quantities of land, some of which he donated to Bowdoin College but another 2352 acres was sold to the school by his children after his death in 1802 - for $2744.

For someone who was such a public figure, little is known about his personal life though there may have been good reason for that.

Wheeler gives us the most information:

> *In regard to his character, it is hardly possible to render Brigadier Thompson exact justice. Nothing has been learned as to his private and social life. It is known, however, that his wife was, at times, insane, and it is said that on one occasion she killed an adopted son, of some five or six years of age, with a pair of steelyards. One of his children was also an imbecile. Under such circumstances, it is hardly probable that his home life could have been a happy one.*
>
> *In regard to his public life, it is not so difficult to form an opinion, though even here, owing to his outspoken and vehement manner, he made so many enemies that it is difficult to know the truth of some statements made in regard to him. One thing*

1. Roser, 231
2. Thompson's War, https://goo.gl/PysDq3, accessed online 13 July 2014.

is sure, that he was one of the leading men of his day, running over with zeal and patriotism. The late Judge Freeman says of him, " He was a portly man, not of very tall stature, but somewhat corpulent, and apparently of a robust constitution, but not supposed to be possessed of much real courage. Nature had furnished him with strong mental powers and a capacity which, if it had been rightly directed and employed, might have rendered him a useful member of society, but his mind needed cultivation." He was strictly a "self-made" man, and was particularly remarkable for his firmness of opinion—often amounting to obstinacy— and for his ready wit, which, when he was in the House of Representatives, often excited the mirth of his brother members.[3]

More information about Samuel Thompson is available in the Thompson genealogy written by a Thompson descendant that has a very favorable picture of Samuel.[4] What is interesting to me is that Rachel's children are not listed though her marriage to John is. Charles Sinnett does list the children of her siblings.

So Rachel's home life could possibly had been a nightmare if the story is true about her mother, Abiel Purington. Very little is known about Rachel; she was only 20 when she married.

Rachel Thompson was born to them July 9th 1763 (Brunswick, 32)
Rachel, widow of John, and dau. of late Brigadier Gen. Sam[ue]l, Thompson, suddenly, Apr. 3, 1844, a. 77 y. 3 m. 24 d. [a. 79 y. 8 m., G.R.2.] (Topsham, II, 399)

John served in the Revolutionary War along with his brother, William, and Rachel started receiving a military pension on 4 March 1836 after his death. He is listed as a private in the pension records.[5]

Thompson Abiel and John Wilson (s. of William the eldest and Inn holder, and [ ] Larrabee), [ ], p.R.80. (Topsham, II, 258)
Rachel & John Wilson, Mar. 10, 1783. [int. adds, he of T., she of Brunswick.] (261)
John and Rachel Thompson, Mar. 10, 1783. [int. he of T., she of Brunswick.] (286)

One of the things I found most interesting is that nearly everything has John and Rachel - not just John as most deeds and official papers would have. I thought it to be really enlightened until I realized that Rachel's inheritance was the reason. When a woman inherited property from her father, she still had no property rights. Legally, she had to have her husband named with her in all trans-

3. Wheeler, 812-813.
4. Rev. Charles N. Sinnett, Our Thompson Family, in Maine, New Hampshire and the West (New Hampshire: Rumford Printing Company, 1907), 18-27.
5. U.S. Pensioners, 1818-1872. Original data: Ledgers of Payments, 1818-1872, to U.S. Pensioners Under Acts of 1818 Through 1858 From Records of the Office of the Third Auditor of the Treasury, 1818-1872..

actions. The good news is she would have had some choice in the proceedings since her name and signature was required. That was way better than having all property pass to her husband.

So there are quite a number of deeds for John and Rachel. The estate from Samuel Thompson was really large and the heirs sold it off piecemeal. Besides land, Samuel still owned part of the saw mill at his death in 1798. John and Rachel sold off bits of the inheritance continually over the next 27 years. Sometimes it was as a group of the heirs and the last I found was Rachel's alone.

There's a mortgage in the deeds dated recorded 12 July 1826 that is a mortgage on the lot of land John and Rachel were living on for $256.29. Interest was to be paid annually and mortgage to be paid off in four years. It was the last recorded land transaction for John and Rachel[6] that I could find. The gap starts there - there were no other deeds in the index for any of the family - that's when I realized there were 30 years of deeds missing in Lincoln County.

John died 15 Aug 1835 - here is the proof of his parentage and his death date is engraved on his gravestone:

> *John, Aug. 15, 1835, a. 78 y., G.R.2. [he was a Revolutionary pensioner, s. of William, the eldest, the Innholder and [ ] Larrabee, p.R.80.] (Topsham II, 398)*

William[4] (John[3], William[2], James[1])

I knew he existed. He shows up in every census until his mother dies after 1840. Born between 1785 and 1790, this child of John and Rachel seems to have lived a full life - without leaving a trace beyond the censuses. I checked censuses in 1850 and 1860 but saw no new Wilsons. He does not show up with any of his siblings in 1850. He was between 50 and 60 years old in 1840. Topsham records list a William who died "William, Feb. 23, 1841, a. 55 y., G.R.2." (Topsham II, 400). Once I got to Haley Cemetery I found the grave next to John Wilson in Haley is a William. The marker is broken and partially illegible but it does say Feb. So he was born about 1786, the same year his uncle William died. At last, a mystery solved!

6. Lincoln County Registry of Deeds, Wicasset, Maine, 301: 128.

Isabella[4] (John[3], William[2], James[1]) & Ezekiel Purinton

Isabella [ ], [Wilson, P.R.22], w. Ezekiel, Jan. 29, 1788, in T . (Topsham I, 149)
Isabella and Capt. Ezekiel Purinton, both of T., int. Apr. 7, 1810. [cert, issued Apr. 27.] [m. Apr. 29, P.R.22.] (II, 285)
Isabella Wilson, w. Capt. Ezekiel, Jan. 8, 1879, a- 91 Y-> G.R.3. [a. 90 y., p.R.22.] [dup. a. 90 y. 11 m. 10 d., p.R.22.] (II, 367)
Ezekiel, ch. James, Sr., and Priscilla (Harding), July 14, 1782, in T. [dup. h. Isabella.] [Feb. 15, p.R.22.] (I, 148)
Ezekiel, Feb. 25, 1841, in T. [Capt., a. 58 y., G.R.3.] [h. Isabella, 58 y. 7 m. 11 d., p.R.22.] (I, 367)

Silence, [twin] ch. Ezekiel and Isabella (Wilson), Apr. 22, 1813, in T . (I, 150)
Silence, Dec. 29, 1814, in T. [d. Capt. Ezekiel and Issabella Purinton, a. 20 m. 8 d., G.R.I.] (I, 368)

John and Rachel's eldest daughter was Isabella[4]. She and Captain Ezekial Purinton had five children, one of whom, Silence[5], died as a child, one of a set of twins. Silence[5] is buried in First Parish Cemetery but the rest of the family is in Riverview. Her gravestone states that she was 20 months old when she died 29 Dec 1819. The age is incorrect on the gravestone but the death year is definitely 1819.

Two of the Purinton sisters married one man, Robert McManus b.12 Aug 1803 d.8 Mar 1887.[7]

Priscilla[5] & Mary[5] (Isabella[4], John[3], William[2], James[1]) - The McMannuses

Priscilla, ch. Ezekiel and Isabella (Wilson), July 31, 1811, in T. (I, 150)

Mcmannus Robert, Capt., of Portland & Priscilla Purinton of T., int. Aug. 17, 1839. [cert. Sept. 10.] [Sept. 10, d. Ezekiel & Isabella (Wilson), p.R.22.] (I, 166)
Priscilla Purinton, w. Capt. Robert [d. Ezekiel and Isabella, p.R.22], July 28, 1844, a. 33 y., G.R.3. (II, 348)

Robert, Capt., and Mary Purinton, both of T., Sept. 16, 1846. [second w., p.R.22.] (I, 119)
Mary, [twin], ch. Ezekiel and Isabella (Wilson), Apr. 22, 1813 , in T. (I, 149)
Robert, Capt., h. Priscilla and Mary (Purinton), Mch. 8, —, a. 83 y. 6 m. 26 d., P.R.22. (II, 166)

Priscilla[5] and Robert had one daughter Priscilla Purinton[6]. Left with a small child, Robert married her sister and the twin survivor, Mary[5], d.21 Jun 1905[8] but they had no children.

7. "Maine, Nathan Hale Cemetery Collection, ca. 1780-1980," (https://goo.gl/YBOhiC).
8. "Maine, Vital Records, 1670-1907 " (https://goo.gl/5RSJFj).

Priscilla P., ch. Robert and Priscilla (Purinton), Apr. 3, 1842, in T. [only child, P.R.22.] (I, 119)
McManus, Priscilla P. (d. Capt. Robert of Brunswick) & Col. Wildes P. Walker of New York City, July 15, 1868, in St. James Hotel, Boston, Mass., N.P.6. (II, 166)
Wildes Perkins, ch. Nathaniel and Jane, May 8, 1814. (I, 193) d.1888

Priscilla[6] married an infamous figure, Col. Wildes Perkins Walker d.1888, whose New York City divorce case made headlines in 1854. He had married Catherine Patten, daughter of a wealthy Bath ship-owning family; she charged him with adultery. The full story was published and is available on line at Harvard if you want the salacious details.[9] He was 30 years older than Priscilla[6] and is buried in Riverview Cemetery in Topsham with Catherine.[10] Priscilla[6] died in 1923 and is buried with her father and step-mother/aunt in Brunswick.[11] I wasn't able to find her in any census after 1870 but she obviously never remarried.

Isabella[5] Purinton (Isabella[4], John[3], William[2], James[1]) - The Fosters

Isabella L., ch. Ezekiel and Isabella (Wilson), Feb. 3, 1821, in T . (Topsham I, 148)
Isabell L. & Capt. Robert H. Foster, of T., Dec. 10, 1851. [Dec. 16, P.R.22.] (II, 209)
Robert H Foster June 1819 Oct. 26 1818 (Brunswick, 419)

The fourth child was Isabella[5] d.5 Sep 1911[12] who married Robert H Foster d.26 Oct 1878.[13] They had one son, Frederic(k)[6] "Freddie". He most likely never married: he was living with his mother in 1910[14] the year before her death.

Frederick F., ch. Capt. Robert H. and Isabella L.(Purinton), May 5,1853, p.R.22. (Topsham I, 68)

Israel[5] Purinton (Isabella[4], John[3], William[2], James[1])

Israel Collins [only son, P.R.22], ch. Ezekiel & Isabella (Wilson), Aug. 26, 1826, in T. [h. Margaret E., G.R.3.] (Topsham, I, 149)
Margaret Ellen and Israel C. Purinton, both of T., Jan. 6, 1863, in T. [Israel Collins, P.R.22.] (II, 209)
Margaret Ellen, ch. Smith and Tamson J., Apr. 3, 1842, in T . (I, 37)

Jennie Isabell, d. Israel Collins and Margaret Ellen (Chase), Feb. 25, 1871, p.R.22.

9. Harvard School Library, C C Childs, Walker, Wildes P. A report of the trial of Walker vs. Walker (New York, 1854). http://goo.gl/u1n2GE Accessed 6 June 2015.
10. Findagrave.com, gravestone, http://goo.gl/aIuGKZ, accessed 6 June 2015.
11. Findagrave.com, gravestone, http://goo.gl/wH56Cg.
12. Maine State Archives; 1908-1922 Vital Records; Roll #: 20
13. "Maine, Births and Christenings, 1739-1900," (https://goo.gl/WJG3iQ)
14. Year: 1910; Census Place: Brunswick, Cumberland, Maine; Roll: T624_538; Page: 3B; District: 0046; FHL microfilm: 1374551.

(I, 149) d.26 Oct 1953[15] unmarried

The fifth child and only son, Israel Collins[5] may have been called Collins. His grave lists his name as I. Collins.[16] His father died when he was 15 and he may have lived at home until he married late at age 36 to Margaret Ellen Chase. According to his gravestone, he died in 1916 and Margaret in 1917.[17] Margaret was only 20 years old when they married.

James C, s. Israel Collins and Margaret Ellen (Chase), Jan. 27, 1864, p.R.22. (Topsham, I, 149)

James C[6] Purinton d.1933[18] married Annie S Drew on 24 May 1899[19] at age 36. I do not believe they had children. She does appear in the 1910 census at age 32, giving her a birth year of around 1878. She is not in the June, 1910 census; James[6] is listed as divorced that year. And marriage records exist for November 1900 with two different surnames for Annie. There's definitely some discrepancies in the records leading me to believe there might have been marriages and divorces alike. She died in 1913 according to the matching headstone.[20]

Mary McMannus, d. Israel Collins & Margaret Ellen Chase, Aug. 17,1865, p.R.22. (I, 149)
May M. of T. and Ellery C. Day of Brunswick, Sept. 16, 1891, in T. [int. Mary.] [Mary McMannus, p.R.22.] (II, 210)

Mary McManus[6] d.1949 and her husband, Ellery Copeland Day b.1869 d.1930[21] had one child, Margaret Emily Day[7] b.10 Apr 1893[22] d.22 June 1964.[23]

Rebecca[4] (John[3], William[2], James[1]) - And Her Puringtons

Humphrey, Capt., of Bowdoinham & Rebecah Wilson of T., int. Oct. 8, 1821. [cert. Oct. 23.] [Oct. 29, p.R.90.] (Topsham II, 209)

15. U.S. City Directories, 1821-1989 Ancestry.com Operations, Inc., 2011.
16. Findagrave.com, gravestone, http://goo.gl/Y3Gs9j, accessed 25 Jan 2015.
17. Findagrave.com, gravestone, http://goo.gl/Y3Gs9j, accessed 25 Jan 2015.
18. Findagrave.com, gravestone, http://goo.gl/L6uDv9
19. "Maine, Marriage Index, 1892-1966, 1977-1996," (https://goo.gl/kQBbYd)
20. Findagrave.com, gravestone, http://goo.gl/6xmTJU.
21. Findagrave.com, gravestone, http://goo.gl/ANB9Ly
22. "Maine, Vital Records, 1670-1907 ", (https://goo.gl/ZKzQbs).
23. Maine Death Index, 1960-1997 Ancestry.com Operations Inc, 2002.

Rebecca ,w. Capt.Humphrey ,b .Mar. 10,1791, d. Jan. 12, 1877 ae 86 y.g.r.20 (Bowdoinham, 95)
Humphrey,Capt., h.Rebecca,b.Mar. 24, 1791, d,Apr.22, 1841 ae 49 y.g.r.20 (War 1812,buried on Verrill Farm,Randall Cem.t.r.4) (Bowdoinham, 94)

Rebecca[5] and Humphrey lived in Bowdoinham and are buried in the Purington Cemetery (Brown's Point Road) along with their children and various other Puringtons according to a hand-drawn diagram of the small family plot.[24] I went looking for the cemetery and had a lovely time out in the area but never found it!

Elinor[5] (Rebecca[4], John[3], William[2], James[1]) - The Merrows

Merrow, Elinor P.,w.J.Marstin,d,Sept.10,1886 ae 64 y . l m.g.r.2 (Bowdoinham, 76)
Josiah M.Major, h.Elinor P., d.Dec.23,1852 ae 30 y.g.r.20 (77)

Robert McManus.s.Josiah M.and Elinor P.,d.Dec. 3,1851 ae 11 m.g.r.20 (78)

Their oldest, Elinor[6], married Josiah Marston Merrow on 21 Jan 1846.[25] She is listed as the sister to George in the 1880 census. Her daughter, Ellen Rebecca[7] b.18 Feb 1848,[26] is listed in that census as well as in the 1870 census. No other records were found for Ellen and she is not buried in the family plot so she may have married.

Their eldest son, Josiah Humphrey Purington Merrow b.7 Dec 1846[27] d.1914,[28] married Adaline A Wood b.1841 d.1921[29] on 4 Jan 1870.[30] By 1880 they and their three children, Gertrude b.abt 1871 d.aft 1940, Arthur Sewell b.abt 1877 d.1890[31] and Samuel b.16 Jan 1882[32] d.1950,[33] had moved to Nassau County, Florida.

George Newhall[5], Albert Watson[5] & Norris W[5] (Rebecca[4], John[3], William[2], James[1])

G.N., d.Mar 11, 1897 ae 71 y.g.r.20 (Bowdoinham, 94)
Albert W. , d.Apr. 7, 1870 ae 42 y.g.r.20 (93)

---

24. Bowdoinham Historical Society: http://goo.gl/1cBgLC, accessed 31 Jan 2015.
25. Maine, Marriages, 1771-1907," (https://goo.gl/6bPOBG)
26. "Maine, Births and Christenings, 1739-1900," (https://goo.gl/Lr0qRI)
27. "Maine, Births and Christenings, 1739-1900," (https://goo.gl/3FY60z)
28. Findagrave.com, http://goo.gl/j19ROh, accessed 18 Oct 2015.
29. Findagrave.com, http://goo.gl/zd4DxR, accessed 18 Oct 2015.
30. "Maine, Marriages, 1771-1907," (https://goo.gl/aD9Jjd)
31. Findagrave.com, http://goo.gl/Uoz0Fl, accessed 26 Aug 2015.
32. World War I Draft Registration Cards, 1917-1918 (https://goo.gl/ttDP6h)
33. "Florida, Death Index, 1877-1998," (https://goo.gl/poQKgj)

George Newhall Purinton b.30 July 1825 (unc) probably never married and his tombstone only lists his initials. He and several of his siblings are found still living with their mother in the 1870 census[34] and he is not buried with a wife. His youngest brother, Norris W b.13 Oct 1831[35] d.1 Jun 1893,[36] also never married and was in the 1870 census along with his sister, Amanda. Norris was living with his sister, Elinor, her daughter, Ellen, and sister Courtney's son, Humphrey in 1880.[37] Albert Watson b.11 April 1827 (unc) is also buried without family in the Purington plot. Since he died before the census was taken in 1870 and no census for any of the siblings can be found for 1860, we cannot be sure he didn't marry but he probably didn't.

Courtney[5] & Amanda[5] (Rebecca[4], John[3], William[2], James[1]) - The Randalls

Amanda,w.Samuel W.,d.Apr.19»1903 ae 69 y.7 m.g. r.32 (Bowdoinham, 97)
Courtney,w.Samuel W.and d.Capt.Humphrey and Rebecca Purington,d.May 11,1870 ae 38 y.6 m.28 d.g.r.32

Courtney Purinton b.13 Oct 1831[38] married Samuel W Randall b.25 August 1823[39] d.18 Nov 1893.[40] They had 6 children. Samuel married Amanda b.22 Sept 1833[41] after Courtney's death before 1880. Such marriage was common and understandable as he still had 4 children ages 14 to 2 at home the year Courtney died.[42]

Three of the total six children either died young or never married:

Randall, George N. , s.Courtney and Samuel W. ,d. Jan.5,1862 ae 3 y.6 m.14 d.g.r.32 (Bowdoinham, 98)
Amanda Purington, infant, d.S.W. and C., d. Dec.21, 1864 g.r.32 (97)
Humphrey P., 1868-1940 g.r.3 (98) b.18 Aug 1868[43]

The other three married but none had children: Ellen R b.22 Feb

---

34. "United States Census, 1870," (https://goo.gl/xo1erB)
35. "Maine, Births and Christenings, 1739-1900," (https://goo.gl/l2pBpp)
36. Maine State Archives; 1892-1907 Vital Records; Roll #: 46
37. 1880; Census Place: Bowdoinham, Sagadahoc, Maine; Roll: 488; Family History Film: 1254488; Page: 102B; Enumeration District: 147; Image: 0213
38. "Maine, Births and Christenings, 1739-1900," (https://goo.gl/oRNiKJ)
39. "Maine, Births and Christenings, 1739-1900," (https://goo.gl/5aozXC)
40. "Maine, Vital Records, 1670-1907 ", (https://goo.gl/ouyPNS)
41. "Maine, Births and Christenings, 1739-1900," (https://goo.gl/XVNh8t)
42. "United States Census, 1870," (https://goo.gl/q7TZ6f)
43. "Maine, Births and Christenings, 1739-1900," (https://goo.gl/zqXAko)

1856 d.3 Dec 1935[44] married John Bailey Curtis. Charles Benjamin b.8 Apr 1860[45] d.1942[46] married Stella May Yeaton. Nettie Amanda b.23 Jun 1866 d.22 Nov 1932[47] married Isaac Franklin Umberhine.

Thankful[4] (John[3], William[2], James[1]) & Charles W Purington

Thankful [ ], w. Charles W., Jan. 9,1792, in T. (Topsham, I, 209)
Thankful, w. Charles, Dec. 20, 1885, a. 94 y., G.R.3. (II, 369)
Charles of Bowdoin and Thankful Wilson of T., int. Jan. 4, 1818. [cert, issued May 27.] (Topsham, II, 208)
Charles W., h. Thankful, Feb. 14, 1793, in Bowdoin. (I, 210)
Charles, h. Thankful, Nov. 14, 1826, a. 36 y., G.R.3. (II, 368)

Like her two older sisters, Thankful[4] d.20 Dec 1885[48] married a Purinton: Charles Woodbury Purington, son of Nathaniel Purington and Hepsebath Snow of Bowdoin. She and Charles owned the land next door to John and Rachel in 1826 and witnessed a mortgage that John agreed on with John and Peletiah Haley.[49] This heightens the possibility of her parentage. There is no proof besides that except circumstantial evidence. First, her birth year fits in this family; secondly, there is a girl that age in the censuses (1800, 3 girls under 10, Thankful, Rebecca and Betsey[50]) and thirdly, dang it, she married a Purington!

Charles was from Bowdoin and they lived there until 1823 or 1824 when they moved to Topsham after the death of Converse but before Frances' birth perhaps to be nearer her family.

Converse, ch. Charles W. & Thankful, Jan. 18, 1820, in Bowdoin. (Topsham I, 148)
Converse, July 31, 1823, in T. (II, 367)
Frances J., ch. Charles W. and Thankful, June 18, 1824, in T (I, 148)
Frances J., Nov. 16, 1886, a. 62 y., G.R.3. (II, 367)

Charles and Thankful[4] had five children, Rebecca[5], Converse[5], Octavia[5] who married a Purinton, Frances J[5] who never married and Charles W[5] who married another Wilson family member.

---

44. Findagrave.com, http://goo.gl/O03H07, accessed 7 June 2015.
45. "Maine, Births and Christenings, 1739-1900," (https://goo.gl/pDYa4y)
46. Findagrave.com, gravestone, http://goo.gl/pWC6IU, accessed 7 June 2015.
47. Findagrave.com, gravestone, http://goo.gl/V2Ndth, accessed 7 June 201
48. Findagrave.com, gravestone: http://goo.gl/u7aeNw, accessed 13 Apr 2014.
49. Lincoln County Registry of Deeds, book 138 page 191-192.
50. Year: 1790; Census Place: Topsham, Lincoln, Maine; Series: M637; Roll: 2; Page: 260; Image: 151; FHL Film: 0568142

Rebecca[5] Purington (Thankful[4], John[3], William[2], James[1]) - The Thomases

Rebecca W, ch. Charles W. & Thankful, Oct. 1, 1821, in Bowdoin. (Topsham I, 150)
Rebecca, Aug. 30, 1861, c.R.4. (II, 385)
George H. of Richmond and Rebecca W. Purinton of T., June 2, 1844. (II, 258)
Thomas, George H., h.Rebecca W.(Purington), d. Aug 24, 186l ae 50 y.g.r.26 (Bowdoinham, 123)

John H. s.George H. and Rebecca W. d.Aug.6,1869 ae 21 y.g.r.26 (123)

Mary Rebecca, infant d. George H. and Rebecca, d.Sept.6,1861 ae 15 d.g.r.26 (123)

So Rebecca died soon after giving birth to Mary Rebecca[6] but George died earlier that week as well. Then Mary Rebecca died at 15 days.

Three of the boys, William Walton[6], Eugene[6], and Charles Frederick[6], were taken in by their uncle Charles, aunt Margaret and grandmother, Thankful, as they are found in the 1870 census together.[51] One boy, the oldest is not there and I was not able to find him after 1860: George Albert[6] b.6 Apr 1845.[52]

All three of the other boys married. Eugene[6] b.12 June 1859[53] married Eva Maud in 1905 but I could find no records after that. Charles Frederick[6] b.9 Aug 1857[54] went Minnesota and married Alice A Rowley b.abt 1861. The Minnesota census of 1895 lists him as a railroad station agent.[55] They had three children, Merle Edna[7] b.20 Feb 1885[56] d.20 Jul 1942,[57] Charles Albert[7] b.18 Jan 1891 d.23 Jan 1965[58] (California), and Howard Milton b.25 Apr 1895 d.5 Jul 1975[59] (California). Based on what I found on ancestry.com, most of these descendants do not know their heritage due to the lack of family ties created by the parents' deaths.

William Walton[6] b.24 Apr 1853[60] stayed and raised his family in

51. Year: 1870; Census Place: Topsham, Sagadahoc, Maine; Roll: M593_557; Page: 450A; Image: 449; FHL Film: 552056
52. "Maine, Vital Records, 1670-1907 ," (https://goo.gl/izDXKA)
53. "Maine, Vital Records, 1670-1907 ," (https://goo.gl/L2QYs9)
54. "Maine, Vital Records, 1670-1907 ," (https://goo.gl/5cTavd)
55. Minnesota, Territorial and State Censuses, 1849-1905 [Ancestry.com.
56. Minnesota, Births and Christenings Index, 1840-1980 Ancestry.com.
57. Minnesota, Death Index, 1908-2002 Ancestry.com Operations Inc, 2001.
58. Social Security Number: 471-16-1328; Issue State: Minnesota; Before 1951
59. Scocial Security Administration, Number: 469-10-1471; Minnesota; Before 1951
60. "Maine, Vital Records, 1670-1907 ," (https://goo.gl/leu6u6)

Maine. He married twice.

Emma F., ch. Isaac E. and Melissia Ann, Oct. 5, 1855, in T. (Topsham I, 121)
Emma F. »w.William W. ,d.Apr.l9,1882 ae 26 y.6 m.g.r.26 (123)
Thomas, Angie J., w.William, d.Feb.12,1917 ae 58 y.3 m.g.r.26 (Bowdoinham, 122)

His first wife, Emma Mallet, was a Purington cousin. They had no children. He and Judith Angie Williams had three children, Charles F[7] b.abt 1887[61] d.aft 1940, Elizabeth[7] and George Howard[7] b.30 Jul 1890.[62] None of them may have had children.

Octavia[5] Purington (Thankful[4], John[3], William[2], James[1]) & Joseph C Purinton

Octavia and her husband, Joseph C, were listed in the previous chapter.

James Frank[5] Purington (Thankful[4], John[3], William[2], James[1])

James Frank[6] Purington b.1857 d.6 Jun 1909[63] married Abbie M Tibbetts b.1860 d.1841.[64] They had two children before he died, Carl Russell[7] b.28 Apr 1887[65] d.1945[66] and Helen b.28 Dec 1894[67] d.1932.[68] Both of them married and had children.

Charles Woodbury[5] Purington (Thankful[4], John[3], William[2], James[1])

Charles Woodbury[5] married his cousin, Margaret P Maxwell[5], daughter of William and Betsy Maxwell,[4] in the next section.

Betsey[4] (John[3], William[2], James[1]) - The Maxwells

William Maxwell was the great-grandson of Topsham neighbor and early settler, Actor Patten, whose lot was several lots away from

61. Year: 1920; Census Place: Bowdoinham, Sagadahoc, Maine; Roll: T625_649; Page: 2B; Enumeration District: 142; Image: 347.
62. Maine State Archives; 1892-1907 Vital Records; Roll #: 56
63. Maine State Archives; 1908-1922 Vital Records; Roll #: 45.
64. "J. Gary Nichols Cemetery Collection, ca. 1780-1999," (https://goo.gl/ROihG6)
65. WWI, Maine; Registration County: Androscoggin; Roll: 1653901; Draft Board:2.
66. Findagrave.com, gravestone photograph, http://goo.gl/HtGswQ
67. "Maine Vital Records, 1670-1907 ", (https://goo.gl/10Ps7S)
68. Findagrave.com, gravestone photograph, http://goo.gl/cIvThj

John's.

Betsy (Wilson), w.William, d.Aug. 3,1874 ae 75 y. g. r.l7(b.Topsham,Nov.l4,1796 p.r.5) (Bowdoinham, 74)
William of Bowdoinham & Betsey Wilson of T., int. Feb. 25, 1826. [cert, issued Mar. 11.] [Mar. 14, in T., p.R.90.] (Topsham II, 172)
William, s. Capt.James & Margaret (Patten), b. in Bowdoinham,Feb.22, 1794 p.r.5 d. in Bowdoinham June 14, 1879 ae 85 y.g.r.l7 (h.Betsy (Wilson) (Bowdoinham, 75)

Noble, s.William and Betsy (Wilson), b.Nov.27,1828, d.Jan.31,1833 ae 4 y.g.r.17 (Bowdoinham, 75)

William and Betsey[4] had 7 other children besides Noble, all born in Bowdoinham just north of Topsham: Margaret[5], Charles[5], Rachel[5], Thomas Cheney[5], Pamelia Hill[5], John Franklin[5] and Abion K[5].

Margaret[5] Maxwell (Betsey[4], John[3], William[2], James[1]) & Charles W Purington

Margaret P. [ ], w. Charles W., Mar. 12, 1827, in Bowdoinham. (Topsham, I, 149)
Margaret P., w. Charles W., June, 1897. (II, 367) gravestone says 18 Aug 1900[69]
Charles W. of T. and Margaret P. Maxwell of Bowdoinham, int. June 10, 1861. [cert, issued June 15.] (Topsham II, 208)
Charles W., Jr., ch. Charles W. and Thankful, Mar. 18, 1826, in T. (148)

The eldest was Margaret P[5] who married her cousin, Charles Woodbury Purington d.31 May 1897[70] from above. They did not have any children.

Charles[5] Maxwell (Betsey[4], John[3], William[2], James[1])

Charles, h. Lydia (Coombs), Dec. 14, 1830, P.R.17. (Bowdoin I, 135)
Charles of Bowdoinham and Lydia Coombs, d. of William B. and Lydia (Harmon), of B., [ ], P.R.17. [Dec. 21, 1860, Lydia J., P.R.10.] (III, 113)
Lydia, ch. William B. and Lydia (Harmon), July —, 1836, P.R.17. (I, 60)

The son that followed was named Charles[5] d.21 Apr 1903.[71] His marriage to Lydia J Coombs d.30 Jan 1898[72] in Bath, Maine, gave him six children, Herbert Dennis[6], Mary L[6], Elvira[6], Bessie Wilson[6], Grace Carr[6] and Charles[6].

Herbert Dennis, ch. Charles and Lydia (Coombs), Nov. 7, 1865, P.R.17. (Bowdoin I, 136)
Grace Carr, ch. Charles and Lydia (Coombs), Apr. 26, 1880, P.R.17. (I, 136)

---

69. Findagrave.com, http://goo.gl/p1SiLy.
70. "Maine, Vital Records, 1670-1907 ", (https://goo.gl/ixEVKG,).
71. "Nathan Hale Cemetery Collection, ca. 1780-1980," (https://goo.gl/Zc1vjc). Maine State Archives; 1892-1907 Vital Records; Roll #: 37
72. Maine State Archives; 1892-1907 Vital Records; Roll #: 37.

Bessie Willson, ch. Charles and Lydia (Coombs), Oct. 3, 1873, P.R.17. (I, 136)
Charles, ch. Charles and Lydia (Coombs), , —, 1875, P.R.17. (I, 136) d.1877[73]

Nothing is known about Elvira[6] except that she appeared in the 1880 census.[74] Mary L[6] b.4 Mar 1862[75] d.9 Jan 1881[76] died at age 18 but Herbert Dennis[6] d.1924[77] supposedly married twice, first to Miriam Caroline Spinney on 29 Oct 1887.[78] They may have divorced. His second marriage to Louise Hodgdon on 16 Jan 1907[79] did result in two children. She may have been a relative of the first wife: her mother was a Spinney. Grace Carr[6] married Arthur Larrabee (17 Oct 1905[80]) but died only two years later on d.28 May 1907.[81]

Bessie[6] d.aft 1940 married on 18 Aug 1897.[82] She and her husband, Frederick Elbridge Heath, b.28 May 1872 d.aft 1940 who was a minister according to his Mason card,[83] had five children born in Maine and Massachusetts after 1900.

Rachel[5] Maxwell (Betsey[4], John[3], William[2], James[1]) & Henry Dunning

Rachel E., w.Henry S Dunning and d.William and Betsy Wilson),b.Aug.29,1842, d.Jan.16,1916 g r.17 (Bowdoinham, 75)
Henry S., ch. Elisha and Lydia, Aug. 11, 1838, in Brunswick. (Topsham I, 58)

The youngest, Rachel[5] d.16 Jan 1916[84], married Henry Sherman Dunning d.24 Sep 1908 on 7 Oct 1884.[85] It appears that Rachel and Henry had no children.

Thomas Cheney[5] Maxwell (Betsey[4], John[3], William[2], James[1])

---

73. "Nathan Hale Cemetery Collection, ca. 1780-1980," (https://goo.gl/Zc1vjc).
74. Year: 1880; Census Place: Wales, Androscoggin, Maine; Roll: 475; FHL: 1254475; Page: 479C; District: 021; Image: 0955
75. Findagrave,com, gravestone: http://goo.gl/ri0N9p.
76. "Maine, Vital Records, 1670-1907 " (https://goo.gl/d3WOqv).
77. "Maine, Nathan Hale Cemetery Collection, ca. 1780-1980," (https://goo.gl/D1orq3).
78. "Maine, Vital Records, 1670-1907 ", (https://goo.gl/PZyfdO).
79. Massachusetts, Marriage Records, 1840-1915 Ancestry.com Operations, Inc., 2013.
80. "Maine, Marriage Index, 1892-1966, 1977-1996," (https://goo.gl/GyJ8Fc).
81. Maine State Archives; 1892-1907 Vital Records; Roll #: 33
82. "Maine, Marriage Index, 1892-1966, 1977-1996," index, (https://goo.gl/t9K4cG).
83. Massachusetts, Mason Membership Cards, Ancestry.com Operations, Inc., 2013.
84. Findagrave.com, gravestone photograph for both, http://goo.gl/4oPsTE.
85. "Maine, Marriages, 1771-1907," (https://goo.gl/8ipZI).

Thomas Cheney[5] b.12 Jan 1833[86] d.10 Apr 1895[87] married Ruth A Sedgely Oct 1860.[88] They had four children, Mattie C[6] b.3 Feb 1862 d.8 Feb 1946,[89] Noble[6] b.21 Aug 1863[90] d.11 Oct 1919,[91] Gilbert[6] b.2 Apr 1866 d.14 Nov 1942[92] and Ruth Marie[6] b.7 Nov 1879 d.22 May 1922.[93]

Pamelia Hill[5] Maxwell (Betsey[4], John[3], William[2], James[1]) - The Reeds

Pawelia H. (Maxwell) ,b.Dec.22,1834,d.0ct.29,1899 g.r.l? (Bowdoinham, 99)
Reed, Andrew J.,h.Pamelia H, b. Apr.16,1826, d.Oct.13,1910 g.r.17 & p.r.5 (99)
Ora E.,d.A.J.and P.H.,b.Oct.l0,1860,d.0ct.ll, 1948 g.r.17 (99)
William M.,s.A.J.and P.H.,b.0ct.l2,l866,d.Mar.5 1874 g.r.17 (99)

Pamelia[5] and Andrew Jackson had two children, Ora Ella Reed[6] who never married and William Reed[6] who died young.

John Franklin[5] Maxwell (Betsey[4], John[3], William[2], James[1])

John F., h.Maria Louise, b.Mar.12,1837, d.Sept.18, I925 g.r.l7 (s.William and Betsy (Wilson) p.r. 5 (Bowdoinham, 74)
Maria Louise.w.John F., b.Nov.l5,l844, d.Pec.20, 1929 g.r.17 (74)
Howard Melville,b.May l6,1879,d.Aug.22,1949 g. r.17 (74)

John[5] and Maria Louise Hatch had two sons, Howard Melville[6] who never married and Arthur William[6] b.26 Apr 1880[94] d.1958[95] who married Eulela Belle Rowell b.1879 d.1953[96] but had no children.

Albion K P[5] Maxwell (Betsey[4], John[3], William[2], James[1])

Albion[5] b.15 Mar 1840[97] d.12 Dec 1908[98] married Emma O Dunlap

86. "Maine, Births and Christenings, 1739-1900," (https://goo.gl/zFMHJ8).
87. "Maine, Vital Records, 1670-1907 ", (https://goo.gl/r5T4bm).
88. "Maine, Marriages, 1771-1907," (https://goo.gl/epidZf).
89. California, Death Index, 1940-1997 [database on-line]. Ancestry.com.
90. "Maine, Births and Christenings, 1739-1900," (https://goo.gl/gYVQ2w)
91. "Maine, Nathan Hale Cemetery Collection, ca. 1780-1980," (https://goo.gl/lpNzMC).
92. California, Death Index, 1940-1997 [database on-line]. Ancestry.com.
93. "Maine, Nathan Hale Cemetery Collection, ca. 1780-1980," (https://goo.gl/12wFqi).
94. "Maine, Births and Christenings, 1739-1900," (https://goo.gl/5iejTZ).
95. Findagrave.com, gravestone, http://goo.gl/u8wIdm
96. Findagrave.com, gravestone photograph, http://goo.gl/Z2SdXq.
97. "Maine, Births and Christenings, 1739-1900," (https://goo.gl/PYqMEl).
98. Maine State Archives; 1908-1922 Vital Records; Roll #: 36

b.16 Apr 1861[99] d.12 May 1941[100] and had a son, Irving William[6] b.5 Dec 1893 d.May 1978[101] who did marry and have children.

And the others....

Supposedly born around 1805, I could find no direct evidence of a daughter for John[3] named Rachel[4]. But there is this:

> *Rachel of T. and Jeremiah Higgins of Lisbon, int. July 30, 1842. [cert, issued Aug. 13.] (Topsham II, 287)*

That Rachel died in 1845 one day after her child was born. I can find no evidence of a Rachel in other Wilson families that matches her. The Irish Wilsons only had one Rachel at all and there are more Rachels in our Wilsons. So it just might be. If so, then there could be another family line that may not doesn't know her mother was a Wilson at all or else don't know which Rachel.

> *Adruana L Higgens was born April 19th AD 1845 (Lisbon, 156)*

Adriana's mother is listed as Phebe (Sawyer) who Jeremiah married after Rachel died. They are all buried in Bowdoin together, Jeremiah, Phebe and Rachel. According to the Lisbon records, that marriage took place in August of 1841 - obviously incorrect since Rachel died in 1845. There's definitely confusion surrounding this family. Some folks have made that Rachel wife of Jeremiah Higgins Sr but with a birth year of 1795. Her grave definitely says 20 April 1845 and age of 40 and 9 months.[102]

Barring a DNA match to a definite descendant of Adriana, we may never know for sure. As it is, I can find no marriage for Adriana.

Humphrey Thompson[4] (John[3], William[2], James[1])

His story is continued in the next chapter.

---

99. National Archives and Records Administration; Washington D.C.; NARA Series: Passport Applications, January 2, 1906 - March 31, 1925; Roll #: 2687; Volume #: Roll 2687 - Certificates: 500850-501349, 26 Dec 1924-29 Dec 1924

100. Findagrave.com, http://goo.gl/m05Gne, accessed 8 June 2015.

101. Social Security Administration, Number: 007-38-7023; Maine; Issue Date: 1956-1957

102. "Maine, J. Gary Nichols Cemetery Collection, ca. 1780-1999," (https://goo.gl/ZusYp4)

Humphrey T and Family

Humphrey Thompson[4] Wilson (John[3], William[2], James[1])

Humphrey Thompson Wilson was born 7 Nov 1794, the second son of John and Rachel Wilson. Thompson was his mother's maiden name and we can only assume that the T of his middle initial stands for it as I cannot find one record with it spelled out. It's listed differently in many records, frequently what looks to be an F. I did find one handwritten record in the Topsham town records where it looked like an F but comparing it to both a F and a T on the same page, it was obviously a T. T's used to be much fancier and a modern reader is more likely to think a T is an F.

That town record was from April of 1833 where Humphrey[4] is listed as a surveyor of lumber along with his cousins, Hugh[4] and Arthur Lee Wilson[4].

He was a veteran of the War of 1812, serving in Lt. Col. A Merrill's regiment under Captain John Wilson. The dates are listed as June 20 - 24, 1814, and Sept. 10 to Sept. 28, 1814 and states the regiment served in Bath.[1] I did find matching pension records; as the pension would have been based on service and not being wounded or killed, the pension would be after 1871. The bounty when he first joined was $31 and 160 acres of land. His pension record does list a land bounty number of Wt 32767 160 55 but does not state how much land he received or where it was. The application to get that land is probably in existence but the files have only been indexed up the K surnames.

The birth record was one entered in his adulthood; not announced in the town or church records at his birth. His family belonged to the Baptist Church Society at his birth; his father was one of the founding members. Those church records have not survived.

Humphry T., h. Nancy C , Nov. 7, 1794, in T. (Topsham I, 210)
Humphrey T., Aug. 23, 1880, a. 87 y., in Lynn, Mass., formerly of T. (II, 398)

He remained at home until his marriage at age twenty-seven to

1. Records of the Massachusetts volunteer militia called out by the Governor of Massachusetts to suppress a threatened invasion during the war of 1812-14 (Boston, Mass.: Wright & Potter printing co., state printers, 1913).

Nancy Low Center who was born in Massachusetts but her family had settled in Bowdoinham between 1800 and 1810, just down the road from Topsham. Her parents, Samuel and Rachel Low Center, and some of her siblings are buried in the Beech Hill Cemetery in Bowdoinham.

Humphrey T. of T. and Nancy Center of Bowdoinham, int. Nov. 24, 1821. [cert. Dec. 9.] [Dec. 28, P.R.90.] (II, 285)
Nancy C. [— — —], w. Humphry T., Mar. 28, 1802, in Charlestown, Mass.
Nancy C , Mrs., w. Humphrey T., Jan. 29, 1878. [Nancy L., a. 76 y. 10 m., N.P.6.]

Humphrey was a farmer just like so many of his generation.

All of their children were born in Topsham except Henry who was born in Bowdoinham in 1830. We don't know if they were living there that year but Rachel's father died in November of 1833; if he had been ill or failing in 1830, she might have been spending more time with her parents than normal.

The family names are nearly all Center names - with Nancy's siblings duplicating the same names, Serena, Maria, Emory/Emery, Thomas, and Carnes. All of Humphrey's children except one, the youngest, have their birth dates recorded in the Topsham records. The youngest was listed in the 1850 census.

Center, ch. Humphrey T. and Nancy C , Mar. 26,1838, in T. (II, 208) d.Oct 1859[2]
Harriet Augusta Carnes, ch. Humphrey T. & Nancy C, Oct. 2, 1840, in T. (II, 209)
Harriet A. C , d. Humphrey T., Jan. 27, 1859, in T. [a. 18 y. 3 m., N.P.6.] (II, 398)
Maria Clark, ch. Humphry T. & Nancy C, June 13, 1826, in T. (II, 211)
Serena Ann Center, ch. Humphry T. & Nancy C, Aug. 30, 1828, in T. (211) d.Feb 1860[3]
Thomas Cheney, ch. Humphry T. and Nancy C , Apr. 14, 1822,in T. (211)

Only four survived to live and marry.

The death toll is upsetting, with Center[5], the sailor, dying of yellow fever at 18 and Serena[5] at 31 from cerebritis (most often associated with Lupus). Thomas Cheney[5] most likely died before turning 18 as no trace of him can be found after 1830. Harriet[5] also had an early death at 18 within a year of Center[5] and Serena[5].

2. U.S. Federal Census Mortality Schedules, 1850-1885 Ancestry.com.
3. U.S. Federal Census Mortality Schedules, 1850-1885 Ancestry.com.

Maria[5] may have married but I cannot find her after 1850 - it's quite possible she died during that decade though. That would be the fourth young adult death for the family in a very short time period. A possible hint to her death could be sister Serena's death: cerebritis is an inflammation of the brain - commonly seen in lupus patients. Back in the 1800s cerebritis could also be due to lead poisoning though was considered to be a rare cause.[4] Definitely, though, the symptoms would be more of dementia with loss of memory and delirium but with a rapid onset.

The reason why I found this to be interesting is because Serena's brother, my great-great-grandfather, also died from cerebritis many years later in 1922.[5] A family with lupus? Something to think about.

By 1860[6], only the ones we know survived are living at home with Humphrey and Nancy - Angeline "Anne"[5], Henry[5], Emery[5] and Lorin[5]. Henry is listed as shoemaker. Five years later, they all, except for Humphrey, are living in Lynn, Massachusetts. Henry[5] has married but Emery[5], Lorin[5] and Anne[5] are still single and all listed as working in the shoe business.[7] In 1870, Humphrey[4] is living with Emery[5] and his family back in Topsham.[8] Nancy is not there, however and I can find no census record for her that year. It is possible that she remained in Massachusetts and is living with Lorin[5]. She died in 1878 but it was a newspaper announcement and we only have the date - not where she died.

Humphrey[4] died in 1880 and is listed in the census with Emery[5] and his family in Lynn that year. His death certificate states that his body was shipped back to Topsham. We have not been able to find his or Nancy's grave or any grave of the children who died while in Topsham. The broken stones next to Isabella Wilson's grave in Haley Cemetery could be the remains of their gravestones.

4. Hamilton, Allan McLane, Nervous Diseases: Their Descriptions & Treatment (Philadelphia: Henry C Lea's Son & Co, 1881), 167-170.

5. New Hampshire, Death and Disinterment Records, 1754-1947 Ancestry.com..

6. Year: 1860; Census Place: Topsham, Sagadahoc, Maine; Roll: M653_448; Page: 441; Image: 439; FHL Film: 803448

7. Massachusetts, State Census, 1865 [database on-line]. Ancestry.com.

8. Year: 1870; Census Place: Topsham, Sagadahoc, Maine; Roll: M593_557; Page: 449A; Image: 447; FHL Film: 552056

Lorin Fisher[5] *(Humphrey*[4]*, John*[3]*, William*[2]*, James*[1]*)*

Lorin F., d. Humphry and Nancy (?), a. 3 y., in u.s.c. (210)

Lorin was the youngest child of the ten, born 26 Apr 1847. I do not have proof of his birth date or his middle name. I thought for a long while that I couldn't find him after the 1865 census but I did turn up a marriage record for him and Martha Dushuttle on 8 Jun 1867.[9] It mentions that Martha is from Lynn and the daughter of Lewis and Orilla. There is no trace of either of them after that in Massachusetts; it makes me think they left the state or died. The more uncommon a name one has such as Lorin, the less likely it will transcribed correctly from old records. This could easily be why a search is not turning up anything.

Jefferson Clark[5] *(Humphrey*[4]*, John*[3]*, William*[2]*, James*[1]*)*

Jefferson Clark, ch. Humphry T. & Nancy C, Apr. 17, 1824, in T. (210)

Jefferson had me chasing my tail for a long time until I was able to get to the Sagadahoc County courthouse in Bath. There I found a number of deeds that helped me make sense of the confusing records.

I found three marriage records for a Jefferson:

Jefferson C. of T. and Cyntha M. Larrabee of Green, int. Apr. 30, 1847. [cert. May 15.] (Topsham, II, 286)

Jefferson and Lissie D. Small, both of Brunswick, June 11, 1860. (286)

The third record is for a Rebecca Lowell who married Jefferson C in Lewiston. There a lots of records for a Jefferson C Wilson in Green with a Cynthia Mower Larrabee and a Rebecca as wives.

Jefferson and Cynthia Mower had multiple children starting in 1848 and continuing on into the next decade. Jefferson, however, is listed in the 1850 census in Topsham with his parents. And there is a Jefferson living with his wife and her parents in Greene that same year. So I initially decided that Jefferson was mostly likely not our Jefferson Clark. Turns out though he got had to have gotten counted twice!

9. "Massachusetts, Marriages, 1841-1915," (https://goo.gl/EzBvBJ).

Jefferson and Lizzie - there's a Jefferson with no middle initial and Elizabeth buried in Brunswick. Elizabeth was his second wife - his first, Sarah, died in 1857. His birth year is 1820 - four years older than Jefferson C. That's definitely not him. Bizarrely, however, the Brunswick Jefferson died only weeks after Jefferson C.

So that leaves Rebecca and it becomes clear that she is Jefferson C in Green's second wife when in 1860 that family includes an elderly couple named Larrabee, who must be Cynthia's parents, and Cynthia's children are listed as well.

That Jefferson C removes to Iowa - yes, Iowa. Since most of these Wilsons do not stray far, I was skeptical that it could be our Jefferson. Even his children were pioneers, settling parts of Alberta, Canada.

Then I discovered deeds that proved Jefferson was a mover. All of those records of transactions with his father state Jefferson is of Green and he was highly involved in Topsham as well. Green is located above Lewiston - a small town on the road to Augusta.

Jefferson's first wife, Cynthia Mower Larrabee, died prior to 1860. Her gravestone is on findagrave.com but it has sunk so that the death date cannot be read.[10] Their children were John Larrabee[6] b.29 Mar 1848[11] d.12 Feb 1916,[12] Thomas[6] b.abt 1849 d.bef 1860, Fanny[6] b.29 Apr 1849[13], Frank[6] S b.1 Sep 1850,[14] Ella A[6] b.23 Dec 1851[15] and Cynthia[6] b.14 Jan 1856[16] d.1890.[17] Thomas[6] is listed in the 1850 census[18] but Fanny[6] is not and he is not in the 1860 when Fanny[6] is.[19] So either the 1859 census was wrong or else Thomas (Fanny's twin?)

10. Findagrave.com, gravestone photograph, http://goo.gl/lPj1Bi.
11. "Maine Births and Christenings, 1739-1900," (https://goo.gl/AJIim5).
12. Findagrave.com, gravestone photograph, http://goo.gl/xJxtcw.
13. "Maine Births and Christenings, 1739-1900," (https://goo.gl/lsjF0w).
14. "Maine Births and Christenings, 1739-1900," (https://goo.gl/Amn1NQ).
15. "Maine Births and Christenings, 1739-1900," (https://goo.gl/mgYWYo).
16. "Maine Births and Christenings, 1739-1900," (https://goo.gl/OpGaK8)
17. Findagrave.com, http://goo.gl/cypobq, accessed 12 Oct 2015.
18. Year: 1850; Census Place: Greene, Maine; Roll: M432_258; Page: 341A; Image: 492.
19. Year: 1860; Census Place: Greene, Androscoggin, Maine; Roll: M653_432; Page: 49; Image: 49; Film: 803432.

died before 1860.

John Larrabee[6] may not have married but he did follow his brother to Canada. I couldn't track Fanny[6] or Ella[6] after the 1860 census nor could I turn up a trace of Frank S[6] after the 1870 census. Cynthia[6] married E S Roming on 23 Feb 1888[20] but died just two years later.

One of the intriguing facts I kept running across was that Lewiston was a marriage locale destination for a consistent number of Topsham residents. I liken it to running away to get married quickly - in Georgia while I was growing up, that was South Carolina. I have not been able to find out why Lewiston would be a choice but that's where Jefferson and Rebecca went.

Marriages Solemnized by Jacob Golder, Apr 13, 1860, Jefferson C. Willson and Miss Rebecca Lowell (Lewiston II, 671)

Jefferson[5] first appears in Iowa in the 1870 census with his sons, John[6] and Frank[6].[21] Rebecca must have still been in Maine, pregnant with Lena[6] who was born there in late 1870. I absolutely cannot find any census record for her or the other children that year for either Iowa or Maine. Jefferson[5] did return to Maine to finalize their move. There is a deed where he sold his land back to Humphrey[5] that he had bought in 1866. It is dated 29 Jan 1871; he did personally appear to sign the transaction.[22]

Congress passed the Homestead Act in 1862, giving away western land for small fees and living on the land for five years. This was probably the impetus for going west[23] but I was wondering how come he seemed to be able to come and go from Iowa.

By land it would really be a trek but then I remembered that the mid-west was frequently accessed via the Mississippi River. They would sail around to the mouth and then go up by steamboat. I was just in Kansas City this summer and went through the Arabia Steamboat Museum. It's an interesting peek into life in the 1850s

20. "Iowa, County Marriages, 1838-1934," (https://goo.gl/QjxdDh).
21. Year: 1870; Census Place: Cass, Cass, Iowa; Roll: M593_380; Page: 69B; Image: 143; Family History Library Film: 545879
22. Sagadahoc County Registry of Deeds, 29:40, 34:459.
23. History.com, The Homestead Act, http://goo.gl/UZA5rN

where people and goods were moved by river.[24]

They could have also traveled by wagon train or train as the Transcontinental Railroad was completed in 1869. That actually might have been a reason for Jefferson going at that time. He could have been thinking about it for a while but Cynthia's parents lived with Jefferson's family until their deaths in the 1860s so he may not been able to leave earlier.

Jefferson[5] died 17 Jan 1899[25] and Rebecca died ten years later on 4 Feb 1909[26] in Pottawattamie County, Iowa. The reason why the river travel came up? The trigger was the grave marker with the anchor. Donna Carano had contacted the findagrave.com person in charge of the profile. In response they uploaded the photo which we had not seen before. Besides sailing, an anchor can denote hope or eternal life but it can also be a masonic symbol for well-grounded hope.

Jefferson and Rebecca had six children, one who did not survive born 16 Sep 1867.[27] All were born in Maine, except the youngest. They were Ida C[6] b.8 Jun 1861 d.26 Jan 1948[28] Charles Emery[6], Burton[6] b.abt 1869, Lena G[6] and Rollin[6]. The others all married but Ida[6] doesn't seem to have had children with George Eichorn whom she married on 7 Mar 1882.[29]

Burton married twice but I couldn't find who his first wife was. He married Alice B Trumbo in Billings, Montana, on 9 Jul 1928. Her father is listed as George Elliott so Trumbo was probably a married name. Burton is listed as widowed.[30] They moved to Newport Beach, California, and were both still alive in 1940.[31]

24. The Arabia Steamboat Museum, http://goo.gl/MWEP97
25. Findagrave.com, http://goo.gl/UpHNhu, accessed 10 Oct 2015.
26. "Iowa, County Death Records, 1880-1992," (https://goo.gl/YTVCmH).
27. "Maine Births and Christenings, 1739-1900," (https://goo.gl/Ycm4Tq).
28. Findagrave.com, gravestone, photograph, http://goo.gl/aHXHdX.
29. "Iowa, Marriages, 1838-1934", (https://goo.gl/RRzpBj).
30. "Montana, County Marriages, 1865-1950," (https://goo.gl/fjy8GE)
31. Year: 1940; Census Place: Newport Beach, Orange, California; Roll: T627_273; Page: 16A; Enumeration District: 30-54

The 1885 Iowa census has John Larrabee[6] working as a schoolteacher and Frank[6] is no longer at home.[32]

Lena G[6] b.16 Dec 1870 d.29 Apr 1950[33] married Elwin C Whitaker b.Sept 1871 d.24 Feb 1936[34] on 26 Nov 1895.[35] They had four children born in Iowa, one in Missouri and one in Colorado. They also lived in Nebraska, Oklahoma and Kansas. He was a minister according to several censuses. In 1930 he is listed as a real estate agent in Oklahoma. They were living with their daughters, Leota[7] (bank secretary and listed as head of household), Iris[7] (secretary, oil company), Margarite[7] (bookkeeper, garage) and Dorothy[7] (tabulator operator, oil company).[36]

There were two other children, Lowell[7] b.16 Oct 1896 d.Mar 1971[37] and Lois Ada[7] b.28 Jun 1901 d.15 Dec 1967.[38] Lowell[7] married Mary Ada Baskett and had two children, Winona Leonora[8] and Earl C[8]. Lois[7] married Horace Milton Aldrich and had Horace Milton[8], Dorcas Ramona[8], Laverna Jean[8], Lawrence Richard[8], Betty Joan[8], Robert D[8] and Ronald Lee[8].

Neither Margarite[7] b.9 Apr 1906 d.2 Nov 1979,[39] Dorothy[7] b.29 Aug 1909 d.23 Oct 1997[40] nor Leota H[7] b.24 Oct 1898 d.28 Feb 1955[41] married; Iris[7] b.1904 d.1962[42] did marry a J. Stewart Hume but I found no children for them but that does not mean there weren't any.

The youngest son of Jefferson and Rebecca was Rollin Noble[6] b.7 Oct 1873 d. 28 Aug 1953.[43] He married Nellie M McAdam b.5 May

32. Iowa, State Census Collection, 1836-1925, Ancestry.com
33. California, Death Index, 1940-1997, Ancestry.com.
34. Findagrave.com, http://goo.gl/CITxQ1, accessed 10 Oct 2015.
35. "Iowa, County Marriages, 1838-1934," (https://goo.gl/reWBac).
36. Year: 1930; Census Place: Ponca City, Kay, Oklahoma; Roll: 1909; Page: 6B; District: 0033; Image: 106.0; FHL microfilm: 2341643.
37. Social Security Administration, Number: 515-01-6523; Kansas; Before 1951.
38. Findagrave.com, gravestone photograph, http://goo.gl/HFa530.
39. California, Death Index, 1940-1997 [database on-line]. Ancestry.com.
40. Social Security Administration, Number: 574-01-8869; Alaska; Before 1951.
41. Findagrave.com, gravestone photograph, http://goo.gl/x0KCyB.
42. Findagrave.com, gravestone photograph, http://goo.gl/z1624a.
43. Findagrave.com, gravestone photograph, http://goo.gl/eYhRR7.

1874 d.14 Mar 1948[44] from New York. They had four children but they may not have had grandchildren. Rollin Noble, Jr., b.1919 d.1943 died in a plane crash in South Carolina five months after his enlistment during WWII.[45] The other three were Jeanie Alice[6] b.26 Dec 1901 d.1 Mar 1987,[46] Irene Ada[6] b.7 Dec 1904 d.30 Apr 1958[47] and Robert Rollin[6] b.24 Jan 1907 d.30 Apr 1958.[48] Irene and Robert died on the same day.

Jefferson's other son, Charles Emery[6], is the most interesting of the lot. He married Mae Merchant and they had their first child in Iowa: Wilbur John[7] b.1902 d.3 Nov 1972. According to Wilbur's obituary, when he was only three months old, they moved to Erskine, Alberta, Canada, as pioneers following his grandfather's path. Erskine was and is a small town but is located near Red Deer which even back then was large comparatively. I did find a book on line that has this family in it and it has more information about that area.[49]

"In regards to why Charles and family would move to the frontier. I really don't know. Economic conditions at that time were not good. Lots of land in Alberta was being set up as homestead land. If you were a Canadian citizen, or a landed immigrant, you could apply. All it cost was ten dollars. You also agreed to build a house, bring an amount of land into production, this was called breaking the land. It was hard work for man and beast both. Charles and an older brother, John Larabee Wilson both both filed for homesteads. This for one quarter(160 acres) each. Charles's father in law(Wilson Merchant) also settled there. The three men had a total of three quarters (480 acres) all on section six township 38 range 21 west of the fourth meridian. When Grampa passed away in 1939, Earl (oldest son) took over the east half of sec, 6 and some other land that they had purchased. I think that he couldn't manage this and by

44. Findagrave.com, gravestone photograph, http://goo.gl/r5msDx.
45. South Carolina, Death Records, 1821-1960, Ancestry.com.
46. California, Death Index, 1940-1997, Ancestry.com
47. Findagrave.com, http://goo.gl/3E0TVh, accessed 10 Oct 2015.
48. Findagrave.com, gravestone photograph, http://goo.gl/9cVHXl.
49. Clark, Edith J. Lawrence, Tails of Tail Creek Country, privately published about 1968, http://goo.gl/LCCUKT

1940 or 1941 they lost it."[50]

It was Wilbur John's profile on findagrave.com that gave me hints to his brothers and sisters. They were Earl Jefferson[7], Frank Burton[7], Eva S[7], Marion[7] and Lester Earl[7]. Wilbur John[7] married Mildred Juanita Ewartz b.12 Oct 1912 d.13 Nov 2004[51] from Oklahoma and had three children, Marion[8], Arnold Wilbur[8] and Charles Emery[8].

Wilbur's brother Earl Jefferson[7] was born in Iowa on 5 July 1901,[52] making him the oldest. He married Margaret Vickers and had two children, Charles Everett[8] and Jean[8]. He died in 1952[53] and Charles in 2006 but Jean is still alive today. Frank Burton[7] b.2 Mar 1904 d.24 Dec 1986[54] married Myrtle Bernice Lambert who died before him. They may not have had children; it was a step-daughter who was the informant on the death certificate.

Eva[7] S b.12 Aug 1905 d.7 May 1982 married Jay Waldo Lohr b.4 Sep 1895 d.12 Feb 1990.[55] They had four children, Marvin[8], Willard[8], Bonita Kay[8] and Marie Mae[8]. Lester E[7] was born in 1910 but I could find nothing about him after 1928.[56] The youngest was Marion Mae[7] b.20 Jan 1911[57] d.1989[58] who married Samuel Warrick Anderson b.30 Sep 1905[59] d.1993.[60] I was not able to find any children for them. Both Marvin[8] and Bonita Kay[8] are still living. Marvin is emailing at age 88 and obviously going strong!

Henry Carnes[5] (Humphrey[4], John[3], William[2], James[1])

Henry Carnes, ch. Humphrey T. and Nancy C, Nov. 4, 1830, in Bowdoinham. (209)

---

50. Email from Marvin Lohr, grandchild of Charles Emery Wilson, 19 Oct 2015.
51. Findagrave.com, http://goo.gl/csSEfJ, accessed 10 Oct 2015.
52. "Iowa, County Births, 1880-1935", (https://goo.gl/zgHMBP).
53. Findagrave.com, http://goo.gl/TGex2p, accessed 10 Oct 1952.
54. "British Columbia Death Registrations", (https://goo.gl/lVil65)
55. Findagrave.com, http://goo.gl/58JM66.
56. Manifests of Alien Arrivals at Eastport, Idaho, 1924-1956; National Archives Microfilm Publication: A3460; Roll: 35.
57. Manifests of Alien Arrivals at Eastport, Idaho, 1924-1956; National Archives Microfilm Publication: A3460; Roll: 1..
58. Findagrave.com, gravestone photograph, http://goo.gl/LZfch4.
59. Manifests of Alien Arrivals at Sweet Grass, Montana, August 1917-June 1954; National Archives Microfilm Publication: A3440; Roll: 1.
60. Findagrave.com, gravestone photograph, http://goo.gl/BGbpVK.

Henry married Catherine Alley Bubier b.29 Jan 1844[61] on 31 May 1863 in Lawrence, Massachusetts.[62] They settled in Lynn and like so many others he worked in the shoe industry. At the time, shoes were made in small scale shops; Lynn became the shoe capital of the world after an inventor patented a revolutionary shoe-lasting machine that cut the price of shoes in half after 1885.

Obviously, there were work outages that affected workers before then. The 1880 census shows that Henry had been out of work for 5 months that year - and so had others in the area who worked in shoe shops.[63]

Henry[5] and Catherine had three children, Mary Wallace[6], Maud Elizabeth[6] and Fred Eugene[6]. Mary[6] b.2 Apr 1864[64] d.21 Dec 1897[65] died from tuberculosis, a very common malady in an industrialized area like Lynn.

Maud Elizabeth[6] b.8 Jul 1866 lived with her father until his death on 11 Nov 1914.[66]

Henry[6] was listed as a shoe heeler in the 1900 census; Maud[6] was a bookkeeper. Frederick's there too as a shoe cutter. Catherine is also in that census which is incredibly bizarre[67] as there is a death certificate for a Catherine born 1844 with the correct parents' names who died in 1883. I don't know who that was in 1900 but I can guess that it was someone without citizenship or a visa using her identity. Catherine is buried with her family with a death date of 6 Apr 1883.[68]

In 1910, however, only Henry[5] and Maud[6] are left at home. That

61. Massachusetts, Town and Vital Records, 1620-1988
62. "Massachusetts, Marriages, 1695-1910," (https://goo.gl/SfIIVR).
63. Year: 1880; Census Place: Lynn, Essex, Massachusetts; Roll: 531; FHL: 1254531; Page: 225D; District: 215; Image: 0452
64. "Massachusetts, Births and Christenings, 1639-1915," (https://goo.gl/YAxUsI).
65. "Massachusetts, Deaths and Burials, 1795-1910," (https://goo.gl/YP5NHr).
66. Findagrave.com, http://goo.gl/68pqfY, accessed 28 Oct 2015.
67. Year: 1900; Census Place: Lynn Ward 5, Essex, Massachusetts; Roll: 645; Page: 2A; District: 0387; FHL microfilm: 1240645
68. "Massachusetts, Deaths and Burials, 1795-1910," (https://goo.gl/rxbBW9).

census states that Maud[6] was a bookkeeper in a shoe factory.[69]

Fred Eugene[6] b.1 Oct 1869[70] is gone before 1910 and there is a grave in Pine Grove for Fred E who died at 31 years old in Jan 1901.[71] The grave plot is the same as his sister's, Alpine Path, Lot-109. With that information I found his death record - consumption on 24 Jan 1901.[72] Maud[6] is also buried in that plot; she died in Oct 1949.[73]

Henry died 11 Nov 1914 having outlived his wife and two of his children. He did not die in the house where all the censuses were taken, on Boston Street. He died in a house that might well have been a rental or boarding house at 16 Mansfield Place.[74] That house is listed on trulia.com so I could access some information about it and see a picture.[75]

Angeline "Anne" Elizabeth[5] (Humphrey[4], John[3], William[2], James[1])

Angelina Elizabeth Carnes, ch. Humphry T. & Nancy C, Oct. 18, 1834, in T. (208)

Angeline "Anne" never married, dying of old age / senility in Concord, New Hampshire, on 11 Sep 1907.[76] She did stay in Lynn after her mother and brother returned to Maine. I found her in the 1870 census as a shoe fitter,[77] the same occupation she had in 1865. I have not found her 1880 or 1900 census to know when she left Massachusetts. Her death record is clear, listing her parents as Humphrey and Nancy of Topsham, Maine. Her brother, Emery, moved to Candia, New Hampshire, as early as 1902 so she may have moved at the same time he did. Concord is only about 30 miles from Candia. If she died of dementia only five years later, she may have been in poor shape by 1900.

69. Year: 1910; Census Place: Lynn Ward 5, Essex, Massachusetts; Roll: T624_584; Page: 9B; District: 0395; FHL microfilm: 1374597
70. "Massachusetts, Births, 1841-1915," (https://goo.gl/dYSOgf).
71. Findagrave.com, http://goo.gl/wP7VDD, accessed 8 June 2015.
72. Massachusetts, Death Records, 1841-1915 Ancestry.com Operations, Inc., 2013.
73. Findagrave.com, http://goo.gl/saH4co, accessed 12 Oct 2015
74. "Massachusetts, Deaths, 1841-1915," (https://goo.gl/CrjrNO).
75. Trulia.com, http://goo.gl/FPUOSm, accessed 13 Oct 2015.
76. New Hampshire Death Records, https://goo.gl/4VHWZ9.
77. Year: 1870; Census Place: Lynn Ward 6, Essex, Massachusetts; Roll: M593_610; Page: 715A; Image: 698; FHL Film: 552109

Emory / Emery Center[5] *(Humphrey*[4]*, John*[3]*, William*[2]*, James*[1]*)*

Emery Center, ch. Humphrey T. and Nancy C, July 2, 1843, in T. [dup. h. Addie F. Faucett.] (209)

Emery C. and Addie F. Fawcett, both of T., June 16, 1869. [Hewey C. Wilson, in Webster, N.P.6.]

So it all comes down to one man, one Wilson standing and, yes, he did father some children. It was only after the Civil War that he married however.

He was a private in the 8th Regiment, Massachusetts Infantry for nine months only according to the official records, 1862 - 1863.[78] His "Personal War Sketch" states he was in from August 1862 to August 1863 and that his term of enlistment expired. That is not what happened to the Maine volunteers but the 8th regiment was more a guard unit that only served three different times and in the case of the 1862 to 1863 time period, it was mustered out in August of 1863. Though the unit itself was only technically active for nine months, some were mustered in and therefore served longer. That unit had 11 deaths - all due to disease.[79] I also found records for the Spanish American war as well that looks to be him. He belonged to Company G, U.S. Volunteer Engineers and appears to been in the band. He enlisted 28 Aug 1898 and was discharged 17 May 1899.[80]

He and Adeline Frances Fawcett b.30 Aug 1849[81] seemed to try to make it up for lack of grandchildren to Humphrey and Nancy by having ten children. Humphrey was living with them in 1870 and 1880. Emory was one of the children with his mother in 1865 in Massachusetts but he returned to Topsham before the birth of his first son Fay Hartwell[6].

78. National Park Service. U.S. Civil War Soldiers, 1861-1865 Ancestry.com, film number M544 roll 44.

79. Acton Memorial Library Civil War Archives, http://goo.gl/cZoBkd, accessed 9 June 2015.

80. Organization Index to Pension Files of Veterans Who Served Between 1861 and 1900, roll 736. Fold3 image: http://www.fold3.com/image/24445244.

81. Massachusetts, Town and Vital Records, 1620-1988 Ancestry.com.

They had three more children before returning to Lynn between 1875 and 1877, Everett Dexter[6], Nellie Mabel[6] b.4 Dec 1872, and Clarence Alton[6] b.24 Apr 1875. Both Nellie[6] and Clarence[6] died in 1875.

Nellie Mabel, Feb. 22, 1875, a. 2 y. 2 m. 18 d., in T.
[—], inf. ch. E. C , June 18, 1875. (Topsham, II, 400) Clarence Alton

Adeline Mabel[6] was born in 1877, followed by Frank Leroy[6], Arthur Edward[6], Clara Geneva[6], Walter Emory[6] and Harold Ernest[6].

Adeline Mabel d.18 Nov 1919[82] never married; she died of heart disease and anemia at 42 years old. Her death certificate lists her occupation as stenographer.

Emery and Addie moved to Candia, New Hampshire, in 1902 as his death certificate says he had lived there for nineteen years when he died 23 May 1922.[83] He died from cerebritis, a brain inflammation or infection frequently caused by lupus, and chronic interstitial nephritis also a lupus result. (His sister Serena had also died of cerebritis.) His wife, Addie, had died only months before on 26 Oct 1921.[84]

I have referred to him as Emery, not Emory, but his birth, death and military records are all spelled as Emery but census records spell it both ways and his son Walter Emory spelled his name with an o.

Emery and Addie's move to Candia was supposedly fueled by their son Fay[6] who bought them a home on the condition that they care for two of his children, Mildred Luella[7] who was mildly retarded and Ruth[7], the third child, which the family says they did for 10 years. The story is that Emery's son, Harold, paid off the mortgage so they could return to Lynn, Mass, but they were living in New Hampshire in both the 1910 and 1920 censuses. Neither of the children were living with them in 1900 or 1910. Their property is listed

82. New Hampshire, Death and Disinterment Records, 1754-1947 Ancestry.com
83. New Hampshire, Death and Disinterment Records, 1754-1947 Ancestry.com.
84. New Hampshire, Death and Burial Records Index, 1654-1949.

as mortgaged in the 1920 census just before their deaths.

Faye Hartwell[6] (Emory Center[5], Humphrey[4], John[3], William[2], James[1])

Fay Hartwell[6] was born 10 Jan 1870 in Topsham, the oldest child and one of the four children born in Topsham. He may have left home very early but he did marry on 15 Jan 1890.[85]

His first wife, Fannie Bell Libbey, was from Lebanon, Maine. They married in Saugus, Massachusetts, but she died following the birth of their child on 21 Aug 1891 from a bowel obstruction.[86] The child did not survive and I can find no records of its birth or death.

On 18 Jul 1894[87] he married again to Edna Alzadia Snow from Thornton, New Hampshire. Edna was eleven or twelve years older than Fay. I found her working as a housekeeper in 1880[88] in Woodstock, NH; they married only a little ways down the road in Plymouth. Woodstock was, and I'm sure must still be, a tourist destination for the city folk in New England. "Several inns and hotels were built to accommodate the wealthy, who sought relief from the summer heat, humidity and pollution of coal-age Boston, Hartford, New York and Philadelphia."[89]

We don't really know what Fay was doing there but I would assume the summer provided lots of work opportunities for young folks there in the White Mountains. It's about 120 miles from Boston.

Nine months later their son, Ashley[7], was born on 13 Mar 1895.[90] His birth was quickly followed by Mildred's on 26 Sep 1896[91] there in Woodstock.

---

85. Massachusetts, Marriage Records, 1840-1915.
86. Massachusetts, Death Records, 1841-1915.
87. "New Hampshire, Marriages, 1720-1920," (https://goo.gl/wX9pb6).
88. Year: 1880; Census Place: Woodstock, Grafton, New Hampshire; Roll: 765; Family History Film: 1254765; Page: 438D; Enumeration District: 103; Image: 0598.
89. Woodstock, New Hampshire, https://goo.gl/gtZZBB, accessed 11 July 2015.
90. "New Hampshire, Birth Records, Early to 1900,"(https://goo.gl/IzPhMq).
91. "New Hampshire, Birth Records, Early to 1900," (https://goo.gl/DL0RM5)

Ruth E[7] was the third child, born 22 Jan 1898 in Stoneham, Massachusetts.[92] The family is found in Concord two years later in the 1900 census. Faye is listed as a farm laborer as is the seven others who are listed as their lodgers. Two of them were from Denmark and there's variety of other French Canadians, Russians and Swedes living on their area, Nine Acre Corner. Even today, this land that lies on the Freedom Trail is still largely rural; it's on the way to the Old North Bridge along Paul Revere's path.

The last daughter, Evelyn May[7], was born two years later on 3 May 1902[93] there in Concord.

Only six years later, Mildred[7] died at age 12 on 27 Dec 1908[94] of tuberculosis while living at the Massachusetts School for the Feeble Minded. Her death certificate says she was sick for eleven months. There's no proof that her grandparents kept her or Ruth[7] but it's certainly possible that they helped out where they could. As Mildred[7] and Ruth[7] had TB and evidently Ashley[7] and Evelyn[7] didn't, it's also possible that the children were separated because of their exposure was greater or they were deemed more susceptible than the others.

The story behind that "school" is a horror though. At center of the eugenics movement, it became a boys only institution and the survivors have their own stories to tell. Most of the worst abuses happened after Mildred[7] was there but the telling bit of this is that the state allowed IQ testing to warrant placement. Children were taken from their parents if they didn't meet certain testing standards. It was used to house orphans and the poor in later years.

Was Mildred[7] placed there voluntarily? Was she really mentally retarded? It has been estimated that half of the inmates were not mentally retarded at all. And the burning question for me is - was that place the source of the tuberculosis that killed her and therefore her mother and sister later? The surviving family was aware

92. "Massachusetts, Births, 1841-1915," (https://goo.gl/DEXdlS).
93. "Massachusetts, Births, 1841-1915," (https://goo.gl/7U5Qrz).
94. Massachusetts, Town and Vital Records, 1620-1988 Ancestry.com.

she was placed in a home but the date and length of that placement was unknown. If you are interested in learning about this institution, I've added a list of sources in the appendix.

Edna is described by her descendants as a "hard-working but sickly woman" and she also died of tuberculosis on 24 Nov 1918 in Methuen, Massachusetts.[95]

Ruth[7] chose to become a registered nurse but developed tuberculosis after finishing her schooling. She was working at the Concord Hospital in New Hampshire in 1920; she is listed as a boarder and a nurse.[96] She died 12 Jan 1926, according to family, in Methuen; though I wasn't able to find a actual death record, I did find her in the Massachusetts Death Index for 1926. One of the reasons I'm sure it's her? Her middle name is listed as Edna.

Her family says she spent a year in the sanitarium there in Methuen before her death. There was a small facility (12 beds) in a house built in 1746. It was called the Barr Sanitarium and Hospital. Today it's the Grace Morgan House, an assisted living home. I assume this is where she stayed.

My grandfather spent time in a Georgia sanitarium in the early 1940s. My family never talked about those years and I realized I did not know where he stayed. Dipping into the history of the sanitariums down there was an interesting sidetrack. One specific statistic that stands out is actually from a University of Virginia faculty member (It's two blocks away from me!). "An estimated 110,000 Americans died each year from tuberculosis in the 1900's. The tuberculosis mortality rates of Virginia were one of the highest in the nation."[97]

I wondered how New England compared to that and in researching it, I stumbled across a mortality report from 1905 which definitely

95. New Hampshire, Death and Disinterment Records, 1754-1947 Ancestry.com.

96. Year: 1920; Census Place: Concord Ward 6, Merrimack, New Hampshire; Roll: T625_1013; Page: 13A; District: 76; Image: 401

97. Sucre, Richard, Blue Ridge Tuberculosis Sanitarium, The Great White Plague, http://goo.gl/rzpVkW, accessed 10 July 2015.

states the highest rates between 1900 and 1905 were in some of the major southern cities. What is the most amazing to me is that we are pretty much oblivious now to the toll exacted by tuberculosis for our parents and grandparents.

Fay[6] died of an "illuminating gas poisoning accident"on 9 Nov 1933.[98] That old-timey explanation is simply carbon monoxide poisoning. At that time gas lamps and gas refrigerators could have been the culprits as well as cars, gas ovens or faulty heaters. Gas refrigerators were phased eventually phased out but it was years before authorities realized the dangers.[99]

Ashley E[7] lived at home working in the woolen mills as his father did as a steam engineer[100] until his marriage in 1923. He married an Elizabeth who had two grown daughters, Esther and Ellen Chapman, who lived with them, but they never had children of their own. Elizabeth was six years older than him - interesting since his father also married an older woman. He had a variety of jobs and became a furniture dealer by 1930.[101] His family says he also had a car repair shop and boat rental business in Methuen. He died on 25 Jan 1955 and is buried in Elmwood Cemetery in Candia according to the Headstone Applications for Military Veterans. He was a World War I veteran.[102]

Evelyn May[7] married James Watson Richards b.12 Sept 1865 d.16 Jan 1947[103] on 27 Apr 1925.[104] He was 31 years older than her and 73 when they had their last child. Evelyn had also gone into nursing and worked a baby nurse for years in addition to being a cook and a seamstress. She was an excellent seamstress and made nearly

98. New Hampshire, Death and Disinterment Records, 1754-1947 Ancestry.com.

99. Jerome B. Trichter, Milton Helpern, M.D. "Accidental Carbon Monoxide Poisoning Due to Domestic Gas Appliances and Gas Refrigerators: The Problem in New York City and Its Control," *American Journal of Public Health*, volume 42 (March 1952): 259.

100. Year: 1920; Census Place: Methuen, Essex, Massachusetts; Roll: T625_689; Page: 16B; Enumeration District: 218; Image: 1121

101. Year: 1930; Census Place: Lawrence, Essex, Massachusetts; Roll: 898; Page: 2B; District: 0114; Image: 786.0; FHL microfilm: 2340633

102. U.S., Headstone Applications for Military Veterans, 1925-1963 Ancestry.com.

103. New Hampshire, Death and Disinterment Records, 1754-1947: Ancestry.com. Original data: "New Hampshire, Death and Disinterment Records, 1754–1947."

104. New Hampshire, Marriage and Divorce Records, 1659-1947 Ancestry.com.

all her children's clothes. She was a superb cook, avid reader and handy in all crafts, including tatting. She was a small woman who never quite reached 5 feet tall and, although she was a baby nurse, she boarded out all of her children except the first child. She died of ovarian cancer in 1959 in Chelsea, Massachusetts.[105]

James and Evelyn[7] had seven children: James Charles[8] 1925-1994, Fay Jeannette[8] 1928-2013, Evelyn Marie[8] 1937-1938, Mildred Esther[8], Adeline Francis[8] 1939-2014, Robert Charles[8], and Katherine Lynda[8].

I've gotten to meet Rob[8] and Katherine[8] who I never knew existed before but Rob was the first "new" cousin I got to actually meet in person. He provided me with all his research to help jump start our part of the genealogy.

Everett Dexter[6] (Emory Center[5], Humphrey[4], John[3], William[2], James[1])

Everett Dexter was born 8 Feb 1871 in Topsham; he married Estella "Stella" Isabel Fairbanks b.2 May 1876[106] on 2 Apr 1895 in Lynnfield, Massachusetts.[107] She had five pregnancies but the first child was stillborn on 11 Jul 1895.[108] They had four children after that but the last only lived four months. Lottie A[7] died on 25 Oct 1904 in Candia, New Hampshire,[109] after being born in Lynnfield on 14 Jun 1904.[110] Her death might actually explain her mother's early death because that baby died of tuberculosis only two weeks after she came to Candia. We don't know when or where Stella died; all we do know is that by 1910, Everett remarried and he had the children.

Since Lottie[7] was the first case of tuberculosis in the immediate family, 4 years before her cousin, Mildred, died in Massachusetts, I can speculate that Stella was the original source of the tuberculosis. Of course, TB was rampant in the Lynn area as we've seen before. Don't forget, however, Everett's first cousins, Henry's children,

105. Massachusetts, Death Index, 1901-1980 Ancestry.com Operations, Inc., 2013.
106. Massachusetts, Town and Vital Records, 1620-1988
107. Massachusetts, Marriage Records, 1840-1915 Ancestry.com Operations, Inc., 2013.
108. "Massachusetts, Deaths and Burials, 1795-1910," (https://goo.gl/d38sfe).
109. New Hampshire, Death and Disinterment Records, 1754-1947 Ancestry.com.
110. Massachusetts, Birth Records, 1840-1915 Ancestry.com Operations, Inc., 2013.

died in 1897 and 1901 of tuberculosis. We of course don't know how close Henry and Emory were but it's reasonable to assume since they were in the same town and were the only surviving married children, that they would be close. I do know that the family appears to have fragmented by 1900 with families in Maine, Massachusetts and Pennsylvania.

Emory and Addie left Massachusetts after the first two grandchildren died and they were probably who Everett fled to when Lottie died a few years later. Perhaps the tuberculosis was one of the reasons why they left Lynn in the first place.

Everett's second wife was Minerva Blanche Fitch b.21 Apr 1886[111] d.14 Nov 1960;[112] they married on 10 Jun 1909 in Manchester, New Hampshire, where she was from.[113] They had four children but by 1920 they were living in Newfields, New Hampshire. That is where Everett was living in 1940 as a divorced man and one child still at home.[114]

The surviving descendants of Minerva and Everett have no knowledge of what happened to their half-siblings. I was able to gain some information including who had descendants.

Ethel Edna[7] was the oldest living child of Everett and Stella, born on 31 Aug 1896 in Lynnfield.[115] On her birth certificate Edna is spelled Ednah and Everett's occupation is listed as farmer. She married M Eugene Hutchinson on 16 March 1917 in Melrose, Massachusetts,[116] but I can find no trace of her after that.

Ernest Fay[7]'s birth record on 9 Aug 1900[117] describes Everett as a teamster. The last time I could find evidence of Ernest was in the 1930 census where he was living as a boarder in Candia. He was a

111. New Hampshire, Birth Records, 1659-1900 Ancestry.com Operations. Inc., 2013.
112. "Maine, Death Index, 1960-1996," (https://goo.gl/8jsuCU).
113. New Hampshire, Marriage and Divorce Records, 1659-1947 Ancestry.com.
114. Year: 1940; Census Place: Newfields, Rockingham, New Hampshire; Roll: T627_2295; Page: 4A; Enumeration District: 8-38
115. Massachusetts, Birth Records, 1840-1915 Ancestry.com Operations, Inc., 2013.
116. "Massachusetts, State Vital Records, 1841-1920," (https://goo.gl/DMZaHd).
117. Massachusetts, Birth Records, 1840-1915 Ancestry.com Operations, Inc., 2013.

"chopper" in the wood industry.

Dexter Raymond[7] b.5 Oct 1902 married Sarah Joseph O'Brien b.abt 1897 from Ireland. He worked for the railroad: by 1920 he and Sarah are living in Mount Vernon, New York,[118] and in 1930 they had moved to Rahway, New Jersey.[119] She states in 1920 that she is a naturalized citizen but I was not able to find a naturalization record prior to 1920, just one for a Sarah O'Brien in 1928.[120] Two censuses say she arrived in the US in 1912, but I was not able to find her entry record.

Sarah was still living in Rahway in 1940; Dexter is not with her but she is listed as married. We have an unconfirmed death date of 9 Sept 1949 in Brentwood, New Hampshire, for him and no answer to that mystery.

Their daughters were Ellen[8] b.abt 1924 and Ethel[8] b.abt 1922. I have no confirmed data for either of them except that another ancestry.com tree has both of them still alive and one married to Robert Francis Tuder b.1913 d.2005.[121] A bit of sleuthing turned up Ethel[8], presently 93 years old, living in New Jersey. Ethel[8] and Robert had two children, a boy, Robert D, and a girl, Linda. It is Linda's daughter that has the ancestry account. She has three other siblings. Hopefully, contact will be made. More new living cousins!

It does look like Ethel's sister, Ellen[8] never married but is also still alive.

The half-siblings, Minerva's children, included Alice[7] b.7 Mar 1911[122] d.16 Nov 1976[123] who never married. Donald R[7] b.abt 1919

118. Year: 1920; Census Place: Mount Vernon Ward 3, Westchester, New York; Roll: T625_1277; Page: 16A; District: 90; Image: 331

119. Year: 1930; Census Place: Rahway, Union, New Jersey; Roll: 1389; Page: 20B; District: 0127; Image: 316.0; FHL microfilm: 2341124

120. National Archives and Records Administration; Washington, D.C.; Index, 1906-1966 Petitions for Naturalization, U.S. District Court, Western Dist. of New York, M1677; Microfilm Serial: M1677; Microfilm Roll: 13

121. U.S., Social Security Death Index, 1935-2014 Ancestry.com Operations Inc, 2011.

122. Social Security Administration, Number: 002-14-2160 New Hampshire.

123. Massachusetts Death Index, 1970-2003 Ancestry.com Operations Inc, 2005.

also disappears after 1930. David Roland[7] b.1921 married Muriel Jeanette Harris b.abt 1923[124] and went to war on 23 Oct 1942.[125] I found two death records for stillborn babies in 1947 and 1957 and no other information.

Nellie Lorena[7] Wilson b.6 June 1923 d.3 June 2001 married Dominic Nunzio Carano b.19 May 1904/5 d.11 Apr 1971.[126] They had four children, Terrance John[8], 1941-2009, Susan Alice[8], 1945-1946, Linda Joyce[8] and Donna[8]. Donna now lives in Las Vegas and had done a lot of work on the genealogy but lost her info. Now that I've been digging into the tree, she's back at it!

Arthur Edward[6] (Emory Center[5], Humphrey[4], John[3], William[2], James[1])

Arthur Edward b.12 Feb 1884[127] d.1948[128] married Edith Molly Wallace b.13 Sept 1888 d.Sept 1973[129] on 3 Apr 1909[130] in Boston. They lived in the Worcester area before moving to Auburn, Maine, by 1930.[131] That year he is listed as a salesman in the shoe manufacturing industry and his daughter is still living at home. He had worked as a draftsman in the construction industry as well.[132]

Their son, Howard[6] A b.8 Aug 1906 d.1 May 1937[133] died in an auto accident (fractured skull) in North Carolina at age 31. His death certificate gives us to more pieces of information: he had a wife named Ruth at that time and he is supposedly buried in Worcester, Massachusetts.

Jeanette Elizabeth[6] b.23 May 1911 d.3 May 1998[134] married Quentin

124. New Hampshire, Marriage and Divorce Records, 1659-1947 Ancestry.com.
125. U.S. World War II Army Enlistment Records, 1938-1946
126. U.S., Social Security Death Index, 1935-2014 Ancestry.com Operations Inc, 2011.
127. Massachusetts, Birth Records, 1840-1915 UT, USA: Ancestry.com.
128. Findagrave.com, gravestone photograph, http://goo.gl/E3oayX.
129. Social Security Index, Number: 006-24-0869; Maine; Issue Date: Before 1951.
130. Massachusetts, Marriages, 1841-1915," (https://goo.gl/ED8AGL),.
131. Year: 1930; Census Place: Auburn, Androscoggin, Maine; Roll: 827; Page: 13A; District: 0003; Image: 97.0; FHL microfilm: 2340562
132. Year: 1910; Census Place: Worcester Ward 2, Worcester, Mass; Roll: T624_631; Page: 24B; District: 1864; FHL microfilm: 1374644
133. North Carolina, Death Certificates, 1909-1975 Ancestry.com Operations Inc, 2007.
134. Social Security Administration, Number: 005-07-3071; Maine; Before 1951.

Whittier b.13 Dec 1910 d.Sept 1982[135] on 24 Jul 1937.[136] They are buried together in the Mount Auburn Cemetery. It appears that they had two children and that there are living descendants.

Clara Geneva[6] (Emory Center[5], Humphrey[4], John[3], William[2], James[1])

Clara never married but left a strong impact on this family. She was born 3 Sep 1886 in Saugus, Massachusetts.[137] She was a librarian and the family genealogist. I actually don't know what degrees she held or where she went to school. That wasn't important to any of us while she was alive. She used to joke that she lived so long after retiring that she earned more than she ever did with a salary.

Since she lived to age 95, dying on 3 Dec 1981,[138] she was able to make sure all that genealogy was saved and her role as family genealogist was passed on to her niece, Priscilla. She was obviously close to Priscilla's father, Harold. She is the source of the story about Harold paying off the mortgage for their parents and I suspect the source for nearly all the family stories. Priscilla was close to Clara, buying groceries and having her over on holidays in those last years.

Clara and Harold were living together as boarders in Derry, New Hampshire in 1910. Both are listed as library clerks.[139] Then in 1930 Clara is living with Harold and his family during a period of unemployment in Boston.[140]

Harold Ernest[6] (Emory Center[5], Humphrey[4], John[3], William[2], James[1])

Harold was the youngest child b.8 Feb 1892 d.2 Mar 1983.[141] He married Ruth Whitaker of New York b.8 Apr 1897 d.2 Jul 1996.

135. Social Security Adminstration, Number: 005-07-3069; Maine; Before 1951,
136. Maine, Marriages, 1892-1996, Ancestry.com.
137. Massachusetts, Birth Records, 1840-1915 Ancestry.com.
138. Massachusetts Death Index, 1970-2003, Ancestry.com.
139. Year: 1910; Census Place: Derry, Rockingham, New Hampshire; Roll: T624_865; Page: 15A; District: 0240; FHL microfilm: 1374878
140. Year: 1930; Census Place: Boston, Suffolk, Mass; Roll: 957; Page: 45A; District: 0507; Image: 331.0; FHL microfilm: 2340692
141. California, Death Index, 1940-1997 Ancestry.com Operations Inc, 2000.

They married on 30 Dec 1916 in Derry, New Hampshire,[142] and were living in Boston by the birth of their first daughter, Priscilla, in 1918.[143] Harold was listed as an auto salesman in 1930[144] and retired in 1940. They moved to California before their deaths to be near their daughter, Faith.

The second daughter, Faith Mabel b.14 Aug 1921[145] d.20 Jul 1991,[146] married Charles Eugene Stanstny and had four children, three who are still living and one who died in 1991, Susan Marya[7]. There are eleven living grandchildren. Charles attended the U.S. Naval Academy and was a naval officer. He retired in California where they both died.

I believe that Priscilla may still be alive and living in the Boston area at age 96 but no one I know has contact with her. She married Lawrence M Tangvik 1921-1999. They had two children, Robin and Heather, and possibly a son named Lawrence.

Walter Emory[6] (Emory Center[5], Humphrey[4], John[3], William[2], James[1])

Walter Emory[6] b.6 Jun 1888[147] d.9 Sep 1957[148] led a life of stability and security. Married at age 19 in 1908, he and Mildred Viola Griffin b.26 May 1889 d.2 Oct 1972[149] lived in her hometown of Wayland, Massachusetts, throughout much of their early married life. By 1930, they had moved to Rye, New Hampshire, where he continued his sales career. According to his obituary, he was a decorated soldier in both world wars and had lived in Miami before returning to Rye. He dropped dead from a sudden heart attack while mowing his grass.[150]

---

142. New Hampshire, Marriage and Divorce Records, 1659-1947 Ancestry.com.
143. Ancestry.com. U.S. Public Records Index, Volume 1 Ancestry.com .
144. Year: 1930; Census Place: Boston, Suffolk, Mass; Roll: 957; Page: 45A; District: 0507; Image: 331.0; FHL microfilm: 2340692
145. Social Security Administration Number: 031-12-7079; Mass; Before 1951.
146. Social Security Administration, Number: 547-84-3593; California; Issue Date: 1966.
147. WWI, Registration State: Massachusetts; Registration County: Middlesex; Roll: 1684689; Draft Board: 32.
148. "New Hampshire, Death Certificates, 1938-1959," (https://goo.gl/gRK5yy).
149. Social Security Administration, Number: 001-52-3910; New Hampshire; 1973
150. Portsmouth Herald, September 10, 1957, page 3. http://goo.gl/UGIZbB

He and Mildred had two children, Walter Emory Jr[7] and Maxine Arabelle[7].

Walter Emory Jr[7] b.7 Mar 1912 d.7 Aug 1960[151] graduated from Emory University Medical School in 1939. He also attended Yale and is listed in the 1932 yearbook.[152] He married Virginia Dillion b.abt 1914 d.3 Sept 1962, a Georgia native, while in Georgia. He did his internship at Union Hospital Fall River, Massachusetts. He served two years as a First Lieutenant in the Medical Corps during WW II. I found some of this information on line. Someone had found a copy of one of the graduation invitations. It includes a picture of all the graduating interns but I was not able to identify which one was Walter.

Virginia died in a major incident - the 1962 plane crash at Orly Airport in France. Many well-known Atlanta public figures died in the crash which has been called "Atlanta's version of September 11 in that the impact on the city in 1962 was comparable to New York of September 11."

I was too young at age 11 to fully realize what had happened; I only vaguely remember the incident at all. The chartered plane was filled with Atlanta Art Museum patrons (106) who were coming back from a month long tour of Europe when the plane crashed on takeoff. "The crash was at the time the worst single-aircraft disaster, the first single civilian jet airliner disaster with more than 100 deaths, and the second deadliest aviation disaster in history."[153]

Little did my family know that we had lost a family member that day.

Walter[7] and Virginia had one child, Walter Emory[8] Wilson III.

Maxine Arabelle[7] Wilson b.10 Nov 1908 d.Apr 1983[154] married

151. U.S., Headstone Applications for Military Veterans, 1925-1963 Ancestry.com.
152. U.S., School Yearbooks, 1880-2012 , Ancestry.com
153. Air France Flight 007, https://goo.gl/t0B8Oe, accessed 12 July 2015.
154. Social Security Administration, 003-30-1971; New Hampshire; Date: 1956-1958.

James Sanders b.9 Aug 1903 d.2 Oct 1988.[155] "Tink" Maxine and James had three children, James and Emory Wilson Sanders, Sr., and one other one whose name I do not know.

Frank Leroy Granville[6] *(Emory Center*[5]*, Humphrey*[4]*, John*[3]*, William*[2]*, James*[1]*)*

Last but not least is Frank Leroy b.26 Jan 1880,[156] my great grandfather. His WWI draft card says his hair is dark and his eyes are blue. Both Walter and Harold also had dark brown hair and blue eyes - a snapshot of my own dad. Frank met his wife in Massachusetts while he was working at the morgue at the Boston City Hospital. Delia Agnes McCarron was from Ireland. He was training to be an undertaker and she a nurse when they met. He became a conductor on the Amesbury-Merrimack trolley after deciding undertaking was not in his future. They moved to New Jersey in 1909 or 1910 and settled in Camden. He contracted typhoid fever and was sick for months, losing his hearing completely. His hearing did improve over time but he never fully recovered. He worked a variety of jobs and even owned his own chemical business until WWII created shortages of the materials. He died only months before I was born on 10 Aug 1951.[157]

His wife, the original Delia, was born in County Donegal on 24 Feb 1876. She was sent when she was 12 to America to live with her half-sister, Nellie Gill, in Dorchester, Massachusetts. Her mother had died when she was born. I wasn't able to find any record of her arrival nor any trace of Nellie, nor any family in Ireland.

The 1900 and 1910 censuses do not have her as naturalized but the 1920 does. Their marriage date is said to be 19 April 1899; their first child was born in January of 1900. I did find a marriage record in Pennsylvania in 1916[158] though so I get the feeling the grandchildren were not aware of that discrepancy. That is about a year after the last child was born.

155. Social Security Adminstration, 001-44-5844; New Hampshire; Issue Date: 1968.
156. WWI, State: New Jersey; County: Camden; Roll: 1711990; Draft Board: 4.
157. Findagrave.com, http://goo.gl/CSUkMq, accessed 12 July 2015.
158. Philadelphia, Pennsylvania, Marriage Index, 1885-1951 Ancestry.com.

Delia lived to age 90 on 31 July 1966[159] dying only months after her son, my grandfather, died. She was in a nursing home then; we came up in March for his funeral but I was not allowed to see her because they didn't want her to know he was dead. I had only been to New Jersey twice before, at age 6 months and at 5 years so I don't remember ever meeting her.

They had six children including Clara Geneva[7] who died at six months in 1909. The four oldest were born in Massachusetts, both Clara[7] and the youngest, Dorothy Elizabeth[7], were born in New Jersey. Dorothy "Dot" b.25 Apr 1914 d.2 Jun 1989[160] never had children and never left Camden. I was told that she married a William Eckhardt in 1963 who died in 1980 but she died as a Wilson. I found no records of the marriage and my understanding was that she never married.

One thing is for sure, what we think we know about our families just sometimes is a mix of true knowledge, faulty memory and assumptions. One such assumption for me was that I was a product of two Irish Catholics. Half of that was correct. I believe Frank converted; he and Delia are buried in the Calvary Cemetery in Cherry Hill, New Jersey - it is a large Catholic cemetery. I had asked my uncle if he knew the story and he wasn't sure who converted, Frank or his son Joseph. It must have been Frank.

The oldest child was Francis Emery[7] (and yes, it is Emery, not Emory). Born in 1 Jan 1923 in Lynnfield, Francis d.19 May 1973[161] was listed as a stenographer in the 1920 census. In 1930 he appears to be in New York working as a chemist and living by himself. The age is correct, the marriage year is correct and the birth locations are all correct for him and his parents. I cannot find a 1940 census record for a Francis born in Massachusetts anywhere.

According to the family information, he married a Mary Wilson on

159. Findagrave.com, http://goo.gl/UXyA5K, accessed 12 July 2015.
160. Social Security Administration, Number: 139-03-6984; New Jersey; Before 1951.
161. Findagrave.com, http://goo.gl/Z5NLhm, accessed 12 July 2015.

21 Aug 1921 and they had Francis Emery[8] II b.1 Jan 1923 d.24 Aug 1982. Though Francis I is buried in Wichita, Kansas, I do not have all the details. I don't know what happened to his first wife and I have been contacted by someone there who says there was another child, William Henry[8] born after 1940. He did marry at least one other time; he is buried with Marjorie Alvena Grindle who is not the mother of Francis II because she was born in 1912.

Gertrude Mary[7] b.14 Oct 1903 d.Jan 1984[162] married Archibald Clinton Luther and had two children, Archibald Clinton[8], Jr, and William Elmer[8]. Archie Jr had three children, Archie III[9], Nicole Marie[9], and Kay Lynn[9]. William and his wife, Joanna Wiley, had two girls, Janna Cezanne[10] and Jessica Clair[10]. Both sons ended up moving to California and having their children late in the 1960s.

Archibald II[7] received an Electrical Engineering degree from MIT in 1950. He married Patricia Morgan in 1964. After his retirement from RCA, he continued in business, developing and marketing a graphics software program.

Helen Agnes[7] b.26 Jan 1906 d.20 Mar 1998[163] married Thomas Francis Larkin and they had one son, Thomas Jr, b.26 Jun 1934 d.18 Jul 2010.[164] Thomas Jr married Kathleen Flynn but they had no children.

Joseph Leroy[7] b.11 Jan 1902[165] d.19 Mar 1966 married Anna Josephine Piejko b.6 Mar 1901 d.25 Apr 1984 in December of 1920. These are my grandparents. I never met my grandfather; he and Anna had a rocky marriage, finally divorcing in the 1940s. We did go up for his funeral - a truly bizarre experience. To meet family for what felt like the first time, to attend a Catholic funeral (my first and only), to not meet my three first cousins who were not brought from Ohio. To say the least, it's a strange memory for me. My most vivid memory is the actual service inside a gorgeous old Catholic church in Philadelphia and the snow. Real powder snow - in

162. Social Security Administration, Number: 137-54-7077; New Jersey; 1972.
163. Social Security Administration, Number: 154-05-1711; New Jersey; Before 1951
164. Social Security Administration, Issue State: New Jersey; Issue Date: Before 1951.
165. "Massachusetts, Births, 1841-1915," (https://goo.gl/7cF6Pb)

March!

Joseph worked a variety of jobs including carpentry and remodeling. A very handy man, just like my father. He worked for the NY Shipbuilding Company during WWI and also worked on ships that traveled the eastern seaboard.

I didn't get to see my grandmother very many times. I think she and her second husband, Melvin Howell, made the trip down to Georgia three times; I only remember two. She was a quiet woman. Very much the solid Polish type like my Dad was. She came to the U.S. in 1910 with her mother, Kalarryna, and her sister, Marya. Her father is not listed on the ship manifest with them when they landed in November but it appears that his name was Marcin. He had been to America at least twice before in 1896 and 1901. They were from the Galicia area, the city of Przemrysh. Poland, like Ireland, exported people more than anything else in the late 19th and early 20th century due to economics.

The immigration officer couldn't spell Piejko so they entered the country as Palmers. They experienced extreme poverty. She spoke of walking the railroad tracks to find bits of coal that fell from the trains for heating their home when she was young. She worked as a sewing machine operator for much of her marriage and married a second time in 1948. Melvin C Howell had also been married before and had his first family and, not surprisingly, little interest in us.

They had two children, my father and my uncle Joe.

Joseph Leroy[8] was the youngest, six years younger and that is major in this family. My father went to work at age twelve so the two boys were not destined to be close. Joe decided he wanted to go to war like everyone else and tried once to join with an altered birth certificate as he was underage. When that didn't work, a friend suggested another route. He signed up for the draft with a fictitious name and then opted to join immediately. This got him in before anyone realized who he really was (or wasn't). And that's how he became a Williams instead of Wilson at age 15. After the war he married Kathryn M Buffo b.1 Jan 1923 d.30 Oct 1992.[166] Joe received his BS degree from Villa Nova and eventually formed his own business.

Joe and Kathy had three children, Joseph John[8], Mary Ann[8] and Beth Ann[8] and three grandchildren. Joe still lives in the same house he and Kathy raised their children in near his daughters in Parma Heights, Ohio. His son, Joe, graduated from Kent State University with a degree in architecture. He was at Kent State when the National Guard opened fire on the demonstrators in 1970. I remember it vividly - calling up there to make sure he was okay. He owns his own firm in Orlando, Florida, and has no children. His wife is from Boston so he's spent more time up there than possibly anyone alive today in our family branch. Mary Ann has twin girls and Beth has one son.

The older brother was Frank Leroy b.29 Sep 1921 d.18 July 1989.[167] My dad.

I would like to say that I know the truth about my father but he just was not a talker. So let me tell you the story the way I heard it - and not from him.

He was forced to quit school at age 12 to go to work as a carpenter so he never had much formal education. He joined the army on 21 August 1942.[168] At that time he was working in typesetting in Camden. The enlistment record I found says he had three years of high school; he never told me what his education was. While stationed in Georgia, he managed to break his leg in a motorcycle accident and while convalescing met my mother, Helen Elam Vance. They married before he was shipped off to Germany and when he returned, he met his daughter, Marianna, for the first time.

They moved to New Jersey but Mother was unhappy up north and they returned in late 1950 for Daddy to take a job with his father-in-

166. Social Security Administration, Number: 444-14-5259; Oklahoma; Before 1951
167. Social Security Administration, Number: 137-18-6799; I New Jersey; Before 1951.
168. "WW II Army Enlistment Records, 1938-1946," (https://goo.gl/ha5QJn).

law in the Vance Saddle Factory in Gainesville, Ga. Mother immediately got pregnant with me (what? location affects fertility? maybe so), followed by my brother, Frank Graham. In 1959, my grandfather's business partner and cousin died, my grandfather died and a few months later the factory burned. It was sold the next year and Daddy became an insurance salesman after that (he really was not a salesman, unfortunately!) and then worked in the moving industry almost up until his death. He died on my honeymoon. He knew on my wedding day that he wouldn't be seeing me again. Our goodbye was sweet: he told Tommy that he was glad that I had someone take care of me. I had been married before - he had never said anything to a husband before.

He was a sweet man, well-read and interested in the world. He was an excellent carpenter and loved to work with wood, something he passed on to both me and my brother. He refused to cuss in front of his children - substituting words like piffly dee dee. My favorite memory (Mother loves it, too) was when he was replacing the wax ring on the toilet by himself. He managed to put that sucker straight down on the floor bolt and cracked the toilet all the way up. He was so good at anything that to have done something so outrageous (it was our only toilet), that Mother and I just thought it was hysterical. He wasn't laughing.

He was the ultimate do-it-yourselfer; I never thought I couldn't do anything if I tried because he always did what he needed to. Mother was the same way about learning. The two together modeled wonderful tools for us to get ahead in the world. Mother is still alive today, living in an assisted living home in Atlanta. Her mother lived to age 96 - I bet Mother will be around longer than that!

All three of us have college degrees. My sister retired from a very long career at the Centers for Disease Control in Atlanta. I'm a self-employed web designer and genealogist living in Virginia. My brother is a software programmer and works for a electric utility company. I'm the only one that had a child. Justin is a truck driver in the Atlanta area and has no children.

There ends this family line. Though we were named Wilsons, there are none to follow us. The only Wilsons left from Joseph Leroy are some out in the Midwest who have nothing to do with the Wilsons at all. It's not unusual with smaller families to have this happen but it is kind of sad. I guess that is one of the reasons why I wrote this!

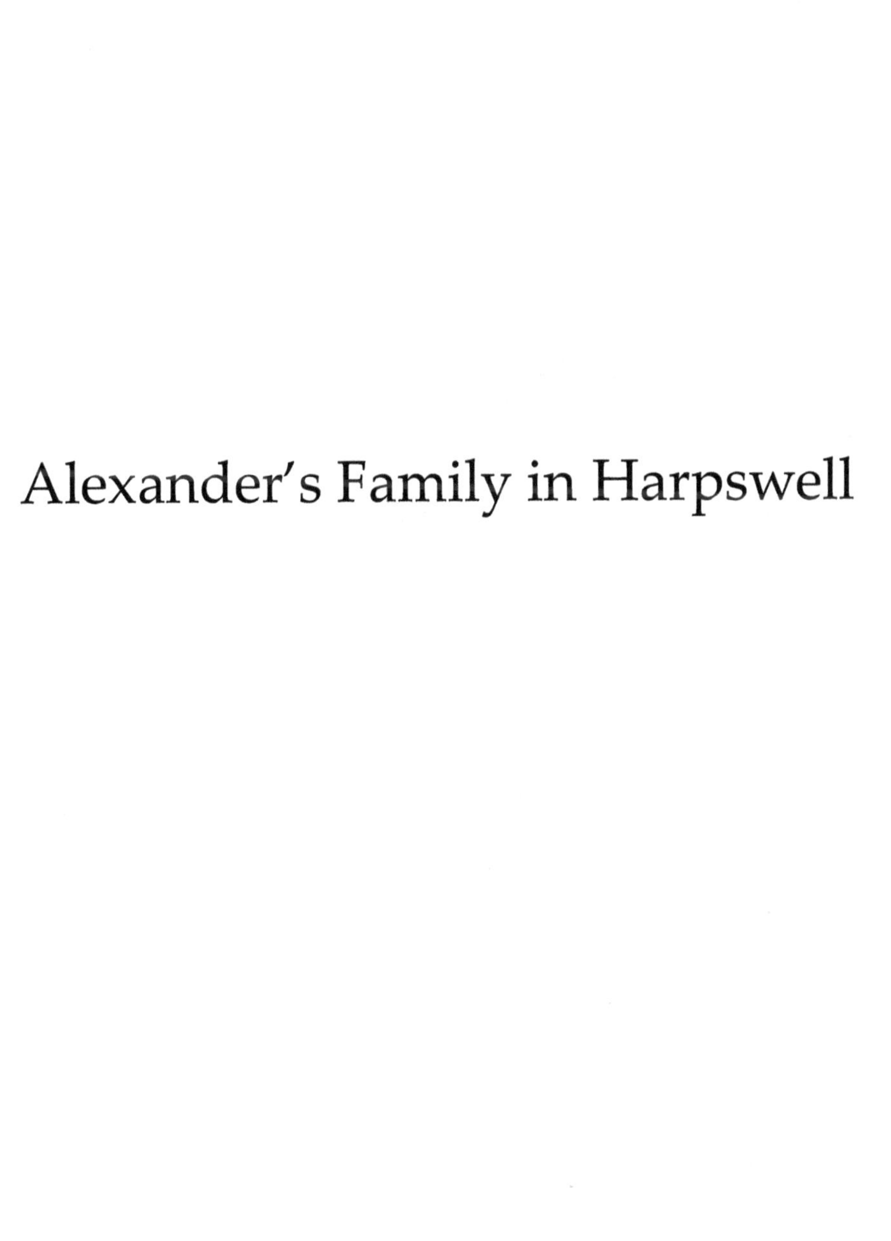

Alexander's Family in Harpswell

As an island family, the birth rate of Alexander and Catharine's descendants is higher than the cousins inland; therefore, the delineating of these families is truncated compared to other lines. Otherwise, I would never get finished with the book or even be able to publish. My family tree on Ancestry.com has been fleshed out as much as possible but Alexander's line has not been as vetted as far as the other lines.

Alexander and Catharine Swansea had nine children, "Deacon" James^3, Mary^3, Elizabeth^3, David^3, Esther^3 b.18 Jan 1756 d.Feb 1756, Jennet^3, Alexander^3, Swansea^3 (Swanzey), and Catharine^3 b.27 Dec 1763 d.10 Apr 1835.[1] Their birth dates and some of the death dates are sourced from the town records.

Alexander did marry again after Catharine's death: after all, the children were under eighteen, five under the age of ten, at the time of her death.

> *Alexander Willson of Harpswell and Sarah Cloof resident at Harpswell were married Aug 12, 1766. (Woodside, Eaton marriages)*

There is no more information about her or anyone named Cloof in Maine however in that time period.

Jennet^3 (Alexander^2, James^1)

Daughter Jennet^3 b.9 Apr 1757 may have married a Jacob Grows in 1789 but I found no confirmation for that nor any trace of a Jacob Grows in Maine during that time frame. Brunswick had Grows, including a Jacob Grows who married there in 1803[2] but there is no other information available.

James^3 (Alexander^2, James^1)

The eldest, James^3 b.16 Nov 1747 d.19 Aug 1839[3], was known as Deacon James^3. He married Keziah Chandler on 21 Mar 1781 and they had eight children. He built a home on his father's land by

1. Findagrave.com, gravestone, http://goo.gl/ukn5kE accessed 24 June 2015.
2. Brunswick, 84.
3. Findagrave.com, gravestone, http://goo.gl/ptQdPN, accessed 29 March 2015.

1784 and became a deacon in the Center Harpswell Church.[4]

A year later, according to Wheeler, a mill in Widgeon Cove was owned in part by Deacon James Wilson and Silas Allen.[5]

The Wilson's early shipyard on their shore was reactivated in 1810 when James built the brig "Two Sisters", 136 tons, and 77 feet in length. A Brunswick resident was her owner and a John Wilson was one of her captains at that time.

James[3] retained ownership of the mill at Widgeon Cove until 1837.[6]

All but one of James and Keziah's children married; the one who did not was Abigail[4] b.13 Jul 1801, the youngest, who appears in a 1870 census in Turner unmarried but with assets valued at $1000.[7] There is also a job title listed but I was not able to decipher it. It does confirm a birth year about 1801 but I was not able to find any other records for her if indeed that is her.

The only child that remained in Harpswell was David[4] who was the child who inherited from his father. All the rest left Harpswell, moving to Brunswick, Bradford and Minot. They didn't leave Harpswell behind though as it becomes clear that they marry Harpswell natives and their descendants.

James[4] (James[3], Alexander[2], James[1])

> *James Wilson of Harpswell and Jane Bartlet of Minor Married May 6th 1827 (Minot, 94)*

James[4] b.11 Jan 1782[8] d. 17 Mar 1867 married Mary Jane Bartlett b.30 Oct 1799[9] d.12 Mar 1891.[10] They had their first two children in Harpswell so they moved to Minot between 1830 and 1834. Jane was originally from there. The children were Alexander[5], Bailey

4. Wheeler, 441.
5. Wheeler, 614.
6. Harpswell Heritage Land Trust.
7. "United States Census, 1870," (https://goo.gl/EC4yAb).
8. "Maine, Births and Christenings, 1739-1900," (https://goo.gl/xDvLyC).
9. "Maine, Births and Christenings, 1739-1900," (https://goo.gl/BhWpgV).
10. Findagrave.com, gravestone, http://goo.gl/cbtKAJ, accessed 20 June 2015.

Bartlett[5], Mary[5] and John[5]. James[5], Jane[5] and two of their children are buried in the Jasper cemetery in Minot.

John[5] (James[4], James[3], Alexander[2], James[1])

John[5] b.2 Feb 1828 (Harpswell, 28) may not have married. I found a military enlistment record for probably the same John with that birth year for Boston in 1864.[11] His place of birth was Harpswell, Maine. According to Charles Sinnett, he died 1852 in Colorado.[12]

Alexander[5] (James[4], James[3], Alexander[2], James[1])

> *Apl.14, 1860, Mr. Alexander Wilson of Minot Miss Elizabeth C. Witham of Lewiston before me R.H. Ford Minister of the Gospel (Lewiston, 661)*

Alexander b.10 Dec 1830 (Harpswell, 28) d.25 Mar 1887[13] married Elizabeth "Lizzie" Curtis Witham b.23 Sep 1834[14] d.1927.[15] They did have one son, John Otis[6] b.13 Jun 1861[16] d.1941[17] who married but most likely did not have had any children.

Bailey Barlett[5] (James[4], James[3], Alexander[2], James[1])

> *Bailey Bartlett Son of James Wilson and Jane his Wife was born Minot May 11th 1839 (Minot, 245)*

Bailey Bartlett d.17 Nov 1903[18] married Mary J Rowe b.9 Dec 1841 d.12 May 1908 on 6 Apr 1862.[19] They had one boy named James R not survive infancy and two boys that did: James R[6] b.7 Jan 1866 d.14 Jan 1895[20] and Fred Henry[6] b.7 Aug 1881.[21] James is buried with his parents but I can find no confirmed trace of Henry after the 1929 Massachusetts Mason card with his birth where he is listed as a gardener.

---

11. United States, Naval Enlistment Rendezvous, 1855-1891. Salt Lake City, Utah: FamilySearch, 2013. Film : 004639551.
12. Sinnett, Charles Nelson, William Wilson Descendants, undated, typewritten manuscript, MHS, call no., 12..
13. Findagrave.com, gravestone, http://goo.gl/SMl36g, accessed 4 June 2015.
14. "Maine, Births and Christenings, 1739-1900," (https://goo.gl/oRVWla).
15. Findagrave.com, gravestone photograph, http://goo.gl/XIH6AK.
16. "Maine, Births and Christenings, 1739-1900," (https://goo.gl/aV4QdQ).
17. Findagrave.com, gravestone, http://goo.gl/GfRi4f, accessed 20 June 2015.
18. Findagrave.com, gravestone, http://goo.gl/nr8Pca, accessed 4 June 2015.
19. Maine Marriages, 1771-1907," (https://goo.gl/SzIkBB)
20. Findagrave.com, http://goo.gl/hbLIQ4, accessed 20 June 2015.
21. Massachusetts, Mason Membership Cards, 1733-1990 Ancestry.com.

Mary[5] (James[4], James[3], Alexander[2], James[1]) - The Jaspers

Mary Daughter of James Wilson and Jane his Wife was born Minot December 11th 1834 (Minot, 245)

Mary[5] d.11 Jan 1875 (unc) married Samuel Branch Jasper on 25 Oct 1856.[22] This was a moving family. According to the 1870 census he was a chair maker. They moved to Ohio before the birth of their first child soon after their marriage[23] and then after Mary's death he moved his children to Indiana.[24] He died in Texas on 27 Oct 1906[25] and is buried with two of his children who never married, Mary Elizabeth "Lizzie"[6] b.26 Aug 1862 d.27 Jan 1940 and Leland Samuel[6] b.26 Aug 1872 d.3 Sept 1927 and another married daughter, Florence Nightingale[6]. One son, Elmer Lincoln[6] b.19 Oct 1864 d.31 Dec 1889 was killed in Guatemala in a railroad accident.[26] There was one other child who must have died at birth or as an infant, Otis M[6], born 16 Jul 1869.[27]

Florence Nightingale[6] Jasper b.1 June 1860 d.1 Apr 1936[28] married Francis Marion Wheeler b.11 Jan 1854 d.10 Feb 1939[29] in Indiana. They had eight children, four in Indiana and four in Texas: they moved to Texas by 1889. Their children were Alvin Hope[7], Leroy Jasper[7], Enola Grace[7], Clyde Francis[7], Elmer Wilson[7], Fred Irvin[7], Charles Francis[7] and Samuel Earle[7].

Francis Jane[6] Jasper b.1857 d.1924 also married in Indiana. She and William Washington Merrill b.1854 d.1940[30] had nine children born between 1884 and 1899, the first two in Kentucky and the others in Texas. They were Blanche[7], Arley Vivian[7], Edna Myrtle[7], Iva Mae[7], Irday M[7], Ray Irvin[7], Elma A[7], Elisha[7], and Ilene Mildred[7].

---

22. "Maine, Marriages, 1771-1907," (https://goo.gl/SfHTuA).
23. Year: 1860; Census Place: Tate, Clermont, Ohio; Roll: M653_944; Page: 293; Image: 392; Family History Library Film: 803944.
24. Year: 1880; Census Place: Vienna, Scott, Indiana; Roll: 309; FHL: 1254309; Page: 86C; Enumeration District: 166; Image: 0173.
25. Findagrave.com, gravestone, http://goo.gl/5gfRJK, accessed 20 June 2015.
26. Sinnett, William Wilson Descendants, 14.
27. Ohio, Births and Christenings Index, 1800-1962 Ancestry.com Inc., 2011.
28. Findagrave.com, gravestone photograph, http://goo.gl/oMOHWX.
29. Texas, Death Certificates, 1903–1982 Ancestry.com Operations, Inc., 2013.
30. Findagrave.com, gravestone photographs, http://goo.gl/JNKd4s.

John Wilson[6] Jasper b.20 Mar 1867 d. 12 Feb 1939[31] was the only son who married. He and his wife, Alice Virginia Covey, had three children, John Earnest Victor[7], Esther Virginia[7] and William Godfrey[7].

Catharine[4] (James[3], Alexander[2], James[1]) - Toothakers Take 2

Catherine married her first cousin, Abraham Toothaker and is included in the next chapter.

Betsey[4] (James[3], Alexander[2], James[1]) - The Hodges

Joseph Hodg of Minot & Betsey Wilson of Harpswell informed of their Intention of marriage April 20 Day AD. 1822 (Minot, 45)

Kezia Lucy Daughter of Joseph Hodge adn Betsey his Wife was born Minot December 4th 1825 (212) d.4 Nov 1838[32]
Lydia Maria Daughter of Joseph Hodge and Betsey his Wife was born Minot November 9th 1827 (212) d.19 Jul 1855[33]
Moses C. Son of Joseph Hodge and Betsey his Wife was born Minot March 30th 1833 (Minot, 213) d.6 Feb 1857[34]
James Wilson Son of Joseph Hodge and Betsey his Wife was born Minot March 31st 1836 (Minot, 213) d.22 Sep 1928[35]

Betsey[4] b.29 May 1791[36] and Joseph Hodge b.7 Jun 1792 d.29 Oct 1879[37] had five children but only Joseph Wilson[5] and Catherine Swanzey[5] had children.

Joseph Wilson Son of Joseph Hodge and Betsey his Wife was born Minot August 29th 1831 (212)

Joseph[5] Wilson Hodge d.1964 married Kezia E Hutchins b.1841 d.1916, a cousin, on 13 Nov 1856.[38] Her mother was Lydia Wilson[4], daughter of Deacon James[3]. Her father was from Minot. Joseph was a Civil War veteran; he served with Company F in the 9th Regi-

31. Findagrave.com, gravestone, http://goo.gl/wNcsnr, accessed 22 June 2015.
32. Findagrave.com, http://goo.gl/dutmBd, accessed 22 June 2015.
33. Findagrave.com, gravestone, http://goo.gl/VBvNo3, accessed 22 June 2015.
34. Findagrave.com, gravestone, http://goo.gl/HmTojh, accessed 22 June 2015.
35. "Florida Deaths, 1877-1939," (https://goo.gl/mqw0Vi).
36. "Maine, Births and Christenings, 1739-1900," (https://goo.gl/t5IXM9).
37. "Maine, Veterans Cemetery Records, 1676-1918," (https://goo.gl/Wys6cv.
38. "Maine, Marriages, 1771-1907," (https://goo.gl/0bqO7e).

ment.[39] He died before June of 1864:[40] Kezia's pension is dated 20 Apr 1865 and the last son was born in early March 1865. He served with Company F in the 9th Regiment.[41]

They had three children, Zillah[6] C b.17 Jan 1858[42] d.1932,[43] Moses C[6] b.13 Feb 1860 d.24 Oct 1943,[44] and Joseph Wilson[6] b.11 Mar 1865[45] d.aft 1940 who married late and had no children. Both Zillah[6] and Moses[6] had children and together had 8 grandchildren for John and Keziah.

Catharina Swansey Daughter of Joseph Hodge and Betsey his Wife was born Minot January 9th 1830 (212)

Catherine Swanzey[5] Hodge d.17 Jun 1860[46] married Edwin Augustus Hackett b.1823[47] d.15 Oct 1910.[48] Months after her death, Edwin married Keziah Yeaton. Their daughter, Evalina A[6] b.abt 1869, married John Otis Wilson[6] (Alexander[5], James[4], James[3], Alexander[2], James[1]). Catherine and Edwin had two children before her death, Maria Lydia[6] and Lizzie C[6] b.abt 1859.

Maria[6] Lydia Hackett b.19 Dec 1857[49] d.aft 1940 married Dennis E Perkins on 5 Dec 1885[50] and lived in Newton, Massachusetts. She had two children.

David[4] (James[3], Alexander[2], James[1])

Feby 17 1819 Mr David Willson 2^d^ of Harpswell & Miss Esther Mountfort both of Brunswick intend marriage. March 16 1819 (Brunswick, 176) by Revd George Lamb (160)

39. Organization Index to Pension Files of Veterans Who Served Between 1861 and 1900 roll 185. Ancestry.com
40. Findagrave.com, gravestone, http://goo.gl/0KuM3n accessed 22 June 2015.
41. Organization Index to Pension Files of Veterans Who Served Between 1861 and 1900 roll 185. Ancestry.com.
42. "Maine, Births and Christenings, 1739-1900," (https://goo.gl/eiLj7k).
43. Findagrave.com, gravestone, http://goo.gl/QVbVVC, accessed 22 June2015.
44. Findagrave.com, gravestone, http://goo.gl/vSLFlh, accessed 22 June 2015.
45. "Maine, Births and Christenings, 1739-1900," (https://goo.gl/XkGZaM).
46. Findagrave.com, gravestone, http://goo.gl/M6bp2u, accessed 22 June 2015.
47. Findagrave.com, gravestone, http://goo.gl/I0aKIv, accessed 22 June 2015.
48. Maine State Archives; 1908-1922 Vital Records; Roll #: 24
49. "Maine, Births and Christenings, 1739-1900," (https://goo.gl/Gfszch).
50. "Maine, Marriages, 1771-1907," (https://goo.gl/DZVV1w).

David[4] b.24 Aug 1793 d.3 May 1840 (Harpswell, 28) remained on the Wilson land in Harpswell. He and Esther Mountfort (Monford) b.11 Jan 1796 d.21 Apr 1882[51] had eight children. One son died as an infant, Paul Randall[5], b.28 May 1837 (Harpswell, 28) d.1837. William Chandler[5] b.13 Aug 1824 d.3 Oct 1841 (Harpswell, 28) was lost at sea. Another son, James[5] b.12 May 1831 d.18 Jul 1853 (Harpswell, 28) may also have been a sailor; he died in New Orleans. Mary[5] b.27 May 1891 (Harpswell, 28), the eldest, married Horatio Toothaker in the next chapter.

John[5] (David[4], James[3], Alexander[2], James[1])

John inherited from his father. During this time the shipyard was still in operation:

> *By 1852, two more vessels had been built in the Wilson Shipyard: the brig "Commodore Stewart", built in 1847, 135 tons, and, five years later, the brig "Mechanic", 219 tons. The "Mechanic" was wrecked in February 1859 off Matinicus Island in Penobscot Bay. Its cargo of lumber was salvaged and used in the construction of the Matinicus Island school house still in use today.*[52]

Captain John[5] b.20 Apr 1835 d.25 Mar 1884 (Harpswell, 28) was born only 5 years before his father died so Esther raised him without remarrying. He was the last one left at home in 1870 with his mother.[53]

He married Jane J Curtis b.26 Aug 1847 first on 17 June 1869 in Brunswick but she died of "purpereal convulsions" or eclampsia during her pregnancy on 19 May 1870[54] right before the census. He then married Mary Given Skolfield b.6 Jul 1838 d.25 Apr 1891.[55] They had one son, Emery Graves Wilson[6] b.15 Jul 1874 d.22 Oct 1938. He was a lawyer. His findagrave.com profile includes his obituary from the Portland Telegram.[56]

Edmund[5] (David[4], James[3], Alexander[2], James[1])

51. Findagrave.com, gravestone, http://goo.gl/kAASm6, accessed 22 June 2015.
52. Harpswell Heritage Land Trust..
53. Year: 1870; Census Place: Harpswell, Cumberland, Maine; Roll: M593_540; Page: 333B; Image: 141; Family History Library Film: 552039.
54. 1870: U.S. Federal Census Mortality Schedules, 1850-1885 Ancestry.com
55. Findagrave.com, http://goo.gl/SVyUU2, accessed 24 June 2015.
56. Findagrave.com, http://goo.gl/0K22gB, accessed 10 Aug 2015.

Edmund[5] b.15 Sept 1822 (Harpswell, 28) d.3 Jan 1913[57] was a sea captain and Civil War veteran (Co K 20 Regiment).[58] He married twice; his first wife was Betsey C A Randall b.24 June 1828[59] d.13 Dec 1862;[60] they had three children before her death. Her mother was an Alexander. Two children died at 11 months: Paul Randall[6] b.21 Dec 1851 d.25 Nov 1852[61] and Frank Otis[6] b.17 Nov 1855 d.5 Nov 1856.[62] The third child, Edmund James[6] b.2 Jan 1861 d.1942[63] did marry but had no children.

Four years after Betsey's death Edmund[5] married Harriet Stover b.30 Jul 1839[64] d.21 Jun 1914[65] and they had seven children including two sets of twins, all of them having children and living until after 1940. They were Betsey Alexander[6], George William[6], Augustus Eaton[6], Jane Stover[6], Delia (!) Stover[6], Nina Clark[6] and Esther[6]. Two married Merrimans, one a Bibber. Two of them were Alexander descendants: the one who was not directly related was an Allen and Toothaker descendant. It does look like it was hard to avoid marrying someone who was blood-related back then!

Rebecca[5] (David[4], James[3], Alexander[2], James[1]) - The Gillespies

Gillespie, Oliver H. of B. and Rebecca Wilson of Harpswell, int. Nov. 8, 1864 (Bowdoin III, 74)

Oliver, ch. Thomas and Catharine B., [ ], P.R.45. [a. 14 y., u.s.c] (I, 94)

Rebecca[5] b.25 Aug 1839 (Harpswell, 28) d.1927 and Oliver H Gillespie b.1836 d.1872[66] had one son, James[6] who married a distant Mountfort cousin. After Oliver's early death Rebecca married Charles Stover Dunning from Harpswell. She is buried with Oliver in Brunswick.

57. Maine State Archives; 1908-1922 Vital Records; Roll #: 60.
58. National Archives and Records Administration. U.S., Civil War Pension Index: General Index to Pension Files, 1861-1934 Ancestry.com Operations Inc, 2000.
59. "Maine, Births and Christenings, 1739-1900," (https://goo.gl/TB2eW5).
60. Findagrave.com, year only, http://goo.gl/1kYnRT, accessed 22 June 2015.
61. Findagrave.com, http://goo.gl/2OayzJ, accessed 22 June 2015.
62. Findagrave.com, http://goo.gl/qYpQHW, accessed 22 June 2015.
63. Findagrave.com, http://goo.gl/QlJ423, accessed 22 June 2015.
64. "Maine, Births and Christenings, 1739-1900," (https://goo.gl/9i4YzS).
65. Maine State Archives; 1908-1922 Vital Records; Roll #: 60.
66. Findagrave.com, gravestone, http://goo.gl/mBC8KM, accessed 23 June 2015.

Esther Ann[5] (David[4], James[3], Alexander[2], James[1]) - The Orrs

Esther Ann[5] b.19 Jul 1829 (Harpswell, 28) d.9 Jan 1898[67] married Arthur Orr b.1825 d.14 Oct 1891.[68] They had at least seven children. Unfortunately, there are no digital records for their births so I may not have found them all. Many birth dates are stated on Findagrave.com without being matched up to a date on the gravestones. The oldest was David[6] b.1850[69] who was gone by the next census. Two others died young, Sylvester Stover[6] b.1851 d.1 Feb 1878 and Joseph[6] b.abt 1859 who probably died between 1870 and 1880.

The youngest daughter, Annie Gertrude[6] Orr b.1871 d.1963, did marry another Alexander descendant, Elwood David Allen, but had no children.

Charles Edwin[6] Orr b.3 Nov 1848 d.27 Sep 1892[70] married Lydia Frances Webber and had five children. According to his death certificate, he was a carriage maker in Bath when he died.[71] His children were Lucy Francis[7], Charles Sylvester[7], Frederick Augustus[7], Carrie Helen[7], and Arthur Richardson[7].

Horatio[6] Orr b.15 Jun 1851 d.3 Apr 1936[72] married Debra Aldrich Bibber b.9 Aug 1855 d.10 May 1941.[73] They had three children but only one survived, Forrest Walker[7].

Cordelia "Delia" M[6] Orr b.24 May 1855 d.15 Jul 1938 also married a Bibber, Orlando M, b.29 Feb 1852 d.7 Nov 1928.[74] They had six children, Charles Alva[7], Susan Maud[7], Orlando Sylvester[7] "Ollie", Annie Esther[7], Bernard Mountfort[7] and Winnifred[7].

Lydia[4] (James[3], Alexander[2], James[1]) - The Hutchins

67. "Maine, Vital Records, 1670-1907 ," (https://goo.gl/kHTDx4).
68. Findagrave.com, gravestone, http://goo.gl/T64ADK, accessed 23 June 2015.
69. Year: 1850; Census: Harpswell, Maine; Roll: M432_251; Page: 262A; Image: 222
70. Findagrave.com, gravestone, http://goo.gl/Q8rEGN, accessed 23 June 2015.
71. Maine State Archives; 1892-1907 Vital Records; Roll #: 43
72. Findagrave.com, http://goo.gl/cTwQ3n, accessed 23 June 2015.
73. Findagrave.com, http://goo.gl/Ri1m2j, accessed 23 June 2015.
74. Findagrave.com, http://goo.gl/F2RaOC, accessed 23 June 2015.

Mr Joseph Hutchins and Miss Lydia WIlson both of Minto informed of their intentions of Marriage July 9th 1837 (Minot, 69)

Lydia[4] b.9 Mar 1798[75] d.2 Dec 1886[76] married Joseph Hutchins b.28 Feb 1803 d.1 Jan 1864 (unc) and had one child, Kezia[5] who married Joseph William Hodge in the previous section of Hodges. They lived in Minot.

Mary[4] (James[3], Alexander[2], James[1]) & Andrew Wilson

Mary[4] "Molly" b.10 Jun 1787[77] d.30 May 1875 (unc) married Andrew Wilson b.13 May 1781 d.1869 (unc). They lived in Bowdoin at first but moved to Bradford by 1840.[78] Though all of their children were born in Bowdoin, they spent the last years in Bradford. Andrew was the son of David Wilson of Freeport, no relation to this family. The children were William[5], Joel C[5], John[5], Keziah[5], Andrew[5] b.2 Apr 1815 d.10 Sept 1848, Betsey[5], Mary[5] b.1822 d.1834 (unc), James Chandler[5], Daniel[5] and Dennis[5].

Joel C[5] (Mary[4], James[3], Alexander[2], James[1])

Joel, ch. Andrew and Mary, Mar. 30, 1809. (Bowdoin I, 234)
Mr Joel C Wilson & Miss Sarah Jane Barker both of Minot informed of their intention of Marriage November 25th 1838 (Minot, 72)
John Henry Son of Joel C. Wilson and Sarah Jane his Wife was born Minot Nov 15 1939 (Minot, 298)
Mary Malissa daughter of Joel C. Wilson and Sarah Jane his Wife was born Minot April 6th 1842 (Minot, 268)

Joel C[5] married Sarah Jane Baker b.14 Feb 1810.[79] They had three children in Minot, John Henry[6], Mary Melissa[6] and Abby Jane[6] b.abt 1849. I could find no death information for anyone besides Melissa[6]. She married Anson Bickmore and moved to Charleston by 1870. Her father is living with them.[80] Sarah disappears between 1850 and 1860, not long after Abby[6] was born.

75. "Maine, Births and Christenings, 1739-1900," (https://goo.gl/xWtVfm).
76. Findagrave.com, gravestone, http://goo.gl/Xe3YP3, accessed 23 June 2015.
77. "Maine, Births and Christenings, 1739-1900," (https://goo.gl/cF4jFi).
78. Year: 1840; Census Place: Bradford, Penobscot, Maine; Roll: 148; Page: 135; Image: 274; Family History Library Film: 0009707.
79. "Maine, Births and Christenings, 1739-1900," (https://goo.gl/nwyqNc).
80. Year: 1870; Census Place: Charleston, Penobscot, Maine; Roll: M593_553; Page: 349A; Image: 220; Family History Film: 552052.

Melissa[6] b.6 Apr 1842[81] d.11 Oct 1929 and Anson b.1836 d.1902[82] had four children, all of whom married. Three of them moved to Massachusetts but Wilbur Anson[7] stayed near his parents in Bradford. The three daughters, Esther[7], Ida[7] and Augusta[7], all had children.

John[5] (Mary[4], James[3], Alexander[2], James[1])
John, ch. Andrew and Mary, Apr. 24, 1813. (Bowdoin I, 234)

John[5] d.14 Jun 1900[83] married Lucy Hobbs b.1827 d.21 Dec 1895[84] on 19 Nov 1845[85] in Bradford. They had six children; Clarissa[6] b.1847 d.4 Nov 1863[86] died at 16 and she is buried with her parents in the Mills Cemetery. There was also a Mary[6] b.abt 1845 who died by 1860. The other four all married and had children. They were John Andrew[6], Lucy Adelaide[6], George W[6] and Oliver D[6].

Keziah[5] (Mary[4], James[3], Alexander[2], James[1]) - The Strouts
Keeziah, ch. Andrew and Mary, May 26, 1811. (Bowdoin, I, 234)

Keziah[5] d.10 Oct 1884[87] married Rev. Alvah D M Strout b.27 Apr 1810 d.24 Apr 1881[88] in Bradford. They had ten children, all of whom lived to adulthood. There are no digital records for births so nearly all are unconfirmed. Two did not have children: Nahum Wilbur[6] b.7 Jul 1846 d.28 Oct 1890 died of consumption in Massachusetts[89] and Andrew[6] b.Oct 1841 d.9 Apr 1864 in Louisiana at the Battle of Pleasant Hill. Even though all the rest married, there were very few children. The other children were Mary Elizabeth[6] b.1836 d.11 Dec 1874, Emeline J[6], Alvah D Merritt[6], George H[6] b.abt 1850 d.1906, Sarah Maria[6] b.15 Jul 1853 d.22 May 1922, Edwin Daniel[6] b.14 Apr 1854 d.19 May 1931[90] and Francis L[6] b.1854.

Enoch B[6] b.12 Jan 1844 was also a Civil War veteran.

81. "Maine, Births and Christenings, 1739-1900," (https://goo.gl/4tXJB3).
82. Findagrave.com, http://goo.gl/uWirHZ, accessed 24 June 2015.
83. Maine State Archives; 1892-1907 Vital Records; Roll #: 61.
84. Maine State Archives; 1892-1907 Vital Records; Roll #: 61.
85. "Maine, Marriages, 1771-1907," (https://goo.gl/XCfHbR).
86. "Maine, Nathan Hale Cemetery Collection, ca. 1780-1980," (https://goo.gl/LgCsfL).
87. Findagrave.com, gravestone, http://goo.gl/p5XUni, accessed 24 June 2015.
88. "Maine, Veterans Cemetery Records, 1676-1918," (https://goo.gl/fz9f7O).
89. Massachusetts, Death Records, 1841-1915 Ancestry.com Operations, Inc., 2013.
90. Findagrave.com, gravestone, http://goo.gl/1cuNdV,accessed 24 June 2015.

Emeline or Emily[6] b.27 Apr 1838 d.20 May 1925 married twice and had children by both husbands, a set of twins by Richard J Soule b.5 Aug 1838 d.4 Aug 1913 and one son by William Moulton Randall b.11 May 1832 d.7 Aug 1865.[91] Emily and both husbands are on the same gravestone in Mills Cemetery.

Merritt D or Alvah D[6] M b.16 Apr 1840 d.8 May 1918[92] had four children by wife Susan J Reed b.4 Dec 1840 d.16 Apr 1932, Addie E[7] b.5 Jul 1865 d.15 Sep 1957, Nellie Agnes[7] b.5 Aug 1868 d.14 Dec 1937, Rollo Guy[7] b.8 Oct 1874[93] d.1942 and Roscoe[7] b.15 Feb 1875 d.1942[94] and Ernest[7] b.abt 1870.[95] It does look like Merritt[7] was named Alvah D M like his father but he declined to use that. He was a Civil War veteran who was wounded. The original pension application was dated 5 Feb 1863.[96]

So out of ten children, all of the boys who were old enough fought in the Civil War. The lack of children is interesting to me because there is a genetic mutation that mothers can carry that causes lack of motility in sperm for their sons. I know this because I have that. I am a Wilson daughter just like Keziah. In some branches of this tree, there is a decided lack of children. No way to tell if this is the cause but it's definitely a working theory.

(Note: the following are families in Bristol. The Bristol vital records were very thorough with a lot of information so I've truncated some of the actual records to make these easier to read.)

William[5] (Mary[4], James[3], Alexander[2], James[1])

William, ch. Andrew and Mary, May 24, 1807. (Bowdoin I, 236)
William & Jane Porterfield, both B., Feb. 14, 1847. (m. in B. N.R.18) (Bristol, 301)
Jane (Porterfleld), w.William, d.Oct.6,1893, a.78y. G.R.15 (Bristol I, 740)

91. Findagrave.com, http://goo.gl/Nq2uGn, accessed 24 June 2015.
92. Maine State Archives; 1908-1922 Vital Records; Roll #: 54
93. WWI, Registration State: Maine; County: Penobscot; Roll: 1654010; Draft Board: 1.
94. Findagrave.com, gravestone, http://goo.gl/oFxuuD, accessed 25 June 2015.
95. "US Census, 1870," (https://goo.gl/UKRxiT).
96. Organization Index to Pension Files of Veterans Who Served Between 1861 and 1900, compiled 1949 - 1949, documenting the period 1861 - 1942, roll 182. Ancestry.com.

William^5 d.21 Mar 1899[97] and Jane Porterfield remained in Bristol to raise their three children.

William, b.Feb. 23, 1850, ch.Wm. Je Jane. T.R.2 (Bristol I, 740)
Sarah Jane, b.Apr.16, 1848, ch.William & Jane. (I, 740)
Edmund Hanson, b.July 7, 1854, ch.Wm. k Jane. T.R.2 (lost st sea,Mar.19,1906 a.51y.8m.l2. G.R.15 (I, 739)

Their daughter, Sarah Jane^6 "Jennie" d.14 Aug 1943,[98] did marry and had two children.

Jennie S. and Edwin D. Bailey, both B., June 7, 1866. (Bristol II, 304)

Robert William^6 Bailey d.29 May 1905[99] never married (I do not think that Robert and William were two children) and Edmund Hanson Bailey was a seaman who was shipwrecked and drowned out of Marblehead, Massachusetts, according to the Massachusetts death record.[100]

James Chandler^5 (Mary^4, James^3, Alexander^2, James^1)

James C , h.Margaret E. (Porterfield), 1826-1919. G.R.15 (d. Jan.29, a.92y.7m. l9d.) (Bristol I, 740)
James C. and Margaret E. Porterfield, both B., Mar. 20, 1849. (II, 304)
Margaret E.(Porterfleld), w.James C , 1829-1919. G.R.15 (d.So.B.,May 21, wld., a.89y.l0m.l5d., T.R.7 (II, 740)
John E., s. James C. & Margaret E., d.Apr.7,1862, a.5m.l6d. G.R.15 (b.Oct. 22, ch.James C. & Hannah. T.R.2) (II, 740)
Charles M., ch.James C. & Hannah, b.May 1,1863. T.R.2 (1863-1929. G.R.15) d. Rockland, Nov. 5, a.66y.6m.4d., b.B., unm. b.B. T.R.2 (II, 439)

James Chandler^5 "Charlie" b.10 June 1826[101] d.29 Jan 1919 and Margaret Eliza had six children: Chandler^6, Everett^6, Andrew^6, Charles^6, Edgar^6 and Hannah^6. They lived in Bowdoinham first; Hannah^6 and Chandler^6 were born there and then moved to Bristol before 1859.

Chandler, h.Mary Louise (Poland), b.July 30,1850, d.Aug.11,1918. G.R.5 (d.Dama., wdr., a.68y. l4d., ship carpenter) (Bristol I, 739)
Chandler of B. & Mary L. Porland of B., Dec. 2, 1874, T.R.3 (II, 301)
Mary Loulse (Poland), w.Chandler, b.Mar.23,1853, d.July 29,1910. G.R.5 (d.Dama. a. 57y.4m.7d.) (I, 740)
Lillian, b.Jan.18,1879, ch.Chandler & Mary Louise, m.Andrew Creamer. P.R.57(b.

97. Maine State Archives; 1892-1907 Vital Records; Roll #: 61.
98. Findagrave.com, http://goo.gl/gVb6gl, accessed 25 June 2015.
99. Maine State Archives; 1892-1907 Vital Records; Roll #: 61.
100. Massachusetts, Death Records, 1841-1915.
101. Maine State Archives; 1908-1922 Vital Records; Roll #: 60.

Jan.8, T.R.2) (I, 740)
Mable, b.Dec.13,1876, ch.Chandler & Mary Louise, m.lst,John Parker, m.2d,Wm. Taft. P.R.57 (I, 740)

Chandler[7] died of TB.[102] Daughter Lillian[7] had no children with Andrew J Creamer but Mabelle[7] and John Parker had one daughter, Priscilla Wilson[7].

Hannah[6] d.16 Jun 1927 and Elbridge Bryant had two children, Anna[7] and Alice[7].

Hannah, wid.Elbridge R.Bryant, b.B., Dec.30, 1848, dau. James C , b.Bowdoinham, & Margaret Porterfield) , b.B. T.R.7 (1848-1927. G.R.33) (Bristol I, 51)
Elbridge, h.Hannah (Wilson), 1840-1926, Co.E.,20th Me.Inf. 0.H.33 Elbridge R., a.9y., under David Sc Ruth. U.S.C.1850,B. see Alice, Annie (Sargt of B., a.22y., unm. W.R.I) (b.E. Oct.6,1641, s.David. T.R.2) (I, 52)
Hannah and Elbridge R. Bryant, both B., Sept. 6, 1868, int Dec. 1, 1867. (I, 52)
Annie R. w. Dana D. Goudy 1871- 1941 G.R. 14 b.B Feb 13, 1871 T.R. 2 (Anna, had one child, Gen 28) (I, 50)
Alice, under Elbridge and Hannah, a.1y U.S.C 1870, B (I, 49)

Alice[6] also married and moved to Massachusetts. She and Thomas E Herald had four children.

Everett James[6] and Georgia had no children.

Everett James, b.May 22,1659, d.May 23,1922. G.R.14 (h.Georgia E.(Goudy),) (a.63y.ld., b.B., s.James, b.B. T.R.7 (Bristol I, 740)
Everett J. and Georgia E Goudy, both of B. May 4, 1888 (II, 304)
Georgia E, wid.Everett J., Feb 16, 1869. dau. Edwin C & Mary F T.R. 3 (I, 266)
Georgia E.(Goudy), wid.Everett J, d.Dama.,Oct.18,1944, a.75y.8m.2d. T.R.3 (I, 740)

Andrew[6] and Susan Barker also had no children.

Andrew, h.Susan M.(Barker), 1852-1923. G.R.5 (b.Mar.14, a.James C. & Hannah. T.R.2) (d.Dama.,Feb.23, carpenter, a.70y.llm.9d., T.R.3) no chn. (Bristol I, 740)
Andrew of B. and Gussie M. Barker of Dama., int . Mar. 9, 1874, cert. Issued Mar. 14, T.R.4 (int., T.R.2) (II, 304)
Susan M.(Barker), w.Andrew, 1850-1926. G.R.5 (Susan Maria, d. Walden, Mass., Apr.7, a.75y.4m.26d., wid., b.Dama., dau.John Barker. T.R.3 (I, 740)

Edgar D[6] b.abt 1871 d.aft 1940 and Carrie J Fossett b.1866 d.1928[103] had four children before her death.

Edgar D., s.James & Margaret, m.Carrie (Fossett). T.R.2 (H.R.6) (I, 739)

---

102. Maine State Archives; 1908-1922 Vital Records; Roll #: 60.
103. Findagrave.com, gravestone, http://goo.gl/wPuhT8, accessed 25 June 2015.

Daniel[5] (Mary[4], James[3], Alexander[2], James[1])

Daniel[5] b.21 Mar 1830 d.1867[104] married Irene D Bailey b.1841 d.1902[105] on 25 Nov 1858 in Bradford. They had five sons, Orris D[6] b.23 Jul 1864[106] d.aft 1940, twins Daniel Otis[6] and Dallas Olin[6] b.27 Apr 1868 d.10 Jul 1915,[107] Oscar[6] b.1 Jan 1861 d.28 Feb 1910,[108] and Orrin Percival[6] b.abt 1866 d.6 Mar 1946.[109]

Orrin[6] never married. He went west at some point and died in Los Angeles. The other four did marry and have children. Oscar's son, Daniel Oscar[7], never married and was last seen in the 1940 census in Massachusetts. Orris[6] had one daughter, Dallas Olin[6] had three and Daniel Otis[6] had two children.

Dennis[5] (Mary[4], James[3], Alexander[2], James[1])

Dennis[5] b.21 Mar 1830 (unc) d.19 Jul 1902[110] was also a Bradford resident. He and Sarah Dunning b.14 Mar 1836 d.5 Aug 1919[111] had eleven children but many seemed to die young, Clifford[6], Kathy L[6], Delma[6], Minnie[6], Dennis[6] and Lizzie[6]. There are only two marriages and no children among the others. They included James R[6], Lewis C[6], Iddo[6], Robert[6] and Sadie[6]. It looks like Dennis[5] also was a Civil War veteran, receiving a pension starting in 1895.[112]

Betsey[5] (Mary[4], James[3], Alexander[2], James[1]) - The Wades

James J., ch. Luther, Jr., and Betsy, Feb. 11,1815. (Topsham I, 192)

Betsey[5] b.12 July 1819 (unc) d.23 Feb 1904[113] married James J Wade d.bef 1860 on 23 Sep 1845.[114] They had three children before his

---

104. "Nathan Hale Cemetery Collection, ca. 1780-1980," (https://goo.gl/SIqH1F).
105. "Nathan Hale Cemetery Collection, ca. 1780-1980," (https://goo.gl/EO7zwI).
106. "Maine, Births and Christenings, 1739-1900," (https://goo.gl/SDuvjc).
107. Maine State Archives; 1908-1922 Vital Records; Roll #: 60.
108. Massachusetts, Death Records, 1841-1915 Ancestry.com Operations, Inc., 2013.
109. "California Death Index, 1940-1997," (https://goo.gl/524jgk).
110. Maine State Archives; 1892-1907 Vital Records; Roll #: 61.
111. Maine State Archives; 1908-1922 Vital Records; Roll #: 60.
112. Organization Index to Pension Files of Veterans Who Served Between 1861 and 1900, compiled 1949 - 1949, documenting the period 1861 - 1942. Ancestry.com.
113. Maine State Archives; 1892-1907 Vital Records; Roll #: 58.
114. "Maine Marriages, 1771-1907," (https://goo.gl/L3N7c0).

death. The youngest was born in 1852 so his death could have been as early as that. I have not been able to find any burial for either James or Betsey[5]. Their youngest, Mary E[6] b.1852, died unmarried on 8 Sep 1897.[115] Both sons did marry.

James Albert[6] Wade b.24 Jun 1846 d.27 Mar 1935 (unc) married Irene D Bailey, the widow of his uncle Daniel[6] Wilson above. After his death in late 1867, she was left with four children under 5 and pregnant with twins. They married 5 May 1869[116] and had two more children, John Bailey[7] b.14 Dec 1877[117] d.21 Dec 1963[118] who did not marry and Bernie Earl[7] b.7 Mar 1876 d.aft 1940 who did marry and have children.

John Emery[6] Wade b.1848 d.1927[119] married Anna L Whitney b.7 Aug 1861 d.27 Dec 1884[120] and had four boys. Jimmie R[7] b.1883 d.1901 never married and he is buried with his parents. Emery Wallace[7] b.25 Jun 1878[121] d.1956[122] married Vivian Roberts b.1882 d.1958 and had six children. Harold Fisher[7] b.9 Sep 1879 d.31 Dec 1962[123] and Elizabeth Elmira Arnold b.7 Feb 1886 d.Feb 1979[124] had two daughters. Arthur Leroy[7] b.1 Oct 1881 d.Nov 1974[125] married Lena Essel Randall b.24 Jun 1892 d.14 March 1964[126] and had five children.

John[4] (James[3], Alexander[2], James[1])

M[r] John Wilson & Miss Hannah Curtis was married Sep[r] 30th 1821
Abiezer Curtis born to them Jan[y] 13th 1823 (Brunswick, 313)

John[4] b.13 July 1783[127] d.28 Jun 1825[128] married Hannah Curtis of

115. Maine State Archives; 1892-1907 Vital Records; Roll #: 58.
116. "Maine Marriages, 1771-1907," (https://goo.gl/75l0Iw)
117. WWWI, State: Maine; County: Penobscot; Roll: 1654011; Draft Board: 1
118. "Maine Death Index, 1960-1996," (https://goo.gl/DYqzuQ).
119. Findagrave.com, gravestone photograph, http://goo.gl/WTZ9ok.
120. Findagrave.com, gravestone photograph, http://goo.gl/veRuwQ.
121. WWI, Maine; Registration County: Penobscot; Roll: 1654011; Draft Board: 1.
122. Findagrave.com, gravestone photograph, http://goo.gl/hIrYaF.
123. Findagrave.com, years only on gravestone, http://goo.gl/VTqnvl.
124. Social Security Administration, Number: 004-14-0961; Maine; Before 1951.
125. Social Security Administration, Number: 005-14-5171; : Maine; Before 1951.
126. Maine Death Index, 1960-1997 Ancestry.com Operations Inc, 2002.
127. "Maine, Births and Christenings, 1739-1900," (https://goo.gl/jsavil.
128. Findagrave.com, gravestone, http://goo.gl/JlgBo1, accessed 4 June 2015.

Freeport b.15 Oct 1792.[129] She was a distant cousin (Jane Curtis^{4}, Elizabeth^{3}, Jennet^{2}, James^{1}). John^{5} was born after his father's death if the year on his father's gravestone is correct.

John^{5} (John^{4}, James^{3}, Alexander^{2}, James^{1})

John and Susan E. Gummer, both of Brunswick, June 10, 1852. (Hill, II, 117) (Brunswick, 506)*

John Wilson	*Feby 10 1826*	*d.9 Feb 1903*[130]	
Susan D Gummer	*Novr 27 1827*	*d.1 Mar 1891*	
Hannah E	*Novr 1 1852 d.27 Jun 1919*[131]		
	Hannah Ellen & Thomas Emery Morse		
Abizer C	*Feby 14 1854*	*d.4 Nov 1918*[132]	
	Abiezer Curtis & Julia Combs		
John E	*Decr 14 1855*	*d.31 Aug 1934*	
	Edwin John & June Simpson		
Samuel G	*Decr 14 1955 d.31 Jul 1916*[133]		
	Samuel Gummer & Jennie L Shurtleff		
Cora A	*June 10 1859*	*d.1 Aug 1912*[134]	
	Cora Ada & Robert Patten Woodside		
Howard	*Augt 1 1863*	*d.30 Apr 1930*	*& Mabel Emily Rogers*
Mary E	*April 10 1866*	*d.23 Jan 1929*	*Mary Emma*

In addition to the above, John and Susan also had Lizette Mabel^{6} b.28 Feb 1868 (unc) d.3 Nov 1942 (unc) (Frank Weldon Rogers) and James Alvah^{6} b.19 Apr 1870 d.20 Sep 1944[135] (Lillian Rogers).

All but Samuel^{6} had married and had children. I counted 22 grandchildren.

David^{3} (Alexander^{2}, James^{1})

David^{3} b.22 Apr 1754[136] married Mary Dunning. Her branch of the Dunnings is not related to the Brunswick Dunnings. Four of her brothers and sisters married Alexanders and one had a granddaughter who married into the Wilson/Maxwell family. There has

129. "Maine, Births and Christenings, 1739-1900," (https://goo.gl/reN2Z7)
130. Maine State Archives; 1892-1907 Vital Records; Roll #: 61.
131. Maine State Archives; 1908-1922 Vital Records; Roll #: 39.
132. Maine State Archives; 1908-1922 Vital Records; Roll #: 60.
133. New York, New York, Death Index, 1862-1948 Ancestry.com.
134. Maine State Archives; 1908-1922 Vital Records; Roll #: 61.
135. Findagrave.com, gravestone, years only, http://goo.gl/FzQJsS.
136. "Maine, Births and Christenings, 1739-1900," (https://goo.gl/0xeRxp).

been some major confusion about this man because there was also a David Wilson of Freeport b.1760 who married Mary Soule and ended up in Bowdoinham but definitely is not part of this family. That said, I can find very little about our David that I can be sure of.

Swanzey[3] (Alexander[2], James[1])

Swansey Willson and Deborah WARD married 24th APRIL 1788 (Woodside)

Swanzey was born 8 Sep 1761 and did marry. Those are the only two known facts, however. His name is spelled as Swanzy on the birth record.

Alexander[3] (Alexander[2], James[1])

Alexander[3] b.8 Jul 1759[137] married Joanna(h) Phinney (Finney) b.abt 1770 d.1830-1840 on 14 Feb 1790. Nothing is known about Joanna; the town records spell her name in varying ways. I can find no grave or death record but it does look like she outlived Alexander as it appears she is in the 1820 census. One of their eleven children, Catharine[4] b.15 Jul 1792[138] disappears without a confirmed trace by the census of 1820.[139]

The 1830[140] Harpswell census record at ancestry is so poor that the names cannot be read; however, the index lists a Jeanne which may be Joanna and several Davids. The Jeanne entry has a woman the right age to be Joanna, 2 or 3 men 20 to 30 and one woman 15 to 20. The three men could be David[4] b.15 Mar 1802 (Harpswell, 28), Elisha[4] and Benjamin F[4], Mary[4] is the correct age for the woman but Betsey[4] b.15 Aug 1799 is not there. One of the Davids appears to have small children but I think is too old. The other for a David P is the right age.

The 1840[141] census has Elisha[4] in a household with 2 men 30 to 40

137. "Maine, Births and Christenings, 1739-1900," (https://goo.gl/fRM0fQ).

138. "Maine Births and Christenings, 1739-1900," (https://goo.gl/3GLaVq) .

139. 1820 U S Census; Census Place: Harpswell, Cumberland, Maine; Page: 383; NARA Roll: M33_34; Image: 224.

140. 1830; Census Place: Harpswell, Cumberland, Maine; Series: M19; Roll: 46; Page: 34; Family History Library Film: 0009700.

141. Year: 1840; Census Place: Harpswell, Cumberland, Maine; Roll: 138; Page: 379;

and two women 20 to 30. As there is a separate household with Benjamin[4], I'm assuming then that the household contains David[4] and Elisha[4]. Mary[4] may have married by 1840 so the two girls could be Anna[4] b.24 Apr 1810[142] and Rachel[4] b.5 Feb 1813.[143] So the children that either never married or I have no adult information for were Alexander[4], Catherine[4], Betsey[4], David[4], Anna[4], and Rachel[4]. The married children are Elisha[4], Benjamin Franklin[4], Seth[4], Swanzey[4] and Mary[4].

Elisha[4] (Alexander[3], Alexander[2], James[1])

Elisha[4] b.20 Oct 1806 (Harpswell, 28) supposed married in 1842 but died within the year on 5 Feb 1843.[144]

Benjamin Franklin[4] (Alexander[3], Alexander[2], James[1])

Benjamin Franklin[4] b.8 Jan 1808 (Harpswell, 28) married Amelia Thorne who had been married to a Dyer previously. She came with at least four children from that marriage. She and Benjamin[4] had six more children but Amelia supposedly died before 1860 (5 May 1857) when their children were young. I cannot find a census for 1860 for either Benjamin[4] or Amelia. Amelia's son, George Dyer, married in 1859 and Benjamin[4] is living with that family in 1870[145] but not in 1860[146] or 1880.[147]

These children either didn't survive, didn't marry or else cannot be definitively traced: Drusilla[5] b.9 Oct 1840,[148] William Henry[5] b.15 Apr 1845 and Ellen C [5] b.27 Dec 1850. It looks like the children might have gotten farmed out after their mother's death. I did find marriages for a William Henry and Ellen in Maine but nothing

---

Image: 689; Family History Library: 0009702

142. "Maine, Births and Christenings, 1739-1900," (https://goo.gl/O9zVje).

143. "Maine, Births and Christenings, 1739-1900," (https://goo.gl/jczRJo).

144. "Maine, Births and Christenings, 1739-1900," (https://goo.gl/cEkNtb).

145. Year: 1870; Census Place: Harpswell, Cumberland, Maine; Roll: M593_540; Page: 347A; Image: 168; F FHL Film: 552039

146. Year: 1860; Census Place: Harpswell, Cumberland, Maine; Roll: M653_436; Page: 947; Image: 948; FHL Film: 803436.

147. Year: 1860; Census Place: Harpswell, Cumberland, Maine; Roll: M653_436; Page: 947; Image: 948; FHL Film: 803436.

148. "Maine Births and Christenings, 1739-1900," (https://goo.gl/gMi7Bl).

in Harpswell. The others did marry: Daniel H[5], Amelia Ann[5] and Mary Ellen[5].

Daniel H[5] (Benjamin[4], Alexander[3], Alexander[2], James[1])

Daniel[5] b.17 Apr 1843 (unc) d.25 Aug 1892[149] married Abigail Southard b.abt 1843 d.aft 1910. Daniel committed suicide by shooting himself. He was a fisherman. Abigail is still alive in 1910, living with her son, Charles W[6], and with her daughter, Grace[6] in 1910.

They had five children who may have all married. They were Charles W[6], Grace Lucia[6], Viola May[6], Lucy Ann[6] and Sabrina Lewis[6].

Sabrina[6] b.6 Nov 1865 (unc) may have married a Benjamin King; Charles W[6] b.abt 1872 married twice but had no children. Lucy Ann[6] b.1875 d.27 Mar 1963[150] also married twice and had no children.

Grace Lucia[6] b.16 Aug 1869 d.24 Dec 1889[151] and Elisha Oakes Leavitt b.5 Oct 1846 d.1903 (unc) had one child, Grace A Leavitt b.13 Nov 1888 d.24 Feb 1892 who died of meningitis and then her mother died about a year later. They had another child that did survive and had children. She was Sarah Angie Bell Leavitt b.11 Apr 1885 (unc) d.aft 1940. She and Patrick Joseph Donohue had five children.

Viola May[6] b.21 Sep 1863 (unc) d.30 Nov 1914[152] married Frederick Ellis Darling b.5 May 1858 d.27 Apr 1931 (unc) and had three children.

Amelia Ann[5] (Benjamin[4], Alexander[3], Alexander[2], James[1]) - The Withingtons

---

149. Maine State Archives; 1892-1907 Vital Records; Roll #: 61.
150. Maine Death Index, 1960-1997: Ancestry.com.
151. Findagrave.com, http://goo.gl/VgkTju, accessed 12 Aug 2015.
152. Maine State Archives; 1908-1922 Vital Records; Roll #: 14.

Amelia Ann[5] b.5 Jul 1847 (unc) d.20 Nov 1942[153] married twice and outlived both husbands. She and her first husband, Charles Henry Withington b.1 Jan 1838 d.1 Mar 1911,[154] had a daughter, Emma May[6] b.5 Oct 1870 d.25 May 1885 who died at age 15 in Lawrence, Massachusetts, from consumption.[155] After Charles' death, she returned to Maine.

Mary Ellen[5] (Benjamin[4], Alexander[3], Alexander[2], James[1]) - The Darlings

Mary Ellen b.1853 d.30 Jan 1913 married William Henry Darling b.1838 d.29 Jun 1919.[156] They had six children, Alpheus[6] b.3 Oct 1873 d.16 Jan 1936 (unc), William H[6] b.1874, Florence[6] b.1878, Idella May[6], Leslie A[6] b.1888 d.10 Oct 1957[157] and Flora Ellen[6].

Idella May b.1882 d.1942 married Joseph H Matthews b.1861 d.1939[158] and had four children and Flora Ellen b.8 Jul 1892 d.21 June 1967[159] married Franklin W Trafton and had two daughters.

Mary[4] (Alexander[3], Alexander[2], James[1]) & Robert Gatchell Wilson

Mary b.10 Feb 1815 d.5 May 1857[160] married Robert Gatchell Wilson b.6 June 1820[161] d.16 Sep 1897,[162] a descendant of an entirely different branch of Wilsons encountered so far. Robert's original ancestor, came from England in the 1600s. The bit I found listed Connecticut, New York and Massachusetts as residences for these pioneering Englishmen. David's grandfather, William, was the first of his line in Maine; he came from Braintree, Massachusetts.

Charles W[5] (Mary[4], Alexander[3], Alexander[2], James[1])

153. New Hampshire, Death and Burial Records Index, 1654-1949, Ancestry.com.
154. Year only, Massachusetts, Death Records, 1841-1915 Ancestry.com.
155. Massachusetts, Death Records, 1841-1915 Ancestry.com Operations, Inc., 2013.
156. Findagrave.com, gravestone photograph, http://goo.gl/NKaNWr.
157. Findagrave.com, http://goo.gl/CcfN6K, accessed 13 Aug 2015.
158. Findagrave.com, gravestone photograph for both, http://goo.gl/auzst3.
159. Maine Death Index, 1960-1997 Ancestry.com Operations Inc, 2002.
160. Findagrave.com, gravestone photograph, http://goo.gl/eRgX5s.
161. Maine Births and Christenings, 1739-1900," (https://goo.gl/OImZ49)
162. Maine State Archives; 1892-1907 Vital Records; Roll #: 61.

David and Mary had one child, Charles W b.1847 d.1876[163] who married Dorcas Miller Colby b.31 Aug 1842 (Topsham I, 40). They had two boys, Harry L b.4 Oct 1871 (unc) and Charles D b.8 July 1873 (unc).

Seth[4] (Alexander[3], Alexander[2], James[1])

> *Mar 13 1823 Marriage is intended between Mr Seth Wilson of Harpswell and Miss Dorcas McGill of this town, cert. April 5 1823 (Brunswick, 184) (166, April 6, by William Allen)*

Seth[4] b.10 May 1794 (Harpswell, 28) and Dorcas had four children in Harpswell and then moved to Bowdoin between 1850 and 1860. I can find no trace of either Seth[4], Dorcas or one of their children, William Alexander[5] b. 3 Jul 1831 (Harpswell, 29), after that. Another child probably died young, Martha Ann[5] b. 21 Feb 1824 (Harpswell, 29). The others were Elizabeth Jane[5] and Charles Henry[5].

Elizabeth Jane[5] (Seth[4], Alexander[3], Alexander[2], James[1])

Elizabeth Jane[5] b.25 Dec 1826 (Harpswell, 29) d.14 Jan 1907[164] married Luther Merrill, a shoemaker and farmer in Monmouth. They had one child William H[6] b.abt 1851.

Charles Henry[5] (Seth[4], Alexander[3], Alexander[2], James[1])

Charles Henry[5] b. 23 Apr 1833 (Harpswell, 29) married Harriett Collins. They had two boys, Charles[6] and Albert[6].

Though it is certain that this family ended up in Bowdoin, not one record for any of them exist in the Bowdoin records.

Swanzey[4] (Alexander[3], Alexander[2], James[1])

> *July 30 1821 Marriage is intended between Mr Swanzy Wilson and Miss Susan Crips cert. Sept 3d 1821 (Brunswick, 181)*
> *Sep 5 Swanzy Wilson & Susan Crips, (163) by Benj Titcomb*

Born 15 Jul 1796 (Harpswell, 28), Swanzey[4] married Susan Crips b.1 Apr 1791 d.26 June 1890.[165] Piecing this together was extremely dif-

163. Findagrave.com gravestone photograph, http://goo.gl/CFu7zc.
164. "Maine, Vital Records, 1670-1907 ," (https://goo.gl/XCMDum)
165. Findagrave.com, http://goo.gl/1lAetQ, accessed 29 Oct 2015.

ficult because none of his children seem to have birth records where they were born. The clue was the existence of a Susan Curtis being buried with his son, Swansey[5], in Riverview Cemetery, Topsham.

It's obviously been a mystery who Susan Curtis might be for a very, very long time. The family stones for his wife Sarah, daughter Annie[6] and Susan Curtis have no dates - only ages. The stone for Sarah and Annie is to the left of Swansey and Susan's is to the left of Sarah's. I found a census record in 1850[166] that had a Samuel, Hannah, Susan, and Sarah Curtis (wrongly identified as Curlis, not Curtis). It was really sneaky because Samuel and Susan are listed at the bottom of one page and Hannah and Sarah at the top of the next.

I found that a good while ago but didn't know what to make of it. Finally, I realized that Susan was actually Swansey's mother. She remarried after his father died. Then the 1880 census record has Susan Curtis listed with the family and notated as mother.[167]

I don't know when Swanzey senior died nor do I know which Curtis Susan married after his death. Because of that 1850 census record, I believe they also had a daughter named Hannah[5] Wilson who was two years older than Swanzey[5].

There is one mention of Swanzey[4] in Wheeler's history in the list of original members of the Free Will Baptist Society in Harpswell that was organized on 17 April 1817.[168]

No occupations are listed for any of them in 1850. The entire listing is incorrect. Samuel is Swansey[5], Susan is Sarah, his wife, and Sarah Curlis is Susan Curtis.

But there's more. I also found a marriage to a Sarah French in Belfast to a Swanzey. That was just months before his marriage to Susan on 7 May 1821. Swanzey being a family name tells me the Swanzey in Belfast was this family. Could it have been the first

166. Year: 1850; Census: Topsham, Lincoln, Maine; Roll: M432_261; Page: 354B:496.

167. Year: 1880; Census Place: Topsham, Sagadahoc, Maine; Roll: 488; FHL: 1254488; Page: 191A; District: 151; Image: 0392.

168. Wheeler, 449.

Swanzey born in 1761, this Swanzey's uncle? There is a birth for a Sarah French there but I could find out no more.

French, Sally and Swanzey Wilson, May 7, 1821. (Belfast II, 129)
French, Sarah, ch. Nathaniel, bp. June 14, 1797, c.R.2. (I, 78)

Swansey[5] (Swanzey[4], Alexander[3], Alexander[2], James[1])

Swansey, h. Sarah F., Mar. 7, 1826, in T. (Topsham I, 211)
Swansey and Sarah A. Nickerson, both of T., July 17, 1850. (II, 288)
Sarah F. [ ], w. Swansey, Aug. 16, 1828, in Bath. (I, 211)

Anna L., ch. Swansey and Sarah F., Sept. 5, 1857, in T. (I, 208)
Anna L., Sept. 29, 1858, in T. (II, 398)

Swansey[5] was born in Freeport: I had suspected that and then found Willard's death record that stated that. (His father was listed there in the 1820 census as a single household before his marriage.)[169] He married right after that 1850 census but I don't know when they moved to Topsham. I cannot find any of them in a census before 1850 when he and his mother appeared in Topsham. That leads me to believe his stepfather Curtis was alive in 1840 but I can not find out his first name. I expect his father died before 1830 probably in Freeport.

Swansey[5] was living in Brunswick at the time of Wheelers' history. "The house now occupied by SWANZEY WILSON, situated on the Bowdoinham road, just beyond Cyrus Purington's, was built about 1794".[170]

William J ch. Swansey & Sarah F., Feb. 9, 1853, in T. [Capt h. Amelia, G.R.3.] (I, 211)
Amelia A. [ ], w. Capt. William J., , —, 1851, G.R.3. (I, 208)

Capt William J[6] d.10 Jan 1912[171] and Amelia A Davis b.1851 d.1930[172] had one child, Annie E. I found her in 1900 at age 19 and wasn't able to find her again.[173]

Willard T., ch. Swansey and Sarah F., Jan. 2, 1851, in T. (Topsham I, 211)

169. 1820 U S Census; Census Place: Freeport, Cumberland, Maine; Page: 435; NARA Roll: M33_34; Image: 250.
170. Wheeler, 659.
171. Maine State Archives; 1908-1922 Vital Records; Roll #: 60
172. Findagrave.com, gravestone photograph, http://goo.gl/Zl7wQp.
173. Year: 1900; Census Place: Topsham, Sagadahoc, Maine; Roll: 599; Page: 3A; Enumeration District: 0217; FHL microfilm: 1240599.

Julia F., w. Willard T., [—], a. 35 y. 7 m. 29 d., G.R.3. (II, 398)

Willard Thomas[6] d.30 Sep 1898[174] and Julia Frances Husband b.6 Jun 1854 d.11 Feb 1890[175] from Ireland lived in Massachusetts after they married. Willard returned to Topsham after her death. At his death there were five children still under 20 all listed on the guardianship petition with birth dates. The ones over 14 chose the younger ones' guardian as William J Wilson, their uncle.[176] The children were Wallace Willard[7] b.2 Aug 1884 d.4 Mar 1968,[177] Swansy George[7] b.8 Jan 1879 d.20 Mar 1952,[178] Sarah "Sadie" May[7] b.1877 d.15 Mar 1907,[179] Bessie F[7] b.9 Aug 1882, Chester Oliver[7] b.11 July 1886 d.1 Jul 1945,[180] and William Percy[7] b.20 Nov 1887 d.1969.[181]

Sarah[7] married Charles C Leavitt and they had six children. Swansy[7] married Gertrude Cunningham and had one child. William[7] married Marretta Geneva Curtis and had two boys. Bessie[7] may have married a Joseph Naulte and Chester[7] may not have married.

Anna C , ch. Swansey and Sarah F., Feb. 20, 1861, in T. (Topsham I, 208)
Annie C. of T. and Eugene L. Temple of Bowdoinham, Jan. 21, 1882, in T. (II, 283)

Annie Camellia[6] d.7 Jan 1934 (unc) and Eugene Lunt Temple b.1861 d.1941[182] had four children, Ernest N[7], Irving Wilson[7], Sarah Lettice[7] and Ethel Rhoana[7]. The boys were twins but only Irving[7] b.24 Dec 1882[183] d.7 Mar 1942[184] survived the birth. Though he married more than once, Irving[7] had no children.

Sarah Lettice[7] Temple b.28 Apr 1888 d.21 Jun 1942 (unc) married twice and had children by each husband. She and John Rufus Cunningham b.12 Jul 1882[185] had two children, one that did not survive

174. Maine State Archives; 1892-1907 Vital Records; Roll #: 61.
175. Massachusetts, Death Records, 1841-1915 Ancestry.com.
176. Sagadahoc County Probate Court guardianship papers, 1898.
177. Massachusetts, Mason Membership Cards, 1733-1990 Ancestry.com.
178. Findagrave.com, gravestone photograph, http://goo.gl/po9ZOp.
179. Findagrave.com, http://goo.gl/eoYvIK, accessed 27 Aug 2015.
180. Massachusetts, Mason Membership Cards, 1733-1990, ancestry.com.
181. Findagrave.com, gravestone photograph, http://goo.gl/8BPp7V.
182. Findagrave.com, gravestone photograph, http://goo.gl/dchKoy.
183. WWI, Registration State: Maine; Registration County: Sagadahoc; Roll: 1654017.
184. Findagrave.com for year only, gravestone photograph, http://goo.gl/w3REeI.
185. Maine State Archives; Pre 1892 Delayed Returns; Roll #: 25.

but Ernest Albert[8] b.8 May 1907[186] d.17 Oct 1982[187] did. Sarah[7] and Raymond William Condon b.16 Aug 1887[188] d.7 Jan 1944[189] had six children. Ethel Rhoana[7] Temple b.25 Jul 1893 d.10 Oct 1918[190] also married died from the flu a week after her husband and son. I don't know if there were any other children.

Charles Franklin, ch. Swansey and Sarah F., Dec. 22, 1865, in T . (Topsham I, 208)

Charles[6] d.12 Oct 1938[191] married Mary Leavitt b.1875 d.1952 and had six children. I could find only three grandchildren but there may be more.

Alexander[4] (Alexander[3], Alexander[2], James[1])

Alexander and Lavina [int. Louvina] French, Dec. 3, 1819. (Belfast II, 471)
Levina, ch. Eliphelet and Abigal, Apr. 10, 1801. (Belfast I, 78)

Alexander[4] b.20 Oct 1790[192] was a late addition to the family - but only because I couldn't find any information on him. Then I was contacted by Terry Wilson of Shamut, Maine, another cousin! He had been working on the genealogy of his family and was hoping I had more information for him. We compared notes and I found a whole 'nother branch.

Alexander married Lovina French and moved to Waldo before the birth of their first child. I found census records for each year from 1820 to 1860. Lovina died 17 Sep 1851[193] but in 1860 Alexander is living next to one of his sons with a woman named Lucena who is about the same age as Lovina.[194] Since Lovina's death record is definite as the wife of Alexander, this would have to be a second wife but it is odd to have another wife with about the same birth year and another unique name starting with L. There are no children left at home.

186. Maine State Archives; 1892-1907 Vital Records; Roll #: 13.
187. Maine Death Index, 1960-1997 Ancestry.com Operations Inc, 2002.
188. Social Security Applications & Claims Index, 1936-2007 Ancestry.com.
189. Findagrave.com for year only, http://goo.gl/hcLo9n, accessed 14 Aug 2014.
190. Maine State Archives; 1908-1922 Vital Records; Roll #: 13.
191. Findagrave.com, gravestone photograph for both, http://goo.gl/RwQbQb.
192. "Maine Births and Christenings, 1739-1900," (https://goo.gl/RFgLsg).
193. Maine State Archives; Pre 1892 Delayed Returns; Roll #: 104.
194. Year: 1860; Census: Waldo, Maine; Roll: M653_453; Page: 11: 513; FHL: 803453.

I can't find a death date for Alexander but a record for one of his sons reveals that Lovina and possibly Alexander are buried in Hadley Cemetery in Waldo.

It is the 1850 census that gives us the names of their children: Abigail[5], John[5], George[5] and William H[5]. Abigail[5] b.abt 1825 most likely married after the 1850 census. I did find marriage records lists a Gilbert Roberts and a Abigail Wilson but nothing else for Abigail.

> *Roberts, Gilbert of Brooks and Abagail S. Wilson of Brooks, June 13, 1856.* [Abigail S. of Brooks, co.r.] (Belfast II, 369)*

I found nothing else for William[5] b.abt 1828 but both the other boys married and had children.

John T[5] (Alexander[4], Alexander[3], Alexander[2], James[1])

John T[5] b.Dec 1827 or Jan 1828 d.11 May 1891[195] married Lovisa Eveline Bradford b.Jan 1831 d.17 Mar 1906[196] of Thorndike. They had four children in Waldo. The youngest, Grace A[6] b.July 1867[197] d.29 Sep 1890, died at 25 in Boston.[198] George A[6] b.22 Apr 1862 also died young on 30 May 1895 in Boston. His death certificate lists his occupation as teamster.[199]

Both the other two children married. Orinda J[6] and Charles Parkman Heath married on 6 Mar 1869 in Boston.[200] They had Charles Oscar[7], Mabel Elsie[7], and Grace Edith[7].

Dr. Erastus Lozier[6] b.Dec 1962 d.22 Feb 1909[201] married Rosa E Munroe on 6 Oct 1886 in Massachusetts.[202] He graduated from College of Physicians and Surgeons of Baltimore in 1889.[203] They had two children, Rosabelle[7] and John Albert[7] neither of whom survived to adulthood.

---

195. "Nathan Hale Cemetery Collection, ca. 1780-1980," (https://goo.gl/SKTE4K)
196. Massachusetts, Death Records, 1841-1915, Ancestry.com.
197. Nathan Hall Cemetery Collection, (https://goo.gl/Idpeo8)
198. Massachusetts, Death Records, 1841-1915, Ancestry.com.
199. Massachusetts, Death Records, 1841-1915, Ancestry.com.
200. Massachusetts, Town and Vital Records, 1620-1988 Ancestry.com.
201. Maine State Archives; 1908-1922 Vital Records; Roll #: 60.
202. Massachusetts, Marriage Records, 1840-1915. Ancestry.com.
203. Directory of Deceased American Physicians, 1804-1929, Ancestry.com

A search for more information on John netted a Nathan Hale Cemetery sheet that lists John^{5}, Lovisa, George^{5}, Grace^{6}, Lovina and Alexander^{4} on the same sheet. There is no death date for Alexander but there is confirmation of Lovina's 1851 death.

George M^{5} (Alexander^{4}, Alexander^{3}, Alexander^{2}, James^{1})

George M^{5} b.1834 d.Oct 1902[204] married Nancy E Bradford on 19 May 1861.[205] Nancy appears to be the much younger sister of Lovisa.[206] They had one child, Henry Burton^{6} b.22 Apr 1871,[207] who married Jenny Adelaide Williams. He gave George and Nancy eleven grandchildren born between 1898 and 1914. They were Elmer George^{7}, Leona Oraville,^{7} Della Verna^{7}, Perley H^{7}, Clarice Nancy^{7}, Daisy M^{7}, Orilla K^{7}, Harry Osborne^{7}, Ruby Adelaide^{7}, Maurice O^{7} and Roy W^{7}.

204. Maine State Archives; 1892-1907 Vital Records; Roll #: 61.
205. "Maine Marriages, 1771-1907," (https://goo.gl/lzPLel)
206. Year: 1850; Census: Thorndike, Waldo, Maine; Roll: M432_270; Page: 7B: 21.
207. U.S., Social Security Applications and Claims Index, 1936-2007.

Mary & the Toothakers

Mary^{2} and Abraham's descendants are only a part of the Toothakers in Maine.

Andrew Toothaker, Abraham's grandfather, was the son of Roger Toothaker, a folk-healer and self-styled killer of witches, who was one of people charged in the Salem witch trials along with his wife, Mary, and daughter, Martha. He died in the Boston jail on 16 June 1692.

His son, Andrew, was thirteen at the time. By 1700 Andrew is in York, Maine, having his first child. He was the only one of his family to come to Maine that I could find in a quick look. He had at least six children who spread out all over Maine. He and his wife moved to Harpswell around 1715-1717 and then died there in 1760. So all of his children except the oldest lived and died in Harpswell. Two were boys to carry on the Toothaker name and one of his daughters' descendants also married into the Wilson tree. Three of his children, Ebenezer, Seth and Elizabeth had descendants that married Wilson descendants. A number married into the Alexander line which means they tend to be island residents with lots of babies. I had to make decisions about who to include in this book and that did become a reason not to go too far down a tree.

But since Abraham Toothaker left Harpswell and he married one of Alexander Wilson's children, I did make a fateful decision to forward with his family. Little did I know then that the Toothakers would warrant a full chapter: I have actually cut some of the genealogy a bit short here and there. I did a surname report that shows how strongly the family plays in this story. The top names in order are Alexander, Wilson, Curtis, Smith, Darling, Allen, Strout and Toothaker. All except the Wilsons are island / Harpswell families. They multiplied and survived - such hardy folk!

Mary^{2} (Alexander^{2}, James^{1}) & Abraham Toothaker

The Harpswell town records list Mary's birth date as 12 Sept 1749 but the Topsham records list 1752 which means she was either seventeen or twenty when she married Abraham Toothaker of

Topsham. I expect the 1749 date is correct. They had nine children. Abraham was living in Brunswick after her death in 1800; he did not remarry even though he still had young children.

Mary (Wilson), w. Abraham, ——, —, 1752. (Topsham I, 189)
Mary, (Willson), w. Abraham, Jan. 24, 1800, P.R.6. (II, 389)
Abraham and Mary Willson, Sept. 7, 1769, in Harpswell, P.R.6. (II, 264)

Abraham, h. Mary (Wilson), Aug. 15, 1747, P.R.6. (II, 189)
Abraham, h. Mary (Willson), Aug. 2, 1829, P.R.6. (II, 389)

Catherine, d. Abraham and Mary (Willson), June 3, 1783, P.R.6. (Topsham I, 190)
Rebeccah Toothaker Daughter to Abram & Mary Toothaker born to them in Harpswell June 3d 1783 Deceased (Brunswick, 58)
Elizabeth, d. Abraham and Mary (Willson), July 14, 1777, P.R.6. (Topsham, I, 189) died 11 April 1861 ?
Isaac, s. Abraham and Mary (Willson), Aug. 22, 1785, P.R.6. (Topsham, I, 189) death unknown - probably before 1800

There remains some confusion. Catherine is not in the Brunswick records but is in Topsham. I can find nothing about her at all. There were two Rebeccas - one born 3 June 1733 which is the same birth date as Catherine's and one who lived born 1789.

Rebecca4 (Mary3, Alexander2, James1) - The Crawfords

Rebecca, d. Abraham and Mary (Willson), May 28, 1789, P.R.6. (Topsham, I, 189)
Feb 23d Archebald Crawford and Rebecca Toothaker (solemnized by Revd Benjamin Titcomb) (Brunswick, 159)
Toothaker, Rebecca, ch. Abraham & Mary, May, 1822, P.R.6. (Topsham II, 389)

The death entry in Topsham was misleading as she did not die as Toothaker but as Crawford. Rebecca and Archibald b.1785 d.5 Jun 1857[1] settled in Warren, Maine, and had three children before she died at or around the birth of her son, Oliver Malcomb b.1822 d.6 Apr 6 1830.[2] The other two children were Mary O5 and Alexander5.

Mary O Crawford5 (Rebecca4, Mary3, Alexander2, James1) - The Halls

Mary5 b.1820 d.21 Apr 1858 (unc) married Elijah Hall b.1814 d.4 Dec 1897[3] on 10 Nov 1842 in Thomaston.[4] They had at least six children, Benjamin6 b.abt 1848 d.bef 1860, Samuel L6 b.abt 1844,

1. Findagrave.com, http://goo.gl/Is8xNc, accessed 6 Aug 2015.
2. Findagrave.com, http://goo.gl/LEjwGl, accessed 6 Aug 2015.
3. Massachusetts, Death Records, 1841-1915 Ancestry.com Operations, Inc., 2013.
4. "Maine Marriages, 1771-1907," (https://goo.gl/fbtJit).

Charles[6] b.abt 1846, Frank L[6], Elizabeth Benson[6] and Fred[6] b.1858.

I could find no confirmed birth, death or burial records for any of the children besides Lizzie[6] and Frank[6]. Elijah died in Massachusetts and his death certificate said he was to be buried in Rockland where they had raised their family but I cannot find any of the family in Knox County. The pattern of disappearances and early death does suggest tuberculosis.

In 1870 the only child left at home was Frank.[5] Lizzie was living with another family and attending school 1870 at age 15 - a sign that the family was in distress.[6] The others may have been living elsewhere as well. With the scarcity of records as well I'm thinking that poverty was a big problem for the family since a number did live to adulthood but never seemed to marry.

Samuel L[6] Hall married Harriet A Coleman in 1867 in Massachusetts[7] but I can find almost no records for the two of them after that. That marriage record lists his father is as a Samuel, his mother is Mary O and his birth place is Rockland. I found a Civil War record that is probably him but he served in Ohio.[8] That led me to a 1892 record of a Samuel L living in a disabled soldiers home in Hampton, Virginia, with his father's name listed. He was suffering from disease of respiratory organs, nervous disability and rheumatism. He is listed as "dropped" 12 Nov 1901. It also records that he was a landsman in the navy and he is presently single.[9]

Elizabeth "Lizzie" Benson Hall[6] b.5 Sep 1855 d.10 Apr 1914[10] married William Goodell Avery of Wisconsin in Conway, Massachusetts, on 1 Nov 1882.[11] They had two boys, William b.abt 1888 and

5. Year: 1870; Census Place: Rockland, Knox, Maine; Roll: M593_548; Page: 215B; Image: 434; Family History Library Film: 552047.
6. Year: 1870; Census Place: Rockland, Knox, Maine; Roll: M593_548; Page: 223A; Image: 449; Family History Library Film: 552047.
7. Massachusetts, Marriage Records, 1840-1915 Ancestry.com Operations, Inc., 2013.
8. "Maine, State Archive Collections, 1718-1957," (https://goo.gl/cpfdjt).
9. "United States National Homes for Disabled Volunteer Soldiers, 1866-1938," (https://goo.gl/ZnRJmn).
10. "Massachusetts Deaths, 1841-1915," (https://goo.gl/9QfC0z.
11. "Massachusetts Marriages, 1841-1915," (https://goo.gl/ixaYNL).

Webb Reed b.24 Jun 1889 d.27 Feb 1946[12] but neither seemed to have had children.

Frank L[6] Hall b.3 Sep 1853 d.17 Oct 1918[13] married Addie Eva Lamb b.24 Apr 1861 d.3 Oct 1928 (unc) on 16 March 1878.[14] Though they had as many as ten children, most did not survive or marry. Only three had children that I could find: Lizzie M[7] had two and both Arthur Gay[7] and Vernald Packard[7] had one.

Alexander Crawford[5] (Rebecca[4], Mary[3], Alexander[2], James[1])

Alexander, h. Sarah R. (Henderson), Sept. — , 1817, G.R.I. (Belfast I, 55) (Alexander of Warren & Sarah R. Henderson, int. Dec. 14, 1844, "Certife Issued January 6th 1845." (Belfast II, 97)
Alexander, lung fever, July 6, 1870, a. 51. [h. Sarah R. (Henderson), bur. in Warren, g.r.i.] (II, 521)

Ellen Frances, d. Alexander and Sarah R. (Henderson), Apr. 9, 1850, G.R.I. (II, 97) d.14 Jul 1910 [15]

Lida Morse [w. [Melvin J.] Staples], d. Alexander and Sarah R. (Henderson), Mar. 4, 1855, g.r.i. (Belfast I, 55)
Lida M. and Melvin J. Staples, May 24, 1875. [Melvin J., s. Miles S. and Sarah (Ellingwood), p.R.33.] (Belfast II, 97)
Staples, Melvin J., h. Lida M. (Crawford), s. Miles S. and Sarah (Ellingwood), Oct. 12, 1851, P.R.33. (I, 181) d.29 Jan 1915[16]

Alexander[5] and Sarah Rebecca Henderson settled in the Belfast / Warren. His children fared way better than Mary's children. They lost one young from whooping cough, Edwin E[17] and Nettie Jane[6] b.17 May 1859 d.5 Mar 1863 also died as a child. Inez Ellis[6] b.10 Aug 1852 d.21 Jun 1935 never married and was not working in any census; neither did Frances Ellen[6]. Oliver[6], Charles[6] and William[6] married and had children. They are all together in the Grove Cemetery in Belfast.[18]

Charles E., Sept. 17, 1857, g.r.i. (Belfast, 55)
Charles E. & Phebe E. Dunbar, Oct. 29, 1888. [Charles E. of New York City, c.r.i.

12. Social Security Applications and Claims Index, 1936-2007 Ancestry.com.
13. Maine State Archives; 1908-1922 Vital Records; Roll #: 24.
14. "Maine Marriages, 1771-1907," (https://goo.gl/LYHIRJ .
15. Findagrave.com, gravestone photograph, http://goo.gl/OQ6Tts.
16. California, Death Index, 1905-1939 Ancestry.com Operations, Inc., 2013.
17. U.S. Census Mortality Schedules, Maine, 1850-1880; Archive Collection: 1.
18. Findagrave.com, http://goo.gl/eh7cJx, accessed 7 Aug 2015.

Phebe Elizabeth, d. Henry Jr. & Sarah J. (Pote), p.r.115.] (Belfast II, 97)
Dunbar, Phebe Elizabeth, w. Charles E. Crawford, d. Henry Jr. and Sarah J. (Pote), Aug. 29, 1859, p.R.115. (Belfast I, 65)

Charles[6], a pharmacist, and Phebe had one child, Edna D[7] b.9 Nov 1893 d.1 Jul 1991[19] who married after her mother's death but had no children.

William[6] b.19 Jan 1862 d.25 Apr 1938 was an educator. According to findagrave.com, he was a member of the first regular graduating class from Belfast High school in 1878 and attended Colby College. He was the principal of Upper Grammar School in Belfast in 1884 and school headmaster in Boston for many years. He married twice: his first wife, Cora Amelia King b.17 Apr 1866 d.19 Mar 1893, died after giving birth to their only child, Cora Amelia b.8 Mar 1893 d.9 Sep 1935, also a teacher.

He and his second wife, Mabel Amelia Spooner b.15 Sep 1870 d.27 Mar 1935, had four children.[20]

Oliver M[6] b.12 Oct 1845 d.May 1906 married Angeline Brimigion b.1844 d.15 Aug 1897.[21] According to the 1900 census he was a bridge builder in Illinois.[22] They had two children but no grandchildren.[23]

Alexander[4] (Mary[3], Alexander[2], James[1])

Alexander, s. Abraham and Mary (Willson), Sept. 7, 1771, P.R.6. (Topsham, I, 189)

Mary Toothackor was born & Abigail Toothakor July 13th 1801 (Brunswick, 197)
Elizebath Toothakor was born October 18th 1805 (death possibly 1859)
Mercy Toothackor was born November 29th 1803 (d.unknown)
Abraham Toothackor was born November 4th 1810 unmarried
John Toothackor was born Febury 2d 1808 (d.unknown)

Alexander[4] d.7 Feb 1844 married Elizabeth Allen b.1767 d.10 Sep 1847[24] in Harpswell. They had six children in Brunswick but most

19. Social Security Administration, Number: 006-12-5529; Maine; Before 1951.
20. Findagrave.com, gravestone photograph, http://goo.gl/qv9qBP.
21. Findagrave.com, http://goo.gl/MIUF7X, accessed 24 Nov 2015.
22. Year: 1900; Census Place: Aurora Ward 1, Kane, Illinois; Roll: 310; Page: 3B; Enumeration District: 0062; FHL microfilm: 1240310.
23. Findagrave.com, http://goo.gl/Nemxsf accessed 7 Aug 2015.
24. Findagrave.com, gravestone, http://goo.gl/GOrlY8, 15 June 2015.

did not survive or marry: Mary[5] who died at birth or infancy, her twin sister, Abigail d.23 Mar 1870[25] who lived but never married, Elizabeth[5], Mercy[5], John[5] and Abraham[5] d.16 Mar 1871.[26] They moved to New Vineyard around 1825 where most of the family is buried.

Isaac[5] (Abraham[4,] Mary[3], Alexander[2], James[1])

Isaac Toothacor was born July 15th 1795 (Brunswick, 197)

Isaac[5] married Lavinia Eliot b.1804 d.7 Feb 1864[27] on 5 Feb 1826.[28] I don't think they had any children. We don't know where he was buried; no grave exists now in the Newell/McLain Cemetery in New Vineyard. Their marriage took place in Strong but the next Toothaker-Eliot marriage took place in Brunswick.

Ephraim[5] (Abraham[4,] Mary[3], Alexander[2], James[1])

Ephraim Toothacor was born March 5th 1797 (Brunswick, 197)
Feby 11 1824, Marriage is intended between Mr Ephraim Toothaker & Miss Mary Elliot both of this town, cert. Mar 10 1824 (186)

Ephraim[5] d.30 Mar 1874[29] married a Mary E Eliot b.14 Oct 1799 d.27 Mar 1889[30] - she was probably Lavinia's sister but there are no birth records for them in Brunswick. They had six children, Ephraim[6], Abizer[6], William[6], Margaret Ann[6] b.18 Aug 1839 d.1 Sept 1856[31], Andrew[6] and Miriam[6].

Captain Abizer Snow[6] b.17 Dec 1827 d.18 Nov 1872[32] married Mary Frances Sinnett b.26 Oct 1843 (unc) d.9 Feb 1910.[33] They have the distinction of divorcing in 1870.[34] When they married in 1858, she was only 15. They did have one child, Lucy Isabelle[7] b.1 Feb 1863 (unc) d.aft 1930 who never married.

---

25. Findagrave.com, gravestone, http://goo.gl/ssneiz, accessed 13 June 2015.
26. Findagravel.com, gravestone, http://goo.gl/mHoO9E, accessed 17 June 2015.
27. Findagrave.com, gravestone, http://goo.gl/509xYv, accessed 15 June 2015.
28. "Maine, Marriages, 1771-1907," (https://goo.gl/8guxOa)
29. Findagrave.com, http://goo.gl/5fs1tm, accessed 13 June 2015.
30. Findagrave.com, http://goo.gl/RWPZ4K, accessed 17 June 2015.
31. Findagrave.com, http://goo.gl/gd9Zr8 accessed 15, 2015.
32. Findagrave.com, http://goo.gl/7qsQnK, accessed 15 June 2015.
33. Maine State Archives; 1908-1922 Vital Records; Roll #: 43.
34. Maine, Divorce Records, 1798-1891 Ancestry.com. Docket number 506, vol 64/104.

Miriam Shaw[6] b.1831-1835 d.4 Apr 1903[35] married John Jones Stewart b.1819 d.23 Mar 1869[36] and had two children. John W[7] b.1867 d.14 Feb 1896[37] died young and daughter Helen[7] b.1863 d.1946[38] may have married Gilbert Handly b.1859 d.1920.[39] Gilbert and Helen[7] had one stillborn child in 1892.[40]

Ephraim Shaw[6] b.17 Dec 1829 d.26 Jan 1874[41] left Maine and settled in Missouri between 1850 and 1858. He married Anna Louisa Watson on 6 Sep 1858[42] in Linn, Missouri, and raised his children there. He was a civil war veteran; his gravestone lists Co.D 62nd MO Eng. Mil as his company. They had seven children: Mary Ann[7], Ephraim[7] Edwin[7], Abizer Elliot[7], Miriam[7], William Shaw[7], Elvira[7] and Andrew Jackson[7].

His oldest daughter, Mary Ann[7], may have married. I found a marriage record for her and a William Werron, probably Warren, but though I found records for William Warrens married to Marys, I wasn't able to confirm that any of them were her.

Both Ephraim Edwin[7] b.11 Jul 1866 d.21 Aug 1934 and Abizer Elliott[7] b.14 Jan 1872 did marry but had no children. Abizer[7] disappeared after his divorce in 1914 according to relatives. Ephraim's gravestone has his and his wife's name as Toothacher, Uncle Eph Toothacher.[43] He had moved to be near his wife's family.

Miriam[7] b.14 Sep 1864 d.5 Mar 1956[44] married Francis Gilbert Adams b.21 Dec 1860 d.18 Dec 1923[45] on 13 Jun 1883.[46] They had at least nine children born between 1884 and 1898. Most either didn't marry or have children but there were eight grandchildren for

35. Maine State Archives; 1892-1907 Vital Records; Roll #: 54
36. Findagrave.com, gravestone photograph, http://goo.gl/JYorJT.
37. Findagrave.com, http://goo.gl/Dv6Gwn accessed 16 June 2015.
38. Findagrave.com, http://goo.gl/siq30R accessed 16 June 2015.
39. Findagrave.com, http://goo.gl/NJhfKz, accessed 16 June 2015.
40. "Maine, Vital Records, 1670-1907 ," (https://goo.gl/fwUJvz).
41. Headstones Provided for Deceased Union Civil War Vets, 1879-1903 Ancestry.com.
42. Missouri, Marriage Records, 1805-2002 Ancestry.com.
43. Findagrave.com, http://goo.gl/T2TwhJ, 15 June 2015.
44. Findagrave.com, http://goo.gl/ekmWq3, accessed 15 June 2015.
45. Findagrave.com, photo of death cert, http://goo.gl/ek9uRQ, accessed 15 June 2015.
46. "Missouri, Marriages, 1750-1920," (https://goo.gl/Fuxywk)

Francis and Miriam[7]. Most of the Adams are buried in the Laclede Cemetery.

Elvira[7] b.12 Oct 1862 d.1909 married Lorenzo Dow Sights b.29 June 1860 d.5 Sep 1937[47] and they had at least six children though marriages cannot be found for three of the daughters.

William Shaw[7] b.16 Dec 1868 d. 4 Jan 1951 married Inez Pembroke Wilson b.23 Apr 1873 d.30 Sep 1957 on 20 Dec 1893.[48] She was a North Carolina Wilson. They had five children but only two survived to adulthood and only one married.

Andrew Jackson[7] b.22 Oct 1880 d.11 May 1926[49] married Mary E Massey b.23 Dec 1888 d.25 Nov 1971.[50] They had at least eight children, several of whom died young. I only found 2 marriages among them.

William Eliot[6] b.25 Aug 1836 d.31 May 1867[51] married Lucy B Pierce b.5 Jul 1835 d.10 Jun 1888.[52] They had two children before William's death at age 30: Caroline[7] b.27 Mar 1866 d.13 Apr 1866[53] and her brother, Ernest Elwood[7] b.14 Aug 1863 d.15 Mar 1960[54] who married and moved to Washington by 1904. William was a Civil War veteran[55] and he received a pension immediately after the war.[56]

Ernest[7] married Norma Lena Marsh and had ten children born between 1893 and 1918 and over 16 grandchildren. He lived to be 96 years old.

Levi[5] (Abraham[4,] Mary[3], Alexander[2], James[1])

---

47. Findagrave.com, http://goo.gl/P13bUp
48. Missouri, Marriage Records, 1805-2002 Ancestry.com Operations, Inc., 2007.
49. Findagrave, gravestone, http://goo.gl/Ez8Lo0, accessed 16 June 2015.
50. Findagrave, gravestone, http://goo.gl/XWTf6x, accessed 16 June 2015.
51. Findagrave.com http://goo.gl/jWFLFh, accessed 16 June 2015.
52. Findagrave.com, http://goo.gl/gczoYq, accessed 16 June 2015.
53. Findagrave.com, http://goo.gl/XL21JM, accessed 16 June 2015.
54. Washington, Deaths, 1883-1960 Ancestry.com Operations Inc, 2008.
55. Historical Data Systems, comp. U.S., Civil War Soldier Records & Profiles, 1861-1865. ncestry.com.
56. Organization Index to Pension Files of Veterans Who Served Between 1861 & 1900.

Levi Toothacor was born March 15th 1799 (Brunswick, 197)
Sept 12 1824, Marriage is intended between Mr Levi Toothaker & Miss Sarah Thomas both of this town, cert. Oct 2d 1824 (187)

Levi[5] d.16 Aug 1881 married Sarah "Sally" Thomas b.1807 d.7 Jun 1881 before his parents left Brunswick but he must have gone with them initially. They had ten children but there were a number of miscarriages or still births while they were in New Vineyard. The first child that survived was Rebecca[6] b.1831 d.1852. Lucinda[6] b.1832 d.1877 never married; nor did Levi[6] b.14 Apr 1839 d.6 Jan 1910 but he was a businessman in Brunswick and Civil War veteran. Daniel[6] b.4 Dec 1841 d.3 Mar 1927 did marry but had no children. He also was a Civil War veteran. Josephine Augusta[6] b.17 Feb 1847 d.1 July 1915 also married but had no children. Nearly all of them are buried in the same cemetery plot in Brunswick where most I pulled most of the dates from.[57]

They had returned to Brunswick about 1840 but Sara and her six surviving children are in Saco in 1860; She was running a boarding house there that year.[58] In 1870, Levi[5] was living with cousin, Elisha Allen Jr, in Harpswell but had moved to son Daniel's in 1880. Sarah was in Brunswick in 1870 and 1880[59] but the last time they were in the census together was 1850.[60] Looks like they were not close the last 30 years but they both died in 1881 and are buried together with several of their children in Pine Grove Cemetery.

Ruth T[6] b.11 Jan 1844 d.27 Mar 1924[61] married Frederick A Milliken b.25 Aug 1839 d.12 May 1904[62] of Saco. They had five children in Saco, Lillian "Lilla" Maud b.14 Jan 1865 d.1940[63] who never married, Edwin A H[7] b.1863, Albert Leroy[7] b.1867, Angie Ella[7] b.4 Apr

57. Findagrave.com, http://goo.gl/cRsY5D, accessed 13 June 2015
58. Year: 1860; Census Place: Saco, York, Maine; Roll: M653_451; Page: 701; Image: 258; Family History Library Film: 803451.
59. Year: 1870; Census Place: Brunswick, Cumberland, Maine; Roll: M593_539; Page: 69A; Image: 142; Family History Library Film: 552038
60. Year: 1850; Census Place: Brunswick, Cumberland, Maine; Roll: M432_251; Page: 211A; Image: 121.
61. Findagrave.com, http://goo.gl/0BIUfn, accessed 14 June 2015.
62. Findagrave.com, http://goo.gl/kkTnYU, accessed 14 June 2015.
63. Findagrave.com, http://goo.gl/iXlBQ5, accessed 14 June 2015.

1874 d.1942[64] and Susan Gertrude[7] b.1876 d.1967. There were at least thirteen children among the four that married.

Charles[6] H b.14 Feb 1849 d.17 May 1921[65] married Mary Eliza "Lizzie" Bragdon of Freeport b.16 Nov 1848 d.28 Oct 1916.[66] They remained in Brunswick and birthed eight children there. Three died early, Joseph L[7] , Laura B[7], and Sarah J[7] but the rest all married and had children: Ella L[7] b.8 Jun 1869 d.31 Mar 1934,[67] Alfred M[7] b.1 Jan 1871[68] d.1935,[69] Ruth Elyadie[7] b.19 Nov 1879 d.15 Aug 1962,[70] Charles Lesley[7] b.10 Mar 1882[71] d.1969[72] and Abby Isabelle[7] b.1884.

Mary[4] (Mary[3], Alexander[2], James[1]) - The Rosses

Mary, d. Abraham and Mary (Willson), Aug. 18, 1780, P.R.6.
June 10 1804, Mr John Ross [of] Lisbon & Miss Mary Toothaker [of] Brunswick (Anderson, 100)

Mary[4] d.7 Mar 1854[73] married Deacon John Ross b.10 Jun 1778[74] d.16 Dec 1851,[75] resided in Wales and had eight children. These never married or had no children: Elizabeth[5] b.22 Aug 1806 d.18 July 1867,[76] Sally S[5] b.15 May 1821[77] d.24 Mar 1848,[78] Jane[5] b.10 Jun 1812,[79] Martha Katherine[5] b.16 Oct 1818[80] d.4 Mar 1899,[81] and John[5] b.23 Mar 1816 d.28 Sep 1855.[82]

The others who had children were William[5], Robert[5], and Rebecca[5],

---

64. Findagrave.com, http://goo.gl/xVsx1B, accessed 14 June 2015.
65. Maine State Archives; 1908-1922 Vital Records; Roll #: 56.
66. Findagrave.com, http://goo.gl/BrpyGa, accessed 14 June 2015.
67. Findagrave.com, http://goo.gl/rbcemV, accessed 14 June 2015.
68. "Maine, Births and Christenings, 1739-1900," (https://goo.gl/KvvAHQ).
69. Findagrave.com, http://goo.gl/4OkgPo, accessed 14 June 2015.
70. Findagrave.com, http://goo.gl/nCV7ys, accessed 14 June 2015.
71. U.S., World War I Draft Registration Cards, 1917-1918 Ancestry.com Operations.
72. Findagrave.com, year only, http://goo.gl/fpQjFA
73. Findagrave.com, gravestone photograph, http://goo.gl/nGbbOz.
74. Maine, Births & Christenings (https://goo.gl/qsDoB1
75. Findagrave.com, http://goo.gl/gBjTTd, accessed 7 Aug 2015.
76. Findagrave.com, gravestone, http://goo.gl/b6OnHd, accessed 16 June 2015.
77. "Maine, Births and Christenings, 1739-1900," (https://goo.gl/eh4h02).
78. Findagrave.com, gravestone photograph, http://goo.gl/ZYODbf
79. "Maine, Births and Christenings, 1739-1900," (https://goo.gl/h0y9d2).
80. "Maine, Births and Christenings, 1739-1900," (https://goo.gl/iJN8YQ).
81. "Maine, Vital Records, 1670-1907 ," (https://goo.gl/FSBtYn).
82. Findagrave.com, gravestone photograph, http://goo.gl/df4M2i.

William[5] Ross (Mary Ross[4,] Mary[3], Alexander[2], James[1])

William[5] b.25 Mar 1805 d.23 Nov 1863 married Nancy Lord b.6 May 1809 d.29 Sept 1882. Two of their three children did not marry, Harriett A[6] b.1831 d.28 Oct 1882 and Judson[6] b.1838 d.23 Aug 1868.[83]

The third, Sarah J[6] Ross b.1835 d.16 Sep 1914,[84] married Addison Joseph Small b.29 May 1824 d.20 Oct 1917[85] on 11 Nov 1861.[86] They had three daughters and one son, all of whom married. The youngest daughter Myrtie[7] Vesta b.29 Jan 1878[87] d.1958 married Redford Estes b.1879 d.1959 but had no children.[88]

Mary Jane[7] Small b.abt 1832 married Ernest W Dyer on 11 May 1884[89] and had one child Elizabeth "Bessie" M[8] b.16 Dec 1885 d.30 Dec 1974.[90] Lydia Aldora[7] "Dora" Small b.17 Jul 1867 d.1950[91] married Herbert M Cole b.27 Jun 1869[92] d.2 Sep 1942.[93] They had four daughters, all of whom married and had children. Frank Vivian[7] Small b.16 Jul 1876 d. 2 Sept 1967[94] married twice and had a total of five children.

Rebecca C[5] Ross (Mary Ross[4,] Mary[3], Alexander[2], James[1]) - The Witherells

Rebecca C[5] b.25 Sep 1814[95] d.8 Feb 1885[96] married Isaac Witherell b.22 June 1810 d.10 Aug 1890[97] and moved to Litchfield. They only had one child, Isaac Mellon[6], who survived childhood. The others that didn't were Humphrey[6] b.5 Aug 1841 d.5 Sept 1848,[98] Mary E[6]

83. "Maine, Nathan Hale Cemetery Collection, ca. 1780-1980," (https://goo.gl/8qMsqB)
84. Maine State Archives; 1908-1922 Vital Records; Roll #: 51
85. Maine State Archives; 1908-1922 Vital Records; Roll #: 51
86. "Maine, Marriages, 1771-1907," (https://goo.gl/sHqBQU).
87. "Maine, Vital Records, 1670-1907 ," (https://goo.gl/NZY89M).
88. Findagrave.com, gravestones, http://goo.gl/7zu6ch, accessed 16 June 2015.
89. "Maine, Marriages, 1771-1907," (https://goo.gl/fgxsrJ).
90. Social Security Death Index, 1935-2014 Number: 004-64-7142; Maine; 1973.
91. Findagrave.com, http://goo.gl/nZKmBs
92. Maine State Archives; Pre 1892 Delayed Returns; Roll #: 21
93. Findagrave.com, year only, http://goo.gl/i5QxPs
94. "United States Social Security Death Index," (https://goo.gl/mzAC8b).
95. "Maine, Births and Christenings, 1739-1900," (https://goo.gl/s1yZZ5).
96. Findagrave.com, http://goo.gl/70AcX4, accessed 16 June 2015.
97. Findagrave.com, gravestone photograph, http://goo.gl/ARxRZR.
98. Findagrave.com, gravestone, http://goo.gl/HNrdyx, accessed 16 June 2015.

b. 7 Sept 1847 d.28 Aug 1848[99] and Sarah A[6] b.4 Mar 1850 d.5 June 1855.[100]

Isaac Mellon[6] b.25 Jan 1854 d.11 Jul 1942[101] first married Margaret Kimball b.23 Nov 1855 d.26 Apr 1888.[102] They had five children before her early death at 33. Isaac then married Eleanor "Nellie" Jordan b.6 Jul 1867 d.19 Sep 1919.[103] They had eight more children. All thirteen lived to adulthood. All but one married.

Robert [5] Ross (Mary Ross[4,] Mary[3], Alexander[2], James[1])

Robert [5] b.8 Mar 1808 d.1 Feb 1877 married Rebecca P Lawrence b.22 July 1804 d.17 Sep 1888. They had Rebecca A[6] b.5 Feb 1844 d.22 Jan 1899[104] who never married and Mary J[6] b.21 Feb 1846 d.2 Jun 1909 who married Daniel Palmer b.9 May 1841 d.15 June 1897 and had one child, Robert R Palmer[7] b.14 Apr 1871 d.6 Apr 1945.[105] They are all buried in the Palmer Road Cemetery in Newport. Robert and both Rebeccas are listed together with their birth and death dates on one page of the Nathan Hale Cemetery Collection.[106]

Jane[4] (Mary[3], Alexander[2], James[1]) - The Knights

Jennet, d. Abraham and Mary (Willson), June 19, 1792, P.R.6 (Topsham, I, 189)
Jannet, d. Abraham and Mary (Willson), Feb. 16, 1863, P.R.6. (II, 289)
1814 June 18, Mr William Knights & Miss Jane Toothaker, both of Brunswick intend marriage, cert. 1814 Aug[t] 2 [?] (Brunswick, 169)

Jane[4] married William Knights/Knight b.26 Mar 1789 from Portland.[107] They lived in Brunswick / Topsham and are buried in Marquoit Cemetery in Brunswick. Their gravestones add the s to Knight.

---

99. Findagrave.com, gravestone, http://goo.gl/N8uaZf, accessed 16 June 2015.
100. Findagrave.com, gravestone, http://goo.gl/uU2zNn, accessed 16 June 2015.
101. Findagrave.com, years only, http://goo.gl/b3kpim, accessed 7 Aug 2015.
102. Findagrave.com, gravestone photograph, http://goo.gl/BbwGSG.
103. Maine State Archives; 1908-1922 Vital Records; Roll #: 61
104. "Maine, Vital Records, 1670-1907 ," (https://goo.gl/bHwH4y)).
105. "Nathan Hale Cemetery Collection, ca. 1780-1980," (https://goo.gl/ngu7QY).
106. Maine, Nathan Hale Cemetery Collection, ca. 1780-1980, (https://goo.gl/Jnpc8R).
107. Maine State Archives; Pre 1892 Delayed Returns; Roll #: 62

Elizabeth R June 18 1815 (Brunswick, 343)
William Storer Sept 7 1819, Elizabeth Knight his Wife June 18 1815 (402)

In addition to Elizabeth[5], the others were Mary Jane[5], Sarah Ann[5], Priscilla Rebecca[5], Hannah T[5], Charles A[5], Catherine W[5] and William James[5] - all of whom married.

Priscilla Rebecca[5] & Mary Jane[5] Knight (Jane[4], Mary[3], Alexander[2], James[1]) & John Alexander, Jr.

Priscilla R July 4 1820 Decr 19, 1848 (Brunswick, 343 & 403)
Jany 2[d] 1842 John Alexander Jr. & Priscilla R Knight both of Brunswick intend marriage, cert. Jany. 16th 1842 (221)
Feb 10, 1842, John Allexander Jr, & Priscilla Knight both of Brunswick (287)

John Alexander Jan[y] 22 1822 (403)
Rhoda Hall Frost By her Second Husband John Alexander
John Jan 9 1821 (349)
Rhoda July 15 1844 Augt 4 1844 (403)
Rebecca J Novr 19 1847 Jan[y] 19 1848 (403)

1849 April 25, John Alexander and Mary Jane Knight both of Brunswick intend marriage, certified 1849 May 9th (245)
Mary J. Sept 6 1817 (343)
Mary J Knight 2nd Wife Sept 1 1817 Oct 1 1854 (403)

Priscilla Rebecca[5] was John's first wife. Rebecca[5] and her two daughters are buried together in Brunswick's Pine Grove Cemetery. After two babies and her death on 18 Dec 1848 (gravestone date), he married her sister, Mary Jane[5].

Children of John Alexander & Mary Jane Knight his Wife (378)
John William Born Octo 24th 1851
John W Oct 21. 1851 (403)

Unfortunately, Mary Jane[5] died only four years after their marriage. John remarried again immediately so son John William[6] was not alone for very long. John moved his family to Wicasset by 1860[108] but they had returned in 1880.[109]

1855 July 14 John Alexander & Miss Harriet Jane Gatchel both of Brunswick intend marriage (266)

---

108. Year: 1860; Census Place: Wiscasset, Lincoln, Maine; Roll: M653_442; Page: 842; Image: 496; FHL Film: 803442.

109. Year: 1880; Census Place: Brunswick, Cumberland, Maine; Roll: 477; FHL: 1254477; Page: 65D; District: 024; Image: 0381

Harriet J *Mar 10, 1830 (511)*

John William[6] was run over and killed by an electric car in Lisbon on 19 Apr 1913.[110] He had married Lena Mae Petersen on 27 June 1887.[111] They had two children, Andrew J[7] b.4 Aug 1893[112] d.27 Apr 1972[113] and John Joseph[7] b.8 May 1891[114] d.15 Apr 1964.[115]

John[5] and Harriet had three additional children. Those children were cousins as well as half-siblings to John William[6]. John Alexander was the son of John Alexander and Rhoda Hall and the great-great-grandson of William Alexander. Their children were Leonard M[6], Harriet Emma[6], Addie[6] and George Edward Alexander[6]. Since I am not taking Alexanders down this far in this book, I will not say more. But figuring out who John was in the first place was a tricky bit of work. I am satisfied!

Sarah Ann[5] Knight (Jane[4], Mary[3], Alexander[2], James[1]) & Joseph Weeman Strout

Sarah A *July 6 1819 (Brunswick, 343)*

Sept 24. 1841 Joseph W. Strout & Sarah A Knight both of Brunswick intend marriage cert. Octo 8. 1841 (220)

Joseph W Strout	*July 15 1813*	*Sep[t] 8. 1878 (402)*
Elbridge A.	*born April 11. 1843*	*died Augt. 12th 1846 (369) or July 25 1845 (402)*
Lydia E	*May 24 1851*	*Augt 15 1851 (402)*
Williard Warren	*born April 11 1858 (369)*	

Sarah Ann[5] d.8 Mar 1892[116] and Joseph Weeman Strout of Durham lived in Brunswick and raised all their children there. They are buried in Varney Cemetery. Joseph's birth date appears to be incorrect. The Durham birth records has 11 July 1811[117] but the gravestone says 66 years old[118] which would make 1812 the correct year. Willard Warren[6] may have married late and had no children.

110. Maine, Death Records, 1617-1922 Ancestry.com.
111. "Maine, Marriages, 1771-1907," (https://goo.gl/f7mWLf)
112. "Maine, Vital Records, 1670-1907 ," (https://goo.gl/lxW0zc)
113. Maine Death Index, 1960-1997 Ancestry.com Operations Inc, 2002.
114. "US World War I Draft Registration Cards, 1917-1918," (https://goo.gl/AkcsXP)
115. Maine Death Index, 1960-1997 Ancestry.com Operations Inc, 2002.
116. Maine State Archives; 1892-1907 Vital Records; Roll #: 54.
117. Maine, Birth Records, 1621-1922 Ancestry.com Operations, Inc., 2010.
118. Findagrave.com, gravestone, http://goo.gl/f68S1h, accessed 18 June 2015.

Ann Elizabeth	*born*	*Jany. 1st 1849 (Brunswick, 369)*
Alexander, Asa James	*July 7 1844 (402)*	

Asa James Alexander's father was a William and his mother was Deborah Wilson, a daughter of James and Patience, the Irish Wilsons. Asa was a Civil War veteran[119] and spent his last years at Togus.[120] I was not able to tell exactly where Asa James' family falls in the Alexander tree nor was I able to pinpoint what other Alexander family he might have been from.

Ann Elizabeth[6] Strout d.24 Jul 1876 and Asa James had Nellie May[7] b.30 Dec 1870 d.Nov 1967,[121] Harry Asa[7] b.20 Oct 1872[122] d. 3 Feb 1962[123] and Giny[7] (probably Virginia) b.abt 1875. Harry Asa[7] had as many as 18 children with 15 living to adulthood and at least 22 grandchildren.

Mary Jane	*born Feby 14. 1846 (369) d.1923*
Mary Jane	*Feby 14 1847 (402) (405)*
Harvey M. Doughty	*May 15 1842 (405) d.1909*[124]
Ada L. Doughty	*March 25 1866 (405)*

Mary Jane[6] Strout and Harvey Doughty had six children. The only marriage I could find for them that produced children was that of Ernest Emery[7] b.27 Feb 1879 d.27 Mar 1960 in Washington state.[125] He and his wife, Edith May Stacey b.16 Mar 1877, had two children before her death on 13 Oct 1916 from tuberculosis in Brunswick.[126] The other children were Ada Lillian[7] d.1958,[127] James Winfield[7] b.30 Aug 1867[128] d.aft 1940, Anna E[7] b.20 Oct 1869 d.24 Sep 1900,[129] Carrie Jeanette[7] b.abt 1875 and Mabel[7] b.1884 d.21 Sep 1914.[130]

---

119. "Maine, State Archive Collections, 1718-1957," (https://goo.gl/QMYRHO).
120. U.S. National Homes for Disabled Volunteer Soldiers, 1866-1938 Ancestry.com.
121. Social Security Adminstration, Number: 007-50-8399; Maine; 1965-1966.
122. "US World War I Draft Registration Cards, 1917-1918," (https://goo.gl/T4jjNE)..
123. Maine Death Index, 1960-1997 Ancestry.com Operations Inc, 2002.
124. Findagrave.com, gravestone photograph, http://goo.gl/pw1hH4.
125. Ancestry.com. Washington, Deaths, 1883-1960 Ancestry.com Operations Inc, 2008.
126. Maine State Archives; 1908-1922 Vital Records; Roll #: 16.
127. Findagrave.com, gravestone photograph, http://goo.gl/zcGxhk
128. Maine State Archives; Pre 1892 Delayed Returns; Roll #: 30.
129. Findagrave.com, gravestone photograph, http://goo.gl/e3hRv9
130. Maine State Archives; 1908-1922 Vital Records; Roll #: 16.

Charles Franklin born May 24th 1852 (369) d.1 Jun 1928[131]

Charles Franklin[6] Strout married Harriet Ellen Southard b.Feb 1855 d.17 Feb 1906 and had four children all of whom married: Nettie M[7] b.abt 1872, Ira b.1880 d.1973, Leroy[7] b.19 Mar 1885 d.3 Oct 1947[132] and Leeman[7] b.12 May 1888 d.1 April 1968.[133]

William H. born Feby 4 1855 (369)

William Henry[6] Strout d.13 Aug 1932 married Nancy Matilda Ward, b.1 Feb 1858 d.21 May 1932[134] and had six children. All six married and had children. They were Anne Maria[7], Milton H[7], Etta Matilda[7], Alice Mildred[7], Charles Linwood[7], and Bertha Belle[7].

Abraham Lincoln born April 29, 1861 (369) d. 2 Feb 1937 (unc)

Abraham Lincoln Strout[6] married Emma J Courson b.1864 d.21 Jun 1899[135] who died in her seventh pregnancy. Four did not survive and the others were Clarence Edward[7] b.8 May 1886[136] d.9 Apr 1940[137], Everett Lincoln[7] b.11 Dec 1894[138] d.aft 1940 and Harold Burton[7] b.24 Apr 1897 d.7 Apr 1957.[139]

Hannah Toothaker[5] Knight (Jane[4], Mary[3], Alexander[2], James[1]) - The Griffins

Hannah T. born Jan[y] 1, 1825 (Brunswick, 343)
Hannah [ ], w. Ephriam, Jan. 1, 1825, in New Vineyard. [Hannah Toothaker (Knights), P.R.12.] (Topsham, I, 84)
1844 Nov. 23[d] Ephraim Griffin of Topsham & Hannah T. Knight of Brunswick intend marriage cert. 1844 Decr. 7th (Brunswick, 229)
Ephriam, h. Hannah, Feb. 5, 1817, in Poland. [1814, p.R.12.] (Topsham, I, 84)
Ephraim, Apr. 24, 1878, a. 64 y., G.R.3. [1879. in T., a. 64, p.R.12.] (II, 329)

Ephriam E., ch. Ephriam and Hannah, Dec. 12, 1848, in T. (I, 84)
Ephriam E., Nov. 8, 1849, in T. [E. Edwin, ch. Ephriam and Hannah, Oct. 9, a. 10 m., G.R.3.] (II, 329)

131. Findagrave.com, http://goo.gl/SGN6Kf, accessed 13 Oct 2015.
132. Social Security Applications and Claims Index, 1936-2007 Ancestry.com.
133. Social Security Adminstration, Number: 043-03-4192; Connecticut; Before 1951.
134. Findagrave.com, http://goo.gl/lUL0oq, accessed 9 Aug 2015.
135. Maine State Archives; 1892-1907 Vital Records; Roll #: 54.
136. WWI, Registration State: Massachusetts; Roll: 1674420.
137. Portland, Maine, 1946, U.S. City Directories, 1821-1989 Ancestry.com.
138. Maine State Archives; 1892-1907 Vital Records; Roll #: 54.
139. Findagrave.com, gravestone photograph, http://goo.gl/T4c3DH

Eudora, ch. Ephriam and Hannah, Sept. 26, 1847, in T. (I, 84)
Eudora, Oct. 10, 1847, in T. [Udora, Oct. 7, a. 11 d. ch. Ephraim and Hannah, G.R.3.] (II, 329)
Franklin O. [Oscar, p.R.12], ch. Ephriam and Hannah, Dec. 2, 1851, in T. (I, 84)

Hannah T., Mrs., and David Work, both of T., int. Apr. 16, 1881. [cert, issued Apr. 21.] [m. Apr. 27, N.P.6.] (Topsham, II, 116)

Only Franklin Oscar[6] survived childhood; both Ephraim and Eudora are buried with their father in Riverview Cemetery in Topsham. After Ephraim died, Hannah married David Work and lived to age 92 dying on 10 Mar 1917.[140]

Franklin[6] d.15 Sep 1933 married twice. I believe he divorced first wife, Lizzie, because she is listed by her maiden name in the 1880 census.[141] They married in Massachusetts.[142]

Franklin O. of T. and Lizza K. Estabrook of Brunswick, int. Feb. 8, 1875. [cert, issued Feb. 13.] (Topsham, II, 116)

His second wife was Annie Mabel Woodside b.1 Apr 1860 d.14 Feb 1905,[143] a distant Alexander cousin. They had two children, Ada Cushman[7] b.20 Dec 1886 d.7 May 1963[144] and Earle Franklin[7] b.25 Oct 1895 d.4 Aug 1976.[145]

Charles A[5] Knight (Jane[4], Mary[3], Alexander[2], James[1])

Charles A. Dec 22, 1828 (Brunswick, 343)
Feb[y] 28th 1850 Charles A Knight to Axey J. Gatchell both of Brunswick (294)
Axey J Augt 31, 1830 (460) (355, Exa Jane)
Children of Charles A. Knight & Exey Gatchell his Wife,
Georgianna Born June 25th 1851 (377)

1859 Dec 21 Mr. Charles A Knight to Miss Mary F Allen of Wiscasett (309)

Charles A died during the Civil War on 14 Jan 1863 in Richmond, Virginia.[146] His unit was Company G 4th Regiment. His second wife, Mary, did get a widow's pension that included a minor child

140. Maine State Archives; 1908-1922 Vital Records; Roll #: 61.
141. Year: 1880; Census Place: Brunswick, Cumberland, Maine; Roll: 477; FHL: 1254477; Page: 91C; District: 025; Image: 0432.
142. Massachusetts, Town and Vital Records, 1620-1988 Ancestry.com.
143. Findagrave.com, gravestone, http://goo.gl/c5BbIq, accessed 19 June 2015.
144. Findagrave.com, http://goo.gl/HkZtBx, accessed 19 June 2015.
145. Massachusetts, Mason Membership Cards, 1733-1990 Ancestry.com.
146. Maine State Archives; Pre 1892 Delayed Returns; Roll #: 62.

which must have been Georgianna6.[147]

George Annah of Brunswick & Abial W. Eaton of T., int. Dec. 15, 1870. [m. Dec. 29, Miss Georgiana, N.P.6.] (Topsham II, 155)
Stanley B., s. A. W. and G. A., Sept. 9,1877, G.R.4. (I, 62)

Georgianna6 d.1906 married Abiel Eaton b.1851 d.1928[148] on 15 Dec 1870[149] and had two children, Stanley7 b.9 Sep 1879 d.16 May 1896[150] and Frank W7 b.1 Jan 1873 d.20 Apr 1911[151] both of whom died of tuberculosis. Frank7 did marry though and had two wives and several children; his obituary listed him as a paper maker so I assume he worked in the paper mill there in Topsham.

Catherine W5 Knight (Jane4, Mary3, Alexander2, James1) - The Stones
Catherine W. Oct 23, 1831 (Brunswick, 343)
Stone, Edwin M. & Kate W. Knight, both of T., int. Dec. 19, 1879. [cert, issued Dec. 24.] [m. Jan. 4, 1880, N.P.6.] (Topsham, II, 250)
Stone, Edwin M., h. Dianna S., June 10, 1825, in New Brunswick. [h. Diana S. Sanborn; also Kate W. Knight, G.R.3.] (I, 178)

Catherine6 "Kate"d.18 Aug 1911[152] and Edwin M Stone d.30 Mar 1901[153] are buried together in Riverview Cemetery in Topsham. It was his second marriage and he had children with his first wife but none with Catherine 6.

William James5 Knight (Jane4, Mary3, Alexander2, James1)
William James Octo 30, 1835 (Brunswick, 343)

William5 married Hannah E Wilson Jack b.27 Sept 1833.[154] She was the daughter of James and Patience Carver Wilson (the Irish Wilsons). Her husband, James M Jack, died in 1865 and she was left with three small children. William6 and Hannah married on 25 August 1867[155] and had a daughter, Katherine "Kate" Arlington7 b.30

147. Organization Index to Pension Files of Veterans Who Served Between 1861 & 1900, roll 183.
148. Gravestone photograph for both posted on Ancestry.com.
149. "Maine, Marriages, 1771-1907," (https://goo.gl/CcE45U).
150. "Maine, Vital Records, 1670-1907 ," (https://goo.gl/LgLQT2)..
151. Maine State Archives; 1908-1922 Vital Records; Roll #: 18
152. Maine State Archives; 1908-1922 Vital Records; Roll #: 54
153. Maine State Archives; 1892-1907 Vital Records; Roll #: 54
154. "Maine, Births and Christenings, 1739-1900," (https://goo.gl/PQgX2H).
155. "Maine, Marriages, 1771-1907," (https://goo.gl/bSQLdW.

Aug 1871 d.1955,[156] before he died on 11 Apr 1872.[157] He, like his brother, served in the Civil War in Company C, 15th Regiment.[158]

Abraham[4] (Mary[3], Alexander[2], James[1])

Abraham, s. Abraham and Mary (Willson), Mar. 10, 1775, P.R.6. (Topsham, I, 189)
Abram Toethaker Jr Son of Abram & Mary Toothaker was born to them in Harpswell March 16th 1774. (Brunswick, 58)
Abraham, s. Abraham and Mary (Willson), July 1, 1833, P.R.6. (Topsham II, 389)

Catherine Wilson Oct 19 1785 (Brunswick, 497)
Children of Abraham Toothaker Junr and Catharine his wife (Brunswick, 497)

(Brunswick, 497 & 65)
1st Keziah was born to them September 23 AD 1803 (d. 23 Oct 1873[159])
2nd Mary W. Toothaker March 7 1806 5 Feb 1861
3rd Catharine Toothaker May 10 1808 (May 20)
4 James Toothaker was born Febury 13 1810
5 Isaac Chandler Toothaker was born Decemr 21 1812 (31) Augt 1865
6 Horatio born Apr 1 1815 (Apr 6)
7 Sarah Feby 27 1817 Oct 1852
8 Abraham Apr 10 1819 (Apr 16)
9 Benj T. July 12 1820 died Jany 1830 (14 Jan 1831?)
10 Rebecca C Augt 6 1822 died July 18 1847

Abraham[4] married Catharine Wilson b.19 Oct 1785,[160] granddaughter of Alexander Wilson[2], and therefore his first cousin. A number of their children never married: Keziah[5], Mary W[5], Sarah[5], Benjamin[5] and Rebecca C[5]. Abraham is buried in Maquoit Cemetery where his stone states his age of 58 at death, making the 1775 birth date the preferred birth year.[161]

Catharine[5] (Abraham[4], Mary[3], Alexander[2], James[1]) - The Gatchells

3rd Catharine Toothaker May 10 1808 (20) (Brunswick, 65) died Feby 28 1849 (497)
Augt 10 1833 Marriage is intended between Mr Francis Gathell & Miss Catherine Gatchell both of this town cert. Aug 25, 1833 (149)
Children of William Gatchell & Elizabeth Bishop,
Francis born Aug 29 1806 (317)
Winfield S Mar 12, 1843 died July 12 1843 (534)

156. Findagrave.com, http://goo.gl/swsTcO, accessed 18 June 2015.
157. Findagrave.com, http://goo.gl/MHqTxx, accessed 9 Aug 2015.
158. Organization Index to Pension Files of Veterans Who Served Between 1861 & 1900.
159. Gravestone, http://goo.gl/5wts9L, accessed 18 June 2015.
160. "Maine, Births and Christenings, 1739-1900," (https://goo.gl/m4RrSe).
161. Findagrave.com, http://goo.gl/mCDmIw.

Keziah July died March

Though the marriage record has Catharine's name incorrect, subsequent records confirm this marriage. She is buried in the Gatchell Cemetery along with Francis d.12 Jun 1884.[162]

All four of the surviving children, Elizabeth[6], Sarah Potter[6], Mary [6] and Abraham C[6] married and had children.

Elizabeth Jany 7 1837 (534) (298)
March 11, 1855 Layfayette Gilbert of Leeds and Elizabeth F Gatchell of Brunswick

Elizabeth F[6] and Lafayette b.abt 1837 d.18 Mar 1924 moved to Massachusetts by 1880. They had six children but the first three died around the same time in Maine: Ida Eugenia[7] b.7 Jan 1856[163] d.26 Mar 1862,[164] Minnie Vaughn[7] b.23 Sep 1857[165] d.21 Mar 1862,[166] and Lafayette Chandler[7] b.2 Apr 1860[167] d.16 Apr 1862.[168] The next three were born before Lafayette enlisted in December of 1861; he served until July of 1862.[169] He was listed as invalided on his pension paperwork 24 Jan 1863.[170] The three children who did survive were Harry C[7], Leonora[7] and Maud Ina[7].

Harry Clinton[7] b.21 Oct 1866 d.1946[171] married Lettie Greenlaw b.14 Dec 1864[172] and had two children in Massachusetts. Leonora[7] b.1864 d.1925[173] married George Feeley b.abt 1954 d.1 Jan 1926[174] from Nova Scotia and had two children. Maud Ina[7] b.2 Jan 1876[175] married Edward W Hamilton b. abt 1868 and they had seven children but I only found a marriage and children for one of those seven.

162. Findagrave.com, gravestone, http://goo.gl/1iU3i9, accessed 18 June 2015.
163. "Maine Births and Christenings, 1739-1900," (https://goo.gl/owHBDw)
164. "Maine Deaths and Burials, 1841-1910," (https://goo.gl/98lG1W)
165. "Maine Births and Christenings, 1739-1900," (https://goo.gl/xVhSvb)
166. "Maine Deaths and Burials, 1841-1910," (https://goo.gl/gw6La3)
167. "Maine Births and Christenings, 1739-1900," (https://goo.gl/dH2qFq)
168. "Maine Vital Records, 1670-1907 ", (https://goo.gl/Q8TrJt)
169. United States Census of Union Veterans and Widows of the Civil War, 1890," (https://goo.gl/f7fmrZ)
170. "United States General Index to Pension Files, 1861-1934", (https://goo.gl/jEL5Nz)
171. U.S., Social Security Applications and Claims Index, 1936-2007, Ancestry.com
172. "Maine Births and Christenings, 1739-1900," (https://goo.gl/Tov2RH)
173. Findagrave.com, http://goo.gl/NK7HvY
174. California, Death Index, 1905-1939 Ancestry.com Operations, Inc., 2013.
175. "Massachusetts Births, 1841-1915," (https://goo.gl/AGZ3Lo)

Sarah P Gatchell *Jany 4 1834 (534)*

Sarah Potter[6] Gatchell d.27 May 1910[176] married Samuel Morrill Chase b.abt 1826 d.9 Nov 1897[177] from New Hampshire on 20 March 1859[178] and they settled in Lewiston. He was a cotton manufacturer. They had two who never married: Walter Burton[7] b.1872 d.12 Feb 1898 (TB)[179] and George S[7] b.abt 1877.

Frank Morrill[7] Chase b.Jan 1859 d.1947[180] married Mary T Mahoney b.abt 1858 d.22 Dec 1932[181] on 21 May 1884[182] in Lewiston. They both died in Massachusetts and are buried in Pittsfield, New Hampshire. They had eight children and 15 grandchildren.

Maria C[7] Chase b.8 Sep 1863[183] married Otis Carpenter and had two daughters in Massachusetts.

Nellie E[7] Chase b.27 Oct 1865 d.6 Sep 1907 (TB)[184] married George Freeman Sawyer b.23 Jul 1858 b.20 May 1940[185] of Gray. They had six children and 13 grandchildren.

Annie Chandler[7] Chase b.1868 d.7 Dec 1931[186] married Lauchlin Charles McLaughlin from Nova Scotia and had 7 children and as many as 11 grandchildren.

Charles Everett[7] Chase b.1 May 1870 d.22 Aug 1901[187] married Grace Mabel Burpee and had four children. Sarah "Sadie" P[7] b.1 Aug 1873[188] also married (George Marcy) and had two children.

---

176. Massachusetts, Town and Vital Records, 1620-1988 Ancestry.com.
177. Massachusetts, Death Records, 1841-1915 Ancestry.com.
178. "Maine, Marriages, 1771-1907," (https://goo.gl/SN4hQ5)
179. Massachusetts, Death Records, 1841-1915 Ancestry.com.
180. Massachusetts, Death Index, 1901-1980 Ancestry.com Operations, Inc., 2013.
181. New Hampshire, Death and Disinterment Records, 1754-1947 Ancestry.com.
182. "Maine, Marriages, 1771-1907," (https://goo.gl/LUsP8d.
183. "Maine, Vital Records, 1670-1907 ," (https://goo.gl/Bb3JSN).
184. "Maine, Vital Records, 1670-1907 ," (https://goo.gl/ou6CAq) .
185. Findagrave.com, http://goo.gl/1VKdcb, accessed 19 June 2015.
186. Boston, Massachusetts, City Directory, 1932, 1267. Ancestry.com.
187. Massachusetts, Death Index, 1901-1980 Ancestry.com Operations, Inc., 2013.
188. "Maine, Vital Records, 1670-1907 ," (https://goo.gl/Lrya3t).

Mary A *Sept 14 1835 (Brunswick, 534)*

Mary A[6] Gatchell d.aft 1910 married Levi Dingley Jepson b.18 Jan 1829[189] d.4 Apr 1900;[190] they had John E[7] who died young and Frank Chandler[7] who married but had no children.

Abram C *Oct 20 1841 (Brunswick, 534)*

Abraham Chander[6] Gatchell d.15 June 1925[191] married Emma Jane Brett b.21 Jan 1864 d.8 Jul 1962 on 19 Nov 1886 in Brunswick.[192] They had five children but only two who lived to adulthood, Leonora Esther[7] b.20 Mar 1894 d.4 Dec 1958[193] and Chester Asa[7] b.4 Mar 1897[194] d.1925.[195]

James[5] (Abraham[4], Mary[3], Alexander[2], James[1])

James Toothaker was born Febury 13 1810 (Brunswick, 65)
1846 Feby 7th James Toothaker & Mrs Harriet K. Bishop both of Brunswick intend marriage, certified Feby 21st (233)
Feby 24th 1846 James Toothaker & Harriett K. Bishop both of Brunswick by Rev. William Johnson (286)
[Kendall] Harriet, ch. "Elder" Henry and Sally [Swasey, P.R.68], Mar.17, 1807, in Litchfield. (Topsham I, 111)
Rebecca Toothaker *Feby 27 1847 (Brunswick, 478)*
Emma *June 12. 1850 (478)*

James[5] married Harriet Kendall Bishop d.28 Feb 1896,[196] a Topsham widow with children. They had two more and are buried in Growstown Cemetery in Brunswick. The eldest daughter, Rebecca[6], did marry before 1870[197] but is divorced by the next census and I couldn't find her after that. Emma[6] married Edwin Augustus Hackett b.8 Jan 1842[198] d.26 Feb 1897[199] They had three children: Nina A[7] b.1 July 1869 d.31 May 1895 and Bertha L[7] b.22 Aug 1886 d.1927[200]

189. "Maine, Births and Christenings, 1739-1900," (https://goo.gl/EOTQUH).
190. Maine State Archives; 1892-1907 Vital Records; Roll #: 29.
191. Brunswick, Maine, City Directory, 1926, 154. Ancestry.com.
192. "Maine, Marriages, 1771-1907," (https://goo.gl/UFVg84).
193. Findagrave.com, gravestone, http://goo.gl/22zk2n, accessed 19 June 2015.
194. Maine State Archives; 1892-1907 Vital Records; Roll #: 21
195. Findagrave.com, gravestone, http://goo.gl/c8d6jp, accessed 19 June 2015.
196. Findagrave.com, gravestone, http://goo.gl/HmUYvC, accessed 18 June 2015.
197. Year: 1870; Census Place: Brunswick, Cumberland, Maine; Roll: M593_539; Page: 59A; Image: 122; Family History Library Film: 552038.
198. "Maine, Births and Christenings, 1739-1900," (https://goo.gl/Xf7rJU).
199. Findagrave.com, gravestone, http://goo.gl/s4JYNL, accessed 18 June 2015.
200. Findagrave.com, gravestone, http://goo.gl/71GYzZ, accessed 18 June 2015.

who never married and James E[7] b.14 June 1872. James[7] did marry and have children. He may have died in New York in 1906. (birth dates, Brunswick, 572)

Isaac Charles[5] (Abraham[4], Mary[3], Alexander[2], James[1])

Isaac Chandler Toothaker was born Decem[r] 31 1812 (Brunswick, 65) died Augt 1865 (497)

Isaac[5] moved to Minot and married Sarah Bartlett b.abt 1815 in Minot on 7 Dec 1840.[201] Sarah and Isaac[5] had a son, Abner B[6] b.29 Nov 1844[202] d.1931.[203] Abner did marry late in life but had no children.

Horatio[5] (Abraham[4], Mary[3], Alexander[2], James[1])

Horatio born Apr 1 1815 (Brunswick, 65) d.20 June 1891

May 7th 1847 Horatio Toothaker of Brunswick to Mary M. Willson of Harpswell by Rev E G Page (291)

Mary b.1819 d.15 June 1891[204] was the daughter of David Wilson, a cousin of Horatio's. They moved to Harpswell and had one child, William C[6] b.30 Jul 1847 d.5 Sep 1927. He married Octavia Curtis b.19 May 1853 d.31 May 1898 of New Hampshire who was a descendant of the Alexanders. They had one son Oliver Henry[7] b.10 Apr 1877 d.1969 who married Grace Elizabeth Mead b.28 Aug 1874 d.31 May 1943[205] and had one child. He is buried in Brunswick but spent his adult life in mainly Massachusetts and New Hampshire. They both were teachers.[206]

Horatio[5] and Mary's daughter, Jeanette Frances[6] b.8 Nov 1881 may never married but had a son, Stanley[7].[207] She moved to Boston and unfortunately both she and Stanley[7] are last seen in the Suffolk County Jail in 1930.[208]

---

201. "Maine, Marriages, 1771-1907," (https://goo.gl/0uGzfq).
202. "Maine, Births and Christenings, 1739-1900," (https://goo.gl/2T0pzF).
203. Findagrave.com, gravestone, http://goo.gl/UL31Bk, accessed 18 June 2015.
204. Findagrave.com, gravestone, http://goo.gl/2dzdxc.
205. Findagrave.com, gravestone, http://goo.gl/p2kVhL, accessed 18 June 2015.
206. Year: 1920; Census Place: Fairhaven, Bristol, Massachusetts; Roll: T625_682; Page: 28A; Enumeration District: 26; Image: 302.
207. Year: 1910; Census Place: Auburn Ward 1, Androscoggin, Maine; Roll: T624_536; Page: 1A; Enumeration District: 0002; FHL microfilm: 1374549.
208. Year: 1930; Census Place: Boston, Suffolk, Massachusetts; Roll: 944; Page: 4A; Enumeration District: 0093; Image: 152.0; (https://goo.gl/cEwISR).

Abraham C[5] (Abraham[4], Mary[3], Alexander[2], James[1])

Abraham Apr 10 1819 (Brunswick, 65)
1846 Decr 19th Abraham C. Toothaker of Brunswick & Merriam C. Gilbert of Green intend marriage cert. 1847 Jany 2d (237)
Mariam Gilbert Oct 11 1824 (497)
Amon Toothaker Jany 15 1847 died June 30, 1849
Ferris A. April 29 1848 Toras Ann April 26, 1849 (371)
Gilbert E Novr 20, 1858 Gilbert Earl (371)
Fred A. April 30 1863

Abraham d.1 Mar 1891 and Mariam d. 28 Jun 1907 and their children are all buried in the Growstown Cemetery in Brunswick. Daughter Teris[6] married Erwin B Clark of Connecticut but died in Walcottville, Connecticut, on 18 Feb 1871. Both Gilbert Earl and Fred who both died in 1935 also married but did not have children.[209]

209. Gravestones for each one, http://goo.gl/12PSdO, accessed 18 June 2015.

William & Jennet Alexander in Harpswell

William Alexander's father, David, is memorialized for sacrificing his life to protect him from the Indians. William "was remarkable when a youth for his agility and uncommon strength. In muscular vigor he far exceeded any of the lads in town who were anywhere near his own age. One day he and another boy by the name of Thorn were on the hill near the river, when suddenly a couple of stout Indians pounced upon them, each Indian singling out one of the boys. Their object was to run the lads off into the woods, where they would be comparatively safe from pursuit. The stout resistance, however, made by young Alexander, although a mere boy, made the Indian feel as if he had more than his hands full. At every step he encountered a resolute resistance, and, although a powerful Indian, he was making slow progress. The boy's outcries at length attracted the attention of the settlers up and down the river, and his father, being first to comprehend the true state of things, outstripped all others in going to the relief of his son, guided partly by the voice of the lad and partly by the zigzag trail of the furrowed earth, which was a conspicuous mark and was made by the boy's stubborn obstinacy and resistance. The father at length came in full sight of his son and was hastening to his rescue, when the Indian, letting the lad go, fired, killing Mr. Alexander, who fell instantly dead. The son, the moment he saw his father fall, ran, and the Indian, fearing pursuit, desisted from attempting his recapture. The inhabitants of the neighborhood, having provided themselves with guns, and guided by the Alexander boy, started off in pursuit. They found Mr. Alexander dead."[1]

This lovely story is always offered up about the Alexanders; however, we don't know when this happened except that it was prior to 1731.

There is a William listed as an early settler of Cathance in 1731[2] preceded by his brother James[3] (J Alexander) in 1738. There is a Robert Alexander who may have been a first cousin on that list in 1746[4] with William as having sold their lots. William had lot number 48

1. Alexander, 10-11.
2. Wheeler, 869.
3. Alexander, 12.
4. Alexander, 12.

and Robert had lot 50. These are the lots very close to the Wilson lots on the Androscoggin.[5] This may have been owned by William's first cousin (or uncle), William.

All of Jane and William's children were born in Harpswell and it is believed their move there took place right before David's birth in 1737[6]. Their children were David[3], James[3], b.1739, William b.1741, Elizabeth[3], John[3], Samuel[3], and Hugh[3].

William was named surveyor of highways in Harpswell in 1758.[7] He was also in the same military company as the Wilson brothers, Captain Adam Hunter's.[8]

William died 2 Aug 1778 and Jennet in 1798 (March 7) as evidenced by their gravestones[9] and, according to Alva Alexander, were buried in the yard back of the old First Church on Harpswell, their graves are next to those of their son David and his wife. Alva is the one that put up those stones though so the dates then are a bit iffy in the end.[10]

Harpswell is sixteen miles south of Topsham on a finger of land jutting out into the Atlantic ocean so it makes sense that the Alexanders became a sea going and ship building family. That fact becomes important as the generations go by.

I have not made an exhaustive study of what Alexanders were in coastal Maine in the 1700s but there is that genealogy written by De Alva Stanwood Alexander in 1898. He states that he believes all Alexanders in coastal Maine were descendants of David.[11] He's wrong, however; some of the Alexanders in Topsham and Bowdoin are descended from a Robert who came with his family to Pennsylvania from Ireland. He was the only one of his siblings who went to

5. Pejebscot Papers, 3:35.
6. Alexander, 17.
7. Wheeler, 162.
8. Wheeler, 879.
9. Findagrave.com, gravestone photo: http://goo.gl/KZ7K0X
10. Alexander, 24-25.
11. Alexander, 12.

Maine instead. Also, the William Alexander family has been thoroughly traced on Ancestry.com by an unknown S Alexander. Without her work, I would have had enormous difficulties in tracing the myriad Alexander descendants and so I am exceedingly grateful for that meticulous work that gave me a head start.

Sinnet did a genealogical study of the Alexanders and a copy of that typewritten manuscript is at the New England Genealogical Society in Boston. Some 80 pages or more long, it's just too large to make a copy of or photograph with any ease. His study is not the last word either; I quickly found records that conflict with some of his data and there is more information available now. Other records of Sinnet have also been incorrect so a thorough look might be my next task!

If there are Topsham / Brunswick / Bowdoin families, they do get precedence since that's the main focus of this study. What follows here then is a very abbreviated and condensed look at the Alexanders.

Hugh³ (Jennet², James¹)

Hugh³ b.21 Mar 1750[12] d.8 May 1807[13] and Catherine Ewing, b.1752, d.1 Jan 1788[14]

> *Hugh and Catherine Ewing, Mar. 25, 1773, p.R.80. (Topsham, II, 36)*
> *Hugh and Hannah Dunning, Sept. 29, 1788, p.R.80. (II, 36)*
> *Hannah, daughter of Andrew Dunning & Hannah Shepherd b.22 Feb 1752[15] d.8 Jan 1846 (Sinnett, 9)*

The children were Benjamin⁴, Betsey⁴, Margaret⁴, Martha⁴, Hugh⁴ and Joseph⁴.

Betsey⁴ (Hugh³, Jennet², James¹) & William Curtis

> *Betsey, d. Hugh and Catherine (Ewing), Mar. 1, 1774, p.R.80. (Topsham, II, 27)*
> *William (s. Ezekiel & Elizabeth (Alexander)), & Betsey Alexander, d. Hugh & Catherine (Ewing). June 13, 1796, P.R.80. (Topsham, II, 78)*

---

12. "Maine, Births and Christenings, 1739-1900," (https://goo.gl/i2gDyS).
13. Findagrave.com, gravestone photo: http://goo.gl/4jilW9
14. Findagrave.com, gravestone, http://goo.gl/mGquxv, accessed 30 June 2015.
15. "Maine, Births and Christenings, 1739-1900," (https://goo.gl/G5JC2d).

Betsey, w.William,d.Mar. 14,1848 ae 72 y.g.r.36 (Bowdoinham, 27), first cousin
Curtis, William, s. Ezekiel & Elizabeth (Alexander), Mar. 18, 1769, p.R.80. (Topsham, II, 10)
Curtis, William, h.Betsey, d.June 22, 1849 ae 80 y.g.r.36 (II, 30)

Mary Ann, d. William and Betsey (Alexander), about 1817, p.R.80. (II, 10)
Mary Ann, d. William & Betsey (Alexander) in childhood, P.R.80. (II, 310)
Andrew, s. William and Betsey (Alexander), Nov. 5, 1796, p.R.80. (II, 9)
Andrew, Capt., s. William & Betsey (Alexander), [ ], killed by negro cook in St. Jago, Cuba. Unmarried, P.R.80. (309)
Simeon, s. William and Betsey (Alexander), , —, 1809, p.R.80. (II,
Simeon, s. William and Betsey (Alexander), [ ], in Jefferson Co., Mo., unmarried, P.R.80. (II, 311)
William, Jr., s. William and Betsey (Alexander), Aug. 26, 1805. Non-sane, had fits, p.R.80. (II, 10)
William Jr., s. William and Betsey (Alexander), about, 1850, p.R.80. (II, 311)
Margaret, d. William and Betsey (Alexander), Sept. 25, 1802, P.R.80.
Hugh, s. William and Betsey (Alexander), Oct. 24, 1800, p.R.80. (II, 10)
Hugh, h. Margaret (Rogers), Mar. 12, 1881, p.R.80. (II, 311)
Hugh of Bowdoinham (s. of William & Betsey (Alexander)) & Margaret Rogers (d. of John & Susanna), 1832, P.R.80. (II, 77)
Margaret (Rogers), w. Hugh, May 21, 1881, p.R.80. (II, 311)

Hugh^4 (Hugh^3, Jennet^2, James^1)

Hugh, Jr., s. Hugh and Catherine (Ewing), Dec. 14, 1781. Removed to Richmond, p.R.80. (Topsham II, 1) d.30 Apr 1862[16] married Anna Wilson (no relation) b.27 Mar 1780 d.26 Mar 1843 (11 chn) gravestone year for Anna, 1791

Never married or no children: Mary Ann^5, Nancy^5, Joseph^5, Simeon^5, Rachel^5, William Curtis^5.

Andrew Dunning^5 m. Maribah Siegars (3 chn), Noah^5 m. Mary Ann Siegars (sister of Maribah) (5 chn), Hugh Wilson^5 m. Mary Dunning Washburn (8 chn), Randal Dunn^5 m. Zerada Watson (8 chn), David Wilson^5 m. Louisa Reed Pray (2 chn),

Joseph^4 (Hugh^3, Jennet^2, James^1)

Joseph, s. Hugh and Catherine (Ewing), Apr. 12, 1784. Unmarried, p.R.80. (II, 10)

Record was incorrect: Joseph^4 did marry Pamelia / Amelia Curtis (9 chn).

Never married or no children: Olive,^{5} Martin^5, Sarah C^5.

16. Findagrave.com, gravestone, http://goo.gl/oIvmU7, accessed 30 June 2015.

Daniel R[5] m. Adeline Nason (4 chn), Joseph[5] m. Jane Thomas Toothaker (1 chd), Ambrose[5] m. Elizabeth L Webb (1 chd), Thomas A[5] m. Betsey Barnes Merryman (5 chn), Catherine Jeanette[5] m. John A Cleaveland (4 chn), Margaret Alexander[5], (2 chn) mother of Edward Paul Dyer, see the next chapter, "Damn Yankee Gone South".

Margaret[4] (Hugh[3], Jennet[2], James[1]) - Paul Randall & Paul Curtis

Margaret, d. Hugh and Catherine (Ewing), Apr. 16, 1772, p.R.80. (II, 10) d.19 Feb 1829 [17] m.Paul Randall & m.Paul Curtis
Randall, Paul and Margaret Alexander, d. Hugh and Catherine (Ewing), p.R.80. (II, 213)

Never married or no children: Daniel[5] Randall, Paul[5] Randall, Martha[5] Curtis, Jeremiah[5] Curtis.

Benjamin[5] Randall m. Paulina Anderson (10 chn), Paul[5] Randall m. Nancy Alexander (cousin) (4 chn), William[5] Randall m. Hannah A Alexander, cousin (11 chn), Eliza[5] Curtis m. Benjamin H S Blake (8 chn), Catherine[5] Curtis m. Isaac Merryman (3 chn), Daniel[5] Curtis m. Betsey Strout (4 chn)

Martha[4] (Hugh[3], Jennet[2], James[1]) & Timothy Merriman

Martha, d. Hugh and Catherine (Ewing), Oct. 14, 1779, p.R.80. (II, 10) m.Timothy Merriman
Merriman, T. of Bowdoin & Martha Alexander, d. Hugh & Catherine (Ewing) P.R.80.

Bailey, h. Mary W., 1793, G.R.3. [ch. Timothy and Martha (Alexander), 1798, P.R.49.] [a. 53 y., u.s.c.] (Bowdoin, I, 137)
Bailey, h. Mary W., 1858, G.R.3. [Jan. 20, P.R.49.] (II, 90) (Mary Wilson, no relation)
Timothy Jr, ch., Timothy and Martha (Alexander), July 21, 1799, P.R.49. (I, 140)
Timothy, Jr., h. Appa Anne (Berry), June 18, 1874 in B., a. 74 y. 10 m. 27 d., Capt. militia co., in Brunswick, moved to B. in 1832, P.R.49. (II, 91)
Paul, ch. Timothy and Martha (Alexander), June 8, 1802,P.R.49. (I, 139) d.4 Oct 1884[18] m. Hannah Chase
Catherine, ch. Timothy and Martha (Alexander), June 8, 1804 P.R.49. (I, 137) d.21 Jan 1890[19] m. Samuel Crockett Moody
Harriet, ch. Timothy and Martha (Alexander), 1806, P.R.49. (I, 138)
Harriet, ch. Timothy and Martha (Alexander), Mar. 6, 1882, unm., P.R.49. (II, 90)

17. Findagrave.com, http://goo.gl/Zjqeww, accessed 30 June 2015.
18. Findagrave.com, http://goo.gl/5bLUxH, accessed 2 July 2015.
19. Findagrave.com, gravestone, http://goo.gl/2OJsRy, 2 July 2015.

Nancy, ch. Timothy and Martha (Alexander), Apr. 27, 1808, P.R.49. (I, 139)
Nancy, ch. Timothy and Martha (Alexander), Feb. 15, 1892,unm., P.R.49. (II, 91)
Sarah, ch. Timothy and Martha (Alexander), May 9, 1810, P.R.49.
Hugh, ch. Timothy and Martha (Alexander), Aug. 27, 1814, P.R.49. (I, 138) d.2 May 1896[20] *Wisconsin m. Julia Ann Winslow (5 chn)*
Martha, ch. Timothy and Martha (Alexander), Apr. 8, 1814, P.R.49. (I, 138) d.15 Dec 1886[21] *m. Charles Cowen Snow (4 chn)*
Cordelia, ch. Timothy and Martha (Alexander), 1816, P.R.49. m. (I, 137) d.8 May 1877 m. Stephen Stone of New Brunswick, (Topsham, II, 382 "Cordelia, consort of late Stephen,") (5 chn)

Benjamin[4] (Hugh[3], Jennet[2], James[1])

Benjamin, only ch. of Hugh and Hannah (Dunning), Apr. 12, 1790, P.R.80. (Topsham, II, 1) d.12 Jun 1844 (unconfirmed)

Benjamin[4] m. Hannah Sewall (9 chn) - possibly only one survived

Harriet[5] m. Bradford Holmes of Massachusetts (3 chn)

David[3] (Jennet[2], James[1])

David[3] b.1737 d.29 Oct 1792[22] m. Anna Ewing b.1738 d.22 Sep 1809 (9 chn)

Never married or no children: Joseph[4], Rebecca[4], James[4].

The others were William[4], David[4], Anna[4], Isaac[4], Isabella[4] and Jennett[4].

William[4] (David[3], Jennet[2], James[1])

William[4] b.13 Nov 1762 d.19 Oct 1847[23] m. Elizabeth "Betsey" Campbell (11 chn)

Never married or no children: Aletta[5], Isaac[5].

James[5] m. Eleanor Dunlap (5 chn), Campbell[5] m. Margaret Stan-

20. Wisconsin, Deaths, 1820-1907 Ancestry.com Operations, Inc., 2000.
21. Findagrave.com, gravestone, http://goo.gl/BQujWd.
22. Findagrave.com, gravestone, http://goo.gl/LZqnuc, accessed 1 July 2015.
23. "Maine, Veterans Cemetery Records, 1676-1918," (https://goo.gl/93hViR)

wood (8 chn), Isabella[5] m. John Henry (8 chn), Eliza[5] m. Robert Patten Woodside (6 chn), Ewing[5] m. Sarah Dunning Melcher (10 chn), Aletta[5] m. Anthony Coombs Raymond (3 chn), Joseph[5] m. Mary G Mosier (4 chn), Ann D[5] m. Thomas Whitehouse (6 chn), Hiram King[5] m. Sarah E Phinney (4 chn).

David[4] (David[3], Jennet[2], James[1])

David[4] b.31 Mar 1767 d.22 Nov 1818[24] m. Sarah Dunning (9 chn)

Never married or no children: David[5], David II[5], Betsey[5].

Margaret[5] m. John S Bishop (11 chn), Nancy[5] m. Paul Randall (4 chn), Rebecca[5] m. Levi Sewall (11 chn), Hannah[5] m. William Randall [5](Paul's brother) (11 chn), Nehemiah Curtis[5] m. Hannah B Currier (6 chn), Deborah Raines [5]m. Otis Thwing Macomber (3 chn).

Anna[4] (David[3], Jennet[2], James[1]) & Benjamin Dunning

Anna[4] b.3 Sep 1769 d.2 Jul 1805 m. Benjamin Dunning (8 chn)

Never married or no children: Jane[5], Francis[5], David[5], Rebecca[5], Charles Stover[5]

James[5] m. Abigail Merryman (1 chd), Abiezer[5] m. Jane Stover (6 chn), Isaac [5]m. Nancy Stover (4 chn),

Isabella[4] (David[3], Jennet[2], James[1]) & Walter Merryman

Isabella[4] (twin to Isaac) b.10 Oct 1774 d.11 Nov 1829[25] m. Walter Merryman (8 chn)

Never married or no children: Walter[5], Thomas[5]

Robert[5] m. Clarissa Douglas (5 chn), David[5] m. Louisa Gaubert (9 chn), Shubael[5] m. Mary Jane Curtis, first cousin, (10 chn), Eli[5] m.

24. Findagrave.com, gravestone photograph, http://goo.gl/7qhlv8
25. Findagrave.com, gravestone photograph, http://goo.gl/CgSeqG

Elizabeth Fusslin (1 chd), Anna[5] m. Elisha Allen Jr (10 chn), Betsey Barnes[5] m. Thomas A Alexander, first cousin, (5 chn)

Jane Alexander[4] (David[3], Jennet[2], James[1]) & Nehemiah Curtis

Jane[4] b.10 May 1776 d.6 Dec 1830 m. Nehemiah Curtis (7 chn)

Margaret[5] m. Benjamin Merryman (7 chn), David[5] m. Lydia Ann Cox (1 chd), Nehemiah[5] m. Jane Douglass (7 chn) m2. Hannah L Beal (4 chn), Mary Jane Curtis[5] m. Shubael Merryman (10 chn), Adaline[5] m. Rufus Dunning (7 chn), Isabel M[5] m. Simon Merryman (5 chn)

Isaac[4] (David[3], Jennet[2], James[1])
(twin to Isabella)

Isaac, h. Mary (Pennell), Oct. 10, 1774, P.R.2. (Topsham, II, 17)
Isaac and Mary Pennell, Dec. 31, 1795, P.R.2. (II, 36)
Isaac, h. Mary (Pennell), Mar. 18, 1851, P.R.2. (II, 19)
Mary (Pennell), w. Isaac, Aug. 28,1776, P.R.2. (II, 17)
Mary (Pennell), w. Isaac, Nov. 10, 1868, P.R.2. (II, 19)

James, s. Isaac and Mary (Pennell), Mar. 20,1814, P.R.2. (II, 17) James E, farmer d.30 Aug 1897[26] m. Frances Stover (4 chn)
David, s. Isaac and Mary (Pennell), Nov. 19, 1798, P.R.2. (II, 17) unmarried

David, s. Isaac and Mary (Pennell), Dec. 12, 1804, P.R.2. (II, 19)
Charles, s. Isaac and Mary (Pennell), Aug. 28, 1819, P.R.2. (II, 16) unmarried
Charles, s. Isaac and Mary (Pennell), Jan. 27, 1852, P.R.2. (II, 19)
Mary, d. Isaac and Mary (Pennell), Mar. 21,1808, P.R.2. (II, 17) m. Hinchman Sylvester (7 chn) gravestone death date Sept 28, 1882
Mary, ch. Isaac and Mary (Pennell), Sept. 24, 1882, P.R.2. (II, 19)
Pennell, ch. Isaac and Mary (Pennell), Jan. 19, 1811, P.R.2. (II, 18) m. Abigail Stover (4 chn)
Pennell, ch. Isaac and Mary (Pennell), Dec. 31, 1890, P.R.2. (II, 19)
Thomas, s. Isaac and Mary (Pennell), June 9, 1803, P.R.2. (II, 18) d.14 Sep 1891 (unc) m. Hannah Dunning (7 chn)
William, s. Isaac and Mary (Pennell), Mar. 20, 1814, P.R.2. (II, 18) d.18 Jul 1896 of typhoid[27] m. Elizabeth Dunning (5 chn)
David, ch. Isaac and Mary (Pennell), Nov. 15, 1805, P.R.2. (II, 16) unmarried
David, ch. Isaac and Mary (Pennell), June 22, 1867, P.R.2. (II, 19)
Isaac, s. Isaac and Mary (Pennell), Sept. 21, 1796, P.R.2. (II, 17) unmarried

---

26. "Maine, Vital Records, 1670-1907 ," (https://goo.gl/vBJyWy).
27. "Maine, Vital Records, 1670-1907 ," (https://goo.gl/fZ5VEY).

Isaac, s. Isaac and Mary (Pennell), Mar. 24, 1817, P.R.2. (II, 19)
Alice, ch. Isaac and Mary (Pennell), Aug. 17, 1801, P.R.2. (II, 16) d.5 Feb 1895[28]
m. John Reed

Elizabeth³ (Jennet², James¹) & Ezekial Curtis

Elizabeth³ b.1743 d.18 Feb 1814[29] m. Ezekial d.23 Feb 1820

Ezekiel and Elizabeth Alexander, int. Feb. 26, 1762, P.R.80. 76

Ezekiel, s. David and Bethiah (Sprague), Apr. 30, 1735, P.R. 80.

Jennie, d. Ezekiel and Elizabeth (Alexander), Feb. 10, 1765, P.R.80. (Topsham II, 10) d.10 May 1825[30] *m. David Curtis (6 chn)*
Bethia, d. Ezekiel and Elizabeth (Alexander), Mar. 12, 1763, p.R.80. (II, 9) (no chn)
Bethia (d. of Ezekiel and Elizabeth) & John Smullen of Lisbon, [—], p.R.80. (II, 76)
Ezekiel, Jr., s. Ezekiel and Elizabeth (Alexander), Mar. 16, 1767, p.R.80. (II, 9)
Hannah, d. Ezekiel and Elizabeth (Alexander), Oct. 5, 1779, p.R.80. (II, 9) d.31 Mar 1859[31] *(7 chn) gravestone year is 1778*
Hannah (d. of Ezekiel and Elizabeth (Alexander)) & Ward of Freeport, [ ], P.R.80. (II, 76) (7 chn) Thomas Ward

John, s. Ezekiel and Elizabeth (Alexander), Aug. 29, 1773, p.R.80. (II, 10) d.Jan 1853[32] *m. Abigail Alexander, cousin (2 chn)*
Simeon, s. Ezekiel and Elizabeth (Alexander), June 18, 1781, P.R.80. (II, 10) m. Ruth Curtis (4 chn)
Simeon, s. Ezekiel and Elizabeth (Alexander), Jan. 27, 1844, p.R.80. (II, 310)
William, s. Ezekiel and Elizabeth, Mar. 18, 1769, p.R.80. (II, 10) (6 chn)
William,h.Betsey,d.June 22,1849 ae 80 y.g.r.36 (Bowdoinham, 30)
William (s. Ezekiel and Elizabeth), & Betsey Alexander, d. Hugh & Catherine (Ewing). June 13, 1796, P.R.80. (Topsham, II, 78) (first cousin)
Ruth, d. Ezekiel and Elizabeth, July 9, 1771, P.R.80. (II, 10) d.6 Sep 1838[33] *(6 chn)*
Ruth (d. Ezekiel and Elizabeth (Alexander)) & C , Skolfield, [ ], P.R.8O. (II, 78)
Hugh, s. Ezekiel and Elizabeth (Alexander), Feb. 8, 1776, P.R.80. (II, 10)
Hugh, s. Ezekiel and Elizabeth (Alexander), of fever when young, p.R.80. (II, 310)
d.27 Sep 1795[34]

John³ (Jennet², James¹)

John³ b.1745 d.1780 killed by a fall into a hold of a ship about 1780[35] m. Elizabeth Clarke

28. Findagrave.com, http://goo.gl/L3tSYV, accessed 13 Oct 2015.
29. Findagrave.com, gravestone photographs for both deaths: http://goo.gl/EMsUWe.
30. Findagrave.com, gravestone photograph, http://goo.gl/PKNxm1
31. Findagrave.com, gravestone photograph, http://goo.gl/ldIw1a
32. "Maine, Births and Christenings, 1739-1900," (https://goo.gl/J72luR).
33. "Nathan Hale Cemetery Collection, ca. 1780-1980," (https://goo.gl/DzMXb4).
34. "Nathan Hale Cemetery Collection, ca. 1780-1980," (https://goo.gl/ZcHcnH)..
35. Sinnett typewritten manuscript, 9.

Never married: Josiah[4]

Those who married were John[4], Martha[4], Ezekial[4] and Henry[4].

John[4] (John[3], Jennet[2], James[1])

John[4] b.9 Feb 1771[36] m. Lydia Rodick (3 chn) m2. Elizabeth Wilson (no relation, English Wilsons) (7 chn)

Never married or no children: Betsey[5], Lydia[5], Catherine[5], Josiah[5], Huldah[5].

Hannah[5] m. Jesse Thomas (2 chn), Elizabeth[5] m. John L Lambert (7 chn), Martha[5] m. Henry Martin Prescott (8 chn), Fanny[5] m. Robert Blake (4 chn), Sarah A[5] m. David Merryman (2 chn).

Martha[4] (John[3], Jennet[2], James[1]) & Nathan Addams

Martha, w. Nathan, Mar. 28, 1849, a. 75 y. 3 mos., G.R.3. [Martha (Alexander), P.R.145.] (Bowdoin II, 26)
Nathan, 11. Martha, Sept. 1, 1855, a. 81 y. 5 mos., G.R.3. [s. Thomas and Sarah (Tarr), P.R.145.] (II, 26)

David, ch. Nathan and Martha, Oct. 23, 1800. (Bowdoin, I, 13) unmarried
David, Col., Mar. 15, 1839, a. 38 y. 5 mos., P.R.3. [s.Nathan & Martha, P.R.145.] (II, 27)
Diana, ch. Nathan and Martha, June 29, 1810. (I, 14) death unknown
Eliza, ch. Nathan and Martha, Sept. 14, 1806. (I, 14) death unknown
Henry, ch. Nathan and Martha, Aug. 19, 1812. (I, 14) never married
Harry, s. Nathan and Martha (Alexander), Jan. 15, 1886, a. 74 y., P.R.145. (II, 27)
Thomas 1st, ch. Nathan and Martha, Oct. 4, 1803. (I, 16)
Thomas, ch. Nathan and Martha, Jan. 4, 1804. (II, 27)
Thomas 2nd, ch. Nathan and Martha, Dec. 4, 1805. (I, 16)
Thomas, ch. Nathan and Martha, Sept. 11, 1808. [Martha (Alexander), P.R.l45.] (II, 27)
Samuel, s. Nathan and Martha (Alexander), , —, 1816, P.R.l45. (II, 10) (8 chn)
Samuel, Jan. 15, 1891, a. 74 y. 4 m., 0.12.3. [h. Mindwell (Small), 5. Nathan and Martha (Alexander), P.R.145.] (II, 27)
William, ch. Nathan and Martha, Apr. 29, 1809. [a. 41 y., u.s.c] (I, 17) m. Susan Thurston (5 chn)

36. "Maine, Births and Christenings, 1739-1900," (https://goo.gl/oOdFZQ).

Ezekial[4] (John[3], Jennet[2], James[1])

Ezekial[4] b.21 Jan 1775 d.23 Sep 1837[37] in Jamestown, Va m. Margaret Curtis (11 chn)

Never married or died young: Ezekial[5], Asenath[5], Henry[5], Paul[5], Jane[5], Susannah[5], James[5].

Sarah "Sally"[5] Curtis[5] m. James M Durgin (10 chn); David[5] m. Isabella Strout (4 chn); Ezekial[5] m. Elizabeth Allen (3 chn)

Henry[4] (John[3], Jennet[2], James[1])

Henry[4] b.13 Apr 1777[38] d.4 Dec 1854[39] m. Mercy Beverage (5 chn) m2. Betsey Wheeler (9 chn)

Never married or no children: Elizabeth[5], Ezekial[5], David[5], Zenas Cory[5], William D[5], Mercy B[5], Abigail[5], Mary[5] and Zenas Cory II[5].

John[5] m. Hannah Randal Crockett (4 chn), Sarah[5] m. Nathaniel Beverage (3 chn), Lydia[5] m. John M. Fuller Jr. (2 chn), Benjamin D[5] m. Harriet Frye (2 chn), Henry[5] m. Julia Frye (3 chn).

Samuel[3] (Jennet[2], James[1])

Samuel[3] b.28 July 1748[40] d.1784 died from a paralytic stroke, sturdy fisherman.[41] m. Rosannah Clark (8 chn)

Never married or no children: Mary[5] and James[5]

The ones who married were Samuel[5], Abigail[5], Elizabeth[5], Hannah[5], John[5] and Jane[5].

Samuel[4] (Samuel[3], Jennet[2], James[1])

37. "Maine, Births and Christenings, 1739-1900," (https://goo.gl/FIHh7F).
38. "Maine Births and Christenings, 1739-1900, (https://goo.gl/FvuaYz)
39. Faylene Hutton Cemetery Collection, ca. 1780-1990, (https://goo.gl/0UZAcH)
40. "Maine, Births and Christenings, 1739-1900," (https://goo.gl/42wiLP).
41. Sinnett, 9.

Samuel[4] b.7 May 1771[42] d.14 Apr 1835 m. Sarah Wilson (no relation) (4 chn)

No children: Susanna[5] and Abigail[5]

William[5] m. Eunice Curtis[5] Alexander (first cousin, s. John & Bethiah) (1 chd), Mary[5] m Revel Ruel[5] Alexander (first cousin, s. John & Bethiah) (1 chd)

Abigail[4] (Samuel[3], Jennet[2], James[1]) & John Curtis

Abigail[4] b.27 Jan 1776 d.1 Oct 1857[43] m. John Curtis (cousin) (2 chn)

John Smulline[5] m. Elizabeth Curtis (4 chn), Rebecca A[5] m. Isaac Alexander Johnson (6 chn)

Elizabeth[4] (Samuel[3], Jennet[2], James[1]) & Isaac Allen

Elizabeth[4] b.17 Nov 1778[44] m. Isaac Allen (2 chn)

Isaac[5] m. Mary Pratt (8 chn), Elizabeth[5] m. Charles Lyman Brown (9 chn)

Hannah[4] (Samuel[3], Jennet[2], James[1]) & Henry Farr & Andrew Webber

Hannah[4] b.20 Dec 1780[45] d.13 Jun 1852[46] m. Henry Farr (8 chn), m. Andrew Webber (1 chd)

Never married or no children: Harrison Farr[5]

Isaac Farr[5] m. Sarah Folson Sinnet (4 chn), Robert Farr[5] m. Ruth Curtis (8 chn), Henry Farr[5] m. Sylvia Willson (2 chn), Rosanna Al-

42. "Maine Births and Christenings, 1739-1900," (https://goo.gl/8EdWwe).
43. "Maine Births and Christenings, 1739-1900," (https://goo.gl/ydE0JF).
44. "Maine Births and Christenings, 1739-1900," (https://goo.gl/frwgwI).
45. "Maine Births and Christenings, 1739-1900," (https://goo.gl/uIqvfT).
46. Findagrave.com, gravestone photograph, http://goo.gl/QGnSmg.

exander Farr[5] m. David Grows (5 chn), Catherine Farr[5] m. Abner Grows (1 chd) m2. Benjamin Merryman, Alexander Farr[5] m. Sarah Cripps (1 chd), Eleanor[5] m. Charles Blake (9 chn), Benjamin Webber[5] m. Sarah Rideout (1 chd)

John[4] (Samuel[3], Jennet[2], James[1])

John, Oct. 27, 1840, a. 58, G.R.3. (Topsham II, 296)

John[4] b.8 Oct 1782[47] m. Mary Jordan (1 chd) m2. Lovina Farr (1 chld) (sister of Henry Farr, Hannah's husband),

David Perry[5] m. Phinetta Greenleaf (11 chn), William Stanwood[5] m. Nancy Merriman (2 ch)

Jane[4] (Samuel[3], Jennet[2], James[1]) - The Perrys

Jane[4] b.15 Apr 1784[48] d.5 Jun 1861 (unc) m. David Perry (8 chn)

Never married: Lucy[5]

Rosannah Perry[5] m. William Blake (12 chn), Abigail Curtis[5] Perry m. Levi Shattuck Reed (7 chn), John Curtis[5] Perry m. Mary E Baston (4 chn), Margaret Philbrook[5] Perry m. Hugh Sinnett (2 chn), Alice Reed[5] Perry m. William Totman Higgins (4 chn)

James[3] (Jennet[2], James[1])

James[3] b.1739 m. Martha Mustard (10 chn)

Never married or no children: Jennet Allen[4], Joseph[4], Elizabeth[4]

John[4] (James[3], Jennet[2], James[1])

John[4] b.15 May 1758[49] m. Priscilla Hinckley (w. James Mustard) (5 chn)

47. "Maine Births and Christenings, 1739-1900," (https://goo.gl/vuK6yh).
48. "Maine Births and Christenings, 1739-1900," (https://goo.gl/MXKmnM).
49. "Maine Births and Christenings, 1739-1900," (https://goo.gl/5nDc5L).

Never married: Lois[5], Rhoda[5], Isaac[5], Jane[5]

John[5] b.5 July 1789 (Bowdoin I, 18) gravestone 1791 d.20 Nov 1846[50] m. Rhoda Hall Frost (6 chn)
(I've made this connection with discrepancies; beware!)

James[4] (James[3], Jennet[2], James[1])

James[4] b.4 Jan 1762[51] m. unknown Mustard (2 chn)

Never had children: Mustard[5]

James[5] m. Elizabeth "Betsey" Hinkley (see Hinkley chapter) (1 chd)

Abigail[4] (James[3], Jennet[2], James[1]) - The Jacques

Abigail[4] b.7 May 1765[52] m. John Jacques (6 chn)

Never married: Abigail[5], John[5]

Betsey Jaques[5] m. William Tandy (1 chd), Rev James Jaques[5] m. Anna Marshall (5 chn), Katherine[5] Jaques m. Joshua Paine (2 chn)

William[4] (James[3], Jennet[2], James[1])

William[4] b.21 Apr 1767[53] d.24 May 1847 (unc) m. Elizabeth Robinson (7 chn)

Never married: David[5], Sarah[5], Catherine[5], Melinda[5]

Charles[5] m. Bethia Hinkley (3 chn), James[5] m. Hannah Thomas (2 chn), William[5] m. Nancy Hedge Bradley (5 chn), Isaac[5] m.Nancy Doyle (2 chn)

Catherine[4] (James[3], Jennet[2], James[1]) & John Hasey

50. Findagrave.com, gravestone photograph, http://goo.gl/U7ufBL.
51. "Maine Births and Christenings, 1739-1900," (https://goo.gl/BrJxuh).
52. "Maine Births and Christenings, 1739-1900," (https://goo.gl/XuEaeQ).
53. "Maine Births and Christenings, 1739-1900," (https://goo.gl/wJSOU9).

Catherine[4] b.13 Jan 1769[54] m. John Hasey, no other information but may have had a family in Bristol

Elisha[4] (James[3], Jennet[2], James[1])

Elisha[4] b.16 Sep 1770[55] m. Elizabeth (2 chn)

Never married and/or died young: John[5], Abner[5]

William[3] (Jennet[2], James[1])

William[3] m. Dorothy (1 chn), John[4]

John[4] (William[3], Jennet[2], James[1])

John[4] b.11 Oct 1795 d.2 Feb 1871[56] m. Bethiah Alexander (unknown parentage) (10 chn)

Never married or had no children: Sarah[5], Coming[5], Lois[5], Charles[5]

James[5] m. Jane Southard (10 chn), Revel Ruel[5] m. Mary[5] Alexander (cousin) (1 chd), Joanna[5] m. George Darling (8 chn), Margaret[5] m. George Barnes (7 chn), Eunice Curtis[5] m. William Brown Pennell (2 chd) m. William Alexander (1 chd), Fidelia[5] m. Joel Southard (5 chn)

---

54. "Maine Births and Christenings, 1739-1900," (https://goo.gl/lRBQFB).
55. "Maine Births and Christenings, 1739-1900," (https://goo.gl/ClRaKB).
56. "Maine Births and Christenings, 1739-1900," (https://goo.gl/LTFkzt)

Damn Yankee Gone South

The Story of Edward Paul Dyer of Maine & Virginia

Edward Paul Dyer[6] (Mary Ann Margaret[5], Joseph Alexander[4], Hugh[3], Jennett[2] Alexander, James[1]) also created a southern family though his story in the south begins during the Civil War. He was born 6 Oct 1840[1] in Topsham to a very young mother and a father, Charles Dyer, who died when he was six.[2] Whether they were ever married is in doubt: I can find no marriage or divorce record, not to mention no official birth notice. The only indications of his birth date comes from the hints in census records and then his death certificate. Mary Ann Margaret Alexander b.30 Sep 1824 d.3 Jan 1861[3] would have just turned sixteen at the time of his birth.

She married William S. Michaels b.24 Sept 1820[4] d.2 Feb 1894[5] on 4 Apr 1843[6] when Edward was just two years old. His half-brother, William H, was born three years later on 14 Feb 1846.[7]

William S was a shoemaker as noted in the 1850 census[8] and on his death certificate. Edward must have been trained as a shoemaker by his step-father as this was the way he made his living from the start in Virginia.[9]

Over a year after their mother died in 1861, both sons enlisted together on 14 August 1862,[10] the day the Company I, 16th Infantry Regiment Maine was mustered into service. The call for volunteers had gone out with a patriotic appeal:

> *CITIZEN SOLDIERS! Remember you have a country to save, and you are the men who can render most efficient aid in this holy and patriotic work. To render success*

1. Edward P. Dyer, death cert no. 3715, Virginia Bureau of Vital Statistics, Richmond.
2. Maine State Archives; Pre 1892 Delayed Returns; Roll #: 32
3. Maine State Archives; Pre 1892 Delayed Returns; Roll #: 75
4. Maine State Archives; Pre 1892 Delayed Returns; Roll #: 75
5. Maine State Archives; 1892-1907 Vital Records; Roll #: 39
6. "Maine, Marriages, 1771-1907," (https://goo.gl/2gepzp).
7. Maine, Births and Christenings, 1739-1900," (https://goo.gl/NrPDjz).
8. Year: 1850; Census Place: Durham, Cumberland, Maine; Roll: M432_249; Page: 170B; Image: 329
9. Henry W. Bashore, Old Rag Mountain, Rebirth of a Wilderness (Heathsville, VA, Northumberland Historical Press: 2006), 22.
10. Historical Data Systems, comp. U.S., Civil War Soldier Records and Profiles, 1861-1865 Ancestry.com.

speedy and certain, and to alleviate and abridge calamities of war, the President of the United States has requested this call to be made.
By order of the Commander-in-Chief,
JOHN L. HODSDOX,
Adjutant- General.[11]

Not only that but the Union also did something unique - offering bounties of $300 for enlisting[12] - much higher than the bounties in the South. A total of 960 men volunteered for the 16th regiment as it mustered in.[13] Those early enlistments were for only three months as everyone thought the war would be over quickly.

Half-brother William was underage as the minimum enlistment age was 18 but his father could have permitted it; however, the only records I could find have his age listed as 18[14] which does look like he lied about his age. They both served in Company I.[15] Interestingly enough, that list of Company I notes Edward's desertion with a date but does not record William's death as other deaths were noted in that table. His death is listed later in the book. Twelve men besides Edward were listed as deserting but no one else on the same day or even the same month.

Edward is listed as deserting on 20 Jan 1863[16] a month before William died on 18 Feb 1863. We don't know where William died or where he was buried nor do we know what he died of.

Maine and the Civil War

After working through so many of my ancestor's descendants, I was sure that my family and Maine sent way more soldiers to war than my southern families. Sure enough, when I started looking at Maine's participation in the war, I found that it contributed a larger number of combatants, in proportion to its population, than any

11. A. R. Small, The Sixteenth Maine Regiment in the War of Rebellion, 1861-1865 (Portland, ME, B.Thurston & Company: 1886), 11.
12. Essential Civil War Curriculum, http://goo.gl/nL1UKb, 3.
13. Small, 323.
14. Historical Data Systems, comp. U.S., Civil War Soldier Records and Profiles, 1861-1865 [Ancestry.com.
15. Small, 290.
16. Historical Data Systems, comp. American Civil War Soldiers Ancestry.com.

other Union state.

This was due to several factors starting with Lincoln's first vice president, Hannibal Hamlin, who was a Maine native and former representative, senator and governor. He was a member of the newly formed Republican party and Maine was the first state in the northeast to embrace the new party. He was considered an asset to Lincoln's ticket during the election of 1860 as a strong orator and known opponent of slavery, but he didn't even meet Lincoln until after the election.[17] He set the example and tone of the War for Maine.

The Maine regiment fought in some of the bloodiest and well-known battles of the war such as Gettysburg, Petersburg and Fredericksburg but Fredericksburg was a breaking point for our Edward. A total of nearly 1900 men served in the 16th Regiment: they suffered a 57% fatality rate[18] which gives an idea of what kind of fighting the regiment participated in. The south managed more victories way into 1863 than the north, leading many northern soldiers to feel it was a lost cause. The desertion rate was much higher for the Union army than the Confederates.[19]

Fredericksburg (Dec, 1862) was one of those losses with the Union army suffering 12,653 casualties compared to only 5,377 for the Confederates. Union Army Maj. Gen. Ambrose Burnside was the commander of the Army of the Potomac and in trying to redeem himself after Fredericksburg, executed a disastrous attempt in January of 1863 called the Mud March. He was replaced that month but not before creating a morale problem. General Newton had traveled to Washington with General to convince President Lincoln that Burnside was a major problem. Newton was not able to fully articulate the situation saying, "I could not have told the president that none of the privates had any confidence in General Burnside."[20]

On the first day of the Mud March, torrential rains came and every-

17. Hannibal Hamlin, https://goo.gl/O1mGqZ, accessed 15 May 2014.
18. 16th Maine Volunteer Infantry Reg, https://goo.gl/xakW48, accessed 15 May 2014.
19. Desertion, https://goo.gl/MK4wqu, accessed 15 May 2014.
20. Mud March, https://goo.gl/HX1SZ3, accessed 15 May 2014.

thing became mired down in the resulting quagmire (a good lesson in how not to wage a war). Burnside decided to cross the Rappahannock River upstream of the Confederates and then sneak up behind them. The Union Army suffered public humiliation instead as Confederate troops watched from the other side of the river taunting the Union soldiers with signs that read "Yanks, if you can't place your pontoons yourself, we will send you help" and "This way to Richmond."[21]

By the end of the 21st of January Burnside gave up. As Edward's desertion is listed on the twentieth, we don't know if he stuck around for the full mud treatment but he was definitely gone by the time the troops returned to base. I did find a reference by one descendant of his being "separated from his unit" but in the end since he chose to keep moving west and ran from Union soldiers who were looking for deserters, he did desert.[22]

Was that the shameful thing it is today? Absolutely not. For his descendants to feel ashamed about his desertion is unnecessary.

I have not been able to find the desertion rates for the Maine contingent specifically but the highest Union rates were from New York, Pennsylvania, and Ohio that accounted for a total of nearly 90,000 out of an estimated 200,000 for the Union Army.

> *The daily hardships of war, deficiency in arms, forced marches (which sometimes made straggling a necessity for less vigorous men), thirst, suffocating heat, disease, delay in pay,~ solicitude for family, impatience at the monotony and futility of inactive service, and (though this was not the leading cause) panic on the eve of battle - these were some of the conditioning factors that produced desertion. Many men absented themselves merely through unfamiliarity with military discipline or through the feeling that they should be "restrained by no other legal requirements than those of the civil law governing a free people"; and such was the general attitude that desertion was often regarded* ***'more as a refusal . . - to ratify a contract than as the commission of a grave crime.'***[23]

In addition, those initial three month enlistments had been extended to three years.

---

21. The Mud March Begins, http://goo.gl/5vO6Bj, accessed 16 Feb 2015.
22. Bashore, 22.
23. Desertion in the Civil War Armies, http://goo.gl/CbzIiP, accessed 15 May 2014.

Deserters fled to the enemy or Canada, turned outlaw or headed to frontier areas as Edward did when he headed west to the mountains of Virginia. Desertion was just more acceptable then. Even though later in the war they started shooting deserters in an attempt to slow down the desertion rate, not many were ever shot. Only 500 or so on both sides were executed during the war. President Lincoln pardoned most that were caught.[24]

Edward's desertion also corresponded to a surge in desertions for the Union following the losses at Fredericksburg in the winter and spring of 1862/1863.[25]

So what really did happen to Edward Dyer?

There are just an incredible number of tales running around in his family and I suspect many are theories as to what happened - theories devised to excuse or explain his desertion. Some of his descendants are just devastated at the thought that he had been a deserter. It's certainly harder brag on your ancestor under those circumstances.

Henry Bashore in his book, *Old Rag Mountain*, had his version but he had Edward's birth date incorrect and that leaves his sources and information in doubt. I've found a number of stories posted on Ancestry.com in addition to his stories. Most of information I've found disproves a number of those tales.

Bashore says Edward was "wrestling and playing around near the camp boundary. As they wrestled they moved closer to the camp boundary and eventually just walked away from camp." That's a truly benign tale and just as possible as running away from the action. The only problem with that tale is that the weather on the 19th or 20th was certainly not conductive to such behavior. Also, the company was on the march starting around noon until 9 on the

24. Essential Civil War Curriculum, 4.
25. Essential Civil War Curriculum, 3.

19th.[26] It appears that he did not answer roll call the next morning.

The records from the Civil War are fraught with errors though so we can't be sure that was the day he left. It is possible, therefore, that he actually left later. In the 16th Regiment there was no one else listed as deserting on the same day and nearly all who all who did desert were much later - towards the end of 1863 or later years.

Definitely separated from the unit is a constant theme and of course it was possible. Bashore keeps mentioning Edward's friend who he left with but he does not call the fellow by name. Even whole units got separated from the main force during the Mud March. So individual soldiers getting separated is quite possible.

To top off the insanity, on January 22th, Burnside issued whiskey in an attempt to lift morale but that resulted in a melee involving as many as 2500 men.[27] The Mud March led to the troops being sent to winter quarters in Falmouth after Jan 22 so there was no more fighting for months.

Numbers of men were lost in those winter months through disease and I suspect that was the cause of William's death. Far more men of the 16th were lost to disease than to the fighting. Major Small lists all the deaths from the 16th at the end of his book and William is listed there with no cause or location of death. Small lists 168 killed in action or from wounds and 240 from disease. He also lists only 80 desertions out of 1876 men who served in the 16th during the whole war.[28] That seems low considering the rate of desertion experienced by the Union. Again, as the records kept were not accurate, we cannot fully depend on Major Small's accounting.

Can you imagine a young man full of patriotic fervor being paid to join up for only three months, his enlistment extended to three years? Losing the bloody battle of Fredricksburg, bogged down in the Mud March, possibly knowing his brother was dying or maybe

26. Small, 91.
27. The Mud March Begins, http://goo.gl/5vO6Bj, accessed 16 Feb 2015.
28. Small, 323.

just not knowing what happened to his brother, maybe witnessing or participating in a drunken brawl in the middle of Virginia?

Remember, they were more likely to think of their enlistments as a contract. It would have been quite easy to look at this mess and think the military had not lived up to its end of the bargain.

No, I see no shame at Edward's leaving.

But one last story remains: one descendant (D) before she died is quoted as saying "but he paid his $20 and got that straightened out!"

Just in case that was true, I did research desertion forgiveness. Of course, during the war, deserters could be welcomed back with minor consequences. Back is the key word though. Everything I found speaks to that being a requirement. July 5, 1184, Congress passed the final law on civil war desertions. There were essentially two requirements: first, that he had returned to service or if he had been wounded or died due to injury or disease in the line of duty.[29]

That may well not have been what actually happened though. During the war, there were bounties offered for the capture of deserters. The bounties ranged from $5 to $30.[30] I wonder if someone found Edward and offered to not take him in if he were paid. The bounty hunter actually could have led Edward to believe that his desertion was forgiven with the payment or D may have just misunderstood what had been told to her. She was a very young child at the time of Edward's death and may have just overheard something.

According to Bashore, "the soldiers came looking for him in the Rag mountain area. They searched all over the mountains, but he was able to evade his pursuers".[31] Perhaps he was found after all.

29. Statues of the United States Passed at the First Session of the Forty-eighth Congress, 1883-'84 (Washinton: Government Printing Office, 1884) 120.
30. New York Times, 28 May 1884, http://goo.gl/vtRVHY
31. Bashore, 22.

The Dyers of Virginia

Edward and that friend of his supposedly moved around a bit in an effort to avoid the Union army spending time in two small communities nearer the mountains up until the fall of 1863. The Union army was definitely active and there was fighting in and around where they were. For example, the Battle of Brandy Station, fought in early June, 1863, was the largest calvary battle ever in America.[32] This was only 20 miles from Slate Mills where Bashore says Edward was at that time.[33]

Eventually they arrived in Berry Hollow on the west side of Old Rag Mountain. That's no small peak but a steep peak at 3,268 feet. Berry Hollow is at a lower elevation around 1700 feet. It is interesting to speculate how Edward got there because Berry Hollow is quite definitely an out of the way spot. Even today it's a narrow, almost one lane road. It was obviously just a wagon track back then.

According to Bashore, finding work in and around Berry Hollow in the fall of 1863 would have been easy with farms harvesting and getting ready for the winter. He met his future wife there, marrying Sarah Catherine Berry b.1835 on 7 Mar 1864.[34] I thought it interesting to find out that Sarah was 5 years older than her husband which was unusual back then. My initial information was that she was born in 1845 but the first clue to her real age was on the marriage certificate. I can't help but think Edward looked like a knight in shining armor as a stranger in a small Virginia mountain hollow back in 1863!

Edward and Sarah are buried in the park near his old home along with son George's wife. Edward died 20 Feb 1927 just as the push to create the Shenandoah Park was ramping up. Sarah died before him as he was listed on the death certificate as widowed.

32. Battle of Brandy Station, https://goo.gl/pgWjq9, accessed 21 Feb 2015.
33. Bashore, 20-21.
34. Virginia, Select Marriages, 1785-1940, film number 2048467. Ancestry.com

Their first child William "Billie" was born possibly as early as 1864 but I doubt it. Searching the indexes at the Library of Virginia netted no birth certificates for any of Edward and Sarah's five children (birth registration was not mandatory during those years) but the 1930 census does list March, 1866, for his birth. The other census birth year estimates range from 1864 to 1867. His marriage license lists 1865 as his birth year.[35] The birth dates of the children from that 1930 census were correct making it look like a possibly accurate record.[36]

According to her gravestone, however, Abby Alice, the next child, was born 1866 making a birth year of 1865 - if his birth month was March - be the likeliest year, one year after his parents' marriage. John C, known as Blind John, was born in 1868. The three youngest children were George Washington Dyer, James N and Charles Elmer.

The Marriages

Keep in mind this family is living in a small area in the mountains and their neighbors provide the names that continue that tale - more Berrys, Nicholsons and Weakleys. Though the names reoccur, they weren't marrying cousins as the popular stories abound about mountain families and intermarrying. I've found throughout my genealogical studies that marrying distant cousins is common because in smaller communities there's simply less choice. I am now fond of saying it seems to be a miracle I didn't marry a cousin since it seems that my families populated most of the state of Georgia. A joke but true - you never know what you find when you start looking. Without the genealogical study no one ever knows who actually might be a relation!

One further note? The Alexanders who remained in Maine did marry cousins frequently.

35. Virginia, Select Marriages, 1785-1940, film number 2048472. Ancestry.com

36. Year: 1900; Census Place: Robertson, Madison, Virginia; Roll: 1717; Page: 7B; Enumeration District: 0039; FHL microfilm: 1241717

And most interesting, three of Edward's sons married three Nicholson sisters, all at age 15 or 16.

The Eviction

The tale of how this family lost their homes in the 1930s is not just a tale of this family but of many families who were living in what is now the Shenandoah National Park. The history of how this park came to be is well described in a number of books but one source stands out, *The UNDYING PAST of* Shenandoah National Park by Darwin Lambert.[37] The facts are simple and clear. Virginia offered up this land for the park. 497 families lost their homes but only 197 were homeowners.[38] They were paid (and probably not enough) but very few left willingly.

The old and infirm were granted the right to live out their years in the park but few stayed. Most had lived there for hundreds of years. Some saw their homes being burned; some were literally carried off physically. None had wealth; in fact many lived in a cashless state by farming to provide for their families.

"A remote family before the Civil War was likely to be successful in proportion to its knowledge of nature and skills in homecrafts. Those whose primary goal was to accumulate wealth, rather than to simply live, weeded themselves out by fitting into plantation life or moving west."[39]

This was still very much a description of these families in 1930. One 80 year old I talked with said they gardened and slaughtered a hog once a year. They knew no deprivation; it was simply how they lived. A lifestyle that had simply been the only life they had known there in the mountains and hollows for many decades.

---

37. Lambert, Darwin, *The UNDYING PAST of* Shenandoah National Park (Latham, MD: Roberts Rinehart, Inc. Publishers, 2001)
38. Lambert, 241.
39. Lambert, 50.

That same woman also told me she witnessed the burning of her grandfather's home. Memories are long there in the mountains. They still feel that it wasn't right to lose the only homes they had ever known. Most stayed close by after leaving the park and are buried close to those old homes. The dislocation still rankles.

In total the Dyers owned over 800 acres among the eight sons and grandsons of Edward Paul. As a family, it is obvious to see what a major disruption the creation of Shenandoah Park was. It appears that most of them were not just subsistence farmers and one had several businesses of note. They owned peach and apple orchards, sawmills and a stave mill.[40] Five were listed as head of households in the 1935 park statistics which may indicate that only three sons and two grandsons (different from the ones that were paid for their land) remained that year.[41]

The park wasn't the only big event that decade because there was also a severe drought and major forest fire in 1930. Of course, the biggest was the recession so in some ways the birth of the park was a blessing in disguise for some but as Darwin Lambert put it:

> *"Though life was sometimes hard, they could do what they had to do when they felt like doing it, not when some schedule imposed upon them, The freedom was greater there, and the security was far more dependable than outsiders ever seem to have understood."*[42]

One of the fascinating things about all of this is that I moved to Charlottesville, Virginia, in 2008. Madison County, where all of this took place, is just next door. There I had started researching a Maine family to have it all come back home to me here in Virginia. Turns out I had cousins within a half hour of my home! The photograph above is a cabin once owned by an Edward Paul descendant. I met the man who lived there as a child

40. Bashore, 24, 30.
41. Lambert, 304.
42. Lambert, 253.

and he was gracious enough to show me where it was and tell me what he knew. The cabin sits just outside of the park and is still in use today - though probably as a hunting or getaway cabin.

William Edward[7] (Edward Paul Dyer[6], Mary Ann Margaret[5], Joseph[4], Hugh[3], Jennett[2], James[1])

Billie b.abt 1865 married Homey Catherine Nichols on 19 Dec 1888.[43] They had two sons, Elmer Sylvester[8] b.28 Aug 1890 d.11 Jun 1963[44] who married Lena Belle Weakley b.12 Sep 1893 d.2 May 1976[45] and Herbert Washington[8] b.18 Aug 1898 d.18 Apr 1950[46] who married Rosa "Rosie" Virginia Seale b.29 Jan 1896 d.Mar 1975.[47] Between them, they gave Edward and Sarah 14 grandchildren.

Homey died prior to 1930 as William was listed as widowed in the 1930 census.[48] William died prior to 1936 as his estate as listed as being paid $478 for 28 acres in that year. Elmer received $847 for 44 acres and Herbert received $233 for 44 acres.[49] Herbert inherited his father's home according to his son, William. That cabin is still used as a residence today but is known as the Henry Smith Cabin.[50]

Abby Alice[7] (Edward Paul Dyer[6], Mary Ann Margaret[5], Joseph[4], Hugh[3], Jennett[2], James[1])

Alice b.24 Aug 1866 d.28 Jan 1943[51] married Henry Smith b.28 Aug 1865 d.17 May 1950[52] on 29 Apr 1885.[53] They had nine children born between 1885 and 1910. According to Bashore, Alice and Henry moved into the original Edward Paul cabin in Berry Hollow after

---

43. Virginia, Select Marriages, 1785-1940 Ancestry.com Operations, Inc, 2014.
44. Virginia, Death Records, 1912-2014 Ancestry.com Operations, Inc., 2015.
45. Social Security Administration, Number: 230-62-9356; Virginia; Issue Date: 1963.
46. Virginia, Death Records, 1912-2014 Ancestry.com Operations, Inc., 2015.
47. Social Security Adminstration, Number: 225-52-0275; Virginia; 1956-1957
48. Year: 1930; Census Place: Robertson, Madison, Virginia; Roll: 2450; Page: 6B; District: 0005; Image: 131.0; FHL microfilm: 2342184
49. Lambert, 293.
50. Bashore, 31.
51. Virginia, Death Records, 1912-2014 Ancestry.com Operations, Inc., 2015.
52. Gravestone photograph, ancestry.com.
53. Virginia, Select Marriages, 1785-1940 Ancestry.com Operations, Inc, 2014.

Edward and Sarah moved to a remote location on Robertson Mountain in 1885.[54]

Maude Vera[8] Smith b.16 Jul 1885 d.1958[55] married Alpheus Gideon Nicholson b.7 June 1878 d.5 Jun 1944,[56] son of John William Nicholson and Jemima Catherine Weakley, on 31 Oct 1900.[57] They had nine children and over 22 grandchildren. They moved to Illinois by 1910 and most of their descendants were still there when I was last able to see traces of them.

Odie Breckenridge[8] Smith was born 20 Aug 1890 and died 20 Jun 1959.[58] He and his wife, Gertrude Virginia Cubbage b.26 Aug 1890 d.27 June 1982,[59] had nine children. George Wilbert[8] b.3 Mar 1892 d.31 May 1961[60] married Mary Ellen Lillard b.20 Sep 1892 d.6 Sep 1953[61] and had five children. Walter Henry b.3 Aug 1897 d.5 Jan 1971[62] married Vergie Dodson b.7 Dec 1901 d.15 Aug 1996.[63] They had at least five children. Mary Alice b.1 Jan 1900 d.27 Jun 1973[64] married George W Nicholson b.1879 d.1940 and they had two children. Hazel Gladys b.5 Feb 1902 d.16 Feb 1977[65] married James E Nichols b.abt 1894[66] and had five children. The last child who married was Oliver Estes b.8 Jul 1909 d.29 Jan 1995[67] who married Sylvia A Berry b.8 Jul 1909 d.21 Mar 2003.[68] Her mother was a Weakley and father was from another Berry branch. They had at least two children.

---

54. Bashore, 22-23.
55. Findagrave.com, gravestone, http://goo.gl/ChIfSZ, accessed 1 March 2015.
56. Findagrave.com, gravestone, http://goo.gl/VWWp9B, accessed 1 Mar 2015.
57. Virginia, Select Marriages, 1785-1940 Ancestry.com Operations, Inc, 2014.
58. Virginia, Death Records, 1912-2014 Ancestry.com Operations, Inc., 2015.
59. Findagrave.com, gravestone photograph, http://goo.gl/4xtWxU.
60. Virginia, Death Records, 1912-2014 Ancestry.com Operations, Inc., 2015.
61. Virginia, Death Records, 1912-2014 Ancestry.com Operations, Inc., 2015.
62. Virginia, Death Records, 1912-2014 [Ancestry.com Operations, Inc., 2015.
63. Findagrave.com, gravestone, http://goo.gl/VhR2r2, accessed 1 March 2015/
64. Virginia, Death Records, 1912-2014 Ancestry.com Operations, Inc., 2015.
65. Findagrave.com and ancestry.com family supplied dates.
66. Year: 1940; Census Place: Leesburg, Loudoun, Virginia; Roll: T627_4274; Page: 1A; Enumeration District: 54-11
67. Social Security Administration Number: 229-03-7044; Virginia; Before 1951
68. U.S., Social Security Administration, Number: 227-18-1167; Virginia; Before 1951.

Ada Elizabeth[8] b.26 Jul 1895 d.20 Apr 1974[69] never married and John Wesley[8] b.16 Oct 1907 d.27 Feb 1969[70] may not have either.

John Chadwell[7] (Edward Paul Dyer[6], Mary Ann Margaret[5], Joseph[4], Hugh[3], Jennett[2], James[1])

Called Blind John, he never married and lived with his parents probably until at least his father's death in 1927. I was not able to find a census record for him in 1930 but John was residing with his brother, George in 1940.[71] John Chadwell Dyer b.27 Feb 1868 died 13 Aug 1957 at age 89.[72]

He was said to make excellent ax handles, chairs and stools[73] so was obviously self-sufficient. He was granted lifetime residency in the park and was paid $1,613 for 312 acres.[74]

George Washington[7] (Edward Paul Dyer[6], Mary Ann Margaret[5], Joseph[4], Hugh[3], Jennett[2], James[1])

George b.23 May 1872[38] d.20 Feb 1945[75] married a Nicholson, Effie Susan b.28 Sep 1877 d.14 Apr 1932,[76] on 26 Apr 1894[77] and had two children, Waverly Turner, b.2 Aug 1895 d.9 Mar 1966[78] and Cliffie Susan b.14 Feb 1897 d.28 Sep 1989.[79] After his wife died, he is found in a 1940 census with a young wife, Dorothy b.4 Apr 1913 d.24 May 1982,[80] and two small children, the oldest born about 1936.

George received the most money of any of the Dyers for his 100

69. Findagrave.com, gravestone, http://goo.gl/19SVdV, accessed 1 March 2015.
70. National Cemetery Administration. U.S. Veterans Gravesites, ca.1775-2006 [database on-line]. Provo, UT, USA: Ancestry.com.
71. Year: 1940; Census Place: Robertson, Madison, Virginia; Roll: T627_4275; Page: 12A; Enumeration District: 57-8
72. Virginia Death Index, certificate number 20085, ancestry.com.
73. Darwin, 233.
74. Darwin, 293.
75. Virginia, Death Records, 1912-2014 Ancestry.com Operations, Inc., 2015.
76. Virginia, Death Records, 1912-2014 Ancestry.com Operations, Inc., 2015.
77. Virginia, Select Marriages, 1785-1940 Ancestry.com Operations, Inc, 2014.
78. Findagrave.com, gravestone, http://goo.gl/DteC6o, accessed 28 March 2015.
79. Social Security Administration, Number: 227-28-9342; Virginia; Before 1951.
80. Findagrave.com, gravestone, http://goo.gl/Vxbpor, accessed 27 March 2015.

acres, $2,092, but George was the owner of a sawmill and a stave mill and was not just a farmer.[81] He was the informant on his father's death certificate. His son, Waverly also received $1,130 for 225 acres.

James Nathan[7] (Edward Paul Dyer[6], Mary Ann Margaret[5], Joseph[4], Hugh[3], Jennett[2] , James[1])

James Nathan b.16 Apr 1875[82] married another Nicholson, Georgiana, b.Apr 1884. Georgiana, a much younger sister of Effie Susan, was born 1883 according to the marriage license from 7 Sep 1899.[83] They had two daughters. James and Georgiana lived with her parents in 1900.

James was paid $338 for 13 acres but I can find no census or death records for any of his family after 1930.

Charles Elmer[7] (Edward Paul Dyer[6], Mary Ann Margaret[5], Joseph[4], Hugh[3], Jennett[2] , James[1])

The youngest son was a study in "mosts", most married and the most children. Charles was born 10 Jul 1880. His first marriage was to Virgie Nicholson b.Feb 1886,[84] the younger sister of Effie Susan and Georgiana, on 1 Aug 1902.[85] Virgie was 14 when James and Georgiana lived in her house so after two sisters had married Dyers, it must have seemed like a natural thing to do later. Virgie died leaving no children so one can speculate she might have died in childbirth but I can find no death date or further information.

He then married Fannie Weakley b.abt 1881[86] on 11 Aug 1906.[87] They had seven children before she died probably in or right after childbirth in either 1918 or 1919. Next he married Elizabeth N Nich-

81. Bashore, 24.
82. WWI, Registration State: Virginia; Registration County: Madison; Roll: 1984810.
83. "Virginia, Marriages, 1785-1940," (https://goo.gl/K4H2KQ).
84. "United States Census, 1900," (https://goo.gl/Rcm7SN).
85. Ancestry.com. Virginia, Select Marriages, 1785-1940 Ancestry.com.
86. "United States Census, 1910," (https://goo.gl/Ft4gnN).
87. Bashore, 27.

olson b.3 Jun 1898 d.24 Jan 1972[88] on 24 Dec 1919.[89] They had eight children.

Charlie died two years after Lizzie on 17 May 1974.[78] He had 64 acres in the '30s that he received $717 for but he was no longer farming by the time of the 1940 census. He is listed as a laborer at the Shenandoah Park as was one of his nephews.[90]

88. Findagrave.com, gravestone, http://goo.gl/f19gqK, accessed 28 March 2015.
89. Bashore, 27.
90. Year: 1940; Census Place: Robertson, Madison, Virginia; Roll: T627_4275; Page: 6A; Enumeration District: 57-10

In Conclusion....

So We're Down to the Living

So my specific branch ends with no one surnamed Wilson to continue the name and only three in the next generation. There are more in that generation further out from us - even a few Wilson males but I don't know the names for some of the living younger descendants of Frank Leroy and Delia much less where they are and even whether their parents are still alive or not. I've contacted various family members trying to get more information but simply can't find everyone or else they have not responded to me.

So if I've got your or your family's information wrong, my apologies. Please let me know. You can contact me either via email delia@cvillegenie.com or the contact form on that website. There is a version of the family tree online at http://cvillegenie.com/james_wilson_family. That cannot be easily kept up to date as the working tree is on ancestry. If you have an account, you can view that tree here: http://trees.ancestry.com/tree/64255859/family.

In Conclusion

Yes, of course, I have conclusions. Some of it is an echo of what I started with.

Consumption, The White Plague

Hugh Wilson II

The first death I could find for consumption in the Wilsons was James[4] (Hugh,[3] Hugh[2], James[1]) who died as a young adult in 1786. His sister, Elizabeth, died early as well three years later in 1789 but we have no evidence that TB was the cause.

Thirteen years after James' death, his father, Hugh II, succumbs to TB in 1799.

Hugh's daughter, Hannah (Cram), and her adult daughter follows this path in 1844 along with her daughter, Catherine, when they die on the same day from TB. Another daughter, Mary Jane, died only months before but no ailment was recorded for her. Much later in 1911 Hannah's granddaughter died in Massachusetts of TB but possibly unconnected with the TB that was being passed around the family.

Hugh's son, Hugh III, had several children who must have died young, James, Hugh, Esther, and Mary, leading me to believe that they also died from TB. No proof and there could be other causes of course. His wife also died relatively young as well. Their adult son Charles left Maine, one of the few who did that early in the 19th century. When I first realized that, I speculated that he left after witnessing the deaths. Now that theory makes even more sense if these deaths were due to consumption.

Samuel Wilson II

Next door to Hugh's family in 1818, Priscilla, Samuel's (William[2], James[1]) wife dies from tuberculosis. Samuel also lost three children before adulthood as did his son, James. He died much later in 1862 of tuberculosis. There were just a lot of child deaths in that family.

Samuel and Priscilla's daughter Mary married David Pearson. In Fairfield, his son's daughters, Louisa d.1903, (miliary) Josephine d.1896 (pthisis) and Josephine's son, Joseph, all died of tuberculosis. Then David's son died at age 2 in 1873, perhaps another victim? Josephine and Louisa actually lived with each other after their marriages.

Esther Pearson's daughter Mae died from TB in Massachusetts in 1895 age 24. There are other Pearson women who I have no death date or marriage for - possibly more victims. Though in Mae's case, she was living in an area with a higher rate of tuberculosis.

Lester Given[7] Purinton (Nathaniel Snow Purinton[6], Rev Albert W[5], Priscilla[4], Samuel[3], William[2], James[1]) was a doctor born in 1879 who died in Lewiston. His brother, Newman Albert b.1882, died at age

18 from acute phthisis, galloping consumption in Bowdoin. Their sister, Francis b.1875 Bowdoin, and brother, Royce Davis b.1877 a teacher in Lewiston d.1919, also died, leaving only two siblings that survived and only one that married. TB nearly killed off the entire family.

Another branch of this family may also have had multiple TB deaths. Sarah[4] (James[3], Samuel[2], James[1]) who married Robert Dickey may have died from TB herself but the proven death was great granddaughter Emma d.1897. There is no proof that this family s deaths were from TB but they experienced a lot of deaths within a 15 year span, including Sarah, son, John, his wife, and 6 children in Northport. Sarah's sister, Mercy, (Frye) did die from TB in 1864. In her family, those that left Maine escaped the TB but the ones who stayed were not so lucky: Annie Celia Boynton (Sarah[5], Mercy[4], James[3], Samuel[2], James[1]) d.1847, Celia J Frye (Mercy[4], James[3], Samuel[2], James[1]) d.1902, Emily P Woods (Celia[5], Mercy[4], James[3], Samuel[2], James[1]) d.1896, Emily's husband, Lendall d.1913 and their son, William Arthur d.1916.

And there more tuberculosis deaths that I found, mainly towards the end of the19th or first of the 20th century but no more groupings.

Belfast death records list the cause of death and consumption as definitely of the most common causes especially between 1860 and 1880.

Humphrey Wilson

Once Humphrey's children and grandchildren get to Massachusetts and the shoe industry, the incidence of tuberculosis is marked.

Henry's oldest daughter died in 1897 and then his son in 1901, both of tuberculosis. His wife had died many earlier in 1883 but her death record says bronchitis, not something one dies of normally. There were a lot of cases of congestion, bronchitis and consumption in Lynn that died at the same time.

Emery's son Fay lost his second wife to tuberculosis in 1918. The family narrative describes her as a hard working but sickly woman. His daughter, Mildred, also died from tuberculosis at age 12 in Massachusetts in 1908. The eldest daughter, Ruth, died seven years after her mother in 1925 as well.

Lynn simply was not a safe place to live in the late 1800s and early 1900s. I suppose it's fortunate that all of Emery's adult children (my great grandfather and his siblings) survived those years.

There is a genetic predisposition to tuberculosis[1] and it seemed to have played a factor in one branch of the Purinton family for many years. As tuberculosis is not a major health threat at this moment in the U.S., most of us don't worry about it; however, since the drug resistant strain of TB is now a reality, I think it important that the descendants do know about this. Fortunately, one of those survivors is a high-profile doctor who is well aware of the threat. I am happy to have been able to detect this possible genetic link.

Genetic Genealogy

We all know about inherited diseases and tendencies. For one cousin who was not raised with his biological family, his genealogy research began when the doctor asked those questions in later life.

I myself have a rare genetic disorder called Ehlers-Danlos Syndrome and was hoping throughout this study that I would find others who might have it. My case is not severe and wasn't diagnosed until about 8 or 9 years ago. There could easily be other cousins who have it and not know. This particular disorder/syndrome can come from a mutation so there might not be anyone else.

I would like to see a study among these descendants that looks at inherited disease and conditions. The cost can be prohibitive so it's highly unlikely that can happen without external funding. Testing

1. Human genetics of tuberculosis: a long and winding road , http://goo.gl/oqWEP4, accessed 14 August 2015.

for my variant of EDS can run $2500 and I haven't even had it done myself.

My point is, though, that DNA not only can tie families together in genealogy work but it also can be a tool beyond that. I have been tested through two different websites, ancestry.com and 23andme.com. It made it possible to connect with my cousins (newly discovered as well as "old" cousins).

It also showed me how large part of my families were. I don't have that many matches from my New England family but the number of matches from one of those southern lines is major. I have found a few Polish matches which I hope someday will give me a family history for my grandmother's family. Maybe I'll even one day have an Irish cousin pop up who can tell me more about my namesake's origins.

I do recommend getting DNA tested. Eventually it will become routine, cheaper and more useful. It's also a way of leaving a little bit of yourself behind. A legacy.

The Wilson Leftovers from Topsham

There are some records in Hill vital records of Topsham that I haven't been able to pinpoint exactly who these folks were. I hate loose ends so I'm offering this listing up just in case someone reads this and is able to say who these folks were:

Births
[ ], s. William, Feb. 9, 1794, C.R.I.
Louisa, ch. Hannah, Aug. 27, 1845

Marriages
Betsey and Harrey M. Merryman, both of Brunswick, July 3, 1859.*
Bial of T. & John Larrabee of Green, int. Apr. 30, 1830. [cert, issued May 18.]
Charles of Lisbon and Margaret A. R. Ward of T., int. June 11, 1858. [cert, issued June 16.]
Eliza S. and William Dennett, both of T., int. Sept. 19, 1835. [cert, issued

Oct. 5.] (same one that Hannah is living with in 1850 census) born 1813 so Hannah is her mother probably in Riverview
Elizabeth, Mrs., of T. and Walter McDonall of Georgetown, int. Dec. 31, 1750, T.R.4. James' widow?
Elizabeth and John Holland, both of T., Mar. 26, 1807.
Hannah D. & Horace M. Eaton, both of T., Feb. 11, 1841, at Lisbon.
Josephine E. of T. and John C. Coffin [int. adds 2d.] of Nantucket, Mass., Oct. 7, 1855.
Mary & Nathaniel Merrill, both of T., int. Aug. 29, 1816. [cert, issued Sept. 12.]
Mary of T. & John N. Mars of Alna, int. Sept. 6, 1818. [cert, issued Oct. 5.]
Mary L. of Bowdoinham and Samuel Dunning of Harpswell, Oct. 3, 1862, in T.*
Mary S. of Bowdoinham and Samuel B. Doughty of T., int. Oct. 5, 1833. [cert, issued Nov. 3.]
Rufus of Harpswell and Ruth Getchell of T., Aug. 21, 1842. (moved to Millbridge/Biddeford) born Dec 1818, died 1880, son of David but not Lettice?
Susan and William Mitchell, both of T., Feb. 18, 1836.

Deaths
Hannah, May 29, 1866, a. 83 y., in T., N.P.6. (maybe the 70 year old in the 1850 census with Dennets?)
Hannah, Sept. 26, 1867, c.R.4. [Mrs., a. 88 y., N.P.6.] birth 1779
Mary, Aug. 23, 1853, a. 70 y., G.R.3. grave missing? born 1773
Mary, Mrs., Sept. 19, 1855, in T., a. 62 y., N.P.6. born 1793
T. N., seaman, lost overboard from ship C. A. Morrison, Jan. 23, 1859, a. 20 y., N.P.6.

Sources & Resources

The Sources and Processes

I started with Ancestry.com and have used it as a repository for information as well as testing. Much of the information there is correct about this family and I've worked to keep my tree updated. I used tree hints to gather more information and then started using FamilySearch.org for cross searches. That kind of searching revealed more children and more vital record information but it was frustrating when a birth record appeared with no parents or other identifying information.

I started looking for more primary sources and was able to find a number of old books in digital form. I gained a copy of Wheelers' History of Topsham, Brunswick and Harpswell which was a nice start. The real coup though came from finding the Vital Records of Topsham, Maine, by Mary Pelham Hill in a PDF format. The website is ArchiveCDBooks.org and it's a great edition. I had purchased one from a site that I will not name and it was impossible to even read. This edition is searchable and has a table of contents to help maneuver around the 500 or so pages. I was also able to find actual bound volumes at the University of Virginia libraries. (They had to retrieve it from storage, not much use for it in central Virginia!) It was great to be able to leaf through the pages but they were not printed on quality paper. I let the library know how fragile those books are and even suggested they donate them to Topsham.

Maine used the Hill volumes and other vital record sets produced by her and others in the 1930s for the actual vital records and therefore the digital records you can find today on line. Hill's two volume set leaves something to be desired sometimes with gaps and missing information but at least the dates seem to be correct. Some of the records are from family Bibles, town records, some from church records, newspaper items and actual gravestones.

The most intriguing source was writings of Cyrus Woodman - "private record, Early History of Topsham, by Cyrus Woodman, in the Maine Historical Society, Portland". I ended up finding two sources of his at the Maine Historical Society; one was the "scrapbook" where he had cut out newspaper articles and pasted them into some sort of business yearbook publication. The other was a duplicated version of his original writings. Thank heavens for someone's penmanship! It has some corrections and information added here and there but is mostly a genealogical listing of many Topsham families.

That answered many of my questions and had some definitive relationships recorded.

In all cases, if I had a verifiable source, whether digital or not, I have footnoted it. Any information not footnoted I could not find but that does not necessarily mean it's incorrect: only that I was not able to find the original source.

If I was assuming relationships, I tried to make that clear. There are definitely missing children and sometimes I think I figured out who belonged to whom. I think. Since the Wilsons mostly remained in Topsham and mostly married into a few families and not at all into others, any Wilsons that I could not find parental proof for, I could see where they might fit into certain families.

I love and adore proof of the truth. I don't mind being wrong. I do mind not knowing the truth. Let me know if you find errors.

Delia Wilson Lunsford

Resources and Records by Family Name and Topic

Alexanders

Alexander, De Alva Stanwood, *The Alexanders of Maine* (Buffalo, NY: The Peter Paul Book Company, 1898) https://books.google.com/books/about/The_Alexanders_of_Maine.html?id=x30tAAAAYAAJ or shortened: https://goo.gl/MrQWiE

Clemens, William M., *Alexander Family Records.* An Account of the First American Settlers and Colonial Families of the Name of Alexander, and Other Genealogical and Historical Data, Mostly New and Original Material Including Early Wills and Marriages Heretofore Unpublished (New York: the author, 1914). https://archive.org/stream/alexanderfamilyr00clem/alexanderfamilyr00clem_djvu.txt or shortened: https://goo.gl/bxSwvb

Sinnett, Charles W., *Ancestor David Alexander and descendants* : with index to the names / compiled by Rev. Chas. N.Sinnett. (Mss A 8690). R Stanton Avery Special Collections, New England Historic Genealogical Society, Boston, Massachusetts.

Typewritten manuscript of maybe 80 pages.

Davis of Massachusetts

The Davis family record : a monthly journal devoted to the history and genealogy of the Davis family (1867)
https://archive.org/details/davisfamilyrecor00davi or shortened https://goo.gl/qe9EuF

Dickeys

Dickey, David, *Genealogy of the Dickey Family* (Worchester, MA: F.S. Blanchard & Co.)
https://archive.org/details/genealogyofdicke00dick or shortened https://goo.gl/o7nwZp

Hinkleys / Hinckleys

Rootsweb, documented work by Frederick R. Boyle, Springville, ME
http://homepages.rootsweb.ancestry.com/~rwhitney/whitney/2/3665.htm accessed 17 March 2014.

Sinnett, Charles N. (Charles Nelson), 1847-1928. *Hinckley family history.* Concord, Mass. : Mrs. W.M. Bush, [1954?]
Hinckley family history (Mss C 3884). R Stanton Avery Special Collections Department, New England Historic Genealogical Society, Boston, Massachusetts.

Typewritten manuscript starting with the Massachusetts Hinckleys and covering some of the Maine Hinckleys. "The original manuscript has many of its records completed from the Vital Records of Brunswick, Hallowell, Georgetown, Phippsburg and other Maine towns, furnished by Mrs. Bertha Vickery, Augusta, Maine. The later generations, as in the Brewster Appendix, were furnished by the owner of the original manuscript. Most information sent 1954. Contributed by Mrs. A. T. Griffith, West Long Branch, New

Jersey.""Copied and indexed by Mrs. Walter M. Bush, Concord, Massachusetts." Include bibliographical references and index.

http://en.wikipedia.org/wiki/Thomas_Hinckley

The Farrins

Sinnett, Charles N. (Charles Nelson), 1847-1928. *The Farrin Family of Brunswick, Maine.* Brainerd, Minn. : [Chas. N. Sinnett, ca. 1922]
The Farrin family of Brunswick, Maine (Mss A 8660). R Stanton Avery Special Collections, New England Historic Genealogical Society, Boston, Massachusetts.

"Typescript genealogy on the descendants of John Farrin and his wife, Hannah, Newman, of Brunswick, Maine." 5 pages and yes only on the Brunswick Farrins. Ebenezer is mentioned with only the birth date.

The Thompsons

Sinnet, Rev. Charles N., *Our Thompson Family, in Maine, New Hampshire and the West* (New Hampshire: Rumford Printing Company, 1907) https://archive.org/details/ourthompsonfamil00lcsinn or shortened https://goo.gl/JNw88u

Goold, Nathan, *General Samuel Thompson of Brunswick and Topsham, Maine* (Portland, Maine: Maine Historical Society, 1903.)

Wilsons

The Wilson DNA project, https://www.familytreedna.com/public/Wilson/

Sinnett, Charles Nelson, Rev. *The Descendants of William Wilson*, undated, typewritten manuscript of James Wilson and Son William Wilson. Maine Historical Society, Portland, Maine.

This is barely 50% correct. I was able to glean a few points for the descendants of Alexander but it is is poor for a genealogy. I suggest not even looking at it.

Charles L. Wilson

http://www.flheritage.com/preservation/markers/markers.cfm?ID=alachua
Ancient Probate Records for Alachua County, Florida, http://www.alachuaclerk.org/archive/

History

Bibber, Joyce K., *Images of America, Brunswick and Topsham* (Charleston, SC: Arcadia Publishing, 1994).

Bolton, Charles Knowles, *Scotch Irish Pioneers in Ulster and America* (Boston: Bacon and Brown, 1910). https://archive.org/details/scotchirish00boltrich

Duncan, Roger E., *Coastal Maine: a Maritime History* (New York: Norton & Company, 1992)

Little, George Thomas, *Genealogical and Family History of the State of Maine* (New York: Lewis Historical Publishing Company, 1909). https://archive.org/details/genealogicalfami-00litt or shortened https://goo.gl/LROIRf

Roser, Susan E. *Mayflower Births and Deaths: From the Files of George Ernest Bowman at the Massachusetts Society of Mayflower Descendants*. Volumes 1 & 2. Baltimore, MD: Genealogical Publishing Company, Inc., 1992, 227.

Stackpole, Everett S, *The History of Durham, Maine, with Genealogical Notes* (Lewiston, Maine: Press of Lewiston Journal Company, 1899). (found errors in this source) https://archive.org/details/historyofdurhamm00stac or shortened https://goo.gl/UhQPZ5

Topsham, Maine, A Brief History, http://www.topshammaine.com/index.asp?SEC=4497727C-A69C-49D6-AF22-BA39CCAFDD56&Type=B_BASIC

Topsham, Maine, Historical Walking Tour, A Publication of the Topsham Historic District Commission, 1995, 1997.

Wheeler, George Augustus, M.D., Wheeler, Henry Warren, *History of Topsham, Brunswick and Harpswell including the ancient territory known as Pejebscot* (Boston: Alfred Mudge and Sons, Printers, 1878) http://community.curtislibrary.com/CML/wheeler/index.html

If you can find a copy (which there are several at the Maine Historical Society in Portland) be sure to checkout the additional maps that are not part of the actual book usually. The digitized version on the Curtis Library website includes information about the book and why it was written - which does make a difference in how the material is viewed. It does contain errors and is not a good overview of the people involved in the first two centuries of the area. It does pull information from town records and the early Pejebscot papers and I found no glaring errors in this type of factual information. Some of his off-hand conclusions are not always on point.

Williams, Robert C., *Topsham Maine from the River to the Highlands* (Topsham, Maine: Just Write Books, 2015).

Williamson, Durkee William, *The History of the State of Maine: from its First Discovery, AD 1602, to the Separation, AD 1820, Inclusive,* Vol. II (Hallowell: Glazier, Masters & Co., 1832)

Woodman, Cyrus, Copy of Manuscript - *History of Topsham, 1829,* Maine Historical Society, Portland, Maine.
The Bath Daily Times, 1924, transcription, http://www.maineulsterscots.com/docs/THE_BATH_DAILY_TIMES.pdf (original source was the scrapbooks and notes of Cyrus Woodman)

Massachusetts School for the Feeble Minded:
http://nhgenealogist.com/2/post/2013/12/those-places-thursday-school-for-the-feeble-mindedwaltham-ma.html or shortened http://goo.gl/lt1GY9
http://www.city.waltham.ma.us/sites/walthamma/files/file/file/fernald_center_history.pdf
http://www.cbsnews.com/news/americas-deep-dark-secret/

Antonio, Michael, *The state boys rebellion* (Simon & Shuster, 2005).

Salem Witch Trials:
History of Massachusetts Blog, http://historyofmassachusetts.org/the-toothaker-family-witches-or-witch-killers/ or shortened http://goo.gl/uuYdb6
Roach, Marilynne K, The Salem Witch Trials: A Day-by-Day Chronicle of a Community Under Siege (Lanham, Maryland: Taylor Trade Publishing, 2004)

Alberta, Canada:
Clark, Edith J. Lawrence, *Tails of Tail Creek Country*, privately published about 1968, http://www.ourroots.ca/e/page.aspx?id=3533496 or shortened http://goo.gl/LCCUKT

Records

Lincoln County Property of Deeds, Wiscasset, Maine, deeds for Topsham from 1764 to 1826.
Lincoln County Probate Court, Wicsasset, Maine, probate records 1764 to 1860.

Sagadahoc County Property of Deeds, Bath, Maine, deeds for Topsham. 1860 and later.
Sagadahoc County Probate Court, Bath, Maine, probate records, 1860 and later.

Maine State Archives, Augusta, Maine, microfilms of early records for Topsham including births, baptisms, deaths, marriages and town records. Rolls 578, 579, 580.

Patterson, William Davis, *The Probate Records of Lincoln County, Maine: 1760 to 1800* (Portland, Me, 1895)

Woodman, Cyrus, *A History of Topsham, Maine, Scrapbook, 1835* (Archival material, Maine Historical Society, Coll. 1498), source for Mary Pelham Hills' P.R. 80 records.

BELFAST Vital Records
Johnson, Alfred, ed., *Vital Records of Belfast, Maine, to the Year 1892*, vols I & II (Boston: Wright & Potter Printing Co, 1919).

BOWDOIN Vital Records
Cox, Rachel Townsend, ed., *Vital Records of Bowdoin, Maine, to the Year 1892*, vols I, II, & III (Auburn: Press of Merrill & Webber company. 1944-45).

BOWDOINHAM Vital Records
Rowland, Doris M, *Death Records of Bowdoinham, Maine*, typed manuscript date March 16, 1967.

BRUNSWICK Vital Records
Anderson, Joseph C., II., *Vital records of Brunswick, Maine, 1740-1860 ; and, the Forsaith book of Brunswick family records, compiled 1876-1880 by Jonathan W. Forsaith, town clerk* / compiled by Joseph Crook Anderson, II. (Rockport, ME: Picton Press, 2004).

BRISTOL Vital Records
Dodge, Christine Huston, *Vital Records of Old Bristol and Nobleboro in the County of Lincoln Maine including the present towns of Bremen, Damariscotta, South Bristol and the Plantation of*

Monhegan, vols I & II (Brunswick: The Record Press, 1947).

GEORGETOWN Vital Records
Hill, Mary Pelham, *Vital records of Georgetown, Maine, to the year 1892*,vols I & II (Maine Historical Society, 1939).

HARPSWELL Vital Records
Putnam, Eben, *Genealogical records of the Town of Harpswell, Cumberland County, Maine : compiled from the original town records with notes and additions. Births, Deaths, Marriages 1769-1892*, Family History Library, microfilm 11033.

Woodside, Frances M., *A copy of records from the old record books of Rev. Elisha Eaton of Harpswell, Maine, 1753-1763, Rev. Samuel Eaton of Harpswell, Maine, 1765-1822, Joseph Eaton, Justice of Peace, Harpswell, Maine, 1823-1843*, Family History Library, microfilm 10933. Certified correct Feb. 12, 1931.

Book compiled of the above Harpswell records at Maine Historical Society, call number Mv H236.1, page numbered.

LEWISTON Vital Records
Hodgkin, Douglas I., *Records of Lewiston, Maine*, vols I & II (Rockport, Maine: Picton Press, 2002).

LISBON Vital Records
Groves, Marlene Alma Hinkley, *Vital Records of Lisbon, Maine, to the Year 1892* (Camden, Maine: Picton Press, 1995).

MINOT Vital Records
Anderson, Joseph Crook, *Early Vital Records of Minot, Maine* (Rockport, Maine: Picton Press, 2005.

TOPSHAM Vital Records
Mary Pelham Hill, *Vital Records of Topsham Maine to 1892*, 2 volumes (Concord, New Hampshire, 1929-30).

Cemeteries

Topsham
Haley Cemetery, (site of the Yellow Meeting House Baptists), on the right Winter St. coming from Hugh Wilson houses and 201. It's actually on River Rd after the Topsham Fair Mall Rd. Findagrave.com : http://goo.gl/NZcXB7
First Parish of Topsham, Middlesex Rd., north on Elm St. from 201, on the right at the intersection of Cathance Rd. which is to the left. Findagrave.com : http://goo.gl/S89mWa
Riverview, on the right Elm Street coming from traffic light at Elm and highway 201 (Main St.) Findagrave.com : http://goo.gl/2AOpJx
Brunswick
First Parish, Maine St., on left. Findagrave.com : http://goo.gl/ADGnK2
The Cemeteries of Brunswick http://www.rootsweb.ancestry.com/~mebrucem/index.html
Maine Old Cemetery Association, pay the low membership fee and get access to searchable PDFs http://www.moca-me.org/

The above were the only cemeteries I spent any time in. There are more in both towns. Copies of the cemetery record books compiled by Donald and Mark Cheatum can be found at the Topsham Public Library and the Curtis Memorial Library in Brunswick.

One location that is now missing is the Ferry Point Cemetery. Samuel Thompson and his son were originally buried there but the names of who else might have been there has been lost. It is noted that by 1747, the Indian attacks scared folks so much that they started taking bodies by water to Ferry Point because the normal burying grounds were too dangerous. The Ferry Point graveyard was removed when the railroad was laid out. Though Wheeler calls it a private burying ground, I think it was more than that. Samuel Thompson did, however, "keep" the ferry there in the years before his death.

There was an additional lot near James Mustard's house, two miles from Topsham "on the road to Merrymeeting Bay". The dates on those stone were 1752 to 1771. (Wheeler, 347)

Online PDFs

Table of Contents:
http://cvillegenie.com/pdfs/wilson_toc.pdf or shortened
http://goo.gl/JklxFm

Zoomable Maps:
Full Topsham Map
http://cvillegenie.com/james_wilson_family/wilson_images/topsham-full-wheeler-map.jpg or shortened: http://goo.gl/jZIDD8

Topsham Roads, Now and Then
http://cvillegenie.com/james_wilson_family/wilson_images/topsham_map_roads.jpg or shortened: http://goo.gl/Nc7qUF

Index of Names:
http://cvillegenie.com/pdfs/index_of_names.pdf or shortened:
http://goo.gl/uiJR6q

Index of Names

This index does not include the TOC names nor names of anyone not either a descendant or pertinent to the story. Also, instead of simply listing names used in the book, I also tried to group according to individuals. So if you are looking for James Wilson, there will be James, James I, James 4, James Jr, etc.